MW01195073

On Borrowed Fame

Author's other credits

Donald Jeffries is the author of the Best-Selling books:

Hidden History: An Expose of Modern Crimes, Conspiracies, and Cover-Ups in American Politics.

Survival of the Richest: How the Corruption of the Marketplace and the Disparity of Wealth Created the Greatest Conspiracy of All.

Crimes and Cover-Ups in American Politics: 1776-1963.

Bullyocracy: How the Social Hierarchy Enables Bullies to Rule Schools, Workplaces, and Society at Large.

His work has been lauded by the likes of Ron Paul, Naomi Wolf, Jesse Ventura, Cindy Sheehan and many others.

On Borrowed Fame:

Money, Mysteries, and Corruption in the Entertainment World

Donald Jeffries

BearManor Media

2021

On Borrowed Fame

© 2021 Donald Jeffries

All rights reserved.

No portion of this publication may be reproduced, stored, and/or copied electronically (except for academic use as a source), nor transmitted in any form or by any means without the prior written permission of the publisher and/or author.

Published in the United States of America by:

BearManor Media

4700 Millenia Blvd.
Suite 175 PMB 90497
Orlando, FL 32839

bearmanormedia.com

Printed in the United States.

Typesetting and layout by BearManor Media
Cover designed by Peter Secosh

ISBN—978-1-62933-807-1

This book is dedicated to all the performers who entertained us and left behind an enduring legacy, while being deceived and ripped off by an exploitative industry.

Table of Contents

Acknowledgements

I WOULD LIKE to thank all the veterans of show business who shared their experiences with me. Lana Wood, Paul Petersen, Jon Provost, and Sally Kirkland were kind enough to appear on my weekly radio show. Susan Olsen was a guest more than once, and was the first person to read this manuscript. Nick Mancuso also made multiple appearances on my show, and provided invaluable insight after reading the manuscript. Billy Gray, Ivor Davis, Kathy Garver, Mary McDonough, Patti D'Arbanville and Graham Parker were also kind enough to read the manuscript. John Barbour is not only the most valued friend I've ever had, he was the first and logical choice to write the Foreword to this book. Bob Wilson, the unassuming JFK assassination researcher and Beatles expert, helped me immensely with his limitless supply of entertainment world contacts and knowledge. I owe a tremendous debt of gratitude to Chris Graves, who is the best researcher anyone could ask for. I also want to especially thank Richard Syrett, S.T. Patrick, Ed Opperman, Meria Heller, Tim Kelly, Sarah Westall, Ella Felder, Billy Ray Valentine, Tony Arterburn, Peter Secosh (who helped design the cover), Alexander Mezentsev, Tracy Ramos, Jude Kessler, William Matson Law, David Wayne, Sharon Bach, Mary Muehleisen, Ernest Henry

Raft, and Lorin Hart. And, of course, my wife Jeanne and children John and Julianna, who tolerated my endless name-dropping; they are the underpaid stars of my life. Finally, thanks to Ben Ohmart and BearManor Media for publishing what I hope is an important and interesting book.

Foreword by John Barbour

I ABSOLUTELY LOVE Donald Jeffries' new book, 'On Borrowed Fame'! What a great imaginative meaningful title, and an even greater fun, informative read. It is almost a veritable history of Showbiz, and how the road to fame more than often turns into quicksand. One moment, one year, one decade, your Star as a talent on stage, screen, or radio glows more brightly than any sun, then dark clouds roll by, then a total eclipse, and you're gone. And as Donald points out so brilliantly and movingly in this book, you got Fame, but often not the Fortune you deserved. What is everlasting for most talent, is the financial screwing they got. And in many cases, as Donald uncovers, the screwing they still get.

Donald is right. Fame in most cases is as fleeting as a puddle in Death Valley on a hot day. Only a handful of real geniuses survive and prosper. Greek Playwrights Aristophanes and Sophocles. England's William Shakespeare, Ireland's George Bernard Shaw. America's Neil Simon. Writers. And a smattering of truly talented practical Musicians, from Al Jolson to Irving Berlin, Cole Porter, Lerner and Lowe, all the way up to the Beatles, Abba, Bob Dylan and a few others. And even fewer actors: Cary Grant and Charlie Chaplin owned most of their films.

This is just a lucky handful of those who starred and stayed. In Donald's riveting disturbing book he profiles scores and scores of equally genuine talents whose star shone as brightly and vividly as any of the above, but now are as forgotten as pet rocks and the hula hoop. The only thing that is lasting, according to Donald, is the fucking they still get. When I was a kid, I grew up watching and loving other kids, such as Spanky McFarland of 'Our Gang.' Like all of you with an oldie favorite, I often wondered what happened to him. Donald's wonderful book tells me. And it breaks my heart, and enrages me. His nickname and image was exploited everywhere selling shit on TV. Without permission or a penny. A pop band stole the name 'Spanky and Our Gang;' They deposited millions, and didn't even send Spanky a CD!! What makes the thievery so enraging is that the talents, and victims were kids. But it also happens to adults. Little Richard, the volcanic talent who almost solely created rock and roll was screwed until he was almost as blind as Stevie Wonder. Donald has uncovered scores of them.

Over and above the writing, which is crisp and to the point, what I admire the most is the endless amount of energy and time Donald put into his research; and then the physical time consuming chore of tracking down and phoning the once upon a time star he wanted to write about, to tell their unknown, untold story anew to the world. As much as I love showbiz, and the talents he speaks of, I could and would never do it. I'd hire somebody...cheap!

I love this book for a number of reasons. First, I love performers. With or without talent. They are the most vulnerable, needy, ambitious, insecure egocentric humans on the planet. Therefore the most interesting...because they reveal to us more of ourselves, what we are. And I am fascinated and bewildered and hurt by those other inhumans who exploit them. How could they? How could they steal and cheat another fellow being? Actually, it is worse than killing them. If they're dead, their pain is over. Left alive, and unknown, is a slow death.

Another reason I love this book; like all good books, I can see me in it. I identified with a lot of the victims. But growing up in a severely dysfunctional home…before it was popular, I learned how to rise above feeling like a victim. Feeling that way makes you that way. Donald could have also included a couple of pages about me. So, I'll just give you a couple of sentences. (The whole story is in MY book, 'Your Mother's Not a Virgin,' to which Donald wrote the Foreword.) In 1978 I created the 'Real People' concept. I was under a 13 week contract to Danny Arnold, co-creator of 'Barney Miller.' Since he was a close friend, we had no contract, just a handshake. If ABC, where he had a development deal, passed on my idea, it would become mine. ABC passed. So, I registered my scripts with the Writers Guild, and asked Danny for a 'goodbye good luck' note. He passed. A year later it was the #1 show on TV on NBC. Danny sued George Schlatter, my Executive Producer. My scripts registered at the Writers Guild gave Danny no legal leg to stand on. Schlatter did not want them in court or made public. He wanted the world to think he created 'Real People,' so his insurance paid millions to Danny to settle out of court.

So, I sued ABC over turning my idea into 'That's Incredible.' I too could have collected millions, but my inept lawyer, George Bane, talked me into settling for 50k, that I'd make my million with 'Real People.' The 50k I got barely covered 2 years for my son at Stanford. I had never designed a contract with Schlatter. In the 3rd year he was offered 30 million to syndicate it…which he did. But without my name on a contract he could not!! Now my bungling lawyer partners with my bungling agent at CAA, Roland Perkins, who talks me into signing it for a share of their NET!! In Hollywood, NET is spelled 'NOT!'

I was not a victim. I was just STUPID! Mark Twain said, 'We're all stupid in some areas!' The performers Donald describes so perfectly were only the victims of their unknowing, their trust, and their vulnerability. You may look upon some of what happened to them as rather dark. Not me. By shining his laptop's light on it, it enlightens us. But there is a shorter darker side to 'On Borrowed Fame,' which adds much, much more dimension to it. It's those Stars whose story went from Fame to Infamy. As you know from listening to Donald's lively Friday Night Show, I've been on a couple of times talking with him about my 2 definitive films on the murder of JFK: 'The Garrison Tapes,' and 'The American Media & the 2nd Assassination of President John F. Kennedy.' I am a sucker for skullduggery and intrigue. So, I was totally emerged in his musings on the deaths of John Lennon, Elvis Presley, Marilyn Monroe, George 'Superman' Reeves, and a few others. Believe me. You will be too.

In 'Hamlet,' Polonius says to his son, 'Brevity is the soul of wit!' Following the world's greatest writer's advice, I have purposely tried to keep this forward brief so that you could get to the joy of reading Donald's delicious doings!!!!

John Barbour

Introduction

All they had to do was put my name on a marquee and watch the money roll in.

- Gloria Swanson

I'VE ALWAYS BEEN fascinated by the concept of fame, especially when it's fleeting. "Greatness is nothing unless it be lasting," Napoleon said. Fame has proven to be fleeting far more often than lasting to those rare individuals who achieved it. I am accustomed to writing about corruption, and unfairness. There are plenty of both in the world of show business, as will be documented in this book.

The idea for this book was born in 1993, with the death of George "Spanky" McFarland, the most famous of all the Little Rascals in Hal Roach's Our Gang. Although he was reportedly prone to dismissing references to his film career with a curt, "That's dust,"[1] I'd heard that Spanky had grown quite frustrated by the time of his death, over the widespread use of his name and likeness, for which he received no financial compensation. I became convinced that Spanky had been the victim of a tremendous injustice. I was aware of McFarland's post-Our Gang career, which included working at a hamburger stand. When he was in his mid-twenties, McFarland rather sadly donned his old Our Gang attire to host *The Spanky Show* on a local television station in Tulsa, Oklahoma. Spanky and the other members of Our Gang were paid a good salary for the 1930s-era short films, considering the time and the fact that they were children. However, no one at that point could have foreseen the advent of television, and the explosion of these films, along with The Three Stooges shorts, into syndication in the 1950s and 1960s. I began to imagine how he must have felt about the new-found popularity of his old films, which had such unexpected appeal to young Baby Boomers. I further pondered how he must have reacted to the band Spanky and Our Gang, which had a few big hit records in the mid-1960s. A 2010 newspaper story about the band matter-of-factly noted, "The Little Rascals never sued, but the original Spanky stayed angry at the band for the rest of his life."[2] Finally, I started noticing just how often the name "Spanky" was used commercially, with or without his likeness. For instance, at the time there was a restaurant around the corner from my home named "Spanky's Clubhouse." Its logo featured an obvious likeness of young George McFarland, along with some less identifiable Little Rascals.

Spanky McFarland was paid as much as $100 per week by the Roach Studios. "I started at the top and worked my way down" was another of his bittersweet regular lines. In a 1993 story, Spanky's then eighty-eight-year-old mother, who survived him, recounted how much the dwindling public recognition meant to him: "There'd be this rousing applause when he was introduced," she said. "It moved him to tears. He was a very emotional man."[3] Spanky, still in touch with some of his fellow Rascals, had famously blown the whistle on an imposter passing himself off as his former Our Gang co-star Billie "Buckwheat" Thomas in 1990. Posthumously, Spanky became one of the two Rascals (the other being Jackie Cooper) to have a star on the Hollywood Walk of Fame. Richard Lamparski, who would write a series of wonderful *Whatever Became Of . . .* books, told talk show host Mike Douglas in the early1970s that McFarland "was the most unpleasant little man I ever met. He did nothing but talk about how everyone was against him and wouldn't give him a job. When I turned the tape off, I said: 'Do you know why no one will give you a job? It's because you're a Nasty Little Man!'" Lamparski had no reason to lie about this, but if Spanky had adopted this kind of bitter attitude, who could blame him? Imagine being such a cultural icon, without really profiting from it. As McFarland would later remark, even while attending some of the nostalgic events like the Sons of the Desert conventions (named after one of Laurel & Hardy's most memorable films), "If I knew then what I know now, I wouldn't have done it. I would have gone to college and by now I'd be the president of some corporation."[4]

My good friend, journalist, historian and podcaster Bob Wilson, told me in a February 1, 2021 email: "There was a restaurant in Ocean Township, New Jersey. It was called 'Spanky McFarland's Restaurant,' and featured about 1,000 photographs of the Little Rascals as decorations. Joseph Miller was the owner. George McFarland sued them in 1989, and eventually won the case posthumously, in 1994. When visiting the area, 'Spanky' went to see New York City. As he walked through Times Square, he saw tee shirts, mugs, buttons, and other memorabilia for sale. He wasn't making a cent off of these items, and he was working for a living. The story goes that he was brought to tears over this, as a lucrative industry was being run at his expense." Bob regularly frequents another restaurant inspired by the late Our Gang star; Spanky's Speakeasy Bar & Grill in Naples, Florida. At least Spanky got a little something for that; he sold the rights to use his name and likeness to the place for a one-time fee of $5000.

Spanky's parents had given the Roach Studios exclusive rights to his name and likeness in a 1936 contract. This practice is still common in the industry; David Letterman made a star out of Calvert DeForest, who was a lowly paid receptionist at a drug rehabilitation center before he became Larry "Bud" Melman on *Late Night with*

David Letterman. When Letterman switched to CBS, NBC refused to let him use the Melman name, claiming it was their intellectual property. On the new *Late Show with David Letterman,* DeForest just used his real name, while playing the exact same character. While Spanky may have been understandably frustrated by the usage of his character, he never appeared to harbor any grudges against Hal Roach. In 1984, he and Jackie Cooper presented the then ninety-two-year-old Roach with an honorary Academy Award, and Spanky made sure to publicly thank him for hiring him fifty-three years earlier.

Other than periodically mulling over these sad tidbits from one individual's life, it wasn't until 2009 that I started suspecting that what happened to Spanky was hardly an isolated case. I began to email, write and telephone many actors and musical performers from the past, primarily those who were most active in the 1960s. One of the first I attempted to contact was Spanky McFarland's widow, going through author Richard W. Bann, who co-wrote a book that had long fascinated me, *The Little Rascals: The Life and Times of Our Gang* with Leonard Maltin. Unfortunately, Doris McFarland never replied to me. The response from other old entertainers was encouraging, but ultimately other projects consumed me. I always intended to revisit the subject, but it wasn't really until about seven years later that I began to dig further and find more information.

When I finally decided to resume the idea for this book, I thought of incorporating much of the dark side of the entertainment world into the story. This wasn't just about performers being underpaid or ripped off by unscrupulous managers, agents, studios, record companies, producers or promoters. It was also about all the unnatural deaths connected to the world of show business, the inexplicable falls from grace, the abrupt retirements, and the figurative, sometimes literal disappearance of some performers. I never realized just how temporary fame more often than not is. I was especially intrigued by the unfairness of the pay structure; why did some entertainers become so incredibly wealthy doing basically the same thing that many of those who were ripped off, and forced to find other work to support themselves, were doing? If you've read my book *Survival of the Richest*, you will understand that this kind of disparity is one of my pet issues. And this disparity continues, generation after generation, in the world of show business.

Bela Lugosi was paid peanuts for his starring role in the iconic 1931 film *Dracula,* while those with lesser roles in the same movie were compensated more than generously. Lugosi received all of $3,500 to portray Dracula[5], only a quarter of what David Manners earned for his supporting role as Jonathan Harker, according to IMDb. Turner Classic Movies reported that later, during the filming of 1939's *Son of Frankenstein*, Universal Studios would try to take advantage of Bela again. While co-stars Boris Karloff and Basil Rathbone were handsomely paid, the studio slashed Lugosi's salary to only $500 a week, and scheduled all his scenes to be shot in one week. Director Rowland V. Lee was incensed by this, and purposefully kept Lugosi on the set from the first day of shooting until the last. In a similar situation, seventy three years later, Jon Heder was paid the initial sum of just $1,000 for playing the title character in the independent cult classic *Napoleon Dynamite*.

Bela Lugosi Jr. became an attorney, and filed a lawsuit against Universal Pictures for using the actor's personality rights, in 1966. It was concentrated primarily on the widespread usage of the Count Dracula character, noting that Universal had advertised Bela "Count Dracula" Lugosi in pictures where he played a different role. Eventually, Lugosi's heirs were awarded $70,000, and Universal was prohibited from further merchandising Lugosi's likeness.[6] However, the California Supreme Court reversed this decision in 1979. The California Celebrities Rights Act of 1985 established an inheritable right to an individual's name and likeness for seventy years after their death. In 2007, the law was amended to include anyone who had died since January 1, 1938. In 1993, Lugosi Jr. successfully represented two of the Three Stooges, Larry Fine and Curly Joe DeRita, who were suing Moe Howard, over merchandising income.[7]

In today's entertainment world, musical artists still have a hit or miss relationship with record companies and their own management, but overall certainly fare worse financially on average than their peers did forty years ago. As singer-songwriter Graham Parker would tell me in 2018, "Money was everywhere" in the music industry in the '70s and '80s. Television actors, on the other hand, began doing a whole lot better financially from the 1980s on, than their predecessors did in the early years of the medium. Near the end of its long run on the air, the entire cast of the hit series *Friends* was making a million dollars per episode. Tina Yothers, who played one of the less featured regulars on *Family Ties,* once admitted to Howard Stern that she was set for life because of the show, which represented almost all of her work in show business. In 2008, the voice actors for *The Simpsons* demanded more money and eventually settled for a staggering $400,000 per episode. For voice work. It wasn't always that way in the entertainment business. Spanky McFarland was not alone. Lots of other performers saw far less money than we imagined, and far less than they deserved. Others were plagued by unknown demons, and oddly clashed with a lifestyle any of us would envy. The fall from fame was so swift for some that it defied all logic. And then there is the continuous slew of unnatural deaths, which have always been uncommonly prevalent in Hollywood. Those are the personalities I've always been attracted to; the ones who were ripped off, or were associated in some way with the stranger aspects of the entertainment world.

This is their story.

Chapter One

No Business Like Show Business

I used to think as I looked at the Hollywood night, 'there must be thousands of girls sitting alone like me, dreaming of becoming a movie star. But I'm not going to worry about them. I'm dreaming the hardest.'

-Marilyn Monroe

WHAT EXACTLY DOES "fame" mean? Most of us have the impression that those who are singing the hit songs we hear on the radio, or starring in a popular television show, or appearing in box office smashes on the big screen are being paid enormous sums of money. We assume they're filthy rich. We also believe that, once someone truly "makes it" in Hollywood or the music business, they will be set financially for life. We picture them happily wiling away their golden years, counting their royalty checks and enjoying an endless supply of great memories. We certainly don't imagine any of them resorting to working menial jobs, or becoming homeless, or taking their own lives.

Stephen Foster is generally considered to be the father of American popular music. Foretelling the fate that would befall so many of his fellow artists a century later, Foster saw very little of the profits his enduring music generated for his publisher, W.C. Peters. Foster's wildly successful song *Oh! Susanna* was sold by twenty-one different publishers; one of them netted the composer all of $100. This same publisher even bragged about making $10,000 in the first year alone from the song.[8] Foster was probably the first person to attempt to make a living as a professional songwriter, but he wasn't helped much by giving away a classic like *Old Folks at Home* for $15.[9] Eventually, he contracted with some New York music publishers, who agreed to pay him 2 cents royalty for every copy sold by them. The persistently impoverished Foster died at only thirty-seven, after accidentally hitting his head in a New York hotel room. In his worn leather wallet, which contained thirty-seven cents, was found a scrap of paper with the words "Dear friends and gentle hearts," written on it, inspiring the title of a later song, *Dear Hearts and Gentle People*. Edgar Allan Poe, the literary equivalent of Foster, had his own financial struggles, which are an integral part of his legend - he was paid all of $9 for *The Raven* and only ten people attended his funeral. It's a delicious irony that the name still most associated with tales of horror, died one of the most mysterious deaths ever recorded. On October 3, 1849, the forty-year-old Poe was found, delirious and dressed in someone else's shabby clothing, lying in a Baltimore gutter. Poe, who had not been seen or heard from since leaving Richmond, Virginia on September 27, died four days later, without ever becoming coherent enough to explain the situation. As the curator of the Poe Museum put it, "Maybe it's fitting that since he invented the detective story, he left us with a real-life mystery."[10] Various theories, ranging from murder to the ravages of alcoholism to a victim of vote fraud (Poe was found at a polling site on election day) have been proposed, but no definitive cause of death has ever been established. Adding to the intrigue was the never identified

"Poe Toaster" (or Toasters), who would appear at his original Baltimore grave early in the morning on his January 19 birthday, for some seventy-five years. The shadowy figure in black would pour a glass of cognac, raise it in a toast, and leave the unfinished bottle along with three distinctly arranged roses behind. The unexplained tradition stopped in 2010.

Renowned poet and painter William Blake died poor and unacclaimed. At the time of his death William Wordsworth wrote of him, "There was no doubt that this poor man was mad, but there is something in the madness of this man which interests me more than the sanity of Lord Byron and Walter Scott." Herman Melville, author of *Moby Dick*, may be recognized as one of the finest novelists in the English language, but he was forced to support himself as a customs inspector and died destitute and unknown. There is a disputed legend that Melville was referred to as "Henry" in his *New York Times* obituary, but it is known that a follow-up story a week later called him "Hiram." Henry David Thoreau couldn't find a publisher, and paid for the printing of 1,000 copies of *A Week on the Concord and Merrimack Rivers* himself, of which only 300 sold. Thoreau's classic *Walden* sold very sparingly during his lifetime; the author made a grand total of $9 from the twelve copies the book sold in 1856.[11] Bram Stoker, the author of *Dracula*, and Lewis Carroll, who wrote *Alice in Wonderland*, two of the most timeless works of English literature, both left modest estates of well under $10,000. Stoker had to petition for a compassionate grant from the Royal Literary Fund less than a year before his 1912 death. His widow was forced to sell his hand-written notes later, for which she received the equivalent of about $300. She would engage in a long legal battle with the makers of the 1922 German film *Nosferatu*, before finally prevailing.[12] After granting the stage rights to her husband's work, she never received fair compensation after it became a hit play in England and then the United States. Vincent Van Gogh was penniless when he took his own life at only thirty-seven. Providing his own epitaph, he wrote, "I can't change the fact that my paintings don't sell. But the time will come when people will recognize that they are worth more than the value of the paints used in the picture." He sold only one painting during his lifetime, for just under $450.[13] Franz Schubert died in financial straits and relative obscurity. Oscar Wilde ended his days deliriously wandering the streets of Paris with no financial resources, leaving just $300 behind him. Franz Kafka was largely unknown during his short life, and supported himself by working in insurance and operating an asbestos factory. According to Jim Christy, author of *The Long Slow Death of Jack Kerouac,* when the famed beat writer died at just forty-seven, he had all of $62 in the bank.[14] J.D. Salinger, on the other hand, who famously spent the last nearly five decades of his life as the world's foremost literary recluse, with only *Catcher in the Rye* and a handful of other short published works to his credit, somehow managed to accrue a $20 million net worth.

Buffalo Bill Cody's Wild West Show earned him great renown, but when he died in 1917 he was flat broke. For unclear reasons, Henry Bishop, composer of *Home! Sweet Home!* and other songs, died in poverty. Ragtime composer Scott Joplin died young of syphilis, and was buried in an unmarked, pauper's grave. His music enjoyed a revival over fifty years later, when Marvin Hamlisch adapted his work into the theme song for the movie *The Sting.* Eva Tanguay was the highest paid star in Vaudeville, earning some $3,500 weekly before her fame began to dip in the 1920s. She quickly drifted into obscurity, and spent her final years in a very modest house worth just over $4,000. The two teenagers who created Superman, Jerry Siegel and Joe Shuster, sold the rights to their character to *Detective Comics* in 1938 for $130.[15] Later, Siegel would pitch his idea of a separate *Superboy* comic without success, only to find when he was in the Army that *Detective Comics* had stolen his idea without any credit. By the 1950s, Shuster was working as a deliveryman. Legend has it that he embarrassed the staff by delivering a package to the

DC Comics building, and the CEO supposedly gave him $100 and told him to get a new coat and another job. Siegel and Shuster filed lawsuits for decades, but kept losing in court. By 1975, Siegel too was working as a courier, making a reported $7500 annually, and Shuster had gone blind and was living with his brother in an apartment.[16] That same year, primarily to avoid what was becoming a public relations nightmare, Warner Brothers (who was in the midst of producing the first in a series of *Superman* films starring Christopher Reeve), agreed to provide the two with a modest yearly stipend and medical benefits, as well as credit them in future *Superman* stories. The heirs of both Siegel and Shuster continued litigation after their deaths, with Siegel's family seeming to fare much better. Bill Finger was never even credited as being the co-creator of Batman by his more famous, and much wealthier, associate Bob Kane, until years after his relatively early death. He left behind a net worth of $300,000, in what was described as a state of poverty.[17]

Hollywood moguls Samuel Goldwyn, Cecil B. DeMille, Jesse Lasky, Mack Sennett, and Charlie Chaplin were honorary pallbearers at the funeral of D.W. Griffith, who died in 1948 in surprising obscurity while living alone in a hotel room. Journalist Ezra Goodman stated that the week before, Griffith "probably could not have gotten any of them on the telephone."[18] Griffith's career had declined in his waning years to such an extent that he was high on director Woody Van Dyke's "panic list," consisting of once successful movie people who now were desperate for work. Oddly, he was buried in Kentucky, and it wasn't until two years later that the Directors Guild of America provided him with a headstone. In 1959, the distribution rights to thirty of Griffith's greatest films were sold at auction for a mere $21,000, to the only bidder. Cutting-edge comedian Lenny Bruce went bankrupt and was declared a pauper by the United States District Court in San Francisco, only months before he died at age forty of a drug overdose in 1966. Bruce claimed to have earned all of $6,000 in 1964.[19] War hero turned movie star

Audie Murphy was reportedly bankrupt a few years before he died in a 1971 plane crash at only forty-five. Sherman Helmsley, best known for starring in the long-running situation comedy *The Jeffersons*, died bankrupt and a long dispute arose over the rights to his future residuals. The legendary Fats Waller supposedly once traded nine of his compositions to bandleader Fletcher Henderson for a bag of hamburgers. Frankie Lymon was never paid songwriting royalties for Frankie Lymon and the Teenagers' huge 1956 hit *Why Do Fools Fall in Love* or anything else he wrote during his very short lifetime. Legendary jazz figure Joe "King" Oliver died when he couldn't afford medical treatment, while working as a janitor in a pool hall. Solomon Linda, the South African composer who inspired the hit single *The Lion Sleeps Tonight*, died impoverished and didn't have a headstone for his grave for eighteen years. In 2006, his family was finally awarded millions in back royalties.[20] Marvin Gaye made millions of dollars for Motown Records in the 1960s, but by 1979, the singer had filed for bankruptcy and moved to Hawaii, where he lived in a van and survived on bananas and pineapples. After a successful comeback, he moved back in his parents' house and was tragically shot by his father, Marvin Gay Sr., on April 1, 1984. At the time he died, Marvin Gaye was supposedly destitute. A story broke in 2015 about Gaye's heirs getting a $7.4 million payout from Robin Thicke and Pharrell Williams for infringing upon his copyright with their song *Blurred Lines*. A heated family dispute arose, between Gaye's sisters, who claimed they "received nothing from his estate" and had been banned from singing his songs, and Gaye's second wife Jan. The value of Gaye's estate seemingly improved significantly after his tragic death, as an article on the payout reported that his three children "receive royalty payments from his vast back catalog." In contrast, Gaye's two sisters were said to be "living effectively in poverty."[21]

Gaye's fellow Motown artist and frequent collaborator Tammi Terrell was tragically cut down just short of her twenty-fifth birthday from brain cancer. Terrell suffered terribly, enduring eight operations, going blind and being confined to a wheelchair as her weight dipped to barely ninety pounds. Some of Gaye and Terrell's timeless duets included *You're All I Need to Get By*, *Ain't Nothing Like the Real Thing*, and *Ain't No Mountain High Enough*. One of those urban legends in the business holds that Terrell's problems began with her husband, volatile Temptations singer David Ruffin, hitting her in the head with a hammer. Multiple witnesses had reported seeing the abusive Ruffin beating Terrell up.[22] Terrell's family banned everyone from Motown from the memorial service except Marvin Gaye, disgusted at the way they'd treated her during the final stages of her life. It is easy to speculate that their feelings probably also stemmed from Terrell being shortchanged financially like so many others in the business. Gaye is said to have never completely recovered from the loss of his beautiful singing partner, which contributed to his abuse of drugs and chronic depression.[23]

Allen Klein, who managed both the Beatles and the Rolling Stones, had a plaque on his office desk, engraved with the 23rd Psalm, which contained the blasphemous addition, "For I am the biggest bastard in the valley." Klein is credited with being the first to demand large advances for artists, but always managed to do especially well for himself. Thanks to one of his characteristically lucrative deals, most of the Rolling Stones' hit songs belonged to ABKCO, one of Klein's companies, and not to the band members. The band would sue Klein over this in 1971.[24] Klein managed Sam Cooke, and when the singer/songwriter was shot to death in still unclear circumstances at just thirty-three, he became the owner of virtually all of Cooke's valuable musical catalog. Klein's comment on the early days of rock and roll is illuminating; "All those guys who sold a lot of records thought they had money...they didn't end up with it." John Lennon was strangely sold on Allen Klein, hoping he would bring the Fab Four financial security. "I don't want to see Ringo playing the Northern working men's clubs to survive when he's in his 60s," Lennon declared. Years later, Lennon would regret his affinity for Klein, and the Beatles were forced into a legal battle to separate from him.[25] The Beatles themselves lost control of music's most cherished catalog, consisting primarily of the countless songs written by John Lennon and Paul McCartney, which was eventually purchased by the BBC. The songs were combined with a great deal of less valuable material, and McCartney was unable to purchase back just the Beatles songs in the early 1980s. Michael Jackson swooped in and bought the entire catalog, giving him control over the Beatles' biggest songs. In 2017, McCartney reached a settlement with Sony, regaining the copyright to the Beatles catalog.[26]

John Fogerty, the front man for the wildly successful band Creedence Clearwater Revival, who also wrote most of the band's songs, fought for many years to regain control of his own material from Fantasy Records. Fantasy owner Saul Zaentz had finagled a deal whereby he owned the copyright to all those songs. In addition to this, much of the money C.C.R. had made was lost in one of Zaentz's off-shore tax shelters. Eventually, Fogerty won back royalties in court, but the ownership of his songs was not returned to him.[27] "We were the only artists that mattered on the label. We were selling almost 99.9% of the company's records," Fogerty explained. "I thought we would share to a great degree in the company's success. But then it didn't happen. Fantasy owns the songs and they're supposed to pay me as the songwriter, but I've had to fight to get royalties from 1980 and every year after that. Basically, to get paid I had to sue them, that was their stance." Sadly, Fogerty's late brother Tom eventually turned against him and sided with Zaentz, whom he called his "best friend." Fogerty became estranged from the other two original members of C.C.R. as well.[28] At the other end of the spectrum, Led Zeppelin's manager Peter Grant managed to land them the highest royalty rate in the business - some five times what the Beatles were earning.[29] At last report, both Robert Plant and Jimmy Page were worth some $170 million each. By startling contrast, band mate John Bonham, voted the greatest drummer of all time by *Rolling Stone,* died with a comparatively low $10 million. The other original member of Led Zeppelin, John Paul Jones, currently has $90 million, according to Celebrity Net Worth. As we shall see, such financial disparities are par for the course in the entertainment industry.

Chuck Berry was probably plagiarized more than any other rock and roll artist. The Beach Boys' hit single *Surfin' USA* was an unofficial remake of Berry's *Sweet Little Sixteen.* In this case, justice was somewhat served, as the Beach Boys' manager Murray Wilson (father of band members Brian, Dennis and Carl) simply gave Berry the copyright to the song when he complained.[30] Evidently they never paid him for copying his lead guitar riff on their classic song *Fun, Fun, Fun.* Berry was surprisingly shrewd in financial matters, and accumulated a fortune of at least $10 million, according to Celebrity Net Worth. Fats Domino was another black artist who was paid well for his music. Chubby Checker, whose last "Twist" hit came in the early 1960s, has a nice $4 million net worth, considering the brevity of his recording success. Chubby Checker was one of many entertainers I attempted to contact while researching this book; on February 3, 2009, he sent me the cryptic email reply, "Thanks for your interest but let it go." Truly mystifying is the fact that Lulu, the British pop singer who scored big with the 1967 song *To Sir, With Love,* but did little else in the business, has a $30 million fortune, according to Celebrity Net Worth. At the other end of the spectrum, the far more successful Billy Joel has declared bankruptcy several times; in one instance because his manager had siphoned off $30 million without Joel's knowledge. By 2001, 1970s teen heartthrob Leif Garrett was so destitute that his only income was the $1,000 monthly allowance from his mother, and he had only $350 in cash.[31] When Stax Records folded in 1975, they owed Isaac Hayes some $5 million, forcing the *Shaft* singer, who also co-wrote hits for other artists such as Sam and Dave's *Hold On! I'm Comin'* and *Soul Man*, to declare bankruptcy and lose all future royalties on his old songs.[32] His later years were notable primarily for his role as the voice of "Chef" on *South Park*.

The "curse" of the Little Rascals is hard to deny. Carl "Alfalfa" Switzer was shot to death over $50 at the age of thirty-one. Darla Hood would tell Richard Lamparski in an interview that the troubled Switzer had been taken in by Roy Rogers and Dale Evans. Billie "Buckwheat" Thomas was found dead from a heart attack in his home, at the age of forty-nine, by a neighbor who hadn't seen him in days. Darla Hood died suddenly, and inexplicably, of hepatitis while in the hospital undergoing minor surgery, at only forty-seven. Darla would tell Richard Lamparski that the most money she ever made was from voice work in Chicken-of-the-Sea commercials, and that her parents never gave her a penny of what she'd earned in the Our Gang shorts. Spanky McFarland noted cryptically, during a 1985 lecture at Murray State University, that Darla's old child co-star "Buckwheat" Thomas had died of a broken heart just a year later, still distraught over the loss of Hood. Darla spoke for all child stars when she said, "I felt I had let my fans down by not remaining a child."[33] Norman "Chubby" Chaney's excessive weight was due in large measure to a glandular disorder, which took his life at the tender age of twenty-one. Bobby "Wheezer" Hutchins was killed in a military training plane crash at only twenty years of age. Donald Haines, who later was a background regular in the East Side Kids' films, was killed in World War II. Scotty Beckett led a troubled life as an adult, including alcohol and drug problems, and run-ins with the law. He died at only thirty-eight after undergoing a severe beating from an unknown assailant.[34] Mickey Daniels, the lead in most of the silent shorts, died alone in a hotel room of cirrhosis of the liver, at age fifty-five. It was years before his remains were claimed by his family, and he still mysteriously was buried in an unmarked grave. Robert "Bonedust" Young was burned to death at thirty-three after falling asleep while smoking. Billy "Froggy" Laughlin, one of the few bright spots in the later MGM shorts that were generally far inferior to the original Hal Roach productions, was killed at only sixteen when a speeding truck ran into his motor scooter. Laughlin had left show business and was delivering newspapers at the time.[35] One of the few Rascals who lived a long life, Jay R. Smith, was stabbed to death at age eighty-seven by a homeless man he'd befriended, who dumped his body in the desert.[36] Darwood "Waldo" Kaye lived to be seventy-two, but died unnaturally when he was struck by a hit-and-run driver while he was on the sidewalk. Hal Roach, meanwhile, scoffed at all the claims about a "curse," telling an interviewer in 1973, "…if you took 176 other kids and followed them through their lives, I believe you would find the same percentage of them having trouble later in life." The predictably non-alarmist website Snopes dismissed any notions about the deaths being disproportionately suspect and premature as well, claiming there was no unusual pattern to the deaths of the children involved in the series. Hal Roach had every reason to be upbeat; he outlived nearly all his child stars, dying in 1992 at age 100, and had accumulated great wealth.

Another of Roach's star performers, the nearly forgotten Charley Chase, died at just forty-six. At his peak, Chase was every bit as big as the Our Gang kids or Laurel and Hardy, the other major stars at Roach's studio. An all-around talent, Chase would often sing songs he'd written himself in his films. After being dismissed by the Roach studios rather curiously, Chase went on to Columbia, where he starred in his own shorts and produced and directed some of the best work of The Three Stooges, including the 1938 classic *Violent is the Word for Curly.* Curly suffered one of his series of physical injuries during filming of the short; while being roasted over a fire, he was badly burned. "Curly was hollering his head off, and I don't blame him. Being roasted alive belongs to the Inquisition, not making two-reel comedies," claimed witness Edward Bernds, who would later direct some of the Stooges' shorts himself.[37] Chase was a heavy drinker, and became devastated over the death of his drug-addicted younger brother James Parrott in 1939. Parrott starred in many silent Roach features, but achieved his greatest success as the director of some of the finest Laurel & Hardy two-reel comedies, including the 1932 Oscar winner *The Music Box*. Parrott died either of a heart ailment or suicide, depending upon the source. Chase died only thirteen months after his brother, wracked with guilt over the fact he'd refused to help him financially until he'd cleaned up his life.

Don Myrick, saxophonist for the band Earth, Wind & Fire, was shot to death on July 30, 1993 by a Los Angeles police officer, while he was in the process of being served a search warrant. Although Myrick's family eventually won a $400,000 lawsuit against the city, he still strangely lies in an unmarked grave in Inglewood, California.[38] Child star Bobby Driscoll, who won an Oscar as a twelve-year-old, died penniless at only thirty-one. With a slew of adult problems including a heroin addiction, Driscoll had drifted into the world of Andy Warhol; a friend of the pop artist described the former child star's presence as "That was Warhol's perversity in full play — you know, dissipated Hollywood." Two boys found his drug-addled corpse in an abandoned tenement, with no identification on it. He was buried in an unmarked, pauper's grave, and remains interred there even after his mother and Disney Studios identified him through fingerprint records. His mother hadn't seen him in years, and only found out about his death a year and a half later, after taking out newspaper ads about his disappearance.[39] There are a surprisingly large number of celebrated figures who were inexplicably buried in unmarked graves, starting with the legendary composer Wolfgang Amadeus Mozart. John Wayne, about as large a star as Hollywood has ever seen, lay in an unmarked grave for nearly twenty years. His family did this allegedly out of concern for the distraction it might cause for the others interred there, but it's still odd in my book. Although thousands attended the funeral of renowned blues singer Bessie Smith, she was buried without a headstone. "It wasn't because she died penniless," noted blues expert Steve Salter. Another unforgettable singer, Roy Orbison, was granted a spot on the Hollywood Walk of Fame after his death, but his family still hasn't seen fit to obtain a marker for his final resting place. George C. Scott lies in the same Westwood Memorial Park alongside Orbison, in an unmarked grave as well, as does musical iconoclast Frank Zappa.[40]

It's unknown why actor Fred Gwynne (most notable as TV's Herman Munster) lies in an unmarked grave in a Maryland Methodist Church cemetery. When Gwynne died in 1993, he left behind a surprisingly modest $2 million estate. Wallace Ford enjoyed a long career in movies and television, but for unclear reasons lies in an unmarked grave in Culver City. The aforementioned Our Gang member Norman "Chubby" Chaney was buried in an unmarked grave due to his family's lack of funds. Finally, after seventy-six years, a fund drive started by Detroit rock musician MIKAL resulted in headstones being placed on the graves of both Cheney and his mother.[41] One of the entertainment world's true superstars, Lon Chaney, lies in an unmarked crypt at Forest Lawn. Even modern icons like Steve Jobs and Michael Jackson were buried in unmarked graves. Scott Michaels, owner of the Dearly Departed Tours and Gallery, has arranged financing for headstones for a number of actors who were buried in unmarked graves. Included among them are Schlitzie, the sideshow performer born with microcephaly, who played the character Pinhead in Tod Browning's controversial 1932 film *Freaks*, Jonathan Hale, who portrayed Mr. Dithers in the *Blondie* movies, Thelma Pelish, who appeared in several big films from the 1950s-1970s, and Johnny Arthur, a very busy actor from the Golden Age, who invariably played fussy, effeminate characters (Michaels called him "the gay Stepin Fetchit"). "To end up in an unmarked hole in North Hollywood is a shame," Michaels stated. "These people spent their lives yearning to be recognized."[42]

Forgotten actress Sheila Terry, who played the lead in early talkies like 1934's 'Neath the Arizona Skies (opposite a young John Wayne), killed herself at either forty-six or forty-nine (like many actors, the source for her birth date varies), and was penniless at the time. No one claimed her body, so she was buried in a Potter's field in New York City. In his February 12, 1957 newspaper column "My New York," Mel Heimer recalled that Terry "could have used some good luck. I first met her in the early 1940s. By that time her movie career was behind her. I never did get to know where she came from—and I guess even she didn't know where she was going exactly—but I did know that back in the middle 1930s she was a young Hollywood starlet. She squeezed out something of a living for it and I remember she said she once got $100 for three days' acting…" Heimer described a situation countless older actors must have found themselves in at the time, when he wrote, "the only thing that ever made her bitter was that television was using her old movies and she wasn't getting any money from them."

Kay Francis wrote in her diary: "When I die, I want to be cremated so that no sign of my existence is left on this earth. I can't wait to be forgotten." Francis was the highest-paid female actress during the early talkies era, and ironically has become perhaps Hollywood's biggest forgotten star. David Bowie was cremated privately with not even family members present, and his ashes were buried in a secret location. He was following the lead of fellow musical star Freddie Mercury (front man for the huge group Queen), whose ashes were interred at a still unknown location following his death in 1991. According to controversial author Albert Goldman, John Lennon "had a horror of cremation, a practice that he inveighed against and once proposed to protest in a song."[43] Jude Kessler, author of a painstakingly detailed series of books on John Lennon, told me that Lennon's fear of the dark and dread of cremation was well known to his family. He had even requested that Procol Harum's hit song *Whiter Shade of Pale* be played at his funeral. All this makes the fact that his widow Yoko Ono had him cremated, apparently without consulting any of his family in England, very peculiar. Lennon's ashes, depending upon the source, were either kept by Yoko or sprinkled on the grounds of the famous Liverpool orphanage Strawberry Field, which inspired the title of one of his most memorable songs. Actor Carl Betz, who starred in the television show *Judd for the Defense,* but is probably best remembered as Donna Reed's husband on *The Donna Reed Show,* was cremated and the location of his ashes is unknown. Author Truman Capote's ashes were in the possession of his good friend Joanne Carson, widow of *Tonight Show* host Johnny Carson, until her death in 2015. They were thereafter included in the auction of the rest of her estate. James Doohan, who played Scotty on *Star Trek,* fittingly had his ashes "beamed up" into space along with the remains of 307 others, by the Space X Corporation.[44] The ashes of Orson Welles lie in a covered well in Spain, on the rural property of a renowned bullfighter.

One of the saddest places in Hollywood is "the Vaultage," an off-limits spot in the Pierce Brothers Chapel of the Pines crematorium and mausoleum. There lie what the chapel refers to as the "abandoned cremated remains" of once renowned actors like Bronco Billy Anderson, Lionel Atwill, Thomas Mitchell, Edmund Gwynn and H.B. Warner. This is all the more mystifying considering that these actors had loved ones and had hardly fallen on hard times. Anderson was married to the same woman for over sixty years, who survived him, and had a daughter. Despite being neglected in such an incomprehensible manner, Anderson was honored in 1998, twenty- seven years after his death, with his own commemorative U.S. postage stamp. Mitchell was married three times, had two children, and his brother was President Eisenhower's Secretary of Labor. While Atwill's eldest son was killed in World War II, and his youngest son was just a baby, he was married to his fourth wife at the time of his death. Gwynn was survived by a sister, an ex-wife with whom he was still cordial enough to leave one-third of his estate, and two close male companions. Warner had three children by his second wife. There also rest the never claimed ashes of Helen Chandler, unforgettable as the fragile Mina Harker in 1931's classic *Dracula*. Chandler's life rivaled any in the history of Tinseltown in terms of tragedy. Her excessive drinking destroyed her film career at a young age, and she spent the last years of her life recovering from a fire (she explained the fire thusly: "I started drinking, because that seemed like a good idea")[45]; in and out of mental institutions, and ultimately as a prematurely aged woman (she was only fifty-six when she died) in a Venice apartment, whom only a few neighbors knew had once been a star in Hollywood.

When Andy Griffith died on July 3, 2012 at the age of eighty six, he was very strangely buried less than five hours later. A spokesman for the family merely said, "It had been planned for some time. This was the wish of his family."[46] The *Hollywood Reporter* quoted Larry F. Stegall, an official with the Funeral Directors Association, as telling CNN, "It's not very common. I don't recall having heard of it, and I've been here 32 years."[47] The only comparable case is that of Frank Zappa, who was laid to rest in his curiously unmarked grave less than twenty-four hours after his death; strangely, his death wasn't announced to the world until the following day.[48] On the other extreme, it took months for radio legend Casey Kasem to be buried, due to an ugly family dispute. When he finally was laid to rest, it was in an unmarked grave in Norway. Decades earlier, comedian Larry Semon, whose $3.6 million contract with Vitagraph in 1919 was second only to Charlie Chaplin's, and who also directed the 1925 silent version of *The Wizard of Oz*, died penniless at only thirty-nine of a supposed combination of pneumonia and nervous breakdown. His obituary noted that "Last March he filed a voluntary petition in bankruptcy, listing debts at nearly $500,000. Ceaseless worry undermined his health making him an easy victim of pneumonia."[49]

As IMDb dramatically understates, "an air of mystery surrounds his death." His wife, actress Dorothy Dwan (who played Dorothy in that 1925 film, opposite a young Oliver Hardy as the Tin Man), was curiously not permitted to view Semon's body, which was cremated immediately after a very quick funeral, which almost no one attended, allegedly per the deceased's "previous instructions." Even odder, the location of Semon's ashes remains unknown, and again according to IMDb, "his widow professed until her death to be mystified by the circumstances of his passing." How could his widow have been left out of the loop to such a degree? Such strangeness is all too common in Hollywood.

It's an intriguing bit of Hollywood lore that Bela Lugosi was buried in his *Dracula* cape. Less known is the fact that Harlan Sanders of Colonel Sanders fame was buried in his familiar white double-breasted suit. Jean Harlow was buried in the negligee she'd worn in her last film, *Saratoga*. A ukulele and tulips were buried along with Tiny Tim. Frank Sinatra, Rat Packer to the end, was buried with a fifth of Jack Daniels and a pack of Camel cigarettes. Tony Curtis had his IPhone buried with him. Leonard Bernstein wanted to be interred with a copy of *Alice in Wonderland*. Andy Warhol carried along a bottle of Estee Lauder perfume into the Great Beyond. Writer William S. Burroughs, best remembered for the novel *Naked Lunch* (which featured a dildo named Steely Dan, later inspiring the name of the successful band), was buried with a loaded revolver, a sword cane, a fedora, and a marijuana joint. Road Dahl, author of beloved children's books like *Charlie and the Chocolate Factory*, was the most eccentric of them all; he insisted on being buried along with snooker cues, pencils, a power saw, chocolates, and red wine. It's probably appropriate that rapper Tupac Shakur's ashes were mixed with marijuana and smoked by his friends. Rolling Stones lead guitarist Keith Richards confirmed in 2010 that he had indeed snorted the ashes of his late father. It is not known what he took to his grave, but Hugh Hefner was fittingly buried next to Marilyn

Monroe's crypt. Monroe, of course, was on the first cover of *Playboy* magazine. Hef did, however, fill a casket with video tapes of his personal sexual activities as well as the orgies he'd held at the Playboy mansion, and had it dumped in the ocean before his death in September 2017. "Hugh [Hefner] was terrified of the world finding out everything about his past. He had kept a treasure chest of memories of his life with all these beautiful women dating back from the 1950s to the mid-1990s," according to an anonymous insider. Hefner allegedly did this primarily out of concern for the numerous married celebrities that were captured on these films.[50]

Former Creed front man Scott Stapp, whose Grammy-winning band sold 28 million albums worldwide and was a huge draw in the late 1990s, announced in 2014 that "Right now I'm living in a Holiday Inn, by the grace of God, because there's been a couple of weeks I had to live in my truck. I had no money, not even for gas or food..." Stapp claimed that his money had been stolen, evidently by those he trusted to manage it, and he had failed to receive royalty payments.[51] Stapp was hardly the first prominent figure in the entertainment world to slide into homelessness. Sylvester "Sly" Stone of the Family Stone went from being one of the biggest names in music to living in his van on the streets of Los Angeles, claiming his ex-manager had cost him $80 million. Stone was awarded $5 million in lost royalties in January, 2015. Former leading lady Margot Kidder, despite getting fairly steady work after starring as Lois Lane in four big-budget *Superman* films from 1978-1987, declared bankruptcy in 1990 and was sleeping in cardboard boxes and other people's backyards by 1996. Suffering from intense paranoia, she eventually was confronted by a Glendale, California homeowner, her front teeth missing and her hair cut off.[52] She was able to recover and become a political activist in Montana. Kidder was one of several celebrities I communicated with on Facebook; she and I agreed on many things politically, and she said nice things about my blog. I was stunned when she abruptly died on May 13, 2018 (Mothers'

Day) at age sixty-nine. Perhaps an indication of how far she'd fallen from the limelight was the fact that a Montana funeral home initially announced her death, not an agent or publicist. Her personal manager subsequently reported that she'd died in her sleep peacefully. However, it would eventually be acknowledged that it was a suicide from a drug and alcohol overdose. Kidder's reported net worth was a startlingly low $300,000. Her last wish was a suitably eccentric desire to have her remains devoured by a pack of wolves, but she was cremated instead. Brett Butler spent some time in a Georgia homeless shelter after her hit television series *Grace Under Fire* was cancelled. Debbie Clark, known as "Storm" on the television series *American Gladiators,* was making some $1500 a day on the show. After an injury ended her physically demanding career, Clark was forced to work menial jobs. Years later, she was discovered to be living on the streets of San Diego with her ten-year-old son. Clark was still trying to get off the streets in January 2018 when she asked for contributions to her Go Fund Me page on Facebook. Sean Young was once all the rage in huge 1980s films like *Blade Runner* and *Wall Street.* She evidently was plagued by a good many demons; in addition to having alcohol problems, following a tumultuous relationship with actor James Woods she reportedly sent him and his girlfriend pictures of corpses and mutilated bodies. In August, 2018, reports broke that Young was wanted for questioning in a New York burglary. Oddly, the actress was said to have worked for the company where the robbery occurred, the School of Old, but had been fired four months previously.[53]

Sultry Barbara Payton was making $5,000 a week in 1950. She was linked romantically to half of Hollywood, and was the cause of a widely publicized fight between B movie actor Tom Neal and Franchot Tone, which left Tone in a coma. Payton's career was marred by the scandal, and she became a heavy drinker. She was later arrested for prostitution on Sunset Boulevard, and was paid a mere $1,000 for her autobiography *I Am Not Ashamed,* published in 1963. Relegated to sleeping on benches, she moved back in with her parents, and died at their home at only thirty-nine. As for Tom Neal, he was blacklisted in Hollywood after the fight with Tone. He eventually moved to Palm Springs and became a gardener. On April 2, 1965, the body of Neal's third wife, Gayle Bennett, was found in their home with a gunshot wound in the back of her head. Neal claimed the shooting was accidental, but was convicted of involuntary manslaughter.[54] After serving six years in prison, Neal went back to landscaping and gardening, before dying the next year in 1972. Neal's acting career was notable primarily for his all too convincing leading role in the ultra low-budget 1945 film noir classic *Detour*. Georgeanna Tillman of the huge girl group the Marvellettes suffered from Lupus and other health issues for years. Forced to leave the band, she worked as a secretary at Motown, and then moved back home to Michigan, where she lived with her mother before dying at only thirty-six.

Tough guy character actor Richard Jaeckel, who appeared in countless television shows and was nominated for an Academy Award in 1970, filed for bankruptcy in 1994, lost his home and most of his possessions, and moved into the Motion Picture and Television Retirement Center, where he died three years later. His good friend, actor Robert Blake, would proclaim that Jaeckel was the only person he'd ever met who was "crazier than me." Natalie Wood's younger sister Lana, who appeared in several television shows and big films, including the 1971 James Bond contribution *Diamonds are Forever*, made the following sad announcement on Facebook on March 23, 2017: "I have just been evicted from my home where I've lived for seven years. I got ten days to move, don't have moving money, don't know if there's anything available, have no one to take in a family of six, My daughters COPD has worsened and her cancer is back. My grandchildren are hysterical. I have to somehow remain calm, and not kill myself." The situation seemed so unbelievable that many on Facebook suspected her account had been hacked. Lana Wood assured everyone that her dilemma was all too real, and updated her friends with heart-wrenching posts like: "Frantically looking for a home. Kids crying and don't want to leave this town. Nothing here unless a miracle occurs, even looking at places with no city water...well only. I don't know I really don't know...my daughter held up well, carrying her oxygen and delaying any other treatments right now." The last reported figure for Lana Wood on Celebrity Net Worth was an almost certainly exaggerated $1 million.

Lana Wood's daughter Evan Taylor Smedley Maldonado revealed some startling details of her own struggles on a Network 54 forum. The post, dated July 7, 2008, was apparently in response to some scurrilous rumors regarding her family. She wrote, "Last year, due to medical bills and having to take out a second mortgage on our home (which we lived in for 12 years), we lost our home to foreclosure. You can look it up online, or I can scan whoever would like them, copies of the trustee sale notices. My husband nor myself are not on "dope" and my husband has worked at the same company for 11 years. He has the same bank account that he opened when he moved to California in 1986. Neither of us has ever been arrested and NO ONE in my house (including Lana) drinks alcohol EVER. None of us smoke. I am in remission from Hodgkins Lymphoma nodular schlerosis. I lost one lung and my thyroid to complications. I have trouble breathing every day of my life. I am 33 years old. I have nothing NOTHING positive come out of being related to Natalie. I have only been hurt, ridiculed, stared at, pointed at, and had perfect strangers speak ill of my family and act like they know everything about us. How many of you would like to have that? I will gladly trade." Tragically, Evan would die at only forty-two in July 2017, which resulted in even more heart-breaking posts from Lana Wood on Facebook.

Successful actors sometimes make an inexplicable exit from the film world, one which can't be logically explained. Jay Underwood, star of the memorable 1986 movie *The Boy Who Could Fly*, only appeared in a few other films, and became the pastor of a Baptist church. His co-star in that film, Lucy Deakins, left the business to become a lawyer. 1980s blonde actress Deborah Foreman, who starred in such films as *Valley Girl, My Chauffer* and *April Fool's Day*, exited movies at a very young age. She worked as a graphics artist, and at last report, was the owner of a Pilates studio in Hollywood. Peter Ostrun's only film role was as Charlie in 1971's *Willy Wonka and the Chocolate Factory.* He turned down a three-picture deal and eventually became a veterinarian in New York State. His co-star in the film, Denise Nickerson, left the biz in 1978 and became a nurse, before dying at sixty-two in July, 2019. Julie Dawn Cole, the only one of the five child stars in the film still acting as of 2013, was paid just under $750 for her role, and reported receiving no royalties from video sales of the film. Ian Weighill's witty and convincing performance as the oldest boy in Disney's 1971 film *Bedknobs and Broomsticks* was his sole screen credit. There is absolutely no further biographical information about him online, not even the date or place of his birth. Danny Lloyd, so chillingly memorable as the youngster in *The Shining*, didn't like acting and became a biology professor. Lloyd's co-stars in the film, real life twins Lisa and Louise Burns, who terrified viewers with their brief hallway scene ("come play with us, Danny") never made another film. Another scary youngster, Harvey Stephens, had only two more screen credits after playing Damien in 1976's *The Omen*. Decades earlier, Brenda Joyce just walked away from Hollywood at age 32 in 1949, following her fifth Tarzan movie. After leaving Hollywood, she moved to Washington, D.C. and worked for ten years with Refugee Services, where she helped people find work and housing. Later she worked with Catholic Resettlement in California.[55] Even earlier, William Janney worked steadily in films, from 1929-1937, but then inexplicably quit the business. He lived to be eighty-four, but was so unknown at the time of his death that sources indicate only that he died in "Idaho,

USA." Tom Hulce was a rising star, including an Oscar nominated performance portraying Mozart in 1984's *Amadeus*. He appears to have unexplainably stopped acting in 2008, when he was fifty-five-years-old, and has no further screen credits.

Eighteen-year-old Sarah Holcomb starred as the drunk and promiscuous daughter of the mayor in the smash 1978 movie *Animal House*. After roles in two less remembered films, she followed that up with another plum part in the similarly successful comedy *Caddyshack*, in 1980. Incredibly, that would prove to be her swan song in the business. Sarah was apparently adversely impacted by the frat-house partying atmosphere on the set of *Animal House*. Her mother had to commit her to a psychiatric institution. As Chris Miller, who co-wrote the screenplay, recounted it, "She was young, younger than the rest of us. We were a fast crowd. Drugs were everywhere. She fell into what, for lack of a better term, you would have to call bad company. And got fucked up on drugs. Coke, primarily, if memory serves. She wound up in some home for fucked-up young girls . . . I don't know what became of her. Sad story. She only made three more films before vanishing into obscurity after Caddyshack."[56] Holcomb is reported to be living in seclusion in Connecticut, with a net worth estimated at only $50,000. Doug Kenney, one of the founders of the legendary humor magazine *National Lampoon,* who co-wrote both of these classic drug-era comedies, died at only thirty-three under bizarre circumstances. Apparently, the edge of a cliff he was standing on in Hawaii collapsed under him.

Barret Oliver, star of *The NeverEnding Story* and several other smash '80s films, quit show business at age 16 for unclear reasons. He reportedly studied nineteenth-century wet-place process and presently teaches photography in Los Angeles. Hal Scardino, young star of 1995's *The Indian in the Cupboard*, fizzled out afterwards and had only one more screen role, in 1996. Steven Anthony Lawrence, who starred as "Beans" on the television series *Even Stevens*, and appeared in other '90s shows, was seen working at a Concord, California mall as a Santa's helper in December, 2015.[57] An online update in November 2018 claimed that Lawrence was conducting seminars at local high schools and colleges. Adam Lamberg, "Gordo" on *Lizzie McGuire*, appears to have pretty much vanished from the business after the show left the air in 2004. Cast mate Ashley Brillault, the mean girl "Kate" who bullied Lizzie, has had no further screen credits. Julia Winter's role as Veronica Salt in 2005's *Charlie and the Chocolate Factory* is her only screen credit. Years before, Sarah Pickering starred in the title role in the 1987 British film *Little Dorrit*, and never had another screen credit. Marlene Lawston, convincing as the youngest daughter in 2007's *Dan in Real Life*, had only one screen credit after that film, and there appears to be no updated information about her. Amber Scott played Robin Williams' daughter in the 1991 film *Hook*, but has had only one small voice credit since then. The last update on her reported that she'd graduated from Connecticut's Trinity College in 2006. A child star in another Robin Williams film, 2002's *One Hour Photo*, Dylan Smith, only had a few more screen credits afterward, the last being in 2006. The latest update had him attending college in Rhode Island. Emily Roeske, who appeared in the Disney Channel's *Halloweentown* series of movies, has no screen credits following 2004's *Halloweentown High*. Gail Edwards, who played Danny Tanner's girlfriend Vicky on *Full House*, and also starred on anther television series, *Blossom*, suddenly retired in 1994 and settled with her husband in Sedona, Arizona. She did re-emerge in 2017 for a guest appearance as her old character on an episode of the Netflix reboot of the series, *Fuller House*. Stories broke in September 2018 that Geoffrey Owens, who played a minor but regular role on *The Cosby Show* in the 1980s, was working as a cashier at a New Jersey Trader Joe's between acting gigs. Rapper Nicki Minaj, incensed at the resultant "job shaming," gave Owens $25,000, which Owens subsequently donated to the Actor's Fund, to help his struggling peers. He did so in the memory of the late Earle Hyman, who played Cosby's father on the show and "lived his last many years and died at the Actors' Home (funded and run by the Actor's Fund)," Owens told TMZ.[58]

Brittany Ashton Holmes, whose most memorable role was as Darla in her first film, 1994's *The Little Rascals*, at last report was working for Starbucks. "I was an actress when I was little," she wrote on her My Space page, "and did this movie called *Little Rascals*. It's like really embarrassing to watch and I don't want to act anymore." Mike Maronna, star of the eclectic 1990s television series *The Adventures of Pete and Pete,* is working as an electrician in the film industry. His co-star in that series, the younger Pete, Danny Tamberelli, had his last known acting gig in a 2006 Wendy's commercial. The two Petes have gone on to host a podcast together. Michael Schoeffling, who starred in the iconic '80s movie *Sixteen Candles*, and other huge films like 1990's *Mermaids,* had no more screen credits after 1991, and wound up moving to Pennsylvania, where at last report he was selling handcrafted furniture. Jenny Wright was another busy '80s star, appearing in films like *St. Elmo's Fire* and *Out of Bounds*. She continued to get meaty roles in films like 1992's *The Lawnmower Man*, but then abruptly quit the business at barely thirty years of age. There is no updated information about her online. Jason Zimbler, who starred on the television series *Clarissa Explains it All*, hasn't had a screen credit since the show ended in 1994. His cast mate on the show, Sean O'Neal, drifted into obscurity as well, with only a few bit parts to his credit. 1990s child star Mike Vitar, best remembered for his roles in films like *The Sandlot* and *D2: The Mighty Ducks,* left show business in 1997 for the unlikely world of the Los Angeles Fire Department. Bradley Kidd, who starred in *Jumanji* and provided the voices of Flounder in *The Little Mermaid* and Chip Cup in *Beauty and the Beast,* was last reportedly working as a bartender. Noah Hathaway, who starred in the 1984 film *The NeverEnding Story* and the original *Battlestar Galactica*, left show business for years, working as a tattoo artist and martial arts instructor. Liesel Matthews, who starred in *A Little*

Princess and a few other big films like *Air Force One,* fell off the map after 2000, but was probably able to console herself as an heiress to the Hotel Hyatt fortune.

Blake Tuomy-Wilhoit, one of the very young twins on *Full House,* became a firefighter in Peachtree City, Georgia. Justin Henry, the little boy Dustin Hoffman and Meryl Streep fought over in 1979's *Kramer vs. Kramer* (a role for which he was paid an underwhelming $5,000), and the youngest actor ever nominated for an Oscar, had a limited acting career afterwards. His last role was in 2007 until recently, when he seems to have landed a few new bit parts. K.C. Martel, who appeared in Steven Spielberg's 1982 classic *E.T. the Extra-Terrestrial,* and had a recurring role in the television series *Growing Pains,* has not acted since that series ended in 1992. I couldn't find out any updated information about him, even in articles covering the thirtieth anniversary of *E.T.* Martel's *E.T.* co-star, Robert McNaughton, wound up working as a mail carrier. Chris Owen, who starred in films like 1999's *American Pie,* while continuing to accrue a decent amount of screen credits, was reported to have had less than 100 followers on Twitter and was working as a server at a sushi restaurant. Ilan Mitchell-Smith, who starred in *Weird Science* and other '80s films, was so enamored of his anonymity by the time he started dating his eventual wife that he never revealed to her that he'd been an actor, even after finding out one of her favorite movies was *The Chocolate War,* in which he'd appeared. At last report, he was a lecturer at Texas A & M University, specializing in medieval English literature. He supposedly abhors having his picture taken, for fear his students will recognize him for his *Weird Science* role. Tina Caspary appeared in several well-known films in the 1980s, but had no screen credits following 1989's *My Mom's a Werewolf.* Few of the primary actors in the 1985 film *Just One of the Guys* worked regularly in the business afterwards, including leading lady Joyce Hyser, who reportedly has a modest net worth of $2 million. Director Lisa Gottlieb only directed a few more feature films and gravitated towards teaching film history. Gabriel Melgar replaced the late Freddie Prinze on *Chico and the Man* after the young comedian's sudden death (officially attributed to suicide, but I delved into this in some detail in my earlier book *Hidden History*, and uncovered a lot more to the story). Melgar had just a few bit roles after the series ended in 1978, and the only updated information about him was that he apparently moved to Colorado. Kaleena Kiff was an adorable child actress, who starred in the television series *Love, Sidney* and was a regular on *The New Leave It to Beaver*. She had only sporadic roles as an adult, with her most recent appearance as a "female victim" in a 2008 episode of *Supernatural*. At last report, she was living in Canada with her husband and daughter. Her Facebook profile makes no mention of her acting career.

Marjoe Gortner was a child evangelist who performed his first marriage ceremony at the age of four. Gortner appeared in several big-budget movies in the 1970s, and his career continued, mostly on television, through the 1980s. His last screen credit was in 1995, and there is little updated information about him. Jan Michael-Vincent was a ruggedly handsome leading man in several 1970s and early 1980s films. His numerous problems with the law, all fueled by his severe drinking problem, landed him in jail by 2000. Vincent was involved in a near fatal car crash in 1996, which resulted in a broken neck and chronic damage to his voice. When asked about the accident in a 2007 interview, the one-time potential superstar responded, "Y'know, I have no idea what you're talking about. I don't remember being in an accident." When the interviewer compared him to Brad Pitt, Vincent answered, "I don't even know who Brad Pitt is."[59] By 2009, he was living in seclusion in Vicksburg, Mississippi. An anonymous poster on an internet forum in 2014 claimed he was working as a security guard in Texas. In 2012, he had to have part of his right foot amputated due to a leg infection from his artery disease. Vincent's last screen credit was in 2002. When he died at age seventy-four in February, 2019, Vincent's net worth was valued at just $200,000. Claudia Wells played Michael J. Fox's girlfriend in the iconic 1985 film *Back to the Future*, but her career strangely fizzled out, and she disappeared from acting completely from 1986-2008 for unclear reasons. She has since resumed her show business career, mostly to voice video game characters or in shorts. Chris Makepeace was a busy actor in the 1980s, including playing the lead in the 1986 film *Vamp*. He only had a handful of smaller roles in the 1990s, and his last screen credit was in 2001. Omri Katz had the starring role in the delightfully quirky early '90s series *Eerie, Indiana*. He found few roles afterward, and his most recent screen credit was in 2002. He was reportedly last working as a hairdresser in Los Angeles, and frequently travels back and forth to Israel.

Nikki Blonsky, who starred in the 2007 film version of the musical *Hairspray*, earned her cosmetology license and started working at a Long Island salon out of financial necessity. "Its true Im workin@ Superstar Salon as a makeup artist & more Im proud 2 b workin & helpin pay bills BUT ill NEVER loose sight of my dreams," Blonsky tweeted. "Just cause Im part time workin doesnt mean Im gonna give up on my dreams n dont give up on urs I might book something big soon keep positive." Gary Coleman, endearing child star of *Diff'rent Strokes*, struggled mightily as an adult, and was relegated to working extensively as a security guard, before his premature death from an allegedly accidental fall in 2010. Tiffany Brissette, young star of the '80s series *Small Wonder*, became a devout Christian and left show business shortly after the end of the show. The most recent update reported her to be working as a counselor in San Diego. Jerry Supiran, Brissette's co-star on the show, later lost most of his earnings to a financial advisor and a stripper he was involved with, and was homeless by 2012. Amy Linker, who starred alongside young Sarah Jessica Parker in the early '80s television series *Square Pegs*, has done very little acting since the show ended. According to IMDB, she was working as an outpatient community therapist as of

2015. Pamelyn Ferdin was one of the most visible child guest stars on 1960s television. She left acting to become a nurse and animal rights activist. She engages fans regularly on Facebook, and shares memories of her acting career.

Brandon Call, young star of the long-running television show *Step by Step*, never had a screen credit after the show ended in 1998. By 2005, he was working at his parents' gas station. He was still reportedly working as a gas station attendant, according to a November 2018 online story. His cast mate Christopher Castille hasn't appeared onscreen since the show ended, either. Neither has yet another cast member, Josh Byrne. Castille's fellow child co-star in the first two *Beethoven* films, Sarah Rose Karr, made only one more screen appearance, in 1995, and then disappeared from the business. Taran Noah Smith played the youngest son on the long-running '90s series *Home Improvement.* His parents evidently squandered his earnings, and Smith left the industry to run a vegan catering service with his wife. After battling his parents in court for his $1.4 million trust fund, Smith later filed suit against his now former wife, for the theft of business funds. He is currently said to have just $300,000, according to Celebrity Net Worth. Jeremy Gelbwaks played the original Chris on *The Partridge Family*, but left after the first season. According to David Cassidy, this was because he "had a personality conflict with every person in the cast and the producers." Gelbwaks left not only the show, but the entertainment business. His family moved to Reston, Virginia, and he later worked in the computer industry, relocated to New Orleans and became a business and technology planner.[60]

The child stars of one of television's earliest successful sitcoms, *The Life of Riley,* never continued on in the business. Wesley Morgan, who played Junior, never had another screen credit after the show ended in 1958, while Lugene Sanders, who portrayed his sister Babs, had only a single role in 1960's *Tormented* before vanishing from the entertainment world. Sanders, who has been married to the same man since 1954, the second year of the series, evidently decided to concentrate on being a mother to their two children. Information about Morgan's subsequent career after show business is scant; Kathy Garver and Fred Ascher, in their book *X Child Stars: Where Are They Now?*, merely state that "Now he pursues a more private and quiet life - a good development, he says."[61] The child star of another big hit show from the Fifties, *The Adventures of Rin Tin Tin*, Lee Aaker, became an admitted "Flower Child" in the 1960s, and eventually wound up a carpenter. "Suddenly after the series was cancelled and I began doing guest shots, I realized that something had changed - I wasn't the center of attention anymore. My folks had always told me that my career might not last, but when it happened, it was still a hard thing for me to adjust to."[62] Lydia Reed, who played young Hassie on another memorable show from this era, *The Real McCoys,* left the business after the series was over. Her onscreen brother in the show, Michael Winkelman, had sporadic guest spots on other shows after the series ended, then joined the Navy and was sent to Vietnam. After his discharge from the service, he became a groundskeeper on the Universal Pictures lot. I could find no cause or details about his death at just fifty three in 1999.

Carla DeLizia starred on the charming Disney original series *So Weird,* and later on the series *Boston Public,* but did little else of note before strangely retiring from show business in 2012, at the age of twenty eight. Young Kathryn Short appeared in more episodes of the popular '90s anthology series *Goosebumps* than any other actress. Amazingly, those handful of episodes represent the extent of her show business career. There is absolutely no further information about her online. Cody Jones appeared in more *Goosebumps* episodes than any other actor, but while he did a few other things, his last screen credit was in 2000. After *Good Times* ended in 1979, Ralph Carter essentially left the business, although he had a New York nightclub act during the '80s. Philip McKeon, who played Linda Lavin's son on the long-running series *Alice,* had his last screen credit in 1994, and eventually became the co-host of a Texas radio show before dying at fifty five in 2019.[63] Lance Kerwin, prolific child actor of the 1970s, has had a tumultuous adult life, culminating in 2010 with a suspended sentence for the theft of falsified documents in order to get medical assistance and food stamps. One of Kerwin's co-stars on the television show *James at 16*, the lovely Deidre Berthrong, died before her time after her show business career effectively ended in the late '70s. Her death at sixty-four in 2017 was curiously attributed to the fact she'd been "battling pneumonia for several years." She may be best remembered for her nude scene in the shower at the beginning of the 1976 film *Carrie.*

Amy O'Neill, one of the kids in *Honey, I Shrunk the Kids*, wound up working in a circus stilt act. Carrie Henn, young star of 1986's *Aliens*, never made another film, and became a teacher. Another young actress, Ariana Richards, didn't parlay her plum role in *Jurassic Park* into an extended film career. She reportedly works as a portrait painter. Craig Warnock, who played the young lead in the 1981 film *Time Bandits*, made only a television movie afterwards and left the business. Mara Wilson, who delightfully played the title role in the 1996 film *Matilda*, grew weary with acting. She would write on her blog: "Every time I see a pretty young girl on the subway reading lines for an audition, my only thought is, 'Man, am I glad I'm not doing that anymore.' I never feel nostalgia, just relief." Despite these sentiments, Wilson has evidently returned to less prominent acting roles, judging from her IMDb listing. Despite an important role in 2003's *Elf*, Daniel Tay has had only limited acting jobs since then, the most recent ones voicing video game characters. He is known to have graduated from Yale in 2014. Butch Patrick, who portrayed Eddie on the 1960s' show *The Munsters*, was rumored to have been paid a paltry $600 a year by Universal Studios, but in a May 21, 2018 email reply, he informed me that he was actually paid $650 an episode. Until recently Patrick was still hiring himself out, at over sixty-years-old, to play his most familiar character at parties. Patrick has just $250,000, according to Celebrity Net Worth. Still, Patrick seemed content with his show business career, telling me in a May 22, 2018 follow-up email: "Good people in all departments. Excellent time." Patrick's series co-star, Beverly Owen (the original "Marilyn" before Pat Priest took over the role), left *The Munsters* early in the initial season and never returned to show business. Butch Patrick posted the following on Facebook, after Owen's death in February, 2019 at age eighty-one: "Beautiful Beverly Owen has left us. What a sweet soul. I had the biggest crush on her. RIP Bev and thanks for your 13 memorable Marilyn Munster episodes."

Dylan Sprouse, one of the twins who starred in Disney's television series *The Suite Life*, was supposedly working as a host for a New York restaurant after the end of the show. Sprouse refuted rumors that he was broke, saying, "I am financially secure, and took this job as a way to primarily feed my over bountiful video game addiction."[64] Maybe Sprouse is just eccentric (he identifies as a Heathen, a modern Pagan religion). With all the servers struggling to break into acting, it's strange and ironic that a successful actor would willingly want to become a restaurant host. Sprouse and his twin brother Cole were paid a combined $40,000 per episode by Disney, and Celebrity Net Worth credits the brothers with a collected wealth of $16 million. Lovely Jan Smithers, who played Bailey Quarters on *WKRP in Cincinnati*, fell out of the limelight completely after the end of the show. This would culminate in a bizarre 2007 incident, when her car broke down and she was struck by another vehicle after she got out. For incomprehensible reasons, she was driving naked. Considering that she hasn't had a screen credit since the mid-1980s, it is pretty shocking to see online reports of her having a $6 million net worth. Justin Berfield, who played the bully brother on the series *Malcolm in the Middle,* has had only one screen credit - a television guest role in 2010 - since the show ended in 2006. His youngest on-screen brother, Erik Per Sullivan, has an almost identical post-series career arc; two screen credits, the last in 2010. While Berfield still has an enviable $10 million net worth, Sullivan is said to have a comparatively meager $3 million.

Tommy Kirk was Disney's biggest male star in the early 1960s. He had leading roles in several smash motion pictures such as *The Shaggy Dog* and *The Monkey's Uncle*. However, his drinking and drug addiction combined to destroy his promising film career. At the time he publicly came out as gay in a 1973 interview, Kirk was working as a bus boy in a Los Angeles restaurant. In the mid-1970s he worked as a waiter and chauffeur. Kirk was philosophic about it, saying, "I made a lot of money and I spent it all. No bitterness. No regrets. I did what I did... I wasn't the boy next door anymore."[65] According to Celebrity Net Worth, Kirk presently has just $500,000. Kevin Corcoran was another '60s Disney staple, playing Tommy Kirk's brother in five different films. More often than not, his character's name was "Moochie." Corcoran retired from acting at just fifteen years of age, and went on to have a lengthy career behind the camera, as an assistant director and producer. Corcoran had several siblings who were child actors as well, including Noreen Corcoran, who starred on the television series *Bachelor Father,* and Donna Corcoran, who was so charming in movies like 1951's *Angels in the Outfield*. Noreen, like Kevin, and their fellow child actor brother Kelly, each died too young. Kevin, despite a long career in the business, left behind a modest estate of $500,000. Kay Panabaker appeared on several television shows, and is best remembered for a recurring role on the Disney Channel's 2000's series *Phil of the Future*. She abruptly retired from show business at just twenty two, and as of 2016, was working as a zoo keeper at Disney's Animal Kingdom.

Kevin Jonas of Jonas Brothers fame shunned the entertainment world to become a contractor, until a recent comeback with his siblings. Danica McKellar, who was every young boy's fantasy girl Winnie Cooper on the retro show *The Wonder Years,* shifted gears considerably after the series ended in 1993, and wound up a Mathematics major who has written four books geared to making math appealing to young girls. Former teen heartthrob Kirk Cameron left the entertainment business at a young age, to focus on his devout Christianity. His brilliant, memorable turn as the title character's brother Kip in the 2004 cult favorite *Napoleon Dynamite* didn't lead to greater fame in the film business for Aaron Ruell, who has only had a handful of minor roles since then. Jon Heder, meanwhile, who played Napoleon, has gravitated to mostly voice work. I exchanged private Facebook messages with actress Ellen Dubin, who played Uncle Rico's girlfriend in *Napoleon Dynamite*, on February 17, 2014. "This movie was a very small indie movie," Dubin wrote; "yes everyone was paid a paltry salary but we were all passionate about it. Not sure what the actor playing Kip is doing now - yes he was wonderful in that film."

Rusty Stevens, fondly recalled by Baby Boomers as Larry Mondello on *Leave it to Beaver,* had only a handful of guest starring roles in other shows after the series ended, and wound up his career by reprising his character a few times on 1983's *Still the Beaver* television movie and the subsequent series *The New Leave it to Beaver.* The producers of the updated show had to hire a private detective to locate the reclusive Stevens. When they knocked on his door and asked his wife if this was the residence of the former child actor, she had no idea what they were talking about. Incredibly, Stevens had never even told his wife about his acting career. Jeri Weil, who played Beaver's classmate, tattletale Judy Hensler, never had another screen credit after the show, except for a guest appearance on an episode of *The New Leave it to Beaver*, where she reprised her role as an adult Judy. Weil became a realtor, and was photographed with Jerry Mathers and Tony Dow at a Hollywood show in 2017. Ronda Jeter appeared in eight episodes of *The Andy Griffith Show*, playing the little girl (variously named Karen Burgess, Sharon Porter or Sharon McCall) that Opie had a crush on. Other than that, she had no screen credits. Leif Garrett's little sister Dawn Lyn, who played

Dodie on *My Three Sons* and appeared in many other shows, had her last screen credit in 1978. Felice Schachter had only one bit role (in 2001) after being a regular on the first season of *The Facts of Life*. She eventually became a special education teacher in New York. Julie Anne Haddock was another first year star on the show who was fired and only had a few more screen credits. IMDb didn't even know the name of her spouse, but in an undated update reported, "Is now married and sings for her church."

Luise Rainer had one of the oddest film careers ever. She was the first actor to win back- to-back Academy Awards, in 1936-1937, but made barely ten films in total before leaving movies in 1943. She worked sporadically in television, and returned to the big screen one last time in 1997, before dying at the ripe old age of 104 in 2014. Vivien Leigh had a similarly unusual Hollywood career. Although considered a legend, especially for her iconic, Academy Award-winning role as Scarlett O'Hara in *Gone With the Wind,* Leigh actually appeared in fewer than twenty motion pictures. She pretty much dropped off the radar after her second biggest role, and another Oscar winner, in 1951's *A Streetcar Named Desire*. She was only fifty-three when she died in 1967, of chronic tuberculosis, no doubt exacerbated by her manic depression and heavy smoking. Eleanor Powell was considered the greatest tap dancer in the business, but while playing the lead in big films like *Born to Dance* (1936), she only made fifteen movies before retiring to become Mrs. Glenn Ford. After divorcing Ford, Powell became an ordained minister in the Unity Church. The incredibly talented Rick Moranis quit Hollywood after his wife died, to be with his children. He has had no screen credits since 2008, but is now involved with *Shrunk,* a reboot of his *Honey I Shrunk the Kids* hit film. Unlikely singing sensation Susan Boyle, always uncomfortable as a sudden middle-age celebrity, made headlines in 2014 when she visited a British betting company, asking how to apply for a low-paid customer service assistant job opening.[66] Publicly acknowledging that she has Aspergers Syndrome, Boyle recently disclosed that she hadn't been on a date in six years and that romance had "never been a priority for me."[67]

Gene Clark was the clear leader of the Byrds in their early years, writing most of their best-known original songs. He was haunted by many demons, first and foremost drug and alcohol abuse, but also from a severe fear of flying and a weird reluctance to promote any of his own work. Clark was apparently one of those entertainers who prospered at least financially; he went into semi-retirement in the early '70s, supported by what Wikipedia described as "still-substantial Byrds royalties." Band mate Roger McGuinn complained, "We were all so busy that we really didn't notice how many songs Gene had written until the first album came out and he bought a sports car. He was into Ferraris and we were still starving."[68] In another reference, Wikipedia reported that Tom Petty's cover of Clark's old Byrds' tune *I'll Feel a Whole Lot Better* in 1989 "yielded huge royalties" to him. There was also a great deal of jealously on the part of band mates McGuinn and David Crosby, over Clark's prolific songwriting, and they were reluctant to include Clark's work on their records. The generous Clark was willing to share writing credits for songs like *Eight Miles High,* which he composed alone, just to get his original material onto the Byrds' albums. [69] Clark died at only forty six (although *The New York Times* reported he was forty nine) in 1991, supposedly of a heart attack. But according to John Einarson, author of the books *For What It's Worth: The Story of Buffalo Springfield,* and *Mr. Tambourine Man: The Life and Legacy of the Byrds' Gene Clark,* "What transpired over the last three days of Gene's life remains clouded by controversy... conspiracy theories abound; accusations have been leveled." After his death, what was conceded to be a vast stockpile of Clark's unreleased material mysteriously disappeared. During Clark's memorial service, actor David Carradine, drunk and/or high on acid, scandalously grabbed his dead friend's corpse by the lapel, pulled it up out of the open coffin and snarled, "You cocksucker. You fucked my daughter when she was thirteen."[70] None of the original members of the Byrds were in attendance.

Stanley Fafara is remembered by Baby Boomers as Whitey Whitney, one of Theodore "Beaver" Cleaver's close friends on *Leave it to Beaver*. After the iconic show ended, Fafara had only a handful of mostly uncredited roles, and began abusing alcohol and drugs. He became a drug dealer and was arrested a number of times for breaking into pharmacies. After a stint in jail, Fafara was clean and sober for the last eight years of his life. He was forced to live in subsidized housing in Oregon, and was dependent upon Social Security checks to survive. He died on his fifty-fourth birthday (presumably, he must have been disabled, to draw Social Security that early), rather inexplicably in my view, of complications from hernia surgery the previous month. Buddy Foster, older brother of Jodie Foster, was a busy child actor in the 1960s, with his biggest role being as Ken Berry's son on *Mayberry RFD*. His career floundered as a teen, while his little sister eventually became a powerful figure in the film industry. His book *Foster Child* was published in 1997 and Jodie Foster reacted angrily, calling it, "a cheap cry for attention and money…Buddy has done nothing but break our mother's heart his whole life." She dismissed her brother as "a distant acquaintance."[71] Foster reportedly shot himself in an unsuccessful suicide attempt in 1988, and in his book charged that his mother had frittered away his childhood earnings from show business. Updated information is hard to find about Buddy Foster; at last report, in the early 2000s, he was living with his third wife in Minnesota and employed as a construction worker. Shirley Ellis, who sang the big hit record *The Name Game* in 1964, was so obscure by the time of her death in 2005 that, according to Wikipedia, "It is not known if she had children."

Kim Tyler, who starred as one of the kids on the 1960s television series *Please Don't Eat the Daisies,* had no further screen credits after the show ended its run in 1967. Neither did his on- screen brothers in the show, real life twins Jeff and Joe Fithian. Harlen Carraher, one of the youngsters on the television show *The Ghost and Mrs. Muir*, left show business a few years after the series ended, and wound up working for the Los Angeles Department of Building and Safety. His series co-star and on-screen sister Kellie Flanagan had no more credits when the series finished in 1970. Karen Valentine, best remembered for her role on television's *Room 222*, was big enough by the early Seventies to serve as a guest host for Johnny Carson on *The Tonight Show*. But fame was fleeting. A May 11, 1992 story in *People* magazine about her, titled, "Just Don't Call Her Cute," quoted Valentine as saying, "People constantly recognize me, even from the back. But the powers that be don't. Room 222 is like one of those gifts that you're handed, but double-edged. It's just hard to keep it dancing." The article also detailed how Valentine spent much of the late 1970s and 1980s "in supper clubs, summer stock and 'anything that came my way'." Jake Lloyd, engaging child star of the 1996 Christmas film *Jingle All the Way* and probably best known for playing young Anakin Skywalker in *Star Wars: Episode 1 – The Phantom Menace*, gravitated to providing voices for a slew of *Star Wars* video games, with the last one being released in 2002. Later updates about him indicated he was attending high school in Carmel, Indiana, working at a mall in 2006, and majoring in film at Chicago's Columbia College in 2008. He made the headlines again in a negative way in June 2015, when he was arrested for reckless driving, resisting arrest and other charges in South Carolina. In 2016, he was transferred to a psychiatric facility after serving 10 months in jail.[72] The previous year, he had assaulted his mother, who told the media that Lloyd was on medication for schizophrenia.[73]

None of this is to cast aspersions on those who decide to switch careers and voluntarily leave show business. As my friend Susan Olsen (who played Cindy on *The Brady Bunch*) reminded me after first reading an early manuscript of this book, we shouldn't automatically brand entertainers who are no longer acting as failures.

But my perspective is that the sheer number of examples I've provided here seem even more incomprehensible given the ambitions and desires of all those who beat astronomical odds to succeed in Hollywood. I remain baffled that any such determined and driven individuals would willingly turn their backs on stardom. Just as mysterious is the enduring entertainment world practice of spitting out those it has given a brief reign of success, the clichéd fifteen minutes of fame if you will, and closing the door on them again. One would think their resumes would guarantee them further work.

Ashleigh Aston Moore, best remembered for a supporting role in the 1995 film *Now and Then,* had no more screen roles after 1997 and died in Canada at twenty-six in 2007 under strange circumstances, supposedly from a combination of pneumonia and bronchitis. Michelle Monkhouse, who played Urkel's girlfriend on *Family Matters,* died from a rare form of stomach cancer when she was but twenty-nine. Kim Walker, fondly remembered from the 1988 film *Heathers,* died of a brain tumor at thirty-two years of age. Eerily, her character spoke a memorable line about a brain tumor in the film. Jeremy Applegate, who also appeared in *Heathers,* shot himself to death at only thirty-four. What makes this truly bizarre is that his character says, "I don't think I could handle suicide" at one point in the film. Prolific child star Brad Renfro's adult acting career was derailed by a series of arrests and chronic drug addiction. He died at only twenty-five in 2008 of what was officially determined to be an accidental overdose of heroin. Gene Anthony Ray, who played Leroy in both the 1980 film *Fame* as well as the 1982 TV series based upon it, was HIV-positive when he died at only forty-one of a stroke in 2003. He'd had but a few acting roles after the series ended in 1987. Gia Carangi, considered to be the first "super model," became a heroin addict and lost all her considerable earnings, dying at just twenty-six of AIDS. She had been forced to work in a clothing store, as a cashier, and in the cafeteria of a nursing home. Her funeral was sparsely attended, and no one from the fashion world came.

Jon Paul Steuer appeared in the 1994 film *Little Giants,* but is best remembered for playing Brett Butler's son in the television series *Grace Under Fire.* Steuer had no screen credits after the series ended in 1996, and became another casualty in the long list of Hollywood suicides when he shot himself at only thirty-three years of age, in January, 2018. That same month, another child actor, Joseph Wayne Miller, died in his sleep at only thirty-six. Miller was best known for the 1995 comedy film *Heavyweights.* That film was only his second screen credit, but it proved to be his last. Very little is known about why his show business career ended, or exactly what ended his life so prematurely. His mother noted that he suffered from sleep apnea, and that he'd worked as a radiology technician, a DJ, and a property manager at her office.[74] Dustin Diamond, who starred on the television show *Saved by the Bell* from 1989 to 1993, died of cancer in early 2021 only three weeks after being diagnosed. He'd had a slew of personal and financial troubles since the series ended, featuring a couple of arrests and a bankruptcy filing. At one point, he was relegated to selling his show business memorabilia in an unsuccessful effort to stop foreclosure on his home. Even after penning the tell-all book *Behind the Bell,* at the time of his death at forty-four, Diamond was worth a mere $300,000.[75]

Decades before this, one time leading lady of silent films and early talkies Esther Ralston lost a fortune after the 1929 stock market crash. She would later have to work for department stores and a utility company. Silent film star Jack Mulhall was making $1000 a week at the height of his fame. He too lost a fortune in the 1929 crash, and his career plummeted so far that he was paid a mere $100 for his final film, 1959's grade B *The Atomic Submarine.* Agnes Ayres suffered a similar fate; a celebrated silent star who is best remembered for playing opposite Rudolph Valentino in 1921's *The Sheik*; she lost it all like so many others, inside and outside Hollywood, on what came to be known as Black Tuesday. After her very premature retirement, Ayres became so despondent she was committed to a sanitarium. She died at only forty-two on Christmas Day, 1940. Charlotte Henry, a young early talkie actress best remembered for playing the title role in the 1933 version of *Alice in Wonderland*, left films less than a decade later, and wound up with an extensive career as an executive secretary to the Roman Catholic Archbishop of San Diego. Early talkie actress Judith Wood saw her career end abruptly for unclear reasons. Wood would vaguely attribute it to numerous affairs with the likes of Robert Montgomery and William Powell in a later interview. She eventually wound up in costume design, working on "everything from operas to porno films." Dorothy Sebastian, who starred alongside Joan Crawford and Anita Page in the smash silent film *Our Dancing Daughters* and the early talkie follow-up *Our Blushing Brides*, saw her career plummet after asking MGM for a raise from her $1,000 weekly salary. During World War II, the one-time movie star worked in a defense plant as an X-ray technician, having been relegated to a handful of uncredited roles. Her *Our Blushing Brides* co-star Raymond Hackett had good looks and screen presence, and was the male lead in the 1930 film *The Cat Creeps*. He abruptly left the film world after just one more screen appearance, and little else is known of him, other than that he died at only fifty-five in 1958. Billy Halop, the original leader of the Dead End Kids (not Leo Gorcey, who played a secondary role to him) in films like 1937's *Dead End*, 1938's *Angels With Dirty Faces*, and 1939's *Hell's Kitchen*, eventually drifted into B roles as an adult, and by the mid-1950s was an appliance salesman, even being named "Most Creative Salesman in the U.S." by the National Association of Manufacturers. He then became a registered nurse, before closing out his career with a recurring role on *All in the Family* as Bert Munson, Archie Bunker's pal and owner of a taxi cab company.

Edwina Booth made a handful of early talkies. After filming *Trader Horn* in 1931, which was an ambitious project filmed on location in Africa, she contracted an infection that was referred to in those less delicate times as "jungle fever," or malaria, according to various sources. Although her screen credits list four films after *Trader Horn*, her biography states that she was bedridden by this infection for an astounding six years and "never acted again in films." Rumors circulated at the time that she'd actually died of the fever. Co-star Harry Carey paid tribute to Booth's willingness to have her picture taken with everyone else when they arrived back in New York, declaring, "If an actress were dying she'd still be there when the camera boys called for a newspaper picture."[76] Booth sued MGM for over a million dollars, and the case was eventually settled out of court. Archives at Brigham Young University report that her settlement was a paltry $35,000. Booth had grown so obscure by 1973 that Katharine Hepburn could matter-of-factly state that she had indeed died from schistosomiasis, in an interview with Dick Cavett. She survived and lived to be eighty-six, after working for the Los Angeles Mormon Temple in her later years. Understandably, Booth had little interest in talking about her brief glory days as a movie star. For her trouble, in catching an ailment that ruined her career and almost took her life, Booth was paid $75 per week for *Trader Horn*.

Mary Beth Hughes was a sexy blonde who appeared in numerous 1940s films. Like so many other actors, she gravitated towards television later and guest starred on everything from *Rawhide* to *Dennis the Menace*. IMDb informs us that for a period in 1961, she was a receptionist for a plastic surgeon in Los Angeles, and went on to work as a telemarketer for Sprint. Ruby Nash, lead singer of Ruby & the Romantics, who scored a number one hit in 1963 with *Our Day Will Come*, returned to her hometown of Akron, Ohio after the band's day in the sun was up, where she worked for AT & T. Betty Hutton, an heiress who was briefly a huge film star in the 1940s-1950s, filed for bankruptcy in 1967, and was later discovered to be working as a cook and housekeeper for a Catholic Church rectory in Rhode Island. Though she'd once inherited $30 million, Hutton died with only $3,500 in the bank.[77] Peggy Ann Garner won a special Oscar as the child star of 1945's *A Tree Grows in Brook-lyn*, but never built on this impressive beginning. She wound up working as a real estate broker and used car manager before succumbing to cancer at only fifty-two. Her only child died just after she did, and her mother outlived them both. No one knows where her Oscar is. Sandy West, the drummer for the teenage girl rock group The Runaways, after her fifteen minutes of fame was up, was forced to work in construction, as a bartender and as a veterinary assistant. She died at just forty-seven of lung cancer, and had once bitterly alleged that the band's manager was "the reason I'm broke now."[78] Diana Serra Cary, who achieved world fame as "Baby Peggy," was earning $1.5 million a year in 1923, at just five years of age. In addition, she was making $300 a day working Vaudeville tours; out of this, Peggy was paid just five cents. Her substantial fortune was gone long before she became an adult, thanks to the irresponsibility of her father. By the advent of the 1930s, the one-time child superstar was poor and relegated to working as an extra. When she died at 101 in February 2020, Cary's worth was said to be $2 million.

Actress Mayo Methot, most famous for her tempestuous, often violent marriage to Humphrey Bogart, died of acute alcoholism at just forty-seven. Her body wasn't discovered in her cheap Oregon hotel room until days after her death. Yvette Vickers is best remembered as the second female lead in the 1958 cult favorite *Attack of the Fifty Foot Woman*. She was also one of *Playboy*'s Playmates of the month. Like so many others, her film career was brief, and she had fallen so deep into obscurity that, when her mummified body was found in her Benedict Canyon house on April 27, 2011, it was concluded that she had been dead for an extremely lengthy time, perhaps as long as a year. Guy Williams, who starred in the television shows *Zorro* and *Lost in Space*, died in 1989. His nude, decomposing body was found in the upscale apartment in Buenos Aires, Argentina where he'd retired. Shirley Hemphill, one of the stars of the 1970s sitcom *What's Happening*, died at age fifty. It wasn't until two weeks after her death that her body was discovered in her West Covina, California home by a gardener. Her *What's Happening* co-star, Fred "Rerun" Berry, had financial difficulties after the show ended. At one point, he was relegated to appearing as a contestant on a predictably ridiculous game show segment of Howard Stern's then local New York television show. Married six times, he died at only fifty-two. Actress Margaux Hemmingway, sister of Mariel and granddaughter of writer Ernest Hemmingway, overdosed in 1996, and when her body was found it was badly decomposed, suggesting she'd been dead for quite a while.

Former Mouseketeer Dennis Day was reported missing by his husband in July, 2018. He had last been seen leaving a friend's house on foot. The story of the missing Mouseketeer was covered by *Dateline* in February, 2019, and Day's family criticized police, calling it a "poorly handled investigation." Concerned fans even started a "Help us Find Dennis Day" Facebook page. Day's car had been located in Oregon, where he resided, with two people inside that were initially reported as being unconnected to him, but later said to have told authorities Day let them borrow it. On April 4, 2019, human remains were found in the seventy-six-year-old Day's home, which Oregon Police stated "have not been identified and the investigation is ongoing."[79] It wasn't until early June that Oregon State Police finally reported that the body was indeed Dennis Day's, but they still weren't releasing the cause of death. In an email to *USA Today*, police Captain Tim Fox said, "As with any investigation, it takes time. Due to the nature of this investigation (and any investigation), police release what they can at the time to not compromise the integrity of the investigation." As even this mainstream media outlet wondered, "Why did he die and why did it take nearly a year to learn his fate?"[80] As *TMZ* noted, when the body eventually identified as Day's was found on April 4, it was "highly suspicious and mysterious, because cops had previously searched the home and found nothing."[81] In July, 2019, Day's handyman was arrested on suspicion of manslaughter and several other charges.[82] Day's fellow Mouseketeer, Annette Funicello, stole the hearts of young Baby Boomers everywhere and quickly became the star of the *The Mickey Mouse Club.* She received up to 8,000 fan letters every week, ten times more than her fellow cast members. In her 1994 autobiography, *A Dream is a Wish Your Heart Makes,* Annette recounted being sent school rings and engagement rings from male admirers, all of which she returned. The lovely young actress contracted a hellacious case of Multiple Sclerosis in her mid-forties, and deteriorated to such an extent that she was confined to a wheelchair and lost the ability to speak in her last years, only communicating by blinking or motioning, before dying at age seventy in 2013.[83]

Benji Gregory, who starred on the late '80s television show *Alf,* became a true rarity in Hollywood, by joining the Navy in 2003. Online information about him is scant; at last report, he was living in Arizona with his wife. An earlier performer who took this curious path was singer Jimmy Soul, fondly remembered for his classic #1 1963 song *If You Wanna Be Happy.* Soul joined the Army after his one-hit musical career evaporated. He died of a heart attack at only forty-six. Three members of the one-hit wonder band the Rivieras, who scored big with 1964's *California Sun,* entered the Marine Corps after their fifteen minutes of fame was up. Ken Weatherwax played Pugsley on *The Addams Family* television series, but found it difficult to find work afterwards and wound up joining the Army at seventeen. Like so many child actors, Weatherwax was typecast and also harassed by other kids. "I was kicked out of like, six or seven schools," he told Bill O'Reilly in a 2008 interview. He would later work as a grip for movie studios. When he died at fifty-nine in December 2014, Weatherwax left behind an estate of only $300,000. The staff of the Dearly Departed Tours & Artifact Museum raised the funds for the internment of his ashes at Valhalla Memorial Park Cemetery, three years later, fittingly on Halloween.[84] Child actor Roger Mobley starred in a number of Disney productions (only

Slim Pickens appeared in more episodes of *Walt Disney's Wonderful World of Color*), and was a regular on the television series *Fury*. He left the business for the Green Berets, and with only $6,000 saved from his twelve year acting career, became a police officer in Texas. Both Ken Osmond, who made such an indelible impression as Eddie Haskell on *Leave it to Beaver,* and teen heartthrob singer Bobby Sherman also made this unlikely transition from entertainer to police officer. One-time leading man Michael O'Shea, who appeared in a number of major films like *Lady of Burlesque* (opposite Barbara Stanwyck), later worked as a deputy sheriff for Ventura County. Yet another entertainer who went on to law enforcement was Nick Santo of the Capris (a one-hit wonder group with 1961's *There's a Moon Out Tonight*), who started working for the NYPD in 1965. Herb Fame, half of the singing duo Peaches & Herb, briefly took this same strange route, leaving the music business in 1970 to become a Washington, D.C. police officer, although he returned to show business in 1976 and enjoyed his biggest hit a few years later, with the triple platinum selling *Reunited*. Most ironic of all, former *CHiPs* star Erik Estrada began working as a full-time deputy sheriff in Virginia in 2009. According to Celebrity Net Worth, at the time of his May 18, 2020 death, Ken Osmond was worth a surprisingly low $500,000. This very modest amount is also the alleged net worth of Ernest Lee Thomas, who starred as "Raj" on the television shows *What's Happening* and the later *What's Happening Now.* Thomas's series co-star Haywood Nelson is also said to be worth just $500,000. Nelson is probably doing okay, however, as his wife is an attorney who is directly related to the Royal Family of Saudi Arabia and Dubai.

Hugh Beaumont, who dealt with the escapades of Ken Osmond's character in his enduring role as Ward Cleaver on *Leave it to Beaver,* became a Christmas tree farmer, in addition to already being an ordained Methodist minister, after retiring from show business. Alona Marlowe was the actress sister of June Marlowe, who played teacher Miss Crabtree in a few memorable *Our Gang* shorts. After accusing Lilyan Tashman of assaulting her in Edmund Lowe's dressing room, Marlowe began taking night classes at Hollywood High School, and went into real estate. Tashman died of cancer at only thirty-four, and had a history of physical altercations with fellow actresses like Lupe Velez and Constance Bennett. Velez, who would go on to become one of Hollywood's countless suicides, was such a fight fan she would regularly enter the ring at Hollywood's Legion Stadium during the popular Friday night fights, in order to encourage the Latin fighters, sometimes provocatively flashing the crowd as she did so. Allan Ramsay, the original bassist for Gary Lewis & the Playboys, left the music business to become a pilot for Northeast Airlines. He died at only forty-two in a plane crash. Terry Chimes, the original drummer for the Clash, gave up the entertainment world to become a chiropractor. Richard Coles played keyboard for the '80s group the Communards. He switched gears dramatically, studying theology and eventually becoming Curate of St Paul's Church in Knightsbridge.[85] David Gorcey, younger brother of East Side Kids' leader Leo Gorcey, who also appeared in several of their films, left show biz to become a Catholic priest. Richie Furay, a member of successful bands like Buffalo Springfield and Poco, would later serve as senior pastor at Calvary Chapel in Colorado.[86]

Young Florrie Dugger starred in 1976's *Bugsy Malone,* but never made another film or television appearance. She went on to a career in the Air Force. Her co-star in her only film, John Cassisi, parlayed his young mobster persona into roles on the television shows *Barney Miller* and *Fish,* but then left the business and wound up working in construction. Evidently, his acting roles weren't a huge stretch, as he was imprisoned for money laundering and bribery in 2015.[87] Pete Birrell, of the 1960s British Invasion group Freddie and the Dreamers, became a taxi driver after the band broke up. Judy Craig, lead singer of the girl group The Chiffons, who hit it big with *He's So Fine* in 1963 and several follow up successes, would leave the group in

1969 to work in a bank. The other band members went on to work regular, nine-to-five jobs. Craig would later form a reconstituted Chiffons group which included her daughter and niece. As Craig acknowledged in an April 23, 2015 interview with newjersey.com, "Of course, they didn't pay well back then." Bernie LaPorta, one of the original members of The Happenings, who had a few big hits in the mid-'60s with remakes like *See You in September* and *I Got Rhythm*, became a music teacher in the New Jersey public schools. Wayne Fontana, lead singer of the group The Mindbenders, really fell off the ledge after peaking with 1965's huge hit *Game of Love*. In 2005, after barely avoiding bankruptcy, he was arrested for setting a car on fire near his Derbyshire home.[88] He would subsequently appear in court dressed as the lady of justice, proclaiming "justice is blind." In 2007, he was sentenced to 11 months for setting fire to the car but was released under the Mental Health Act of 1983.[89] The strangest transition of all involved gorgeous starlet Dolores Hart, who abruptly left Hollywood in 1963 to become a strictly cloistered Benedictine nun in Connecticut, where she remains today. Her last screen appearance was on an episode of *The Virginian*, where her character oddly foretold the near future, as she portrayed a Catholic missionary.

The Clint Eastwood-directed 2014 film *Jersey Boys* chronicled the rise and career of the sensational 1960s band The Four Seasons. Just looking at IMDb, I found some curious facts regarding the cast. Oddly, and without explanation, John Lloyd Young, who starred as front man Frankie Valli, and had made only one film prior to this, hasn't had a screen credit since. This seems all the more strange since Young's performance was critically acclaimed, and he had previously won a Tony award for playing the same character in the long-running Broadway version of *Jersey Boys*. The only updated information about Young had him appointed to Barack Obama's President's Committee on the Arts and Humanities (which he actually joined in 2013, before the film), from which he resigned in protest of Donald Trump's policies in 2017, and then launching his own New York cabaret show in 2018. Lou Volpe, who played Valli's father, died in a 2017 construction accident, about which there seem to be no details available. Was the veteran sixty-one-year-old actor working in construction for some reason? Michael Lomenda, who played band member Nick Massi, has no other screen credit to his name. A pretty substantial role in a big-budget film, and no work since then? Renee Marino, who played Valli's wife, has had only one other screen credit. Grace Kelley, who portrayed Valli's daughter Francine, has only had one screen credit since.

Singer George Alan O'Dowd, better known as Boy George, who hit it big in the 1980s while fronting the band Culture Club, struggled after his moment in the sun was up. He hit rock bottom in 2009, when he was sentenced to fifteen months in jail for false imprisonment of a male escort. Despite not being relevant in the music world for decades, he is said to be worth $35 million. Amanda Bynes, the supremely talented child star of *The Amanda Show*, went into a downward spiral as an adult, and has had continual run-ins with the law. She was expelled from a Fashion Institute in 2014. Funk legend George Clinton was never paid properly for his recording success. His managers and business partners owned the rights to his music catalog, and he was forced to declare bankruptcy in 1984. Rock and roll legend Jerry Lee Lewis went bankrupt in 1988. David Blatt, who as Jay Black sang the lead on several big 1960s hits for Jay & the Americans, declared bankruptcy in 2006, in order to satisfy $500,000 in back taxes. The IRS also forced him to sell the trademark rights to Jay & the Americans; he kept performing as "Jay Black the Voice." In an October 22, 2014 interview with *The Schmooze*, it was revealed that the IRS garnishes 15 percent of Black's Social Security checks. The Goo Goo Dolls, who sold more than 2 million records in the 1990s, were one of the more recent bands to sign an awful contract, and they wound up owing Warner Bros. money years later. Leonard Cohen, due to his manager's mishandling of his money, was said to have almost nothing to show for all his years in the music business, and was forced to start touring again in his seventies. The touring must have been quite successful; when he died in 2016, Cohen left behind a $40 million fortune. Dionne Warwick, despite lots of hit records during a half century career in show business, filed for bankruptcy in 2013, claiming assets of just over $25,000. Burt Reynolds, the biggest movie star in the world during the 1970s, had his waterfront Florida home foreclosed on in 2011. Reynolds, who once earned at least $10 million annually, shortly before his death in September 2018 was said to have just a $5 million net worth. "I've lost more money than is possible, because I just haven't watched it…."[90] Reynolds stated. Dick Smothers, the straight man for the Smothers Brothers comedy duo, declared bankruptcy in 2010. He presently has just $1 million, according to Celebrity Net Worth. This same surprisingly low figure was said to be the net worth of another entertainer who died in late 2018, guitarist, singer and actor Roy Clark.

Legendary "king of the surf" guitarist Dick Dale was still touring regularly into his eighties. Dale suffered from a variety of serious medical conditions, for which the medication alone cost over $3000 monthly. The elderly Dale was forced to summon up the energy for live shows, despite wearing a colostomy bag, in order to pay for his exorbitant medical bills. A story about this sad situation in Billboard quoted Dale as saying the perfect way to die would be "On stage from an explosion of body parts."[91] Dale died far more conventionally and quietly than that, on March 16, 2019, at eighty-one. According to celebrity net worth, Dale had no choice but to tour, being worth just a measly $200,000. When distinguished actor Sir John Mills died at age ninety-seven in 2005, it was shocking to discover that despite his decades of work in top-class productions, he left an estate worth only just over $530,000 in US dollars. It was reported that his fortune had been decimated due to the expense of taking care of his elderly wife of sixty-four years, Mary, who had been suffering from Alzheimer's disease for a long time. Mills' daughter Hayley was Walt Disney's biggest star in the early 1960s, but she too has a comparatively modest estate of $5 million, according to Celebrity Net Worth.

Jack Wild, young star of 1968's *Oliver!* and the television show *H.R. Pufnstuf,* wound up with a severe drinking problem, which drained him financially and led to him moving back home with his retired father. He died at only fifty-three. Shelley Duvall, the wonderfully quirky actress who brightened so many films in the '70s and '80s, including *The Shining,* made headlines for the first time in many years in late 2016, when she was interviewed by Dr. Phil. Appearing unrecognizable, Duvall confessed to her struggles with mental illness, and memorably stated that she didn't believe Robin Williams was actually dead, but was only shape-shifting. According to Shelley's mother, her daughter had been living on "government benefits."[92] Randy Quaid, once a highly sought after character actor who starred in numerous films, including *National Lampoon's Vacation* and *Midnight Express,* has become increasingly eccentric over the years, being caught squatting with his wife in a home they'd formerly owned, charged with defrauding an innkeeper of $10,000, and publicly calling out what he calls the "Hollywood Star Whackers," whom he infers have been responsible for the deaths of various celebrities.[93] In 2008, Quaid was banned for life from the Actors' Equity Association due to his peers complaining about his bizarre behavior. Despite a lengthy career in numerous big-budget films, and salaries like the $2.25 million he earned for 1996's *Kingpin,* Quaid is reportedly worth less than $1 million currently. The eccentric actor has even claimed that his brother Dennis, a higher profile name in the film business, had ordered a "hit" on him.[94] Quaid hasn't talked to his brother since 2000.[95]

Steve Martin Caro was the lead singer for The Left Banke, best remembered for the classic '60s tune *Walk Away Renee.* Online, one can find Caro's bitter recollections of his time in the industry. "Looking back, The Left Banke was only a positive experience for a few months." Caro stated. "Mostly it was negatives – bad management, bad vibes. The initial talent was there on my part; I gave it all I had, but I came from European ancestry and I wasn't ready for New York in the sense of everyone lyin' and cheatin'. The way we did things in Europe wasn't cut-throat…But there were people in New York who just tore me apart. Nobody ever treated me fairly, nobody gave me a fair shake. I'm not retired. I plan to regain my rightful place in the music industry; a lot of people wanna work with me. I never asked for any publicity, I never bother anybody, I never want anything from anybody, but people call me all the time. I'll never work with The Left Banke or any people from the past again." Billy J. Kramer, by contrast, who scored multiple hits of Lennon-McCartney tunes with his band the Dakotas, seemed quite content in an October 2, 2016 interview with *The Telegraph*. Kramer had nothing but great things to say about Brian Epstein, who was also his manager, and admitted, "I still get royalties now." Kramer did state, however, that "My biggest cheque for a song was about £12,000." That's just over $16,000, a modest return for smash hits like *Bad to Me, Do You Want to Know a Secret,* and *Little Children.*

Legendary film star Hedy Lamarr died practically penniless. She'd made millions; the public and the film industry routinely touted her as the most beautiful actress, but by the 1960s she had to struggle to pay her utility bills. Too often, she had to rely on the charity of friends even for her meals. In 1966, she was arrested for shoplifting, and once again in 1991, when the seventy-six year-old was caught stealing just over $20 worth of laxatives and eye drops from a drugstore.[96] Although she was a lavish spender, Hedy was a brilliant woman who is in the Inventor's Hall of Fame. It is difficult to understand how she mismanaged such a significant income to that extent. Following her tragically young death in 1969, Judy Garland left an estate with over $4 million in debts. Redd Foxx was wiped out financially by back taxes owed to the IRS, and died broke. His extravagant funeral was paid for by comedian Eddie Murphy. Michael Jackson, while earning close to a billion dollars during his career, was in the red to the tune of some $500 million at the time of his 2009 death. Jazzman Charlie Parker died at only thirty-four with no financial assets. Former child star Corey Haim died broke and little remembered at only thirty-eight. He didn't even own a car at the time of his death, and had become so desperate for money that he'd tried selling a tooth and his hair on Ebay. After his death, other personal items were being auctioned online, to pay for his funeral. Haim's close friend Scott Schwartz, best remembered for his role in 1983's *A Christmas Story* (who would later work in adult films), was quoted as saying, "He was 38 and he had maybe a half a closet full of clothes and a drawer full of T-shirts. That was it. [His father] gave him $500 last month to cover his rent."[97] John Wayne's generous nature, three wives, and unwise investments left him essentially broke after starring in 150 movies. Mike Smith, songwriter, keyboardist and lead singer for the Dave Clark Five, lost his twenty-four-year-old son in a diving accident, then only a few months later was paralyzed in a freak incident at his home. He experienced a myriad of associated complications for the remaining four years of his life, before dying at sixty-four in 2008, only eleven days before the Dave Clark Five was to be inducted into the Rock and Roll Hall of Fame. Topping off this sad story, one of the great singers of the British Invasion era left an estate behind of only $89,000. Smith's Dave Clark Five band mate Denis Payton left an even smaller estate behind when he died at sixty-three in 2006, of just over $62,000. Dave Clark, himself, meanwhile, is said to be worth $30 million. Jerry Garcia of the Grateful Dead left an estate of some $40 million, while Syd Barrett, founder and vocalist of Pink Floyd, left just $5 million. At the time of his tragically early death at age thirty, Andy Gibb was said to be spending $1,000 daily on drugs, and had depleted his fortune, owing millions to his manager and debt collectors. When Billie Holiday died in 1959, it's said that she possessed just $750.[98]

Despite one of the longest, if not *the* longest career in the history of show business, Mickey Rooney left an estate worth only $18,000. One of Rooney's eight wives was lovely star Ava Gardner. Gardner's numerous health issues in later life drained her financial resources, and when she died she had almost nothing left. Cliff Edwards, known as Ukulele Ike and remembered best as the voice of Disney's Jiminy Cricket, became an alcoholic and drug addict, went through all his earnings and died in a hospital as a charity patient after living for years in a home for indigent actors. His body initially went unclaimed and was donated to medical science. Disney belatedly offered to pay for his burial, but the Actors Fund of America and Motion Picture and Television Relief Fund eventually footed the bill. Disney did pay for his grave marker. It is doubtful Edwards ever saw much money for his timeless performance of one of Disney's seminal songs, *When You Wish Upon a Star.* Legendary producer Florenz Ziegfeld died nearly penniless. His widow, Billie Burke, was forced to resume her acting career to pay off his debts, which would culminate in her being cast as Glinda the Good Witch of the North in 1939's *The Wizard of Oz.* Victor Sen Yung, who played Charlie Chan's number two son in many films but is probably best remembered as the cook Hop Sing on *Bonanza,* was nearly destitute when he died accidentally of a gas leak from his stove at age sixty-five.[99] Funeral expenses were paid for and the eulogy was delivered by former *Bonanza* co-star Pernell Roberts. Singer-songwriter Lesley Gore, who had a string of big hits in the 1960s, left a meager estate of only $50,000 to her long-time lesbian partner.[100] In a 1969 interview, Gore had disclosed that she owed Mercury Records $175,000 when she left them. Donna Douglas, who played the lovely Elly May Clampett on *The Beverly Hillbillies,* left a quite modest estate of only $500,000. The star-crossed horror legend Bela Lugosi died with a few insurance policies totaling $15,000, and properties worth an estimated $1,900.[101] We don't know what the extent of his estate was, but Omar Sharif claimed, near the end of his life, that he was "all alone and completely broke…I don't own anything at all apart from a few clothes."[102] One time sex symbol Anita Ekberg was in the hospital in 2011, recovering from a broken hip, when her home was robbed of all her most valuable possessions. She died in 2015 at an Italian clinic after unsuccessfully attempting to receive financial aid, with very little left to her name.[103] One of the most celebrated film directors of them all, John Ford, left an estate of only $500,000 when he died in 1973. It is said that Ford only earned about 20 percent of what Alfred Hitchcock was making during the 1950s and 1960s.[104] Agnes Moorehead, who starred in many films before playing her most memorable role as Endora, Samantha's mother, on the television series *Bewitched,* left a modest estate of $400,000.[105] Golden Age movie star Myrna Loy left an estate of just $600,000.[106]

Fred MacMurray, a long time leading man in Hollywood who made one of the most successful transitions to television as the star of *My Three Sons,* and was rumored to be one of tinsel town's legendary cheapskates, fittingly died one of the richest men in Hollywood. Charles Tranberg claimed, in his 2007 book *Fred MacMurray: A Biography,* that MacMurray left behind a massive $500 million plus fortune.[107] Walt Disney's housekeeper for more than thirty years, Thelma Pearl Howard (whom Walt himself called "the real life Mary Poppins") amassed an estate of nearly $10 million, thanks to Walt's yearly bonuses of increasingly valuable company stock. In contrast, Bette Davis was one of the biggest stars in the history of Hollywood, yet her estate was a shockingly low close to $1 million, of which she left nothing to her daughters and grandsons.[108] On the other hand, long after the peak of her career, Elizabeth Taylor was said to be earning some $2 *per second* in the 1990s, and left an estate worth at least $600 million.[109] Sexy Connie Stevens appeared on several television shows and in films, and recorded the 1959 novelty hit *Kookie, Kookie, Lend me Your Comb* with *77 Sunset Strip* star Edd Byrnes, but doesn't seem to have done nearly enough in show business to have $50 million, according to Celebrity Net

Worth. I love Tracey Ullman, but it floored me to learn that she was Britain's wealthiest comedian; according to a 2006 report in the *Daily Mirror*, worth an incredible $120 million. When powerful movie mogul David O. Selznick died, his widow actress Jennifer Jones was shocked to discover he left behind only enormous debts. Popular singer and variety show host Glen Campbell's estate was initially said to be worth at least $50 million (along with reports that three of his eight children were being excluded from it), but subsequently it was revealed that Campbell had actually left just a meager $410,000 behind after decades as a highly successful entertainer.[110] Bob Denver, who starred in both *The Many Loves of Dobie Gillis* and *Gilligan's Island*, but did little onscreen afterwards, was worth an impressive $20 million at the time of his death, according to Celebrity Net Worth.

The now well-known "bad" film director Ed Wood was hardly celebrated during his lifetime, and had turned to cheap sexploitation films before his death at only fifty-three. He was nearly broke, and resided in a tiny apartment in Hollywood. Ted Healey, leader of the original Three Stooges, may well have been beaten to death by actor Wallace Beery, a crime covered up by the studio, but it's just as sad that, despite a successful, well-paid career, he left his wife and child in such financial straits after his death that they had no money to bury him. MGM staff members set up a fund to pay the expenses. One of the greatest, underrated singers of all time, Mildred Bailey, died penniless at only forty-four. Hattie McDaniel, the first black to win an Academy Award, left an estate worth only $10,000, despite being paid very well during her film career. She left her fourth and last husband $1. McDaniel is supposed to have pragmatically responded to criticism of her stereotypical roles by saying, "Why should I complain about making $700 a week playing a maid? If I didn't I'd be making $7 a week being one."[111] Joe Higgs was the under-recognized father of Reggae music. He taught Bob Marley, Peter Tosh and many other notables. He died penniless in 1999.

Renowned session guitarist David Williams, who had played with Madonna, Michael Jackson, Lionel Ritchie and other top names in the music business, died in 2009. The Hampton, Virginia hospital he was in advised his family to "pull the plug" since he had no medical coverage. Williams was a Vietnam veteran, and the music industry was criticized for failing to step in and help defray his medical costs.[112] When Jack Hammer, who wrote the classic *Great Balls of Fire* for Jerry Lee Lewis, died in 2016, a Go Fund Me page was started to pay his burial expenses. As the page put it, Hammer "died broke, but not broken!"

Ernie Kovacs was an early-day tax protester, and owed hundreds of thousands of dollars to the IRS when he was tragically killed in a car crash at age forty-two in 1962. His widow, Edie Adams, paid the money back primarily by making a series of well-remembered television commercials. Kovacs's daughter Mia would die in an auto accident as well, at just twenty-two, in 1982. Judy Holliday, typically cast as a "dumb blonde," had an IQ of 172. She never parlayed her 1950 Oscar for *Born Yesterday* into lasting stardom, probably because of blacklisting during the McCarthy era, and her career was cut tragically short by breast cancer, as she died just before her forty-fourth birthday. According to Hollywood lore, Vivian Vance and her fourth husband were dining out when they received news of her former *I Love Lucy* co-star William Frawley's death on March 3, 1966. Vance is reported to have exclaimed, "Champagne for everybody!" Frawley had snarled at Desi Arnaz, after meeting Vance, "Where did you dig up that bitch?" Years after the end of the show, Frawley told an interviewer, "I don't know where she is now and she doesn't know where I am and that's exactly the way I like it."[113] Vance was never happy playing Ethel, and resented everything from having a husband that was twenty-five years older, and "should be playing my father," to the fact she had to stay pleasingly plump so that Lucille Ball would always look slimmer. Frawley would refer to her by the pet name, "Old fat ass." Frawley was a rare early television star whose contract set up a residual payment in perpetuity. Although he had no children and was a long-time bachelor, his heirs were paid rerun royalties for decades. By 1957, *I Love Lucy*'s final season, he was being paid a handsome $7,500 per week.[114]

Maurice Gosfield pleased '50s audiences with his role on *The Phil Silvers Show*, but the series star hated him. "Offstage, he thought of himself as Cary Grant playing a short, plump man," Silvers described Gosfield. "He had no professional discipline…If he missed an entrance, he'd say he tripped over a piece of paper."[115] Dwayne Hickman found his *The Many Loves of Dobie Gillis* co-star Tuesday Weld to be just as obnoxious as the unattainable ice princess she played in the series. "She just wasn't a pro," Hickman explained. "Late to work, late getting back from lunch. No sense of responsibility to the show." Louella Parsons called Weld "a disgrace to Hollywood." Weld had a tragic upbringing, and the early death of her father forced her to become the family breadwinner. She had a difficult relationship with her mother, suffered a nervous breakdown at the incredibly early age of *nine,* and was an alcoholic with a suicide attempt under her belt at twelve. She was Stanley Kramer's first choice to play the title role in his 1962 film *Lolita.* Known for her affairs with older men, Weld commented, "I didn't have to play it. I was Lolita."[116] The cast of *Good Times* resented the surprising success of Jimmie "J.J." Walker. Gabe Kaplan and his *Welcome Back, Kotter* wife Marcia Strassman couldn't stand each other. Neither could *Cheers* stars Ted Danson and Shelley Long. Her *Three's Company* co-stars grew to loathe Suzanne Somers. The same thing happened on *Family Ties* when Michael J. Fox took over the show. Alan "Wilbur" Young didn't like the horse that played *Mr. Ed. Laverne and Shirley* stars Penny Marshall and Cindy Williams feuded constantly. Maureen O'Sullivan, who starred as Jane in a classic series of Tarzan films with Johnny Weissmuller, constantly complained about Cheetah, privately referring to the chimp as "that ape son of a bitch." The list goes on.

Howard Hughes was that extreme rarity - a billionaire who died without a will; resulting in his extensive estate being divided between twenty-two cousins (Hughes wasn't married at his death, and never had any children). Orson Welles died "alone and broke" in 1985, leaving behind a messy estate for his heirs to settle. The man considered by many to be one of the greatest directors in the history of the business never directed a picture that made a profit.[117] "I'm not rich. Never have been." Welles once claimed. "I often make bad films in order to live." For his appearance in 1958's *The Roots of Heaven,* Welles was compensated by having $15,000 of his debts settled. Some celebrities leave large amounts to their pets. Michael Jackson bequeathed $2 million to his chimpanzee Bubbles. *Star Trek* creator Gene Roddenberry's widow Majel left an astounding $4 million trust fund for their dogs. Oprah Winfrey has established a ridiculous bequest of $30 million for her five dogs. Oscar winning actress Joan Fontaine left most of her estate to animal rights groups, and it is unclear what, if anything, was bequeathed to her two daughters. Her estranged sister, actress Olivia de Havilland, sued Warner Brothers over the studio's lengthy, inflexible contracts, and won in the Supreme Court. She left behind a healthy $50 million estate when she died at a remarkable 104 years of age in July, 2020.[118] Betty White, who like a startling number of renowned members of the film colony is childless, has decreed that $5 million be left to her beloved golden retriever. On the other hand, numerous celebrities, in recent years, have followed the chic trend of leaving their children nothing. Gordon "Sting" Sumner, George Lucas and Jackie Chan are just a few of these incredibly wealthy "One Percenters" who are not passing on their riches to their loved ones.

Show business families appear to be on average even more dysfunctional than the rest of us. When Jerry Lewis died in 2017, he was yet another star who intentionally wrote his own children out of his will. Lewis's $50 million estate was to be inherited solely by his second wife, and his adopted daughter. His five surviving sons, including 1960s pop sensation Gary Lewis, received nothing. Tony Curtis wrote his five children out of his will shortly before his death, and his estate went solely to his fifth wife. Teen idol David Cassidy left his daughter completely out of his will.[119] Peter Ustinov's substantial estate was dragged through the court for years, and his son went bankrupt in a fruitless effort to claim his share of the inheritance. Ustinov's only will was written in pencil decades earlier, and thus was ruled invalid, with his third wife granted everything. The stepmother versus biological children battle is a familiar one in Hollywood. Peter Falk's daughter Catherine and Casey Kasem's daughter Kerri were both shut out from their fathers' lives by stepmothers, and they launched separate efforts to get legislation passed that would make it easier for friends and relatives to visit elders in such estranged situations.[120] The perpetually troubled Griffin O'Neal leveled some awful accusations at his actor father Ryan, following the 2009 death of the love of his life, Farrah Fawcett. Referring to Ryan's proclamations of affection for the ailing beauty near the end of her illness, Griffin scoffed, "All those crocodile tears. My dad's only goal was to make sure he would be in the will. It was so disgustingly transparent as soon as he found out she was terminal. I consider him a vulture presiding over a carcass. Ryan thought he was going to get everything."[121] In fact, Ryan was completely left out of Farrah's will, the great bulk of which ($4.5 million) went to their son Redmond Fawcett O'Neal. Silent western star William S. Hart (who was paid an impressive $150,000 for his 1917 film *The Narrow Trail*) oddly left his estate to the city of Los Angeles, even though he had a child.

Ronnie Spector's sister and fellow Ronette Estelle Bennett really floundered after the group split up. She suffered from mental illness, and while often homeless, "she sometimes wandered the streets of New York, telling people that she would be singing with the Ronettes in a jazz club."[122] Like so many successful recording artists, the Ronettes had to resort to legal measures in order to get their royalties. According to the same article, "In 1988 the Ronettes sued Mr. Spector for back royalties, and the suit dragged on for 14 years. Part of the case was dismissed, but the three women won the right to some royalties, and according to Jonathan Greenfield, Ms. Spector's husband, they received 'in excess of $1 million.' After lawyers' fees, Ms. Hunter said, each woman took home about $100,000." Another singer from an even bigger girl band of the 1960s, Florence Ballard of The Supremes, was on welfare when she died at only thirty-two years of age. In 1971, Ballard had sued Motown for unpaid royalties, but predictably lost in court. After the tragic early death of original member Georgeanna Tillman, the Marvelettes, another successful girl group from the era, also filed suit against Motown, claiming they hadn't received any royalties despite several big hits. The Vandellas, led by Martha Reeves, sued Motown at the same time.[123] Martha Reeves is said to have a $5 million net worth. The Shirelles left Scepter Records when they found that the trust supposedly holding all their royalty payments until they turned twenty-one, didn't exist. Two of the original members of the tremendously successful Coasters left the group in protest over the incredibly paltry pay. The Platters were unique in that each band member was granted a share of the band and their Social Security was paid. Their legal battles that later ensued were over rights to the original name, a problem that has plagued many of the black singing groups of the past, with imposters performing under a trademark they had nothing to do with.

"Little Eva" Boyd was working as a babysitter for '60s songwriting duo Gerry Goffin and Carole King, when they wrote the huge hit *The Loco-Motion* for her. The song went all the way to #1 in 1962, but Boyd's career fizzled out afterwards, with her only other notable success being a duet with Big Dee Irwin on a remake of Bing Crosby's *Swinging on a Star*, for which she was strangely not credited. She eventually returned to North Carolina with her three children and had almost nothing to show financially for her singing career. It's probably a legend that she was paid just $50 for *The Loco-Motion*; more recent evidence indicates she was paid $50 a week in her recording days, which was only $15 more than she was being paid as King and Goffin's nanny. Another source, however, claims Boyd received $30,000 in royalties.[124] Dee Dee Sharp, who scored with hits like 1962's *Mashed Potato Time*, was the singer *The Loco-Motion* was originally intended for. In a 2008 interview, Sharp was asked if she'd been treated fairly in terms of royalties, and replied, "No. No. No. No. As a matter of fact, they've just started paying me royalties over the last two years….They definitely did not do what they were supposed to do by us. I'm far from the only artist. The Tymes. The Orlons. The Dovells. Even Chubby [Checker]."[125] Darlene Love, whose dynamic voice was featured on many of Phil Spector's 1960s classic recordings, was forced to seek work as a maid cleaning homes in Beverly Hills by the early 1980s. Love claimed that while cleaning in one of these residences, she heard her timeless version of *Christmas (Baby Please Come Home)* on the radio, and took it as a sign to jump start her musical career.[126] Singer-songwriter Melanie Safka, who under the sole name Melanie had some huge hits in the early '70s like *Lay Down (Candles in the Rain), Look What They've Done to my Song Ma* and *Brand New Key,* told an interviewer in 2014 that she doesn't receive any royalties for the songs she wrote prior to 2004, because her husband, who was also her manager, had sold her publishing and performance rights without her knowledge. "He, without my knowing, sold my writer's share," Safka related. "In some countries, that's not even legal…Not just that, but my performances are owned by another company. My publishing is owned by two other companies."[127] Melanie blamed the record company, not her husband, whom she felt had been trying to protect her. In a 2018 story, she was described as looking at very modest homes in Tampa Bay, Florida (one with just 1000 square feet of living space), with her then 38-year-old son, who was living with her.[128]

The Vogues were a popular Sixties group that scored with a string of hits like *You're the One* and *Five O'Clock World.* One of the original band members, Hugh Geyer, described what this sudden success was like in an interview with Gary James on the Classic Bands web site. "A gentleman who had a small record in Pittsburgh liked what he heard, but he didn't like what we had recorded," Geyer recalled. "So he took us back in, and that was back in '65. He found the 'You're The One' song on a Petula Clark album. So we recorded that one. We didn't even have a name. We all had full-time jobs when 'You're The One' came out. I came home from work one day and my wife said 'They're playing your song on the radio.' I said 'What? How could anybody be doing that?' She said 'They're calling you The Vogues.'" Geyer continued, "We all had day jobs…. 'You're The One' came out and was a big hit and guys used to come up to Bill and say 'What are you guys still doing here? You have a hit record! What are you waitin' on?'"

Stan Laurel was living in a $60-a-month small Santa Monica apartment by the early 1960s. Dick Van Dyke has told the story many times of calling Laurel, whose phone number was listed publicly, when he was a young aspiring entertainer, and how receptive the legendary comedian was. Evidently other fans were in the habit of phoning the old star, and he was happy to welcome them into his decidedly humble home. Hal Roach produced the Laurel and Hardy films, and owned the rights to all of them. I spoke to Lois Laurel, Stan's daughter, on the telephone in 2009. She was a wonderfully gracious woman, but had little to offer in terms of her father's career. It was well known that Laurel's contract with Roach paid him considerably more than Oliver Hardy's, but "Babe," as Hardy was known affectionately, didn't seem to care, and acknowledged that Laurel, who wrote their bits, was more important to the act. A revealing anecdote concerned the comedy duo browsing in a London airport's gift shop, where they saw some miniature Laurel and Hardy figurines. Thinking they would make wonderful gifts, the real Laurel and Hardy bought them at full price. According to the Life and Times of Hollywood web site, "When Babe Hardy passed away, he was not well off and living in a tiny starter home." The web site, perhaps not exaggerating all that much, claimed that "20 year olds, just out of school who live far better" than Hardy did, while" Butchers or deli counter men in Cleveland lived far more extravagant lives than Stan Laurel." The 2018 film *Stan & Ollie* examined "the boys" in their declining years, focusing on their 1953 tour of the United Kingdom, during which they sometimes played to astonishingly small audiences in tiny houses.

Stan Laurel's obituary revealed that on the wall of his small apartment hung an autographed picture of President Kennedy, which according to him, "just came in the mail one day." Presumably, JFK was a fan. Laurel bemoaned the editing of his classic shorts, and said, "I never watch myself on TV anymore." He was philosophical about not getting paid for all this increased exposure from television, declaring, "But it doesn't upset me. I don't care. Why would I? There's nothing I can do about it." In 1961, the comedian had reflected, "It's been a great life, and I'm happy that I have made people forget some of their sorrows—but it would have been nice to have made a little money along the way. I'm not complaining. I've got all I want in this little apartment." Laurel was married a total of eight times (rather oddly, to only four women). Laurel noted that "Nobody lifted gags in my time like they do now. There was more ethics then, hence more creativity."[129] Oliver Hardy died with a very modest estate of $500,000, and Laurel was too sick to attend his funeral, declaring "Babe would understand."[130] When he died eight years later, Stan Laurel left a stunningly small estate of just $50,000, according to Celebrity Net Worth.

Author Richard W. Bann is one of my Facebook friends. He strongly disagrees with those who claim that Hal Roach took advantage of talents like the Our Gang kids and Laurel & Hardy. Angered at articles on the Life and Times of Hollywood web site that alleged "the boys" were underpaid, he wrote a response which they published. "I have all of the Laurel and Hardy contracts. I knew Hal Roach as a close personal friend the last 25 years of his life," Bann declared. "There is a book by Christopher Finch and Linda Rosenkrantz titled GONE HOLLYWOOD published by Doubleday & Co. in 1979. In this book they publish figures obtained from a reliable source, the United States Internal Revenue Service. In 1935, 1936 and 1937 Hal Roach paid himself $104,000; $129,000; and $104,000 respectively. For the same years he paid Stan Laurel $156,366; $135,000; and $75,000. And accordingly Roach paid Oliver Hardy $85,316; $88,600; and $101,200. For further comparison and perspective, in 1935, Spencer Tracy was paid $36,250 and Shirley Temple $69,999 and Jack Warner $88,333 and W.C. Fields $76,875... you have defamed Hal Roach, and I ask you to apologize for your insulting and inaccurate representation." The web site, after noting that they were film historians who had been published by the likes of Simon & Schuster, wrote this response to Bann: "Our upcoming comprehensive biography on Jerry Lewis will include records from his estate that he had paid Stan Laurel as a 'consultant' that were made because of pity for Stan Laurel who was dead broke and living in a $60 a month apartment in Santa Monica. Laurel deserved far more....Hal Roach took advantage of two naive performers who had zero business acumen.... Roach owned the likeness of L&H and cashed in on them. He eventually sold those images to the former Bozo the Clown, Larry Harmon, whose company still licensed those images worldwide, returning millions of dollars. Not a dollar went to the estates of Laurel nor Hardy." The web site continued, comparing Laurel & Hardy to Shirley Temple and W.C. Fields, "Both Fields and Temple owned their images. Temple made a fortune on her name and image as did Bill Fields, whose family still collects on his image." Somewhat surprisingly, they also claimed that "The Three Stooges (mostly the Benjamin brothers) have made millions on their images at Comedy Three. Other film actors estates, such from Fred Astaire to James Dean, have produced income for their families. Not Laurel & Hardy." Also here, it was disclosed that the Three Stooges (presumably collectively) were paid $500 a week by Columbia, and this was compared to Johnny Galecki getting paid $2 million for every episode of *The Big Bang Theory*, which when factoring in residuals amounts to an amazing $100 million or so a year. In another of those startling contrasts, the mostly forgotten comedian Harry Langdon was being paid $7500 weekly in the mid-1920s by Mack Sennett.

Another Roach staple, the great comedian Billy Gilbert, died penniless. Despite living to be 100, Hal Roach had been given a medical deferment during WWII because he had "an 80-year-old heart," and was still smoking cigarettes and drinking for pleasure when he was 96.[131] When Peter Lorre died at fifty-nine in 1964, it was reported that the veteran horror actor's body had been found in his "tiny Hollywood apartment." Lorre was in the process of divorcing his third wife, Anna Marie Stoldt, at the time of his death. Stoldt had filed for divorce on grounds of cruelty, and alleged that "He rarely earned less than $70,000 a year, all of which he irresponsibly wasted and squandered."[132] Wu-Tan Clan member Darryl "Cappadonna" Hill gave up all his worldly possessions to live on the streets. He became a cab driver, and reportedly only received one royalty payment in his career. After his brief excursion into the world of the unwashed masses, he moved back home and resumed his recording career.

Richard Lamparski, who had been a long-time public relations man in the television and radio industry, began writing a small fanzine, which later became a series of books called "Whatever Became Of . . ." in the late 1960s. His story on veteran B-movie actress June Lang, once married to notorious Mafia personality Johnny Roselli, illustrated a living anachronism, betrothed to a generation that couldn't adjust to a changing world. She told an interviewer, "I don't like these times and I do not wish to be a part of them." In a May,

1994 letter to author Colin Briggs, Lang lamented, "I have been trying to give up all ties to the world of Motion Pictures. For starters, no answering so called 'fan mail' or attending their functions. I agree with Garbo, 'I want to be alone.'" Lamparski's feature on Burt Ward, whose career fizzled out after a starring role as Robin on the '60s camp series *Batman*, revealed that his apartment was filled with books on the occult, and that he believed himself to be a medium. Alan Napier, who co-starred with Ward as Alfred the butler on *Batman*, was quoted as sadly declaring, "As to my heart: I discovered at a crucial point in my life that my first wife was a lesbian. That sort of thing has a very discouraging effect on a young man." Veteran character actor John Carroll was shown to be a quirky collector, with his treasures including the guns that killed both Billy the Kid and singer Russ Columbo, as well as an autographed copy of *Mein Kampf*. Former East Side Kids' leader Leo Gorcey was depicted as such an unconventional dresser that he was refused service in a New York bar, and who bragged about always keeping a loaded revolver tucked inside his belt. Readers learned fascinating tidbits like when Tommy Rettig, who starred as Jeff on the first Lassie series, *Jeff's Collie*, was arrested for growing marijuana in 1972, Richard Deacon, beloved to Baby Boomers for his roles as Fred Rutherford on *Leave it to Beaver* and Mel Cooley on *The Dick Van Dyke Show*, had offered to post bail. John Drew Barrymore was revealed to be living alone in a shack in the California desert, claiming to fast regularly and be celibate. Old western star Alfred "Lash" LaRue's history of encounters with the law, and his eventual spiritual awakening, as he drove a black hearse around Hollywood, living off Social Security and "love offerings," was reported to readers. Vaughn Meader had his fifteen minutes of fame in the early 1960s, when his album featuring impersonations of JFK and the other Kennedys became a hit. Lamparski detailed how Meader struggled afterwards, as he admitted, "I lived in windowless shacks in the woods and in other people's basements." Meader recovered from a serious drinking problem and chronic LSD use through religion, exclaiming, "I'm a Jesus freak." Johnny Sheffield, whose chief claim to notoriety was his role as "Boy" in a series of Tarzan films, was rather nastily described this way; "After leaving school he married, became a father, and added a great deal of weight…Other than looking after his holdings Johnny does not do much these days…" Old western star Ken Maynard was extremely drunk, and wouldn't let Lamparski's black photographer into his residence, which was a trailer in a trailer park.

The once good-looking, decidedly gay Lamparski claimed that a few of the aging stars he'd interviewed had tried to hit on him. One of these was Mae Clarke, best remembered for getting a grapefruit to the face from James Cagney in 1931's *The Public Enemy* and as Colin Clive's love interest in the original *Frankenstein,* who was a quirky favorite of mine. Clarke was Barbara Stanwyck's best friend and roommate when they arrived in Hollywood, and if one of those countless gay rumors is to be believed, her lover. While Stanwyck went on to screen immortality, Clarke suffered a nervous breakdown, resulting in extensive stays in sanitariums. When she attempted to resume her acting career in 1940, she was relegated to bit roles for the next three decades, which often were uncredited. Lamparski described how forgotten early talkies leading lady Sally Eilers went on a drunken tirade during their interview, screaming profanities at neighbors from a balcony. Listening to some of Lamparski's archived interviews, it was interesting to hear Huntz Hall - who in reality was probably the toughest of all the Bowery Boys, despite his role as Leo Gorcey's goofy sidekick, proudly describe the 1937 film *Dead End* as "a real piece of art." His separate interviews with East Side Kids Hall, Gorcey and Billy Halop revealed that the boys didn't really get along with each other off set. Gorcey admitted to having "no real problems in life," and talked about "raising horses, and dogs, and wives" on his ranch. He also provided a memorable anecdote about how they'd all driven to star-crossed East Side Kid Bobby Jordan's funeral in regular, modest automobiles, except for the lone black member of the gang, "Sunshine" Sammy Morrison, who arrived in a huge Cadillac. Gorcey's interview was filled with fascinating anecdotes, including one where he shot up a toilet bowl, and the next day actress Martha Raye used it and cut herself badly, which caused her to try and sue him. The outspoken Gorcey, who was half-Jewish himself, remarked at one point that he'd "never met a poor Jew." He said he was always paid well, and made as much as $25,000 for eight days of work. In Huntz Hall's obituary, it was noted that he'd lived a comfortable life, "wealthy from offshore oil investments and a 10 percent percentage of the Bowery Boys films."[133]

Robert Montgomery, and later his actress daughter Elizabeth Montgomery both told Lamparski how difficult it was when his father committed suicide. Montgomery had been raised in great wealth, but his father not only shattered the family by taking his own life, he also left them without any money, forcing Robert to quit school and go to work. Henry Montgomery went out dramatically, jumping from the Brooklyn Bridge in front of hundreds of witnesses. It is unclear why the wealthy New York rubber firm magnate left his heirs penniless. Reminding us all just how fickle the publishing industry has always been, the legendary Busby Berkeley disclosed to Lamparski that his memoirs had been rejected by publishers. Lamparski interviewed Cliff "Ukulele Ike" Edwards in 1969, when the once very popular and successful performer, who'd been discovered by Irving Thalberg on the Vaudeville stage, was destitute and living on welfare. Lamparski found poor Edmond O'Brien, who'd starred in such film classics as 1949's *D.O.A.* and played Winston Smith in the original, 1956 version of *1984*, in a Santa Monica "rest home." The Motion Picture Home didn't take patients with a mental disorder. Lamparski interviewed lesser known names like Joyce Compton, a busy actress who appeared with some big names, but often worked in uncredited roles before she gave up acting to become a part-time nurse. Compton was one of the more religious people in the film colony; on her gravestone is carved "Christian

Actress." Outside of a brief marriage of less than a year, Compton always lived with her parents. The notoriously private Kay Francis, who also refused to sign autographs, was one of the old stars who turned Lamparski down. Charming veteran actress Una Merkel, who was rarely a leading lady, told Lamparski frankly that "fortunately, I don't have to work." Merkel seemed like a wonderful woman, remarking at one point that she was very lucky, and that it was "quite marvelous" to still have people come up to her in stores, or on the street, and tell her how much they loved her work.

Stunning Vilma Banky was a huge silent film star, Goldwyn's biggest money-maker during the 1920s, and starred opposite the ill-fated Rudolph Valentino in his last film, *The Son of the Sheik*. Banky retired from movies with the advent of sound, and settled into a forty-two year marriage to matinee idol Rod La Rocque (which, like so many other unions in Hollywood, produced no children). Their marriage was paid for by Sam Goldwyn, who also gave the bride away, and was one of the biggest weddings Hollywood had ever seen. Cecil B. DeMille was best man and Louella Parsons the maid of honor. Although Banky was very active, playing golf well into her eighties, her death at age ninety-three was not announced publicly for several months. This was apparently due to the fact that Banky felt she'd been forgotten by fans and friends alike. Banky's obituary in the December 12, 1992 *New York Times* explained: "Only now has a spokesman revealed the actress died in a Los Angeles nursing home on March 18, 1991, at the age of about 90. Word of Banky's death began appearing in publications this fall. Yet her passing went largely unnoticed until this week, when her attorney confirmed the death following an inquiry from The Associated Press. 'Banky was ill at home for five years and for another five years at the St. John of God Convalescent Hospital,' attorney Robert Vossler said Thursday. 'During all that time, not a single soul came to visit her. She was so upset that she wanted no notice and no service when she died," he said. "I followed her wishes.'"

Some entertainers make a more dramatic and final exit. Jean Spangler had the same dreams so many other young women did in Hollywood, before she vanished without a trace on October 7, 1949. Among those questioned by the authorities was Kirk Douglas. Many have speculated that Spangler was about to undergo an abortion, very rare at the time in America, but quite common in the Golden Age of Hollywood. Italian TV star Ylenia Carrisi, granddaughter of Tyrone Power, literally disappeared during a vacation in New Orleans in 1994. The Italian media hinted at some kind of voodoo being involved. Carrisi had initially fled from New Orleans to Florida, telling her parents that she feared two men were trying to kill her, but strangely returned there to, in her mother's words, "find characters for a book she was writing."[134] No trace of her has ever been found. Actor Joe Pichler, best known for starring in two of the later, direct-to-video installments of the *Beethoven* movies, hasn't been seen since January 5, 2006, when he was just short of nineteen-years-old. Interestingly, although he hadn't acted since 2002, Pichler was said to have received "a substantial amount of money" from his trust fund after turning eighteen. Despite this, two months before he vanished, he'd taken a job as a full-time telephone technician.[135] Errol Flynn's son Sean (his mother was Lili Damita) vanished in the jungles of Cambodia in 1970, while serving as a freelance journalist for *Time* magazine. Promising young singer-songwriter Jim Sullivan's abandoned car was found on a remote New Mexico ranch on March 6, 1975, and he was never seen again. Sullivan had a cameo role in the classic 1969 film *Easy Rider,* and his debut album *U.F.O.* was recorded the same year, with the illustrious Wrecking Crew session musicians playing on it. Some in the UFO research community have connected the album title to his mysterious disappearance.[136] Tammy Lynn Leppert, a model and aspiring actress, most notable as an extra in 1983's *Scarface,* disappeared on July 6, 1983. Her mother would testify that upon returning home from filming the movie, Tammy had been extremely paranoid, refusing to eat or drink out of any containers, and terrified that someone was out to harm her. Her mother steadfastly believed that her daughter was being targeted by a sinister drug and money laundering ring. Her disappearance has never been solved. Richey Edwards, of the band Manic Street Preachers, simply vanished at age 23. Scott Smith, bassist for the band Loverboy, was presumed lost when his sailboat was hit by a freak wave near the Golden Gate Bridge on November 30, 2000. Audrey Hepburn's father was a Nazi sympathizer and found himself in a British internment camp, where he subsequently disappeared.

Singer Arthur Conley, who hit it big in 1967 with *Sweet Soul Music,* performed a figurative disappearing act within a decade, moving to London, then Brussels, then Amsterdam where he changed his name to Lee Roberts. He allegedly did all this to conceal the fact he was gay. Queen's bassist John Deacon all but disappeared from the business following the 1991 death of the band's front man Freddy Mercury. Deacon, who wrote several of Queen's songs, including the huge hit *Another One Bites the Dust*, didn't even attend the band's induction ceremony into the Rock & Roll Hall of Fame. Tandyn Almer, once a promising songwriter, whose credits included the Association's smash 1966 hit *Along Comes Mary,* and collaborations like *Sail On, Sailor* with the Beach Boys' Brian Wilson, vanished from the entertainment world in 1974. For decades, no one knew what had happened to him. When Almer died on January 8, 2013, he'd been living anonymously in the Washington, D.C. suburbs for almost forty years, and at the time of his death was residing in a small basement apartment in McLean, Virginia.[137]

Teen pop idol Barry Cowsill, of the singing Cowsills family, was washed away along with so many others in Hurricane Katrina, and his body was found months later in the Mississippi River. His life had plummeted after the Cowsills' string of hit records dried up, and he'd been forced to support himself by working construction and being a waiter. Compounding the family tragedy, the surviving siblings learned about the death of their fifty-eight-year-old brother Bill, who'd been the group's lead singer, as they were holding a memorial service for Barry. All the Cowsills suffered under their abusive father Bud, who evidently squandered some $20 million in earnings. Porn star Bambi Woods, whose real name has never been established, starred in what was then the biggest XXX-rated film of all time, 1978's *Debbie Does Dallas*. Although those who produced the film made plenty of money from it, "Bambi" didn't see much of that, which has always been the case for female stars in the porn industry. Repelled at the sudden fame her explicit role brought her, "Bambi" simply vanished. Rumors that she either died of a drug overdose (as so many porn stars do) in 1986, or retired to the anonymity of Des Moines, Iowa have not been verified. And the individual who probably really should be credited with inventing motion pictures, Louis Le Prince, disappeared somehow during a September 1890 train ride to Paris. The man and his luggage were missing from his cabin, but the windows were all locked, there were no train stops, etc.[138] The mystery grows deeper when one learns that Le Prince, who had actually recorded the first moving images on film, often spoke to friends about unnamed forces trying to steal his invention. Thomas Edison publicly denied any involvement in Le Prince's disappearance, but quickly swooped in and grabbed the patent.

Young Native American actress Misty Upham's death was as mysterious as it was under publicized. The thirty-two-year-old was found dead in October 2014, with her skull and ribs broken, in a wooded Washington state ravine. She'd been missing for eleven days, and the medical examiner ruled that her death was the result of a fall down a steep embankment. Her blood alcohol level was said to be an unbelievable .33 - which makes it difficult to believe she could have been conscious enough to fall. Despite acting with some of the top stars in the business, Upham was living in a low-income community and dependent upon the Indian Health Service.[139] Misty had allegedly been raped at the 2013 Golden Globe Awards by one of Harvey Weinstein's executive team. The rape purportedly occurred in a men's room, as powerful men in formal wear cheered the assault as if it were a "beer drinking contest," in the words of Misty's father Charles Upham. After being raped, Misty was forced to endure the "walk of shame," again quoting her father, back to the event. The rapist was given congratulatory high fives along the way. Misty's parents pleaded with her afterwards to report the crime, but she was terrified to do so. Charles Upham claimed they even had DNA evidence, preserved on the dress Misty had been wearing, and explained that his daughter recognized that Harvey Weinstein could "ruin her existence." Misty knew enough about Weinstein to realize he had the power to "make people disappear." Misty claimed to have witnessed Weinstein order a man who'd had the audacity to interrupt his conversation with director Quentin Tarantino to be thrown from a car in the middle of nowhere, during a violent Utah snowstorm. When the young girl objected that the man would freeze to death, Weinstein replied, "Someone will come along and pick him up." It was a year after the rape when Misty Upham's body was discovered in a ravine about thirty miles from Seattle. It was determined that her death was caused by blunt force trauma to the head and torso, and conveniently found that these were entirely the result of, and not the cause of, a fall. Misty's family contended that she had indeed fallen, after being chased by police. They also alleged that she'd been a victim of significant harassment from the Oregon Police Department.[140]

Model and actress Linda Sobek was brutally sodomized and strangled during a November 1995 photo shoot by photographer Charles Rathbun. Olivia Newton John's one-time boyfriend, cameraman Patrick McDermott, went missing during a fishing trip in San Pedro, California in 2005. Other passengers on the ship gave conflicting reports, and it remains an unsolved missing persons' case. In November, 2017, a story broke about McDermott being alive in Mexico, after supposedly faking his death. There was no follow-up beyond the single story.[141] Busy child actor Lisa Gerritsen, who starred in *My World and Welcome to It*, *The Mary Tyler Moore Show, Phyllis* and many other television shows, pulled a figurative vanishing act following her last screen credit in 1978. The web site Former Child Star Central tried hard to find her, and eventually she was discovered to be working for a software company. At last report, she was living very privately in northern California with her husband and son. There have been heartfelt remembrances written on the internet by bloggers who'd had a crush on her decades earlier, but Gerritsen evidently remains curiously detached from Hollywood, and has not granted an interview since she left the business.

If the history of Hollywood teaches us anything, it is that once a star frequently does not mean *always* a star.

Chapter Two

Communicating With The Old Entertainers

The music business is a cruel and shallow money trench, a long plastic hallway where thieves and pimps run free, and good men die like dogs. There's also a negative side.

- Hunter S. Thompson

WHEN I WAS a young child, I loved the music of the Beatles, the Beach Boys, Lesley Gore, Lou Christie, the Four Seasons, Del Shannon, Paul Revere and the Raiders, Gary Lewis and the Playboys, Tommy James and the Shondells and so many others. I simply took it for granted that anyone with a hit record must be "rich," at least compared to lower middle-class families like mine. I would read stories here and there about former stars that had fallen on hard times, but I really had no idea of just how many entertainers either never received what they were due financially, or had to fight for years to get it. Forty years later, I began emailing entertainers from the era of my childhood - the 1960s and 1970s - and asked them each about their experiences in regards to royalties and residuals.

Before I began thinking in terms of a book about the subject, I tried to track down some of my typically obscure favorites, to satisfy my own curiosity. For instance, I was enamored with a song called *It's Not Easy Loving You Baby*, which briefly cracked the Top 40 in 1968. I couldn't understand why it never became a big hit. In 2005, while searching on the internet for information about the Will-O-Bees, the forgotten band who recorded the song, I found some contact information for Janet Lussier, the group's singer. She was working as a receptionist in Massachusetts, and seemed pleasantly surprised that someone remembered her. "You found me!" She replied to me in an email dated April 18, 2005. "We released a few 45's. We never released an album....When our songs didn't get picked up by the radio DJ's, Screen Gems Columbia would pass them on to established artists who would then get the air time. We released 'Shades of Gray' to be re-released by The Monkees. (Our version was better). Then also we released a song titled 'It's Gettin Better' to be later released by Mama Cass. (our version was better). Then again when we actually thought we had a full blown hit on our hands titled 'Make Your Own Kind Of Music'. It never seemed to really get off the ground, so low and behold Mama Cass released it and sure enough, it was a smash. (Our version was better). After that, I quit the group and that was the end of The Will-O-Bees. We also did the theme song for a show called Ugliest Girl in Town." I found some of the Will-O-Bees songs online, and Lussier was right - while those recordings by bigger artists were wonderful, their versions *were* better.

On December 9, 2009, Laurie Jacobson, author of *Haunted Hollywood* and other books, replied to my email to her husband Jon Provost, who starred as Timmy Martin in the old *Lassie* series. She wrote, "Hmmm, well, of course, all were underpaid in royalties. No one dreamed of videos, dvds, internet. All contracts read 'in perpetuity' and everyone signed them. I believe Jon's royalties for Lassie lasted for 3 airings, then nothing more. It is on the air currently in close to 50 countries." Provost is one of my many older celebrity friends on Facebook. He enjoys posting about political issues, and loathes Donald Trump, like most of Hollywood. Provost broached the subject of royalties in a February 3, 2019 Facebook post, writing: "When I was filming Lassie ,1957-64, I made an average of $325.00 a week and I was paying 65% Tax and that didn't include my agents 10% before taxes. So that's a total of 75% of my pay check, which was about $12K a year, sure it's 'old' money but in no way does it equal $10 million today. Residuals you ask? I have not received a Lassie residual, not $0.01 in over 45 years and the show is shown on over a dozen cable networks here in the U.S. and in over 60 countries. Someone is getting rich off our backs."

Alan Warner, guitarist and songwriter for The Foundations, whose hits included *Build Me Up, Buttercup* and *Baby, Now That I've Found You*, was very interested in the subject and we exchanged several emails. On November 19, 2009, Warner told me that, "These records were released between 1967 and 1971. We didn't receive any recording royalties until about 10 or 12 years later, by which time of course, the main bulk of the monies were dried up. We only started to receive current royalties from then on. Of course this was nothing like the 'Golden' years when we were selling millions. Even worse! I co-wrote a song called 'New direction' with two other members of The Foundations which was on the B side of 'Build me up Buttercup', This was number one all over the world, selling millions, and was published with Sparta Music, (later to become Sparta Florida). Neither myself nor any of the others have received a single penny to this day, and no explanation as to why, despite numerous requests over the years."

On February 9, 2009, Barry McGuire - best known for his #1 1965 song *Eve of Destruction*, wrote me, "Well, I could get into all the moaning and groaning, but suffice it to say, 'What royalties????'

LOL!" As of 2019, McGuire's net worth was estimated online to be between $100,000-$1 million. Sal Valentino, lead singer of the band Beau Brummels, whose 1965 hit *Laugh, Laugh* was so popular it was spoofed on *The Flintstones*, replied to my email on April 17, 2009 by saying, "I've been told that where there are royalties there are more, it takes a Lawyer to get them. Most artist's in the past were not confident enough to pursue it seems and so go without. I've been receiving royalties from Rhino Records for at least the last 20 years since they secured the Masters of the recordings that I have been a part of. I have finally been paid for what I did over 40 years ago." A story about Valentino from 2006 reported that at one point in the mid-1980s, he took his father's old job of selling racing forms at Bay Meadows race track in San Mateo, California. It wasn't until 1994, when he married a school teacher, that he was able to get the insurance he needed to replace his front teeth. Apparently, the most money he made after his salad days with Beau Brummels was the $5,000 finder's fee he received for bringing Rickie Lee Jones to Warner Brothers Records.[142]

Some artists fared better than others, again for unclear reasons. Johnny Tillotson - primarily known for his huge 1960 hit *Poetry in Motion*, was evidently one of those. His wife Nancy replied to my email on March 21, 2009 by explaining, "I'm sorry to say that we don't have any specific information to relay to you on the subject. Naturally we have heard of artists who did not receive compensation for their work. Fortunately, Johnny was not one of them and Cadence Records was a very reputable company. Of course the artists at the beginning of Rock N Roll were not compensated in the fashion of today's artists…. Royalty rates in general were much much less. Many more things were done for free and for promotion. And merchandising and licensing wasn't as sophisticated and or artists just weren't compensated. Hops and things as I said were done for free and promotion, where as today people can be paid just to show up at a party. So very different times." Max Crook, who co-wrote Del Shannon's #1 1961 hit single *Runaway* and played the iconic solo on the song, using the unique musitron instrument he invented, replied to me on February 6, 2009. "As far as artist royalties went, Del was compensated for his live performances," Crook wrote. "For the first ten to fifteen years, his compensation for his artistry on his recordings was spotty, at best. At one point, his catalogue was gambled away by the record execs, and was later found in an attic in New York. He and Dan Burgoise of 'Bug' Music in L.A. recovered the catalogue for a fairly large sum (which also included my recordings as 'Maxmilian'). Since that time, Bug Music has been faithful in paying royalties for sales, recording covers, etc. The radio, TV, internet, movie use for his songs has always been well handled by B.M.I."

Steve Boone, guitarist for the Lovin' Spoonful, whose many hits in the 1960s included *Do You Believe in Magic* and *Summer in the City,* replied to me on March 12, 2009 thusly: "The answer to your questions are obviously YES we and virtually all of our contemporaries were underpaid or not paid at all. Your question had many facets to it and trying to be specific would be a difficult task. If you have specific questions I would be glad to try and answer them although the topic is very broad. Good luck with your book." Boone later wrote his own book (with Tony Moss), *Hotter Than a Match Head: Life on the Run With the Lovin' Spoonful.* In the book, Boone detailed his financial issues, as well as his drug bust, subsequent turns as an informer, and later as a drug smuggler. We are also friends on Facebook.

I'd read where Mary Weiss of the successful girl group The Shangri-Las (whose most memorable hit was 1964's #1 *Leader of the Pack*) had tried for years to obtain royalties she felt she was owed. Thus, it was little surprise that she sent me the following curt reply on February 17, 2009: "This is not an issue I discuss with anyone. I have been in court too many times over the years. Enough said." Mary had worked as a secretary after her musical career ended, and eventually wound up in the accounting department of a New York architectural firm. Another girl group, the Angels, had a #1 pop hit in 1963 with *My Boyfriend's Back*. On January 26, 2009, attorney Diane Leigh Davison emailed me and said, "Thanks for contacting me about your research. The Angels are currently in litigation over non-payment of royalties. They were accounted to once in 1963 or 1964 but never since, and never having received a single cent. Even in the face of litigation, the producers refuse to escrow monies, account, or even now pay. I can also put you in touch with many other 60's artists who did not receive royalties…" Diane and I became friends on Facebook, and when I asked her if there were any updates on this, she replied via a Facebook personal message on July 24, 2019, that "So they settled for a very small sum that barely even covered their legal costs, but FGG no longer controls or pays their royalties, the record company now does that. That's all the info I have and can share."

Uriah Heep's lead guitarist Mick Box sent me an email reply on February 16, 2009, stating, "I hope this will be what you are looking for! Well we were not a lot different to most of the artists that came up in the late 60's to early 70's. I do not think I know a band that has not been ripped off by someone in the business. After all we are in the Music Business and the Music part comes easily but the Business side is usually hell. We signed contracts in good faith and were very happy to have a recording contract or indeed contractual live work. All our energies were put into the music and a lot of trust was given to managers, accountants and record companies. Often this trust proved to be most artists downfall as they were never given good advice and signed contracts that gave a ridiculous income to each individual as the royalty rates were so low. Sometimes tying the artist up for years. We never had anything to judge the royalty rate by so we signed in good faith."

I had an interesting series of email exchanges with singer Trini Lopez, who enjoyed a series of hit singles in the early to mid-'60s like *If I Had a Hammer* and *Lemon Tree,* and had a prominent acting role in the huge 1967 film *The Dirty Dozen,* and his personal assistant. On January 29, 2009, Personal Assistant Oralee Walker frankly stated, "Yes, Mr. Trini Lopez is very suspicious that several companies, especially Reprise/Warner Brothers Records, grossly under compensated him for the last 40 years." Then, apparently under the misimpression that I was an attorney, she added, "Please send more information on what you and your office does for the recording artist you mentioned on your email of 1/29/09." Two days later, I received another email from Walker, which read, "We were under the assumption that your office would have auditors go into the record companies to audit the books for the recording artist. If you know of such a company that could help recording artist to get their money from these big recording companies, please let us know at your earliest convenience." On February 4, 2009, Trini Lopez himself emailed me, and advised me, "I don't think it is a good idea to have anything published by me about me not receiving my correct royalties from different record companies. I think it would hurt me more than help." A few days later, on February 9, Lopez changed his stance and wrote back, "If you want to mention in your book that people like Trini Lopez has and is still experiencing major record companies not reporting his due royalties, that is ok with me. Just maybe a major auditing firm will read your book and try to help artist such as myself and others. Wishing you all the best with your book." I was never able to get specific details from Lopez or his assistant, regarding his situation, but clearly he still felt, decades after the height of his career, that he'd been cheated financially. Trini Lopez died on August 11, 2020. Somewhat surprisingly, he had a reported net worth of $5 million.

Howard Kaylan, former lead singer of the '60s band The Turtles, who scored with a slew of huge hits in the 1960s like *Happy Together* and *She'd Rather Be with Me,* and later "Eddie" of Flo (Turtles' band mate Mark Volman) and Eddie, sent me a February 7, 2009 email which stated, "We were screwed, blued and tattooed. I highly recommend that you go to You Tube and type in The Turtles/Managers/lecture or something like that, you'll be directed to an excerpt from a documentary that Rhino did about us a few years ago, wherein Mark and I discuss, in length, how we were taken advantage of in the Sixties. The clip is about seven minutes long, but it says it all better than I could convey in this email." It is indeed an interesting little video, describing how their series of managers screwed them over, while at the peak of their fame they were borrowing $250,000 from their record company. Nick Gravenites, a singer, songwriter and producer who worked with Janis Joplin and numerous other industry icons, replied to me on January 27, 2009. "If you research the history of Jimi Hendrix's recordings and management, you'll know all you need to know about undercompensate," Gravenities wrote. "My first recorded song was BORN IN CHICAGO by the Paul Butterfield Blues Band in 1965. Forty – four years of experience have taught me that it is better to have the money and be sued than not have the money and do the suing. Thieves rule. Good luck with your project."

John Hall, formerly a member of the '70s band Orleans, which charted top hits like *Still the One*, went on to rather inexplicably graduate to the United States Congress. I sent Rep. Hall an email in February 2009, but received only a form response, which didn't address the subject matter. This brought to mind the similarly confounding transition Jeff "Skunk" Baxter made, from Doobie Brothers and Steely Dan guitarist to one of the Pentagon's top missile defense consultants. Perhaps the most touching email response I received came from singer Brenton Wood, who hit it big with 1967's *Gimme Little Sign*. Wood wrote me on January 27, 2009, that, "Don, do artist get paid or in fame? I wrote singed and performed my music, I did not receive any royalties from double shot records Irwin Zucker. Seymore Zucker thought if they bought me a car I would be happy. Al Bennett of liberty records started a record label for his son

Wayne Bennet and now the songs are on universal and I still dont receive any royalties from them. so I feel record companies only pay current artist with hits on the charts. Best wishes."

On January 29, 2009, Kay Bryson, presumably the wife of Raspberries' band member Wally Bryson, replied to my email this way, "Please formulate a few specific questions once your book is more in the definite stage for Wally to answer. I'm in the process of writing a book myself about Wally's music business experiences, so there's lots to tell." She didn't reply to my subsequent list of questions. More than one person told me they were writing their own book. A November 24, 2015 story on Cleveland.com reported that Raspberries lead singer Eric Carmen had filed a complaint in Cuyahoga County Probate Court, accusing his brother of making a "financial mess" out of his trust fund. The story noted that Carmen's royalties were running between $600,000-800,000 per year. I wrote to The Band's drummer and vocalist Levon Helm, and his assistant Barbara O'Brian sent the following very interesting reply on January 27, 2009, "The whole world of royalties is a cobweb that I'd love to be able to fully understand. i personally think the industry and the 'suits' have designed it so that the artist or layman will never be able to decypher the information and figure out what they're supposed to be getting. Levon, right now, is engrossed in several projects that have been instrumental in pulling him out of bankruptcy and near foreclosure (could royalties have been responsible????) I'm not sure he'll have the time to talk to you, but I can pass you along to Levon's attorney, Mr. Michael Pinsky, who has helped us tremendously in navigating through that cobweb...." I never heard back from Helm's lawyer. Levon Helm was only one of the entertainers I contacted who have since sadly passed on.

Sonny Geraci, who died at age sixty-nine in 2017, was the lead singer of the '60s group The Outsiders, remembered for their #5 1966 single *Time Won't Let Me,* and later sang for the band Climax, who had the huge 1972 hit *Precious and Few.* Geraci replied to me on January 26, 2009. "Well, I can pretty much tell you that we were underpaid. Actually in most cases, never paid. Always had excuses. We were not accountants. Most of us probably could not afford a lawyer or accountant. I have been in this business since 1965. I was born and raised in Cleveland Ohio. Moved to LA in 1968. Lived there til 1976. I wanted to write a book myself. I believe it would be very interesting. I'm still performing about 40-50 one nighters a year with my band. If I can be of any further help let me know."

The late Don Grady, who starred as Robbie Douglass on the long-running television show *My Three Sons*, was one of those who preferred not to dwell on such things. "Donald - Your request is not intrusive at all...I welcome any correspondence, especially from another writer," Grady wrote me on January 25, 2009. "However, and unfortunately, speaking about compensation and residuals from the past is not my idea of a good time...sorry, Donald. Yes, the performers of the '60's have not benefited from the Cable and Internet explosion...so be it. It's the past. Onward. Best with your project..." Lori Saunders, who starred as Bobbi Joe Bradley on the television show *Petticoat Junction*, sent me the following brief response on January 14, 2009: "When I did pcj they gave us 3 rerun royalties...they have paid nothing over the past many years.....that was the deal then…" Florence Henderson, who was one of the most beautiful eighty-two-year-old women ever when she died in 2016, starred as Carol Brady on *The Brady Bunch*. She sent the following predictably upbeat reply to me on February 5, 2009: "Thank you for your message. Unfortunately in the 70's contracts were different. Payment was much less and residuals only lasted for a few years. Of course people made millions on the Brady Bunch as the series has never been off the air and is in 122 countries all over the world, for which I have never received a cent. There is also much memorabilia which is sold for which I am not compensated but I'm grateful for the Brady Bunch." Jean Darling, who starred in lots of silent and some of the early talkie Our Gang shorts, was still sharp on January

16, 2009, when she replied to me by saying, "Hi! No, I never received a cent from the GANG after I left the Roach Studio. However I have never been one to fret. After all back then there was no deal as far as residuals were concerned. Seeing that was the case why waste time giving it a moment's thought? Anyway as today I belong to a dying breed i.e. someone who began a career in silent movies, I am rather proud of still being extant despite never receiving residuals, royalties or otherwise from Little Rascals/Our Gang!!!!!" One of the rare Our Gang kids who lived a long life, Darling was ninety- three when she passed away in 2015.

On November 9, 2009, Henry Gross, a founding member of the retro group Sha Na Na, who also played lead guitar on Jim Croce's 1973 LP *I Got a Name*, but is probably best known for his 1976 hit song *Shannon* (written about Beach Boy Carl Wilson's dog), replied to my email with, "In response to your question, though I have had problems in the past vis a vis royalties and abuse by the record business I choose to focus on the joy and satisfaction of having made a life making and bringing music to people all over the world. No business is without it's problems. Artists will be artists, good businessmen will be good and honest and thieves will be thieves. The same can be said of any business. Focusing on those darker, painful realities serves no purpose other than the venting of anger that should have been dealt with years ago. It's a new business and a new day where artists are more in control of their careers. Better to write about the possibilities for the future. The old record business model is doomed and nearly dead. It has flogged itself to death through greed and gluttony. Old news! Time for the new world. May we bring joy to audiences large and small with our visions of love and laughter. Rock on." The next day, he followed up with, "Don, Without naming names, certain 'artists' on your list of initial responders are well known whiners who can't seem to move on. One in particular might be the all time champion. He's a rich man who can't just accept that when you build a house, some wood winds up in the dumpster. I lost a fortune to the 'honest' record company accountants. I prefer the music to be the legacy. Glad you understand."

On January 24, 2009, I received a response from one of my favorites as a youth, recording artist Kent LaVoie, better known as Lobo, whose memorable hit singles in the early 1970s included *I'd Love You to Want Me* and *Me and You and a Dog Named Boo*. "All of my contracts for my hits were with Phil Gernard, my producer. He demanded all of the publishing and paid me a royalty on records sold. Therefore I didn't make any of the advance money he collected after the big hits." LaVoie wrote. "When my manager figured this out I refused to record unless he shared the advances. He refused and that was the end of that. After a year of legal battles I was released and he got no more of the advances. To this day I don't know why he couldn't compromise. I got a clue just this last year when he committed suicide. Look up 'Number One with a Bullit' about Phil Gernhard. But dont cry for me because he sold his rights to Famous Music, now Sony, and they still pay me more than I need to live the lifestyle I prefer. I finally started receiving royalties a few years after getting someone to collect them for me. After the legal battles of the 70s I just didn't have the stomach to go after Gernhard, it wasn't important to me. By the way everyone he worked faced similar problems, maybe that's why he couldn't live with himself. He did always know what was a Hit. Hope this helps."

Eve Plumb, remembered as Jan Brady on *The Brady Bunch*, and now a Laguna Beach artist, was very forthcoming to me in a January 16, 2009 email, writing, "Hi Don - Sorry, I was a kid at the time and had no idea of how much I was being paid. My father was also in the music business for many years, Neely Plumb, and I know he missed out on being paid at times. What I do know is that under our contract, we were paid residuals for up to 10 repeats of each episode, which seemed like a good deal at the time. No one expected the Spanish Inquisition of endless repeats on local channels, cable, etc. When cable started up they cried poor and got reduced rates, or even free content, as in the case of TVLand, which, because it's a basic channel is considered to come under the same agreement that allowed channels to not have to pay actors residuals. This has built their channel, since all of their content is mainly free, as far as I can tell. I'm guessing that the studios and the producers got paid, as usual. This is a sore point for me and is why I haven't gone to their award show, and often have to fight them to be paid even the minimum to use a clip on that show, which is the rule now. I have a lumbering saying, which is 'Artists are the only people who are expected to be grateful for being paid.' Whenever I am fighting to get compensation, I remember that even Mary Pickford had to fight with D.W. Griffith on the same issue. Good luck on the book." Plumb made headlines again in 2016, when her Malibu beachfront home sold for $3.9 million. It was reported that Plumb had purchased the home in 1969, at a mere eleven years of age, for just over $55,000.[143]

I contacted both the son and daughter of Three Stooges star Moe Howard. On January 15, 2009, Paul Howard sent me this tantalizing, cryptic reply: "To get the info you desire, I recommend that you contact my sister, Joan Maurer. She is MUCH more knowledgeable than I am about the Stooges. I spent a lot of my life in denial of who my dad was." Later that same day, Moe's daughter Joan Maurer replied to me thusly: "To my knowledge Columbia never paid a cent in royalties to the Stooges for the old shorts when they were released to TV. Some money may have been paid to the people who took over Comedy III Prod. in the nineties. You would have to contact them for that information. My understanding is that there was a cut off date re: compensation and the comedies, sadly, fell before that date." On a recent broadcast of ME-TV's television show *Svengoolie,* it was casually mentioned that the Stooges never made more than $60,000 combined in any one year.

Matthew Fisher, who played keyboard on Procol Harum's unforgettable 1967 hit *Whiter Shade of Pale,* sent me a lengthy email response on January 14, 2009. "If you give me an address, I can send you a copy of the original recording contract between the band Procol Harum and Essex Music…. I've never received very much in terms of artists' royalties in respect of Procol recordings," Fisher wrote. "When I was first in the band (between 1967 and 1969) I never even saw a royalty check. All royalties were paid into the group's collective account and were used to pay off group debts. You might think it strange that a band that had sold around six million singles around the world could be constantly in debt and I can only assume that this is because we had a succession of really dreadful managers. When I left the band in 1969 I was forced to sign a document relinquishing my rights to record royalties in return for being freed from any kind of responsibility for the band's ever-present debts. This was rather strange because:

1. Never having seen a royalty check, I'd no idea what I was giving up
2. I had absolutely no idea what the group debts were
3. I was instructed to sign the document by my then manager (a Mr Ronnie Lyons) who was also managing Procol at the time. I believe this is known in legal circles as 'a conflict of interests'.

This document was also (mis)used as an excuse not to account to me my producer's royalties for Procol's third album, A Salty Dog, which I had produced. I rejoined Procol around 1990 and after a few years, managed to persuade Brooker and Reid to reinstate my artists' and producer's royalties. However, when I left the band in 2003 all these payments ceased. Against this background you can see why I've had such a long, hard battle trying to get my rights as a co-composer of A Whiter Shade of Pale. The fight isn't over yet - we're going to the House of Lords in April. Maybe sanity will finally win the day." Later that year, it was reported that Fisher had won a share of the royalties for *A Whiter Shade of Pale*. Fisher was quoted as saying, "This was never about money. There will not be a lot of that anyway. But this was about making sure everyone knew about my part in the authorship."[144] For what it's worth, Matthew Fisher's current net worth online is estimated to be between $100,000 and $1 million. By comparison, his Procol Harum band mate (and lead singer) Gary Brooker is said to be worth $10 million. The band's lyricist, Keith Reid, has a current estimated net worth of $1.5 million. When I emailed Peter Noone, lead singer of Herman's Hermits, one of the more successful bands from the 1960s' British Invasion, I mentioned something about the situation bands like Procol Harum had experienced. He replied to me on January 25, 2009, with the simple statement, "We were like Procul Harum" and Barry Whitwam, his fellow band member, on February 3, 2009 told me that "My situation was the same as Peter Noone's." On June 29, 2018, Peter Noone replied to my updated email inquiry teasingly with, "I have a good story about royalties and how musicians are not good at math," but never elaborated.

Mary McDonough, who played Erin Walton on the popular '70s show *The Waltons*, provided me with the following information in a February 5, 2009 email: "I was so young I don't know what we made on the show. I know it was about $400 an episode, our residuals were based on the time frame set by the guild - SAG at the time. We were only paid reruns for the first 6 airings. It is not like it is now, that's for sure. The kids always made the least. Sorry to not be of more help. I don't have old contracts." I was truly astonished to learn that a regular cast member of one of the decade's most successful television programs was only being paid $400 an episode. That just seemed like a pittance to me, even considering it was forty years ago. By comparison, Jay North, the young star of an earlier series, *Dennis the Menace*, was initially paid $500 per episode and was earning $3,500 for each show by the final 1963 season, while the cast members on another earlier series, the long-running western *Bonanza,* were making $19,000 per episode by the final 1972 season, and an additional $20,000 per summer rerun during the years 1970-71. Not to mention that NBC paid Lorne Greene, Dan Blocker and Michael Landon $1 million each in 1970, in lieu of future residuals. Don Adams, who starred in the sitcom *Get Smart,* shrewdly turned down what was at the time a very generous salary offer of $12,500 per week in exchange for a percentage of the show's profits. Pernell Roberts, who played Adam during the early years of *Bonanza,* left the show in 1965 due to his blossoming social conscience, which told him that gun control and improving the lives of Native Americans were more important than the $10,000 he was earning per episode.

The cast of *Star Trek,* on the other hand, opted to take the offer of a few thousand dollars each instead of rerun residuals. Series creator Gene Roddenberry clearly fared much better, dying with a net worth of $500 million. The stars of the show eventually earned their fortunes, especially with later big-budget films based on the series. Leonard Nimoy left behind a $45 million estate, and William Shatner is worth an impressive $150 million. In contrast, James Doohan died with some $7 million to his name, and DeForest Kelley had even less, at $5 million. Anne Serling, daughter of Rod Serling, told my friend John Barbour in a 2015 interview that her father unfortunately had sold the rights to all *The Twilight Zone* episodes to CBS. Like many others from the early days of television, Serling just never envisioned how valuable his work would become. *The Mighty Morphin Power Rangers* were all the rage in the early nineties, and kids like my son loved watching them. Evidently, the actors who portrayed the action heroes were shamefully underpaid. The lovely Amy Jo Johnson, who played the original Pink Ranger, revealed on a 2012 No Pink Spandex podcast that the Rangers received a paltry, 1960s-like $600 weekly and were given "zero" residuals. The original Yellow Ranger, Karan Ashley, added that "When we first got on the show we were doing six days a week, 12 to 15 hour days. …" The original Red Ranger, Austin St. John, bitterly commented that "I could have worked the window at McDonalds and probably made the same money the first season." St. John told the *Huffington Post* that he wound up homeless after leaving the show.[145] Both Austin St. John and Amy Jo Johnson are said to have a meager present net worth of just $300,000. Karan Ashley, on the other hand, is doing quite nicely with an estimated $7 million.

Jean Vander Pyl, best known as the voice of Wilma Flintstone, revealed that she'd been paid a mere $250 for each episode of *The Flintstones,* and eagerly accepted a one-time payment of $15,000 when the series ended, in lieu of residuals from syndication, never thinking the show would have such enduring popularity. The cast of *The Partridge Family* were all underpaid. Teen heartthrob and series star David Cassidy was supposedly only making $600 a week on the show. Barry Williams, who played Greg on *The Brady Bunch,* disclosed in his 1992 memoir *Growing Up Brady* that the kids on the show earned a much better top salary of $1,100 weekly. Betty Lynn, who played Barney Fife's girlfriend Thelma Lou on the iconic *The Andy Griffith Show,* was only paid $500 for each of the surprisingly sparse twenty-six episodes she appeared in. In a life imitating art twist, Lynn wound up retiring to Mount Airy, Andy Griffith's hometown that served as the model for Mayberry.[146] I attempted to reach Betty Lynn through the Andy Griffith Museum, and the representative I spoke with seemed interested, and promised they'd ask her if she'd speak with me, but I never heard back. The cast of *Lost in Space* were paid pretty well; anywhere from $1,250 per episode (Angela Cartwright) to $3,500 per show (Jonathan Harris). Dick Tufeld, who provided both the narration as well as the Robot's voice, was paid $400 per show. The salaries of the kid stars of *The Waltons* seem even more mystifying considering a September 4, 1999 article in *South Coast Today,* which detailed the squandering of sizable fortunes earned by earlier child stars Paul Petersen (*The Donna Reed Show*), Brandon Cruz (*The Courtship of Eddie's Father*), and Jon Provost (*Lassie*). In Provost's case, this seemed to contradict his earlier quoted post on Facebook. Gloria Stuart, the leading lady of early Thirties horror classics like *The Old Dark House* and *The Invisible Man*, was paid what seems a startlingly modest $10,000 to play the part of Old Rose in the 1997 megahit *Titanic*.

On April 1, 2016, I had a brief telephone conversation with Mary McDonough's *Waltons'* co-star Eric Scott, who played her brother Ben on the show. Eric was very polite, but seemed uninterested in the concept of the book, basically telling me he saw no purpose in it, beyond "tugging at the heartstrings," and noted, as others had to me, that it couldn't have been foreseen how often these programs would be re-run, and thus no one could be held responsible. Ironically, the surviving cast members of *The Waltons* - including Scott, had recently been interviewed by *Closer Weekly*, which resulted in a December 22, 2015 story headlined, "The Cast of 'The Waltons' Speak Out: 'We Were Taken Advantage Of.'" Eric Scott himself was quoted as saying, "We did not get rich from that show" and "we never felt the studio appreciated us." In another startling contrast, Willie Aames, one of the kids on *Eight is Enough,* was reportedly making $1 million a year by the end of the show's run in 1984. Despite starring on another hit show, *Charles in Charge,* afterward, Aames went bankrupt, his car was repossessed, and he couldn't pay the medical bills for his wife. He eventually became homeless.[147]

Several performers, including Janis Ian, Helen Reddy, Steve Forbert, Walter Koenig (Chekov on *Star Trek*), Alan Sues, Mr. Acker Bilk, Petula Clark, Diane Renay, Dick Gautier, Chris Hillman (guitarist for the Byrds, the Flying Burrito Brothers and Souther-Hillman-Furay), Sheila Kuehl (Zelda on *The Many Loves of Dobie Gillis*), Ann Jillian, Mary Hopkin, Marshall Crenshaw, Rhonda Fleming, Gilbert O'Sullivan and others politely declined to share their experiences. A representative for actor Roy Thinnes, best known for starring in the '60s series *The Invaders,* wrote me back on May 23, 2018 that, "I'll ask him, but he rarely sees any compensation."

On January 27, 2009, singer Bobby Vee wrote, "interesting topic… send me more information and we can chat." He never replied to my subsequent emails. Sadly, Vee announced in 2011 that he'd been diagnosed with Alzheimer's disease, and was forced to stop touring. Vee would die in 2016 at seventy-three. Vee apparently did pretty well financially, as at last report he had $10 million, according to Celebrity Net Worth. I emailed the web site for Cass Elliot, ill-fated star of the Mamas and the Papas, and on February 2, 2009, someone named Charles replied, saying he'd forwarded my email to Cass's sister Leah Kunkel and her daughter, Owen Elliot, and added, "This is a subject that has always interested me, too." Later the same day, Charles emailed back and asked, "Is there a phone number at which Owen (Cass's daughter) may reach you?" Unfortunately, no one ever called me. When I began working on this book again years later, I sent him another email, but didn't receive a reply. Johnnie Whitaker, star of the TV series *Family Affair* and several movies, seemed to think I was someone else, writing on November 10, 2009: "You haven't responded to my question, are you the same Don Jeffries who is/was with the STAR awards? Yes, I was one of the unfortunate ones as the SAG/AFTRA contracts for residuals started in 1971 just as Family Affair was ending." Sheila Kuehl, Lori Saunders and Chris Hillman all added me to their regular email list; Kuehl has gravitated to politics and serves on the Los Angeles County Board of Supervisors, Hillman is still touring regularly with a new band and Saunders sells her art, photos and sculptures.

I exchanged some interesting emails with Lonnie Burr, one of the original Mouseketeers on Walt Disney's *Mouseketeer Club*. I think he resented my attempt to broach his territory, as he told me he was writing his own book. On February 12, 2009, I expressed astonishment at his earlier claim that he'd been getting regular residuals for over 50 years. In his often brusque style, Burr declared, "If you are actually writing a book, you need to do some research. Start with SAG history, which is easily accessible online. SAG got residuals for

TV in discussions in 1948 and they wer into effec n 1950-51 or so. Our 7 year contracts in 1955 allowed esidua rough sixth run. Films were not negoti ed until the early '60s." When I noted that he was fortunate in ving a much better deal than the vast majority of his peers, he replied, "Not so. We got minimum SAG wages and residuals. Spin & Marty actors, kids and adults, made much more than th Mouseketeers." When I asked if this applied to the other Mouseketeers, he said, "All the first 24 (+4 fired early the first season) had the same 7 year contract. I can only ASSUME that the ones who followed got the same deal." I noted that members of Guy Williams' (who played the title character in Disney's *Zorro* television series) family had been battling Disney for years, attempting to get unp d royalties. Burr replied, "This is a fallacious assumption based on your not understanding the subject. It is objective, not subjective. My feelings about are subjective. Did you not hear about the six year arbitration SAG brought against Disney vis-a-vis the residuals of all on the MMC? The press, obtuse and misguided as usual, focused on the 39 Mouseketeers, most particularly the 9 of us who lasted the entire filming but there were MANY MORE actors on the various teen soaps…." He closed with, "I think we best leave discussions UNTIL you do some research and, for that matter, read my book which has more about our situation than anything ever published before."

Sam Bobrick, who wrote for television shows like *The Andy Griffith Show, Gomer Pyle, USMC, The Flintstones, The Smothers Brothers Comedy Hour, Get Smart* and *Saved By The Bell* during his lengthy career, sent me the following response on January 16, 2009: "Dear Don: There are so many different types of royalty structures so I couldn't possibly provide you with all the information you need. However if you contact the Writers Guild Of America for TV, ASCAP or BMI for music royalties and the Dramatists Guild for plays and musicals I'm sure they will have that information. In TV so much depends on the kind show you do, half hour, hour, drama, comedy, network, cable. For theatre a lot of payment is structured based on the size of the theatres, whether it's a first class production or community oriented production, off Broadway, off off Broadway, etc. You probably can get much of that information over the internet. I no longer write for TV and have no idea what the rates are there. They do change and on some TV shows you get residuals and on others you don't. Depends on when you wrote them since the contracts change every three or four years. The royalties on music records used to be a penny a song. Now I have no idea what it is. Maybe an agent might be able to help you. Good luck. Sam."

Sharon Bach, widow of Spanky and Our Gang band member Oz Bach, was very forthcoming in our January, 2009 email exchanges. We have since become good Facebook friends. Sharon told me that Spanky and Our Gang didn't receive much of anything in the way of financial compensation, in spite of huge hits like *Lazy Day, Sunday Will Never Be the Same*, and *I'd Like to Get to Know You*. I'm not sure if that would have made George "Spanky" McFarland feel better. On January 20, 2009, she wrote, "I am Sharon Bach, widow of Oz Bach, founding member, arranger and bass player for Spanky and Our Gang. There is much to the story of this band. I have it from Oz's perspective. I will call Spanky and tell her about your project. Oz sadly passed away in 1998....As for royalties, when I met Oz he said he did not get royalties but that there was money in a trust, a special recording organization (can't remember the name) which he had set up for his children from a previous marriage. That seemed like a nice thing he had done for them. When he looked into it years later, sadly there was very little money in it. When Oz left the group, his Aunt Dorothy demanded to be repaid for the money she had invested in Spanky and Our Gang....Oz had told me that in the recording industry, all the money was in publishing. Spanky and Our Gang performed other people's stuff....When the complete Mercury recordings collection was released by Universal, a friend of Spanky's, Leslie, "helped" with the contract. What they came up with was a microfilm copy of an amendment to the original contract but not the contract itself. It was apparently enough for Universal to grant some sort of royalties to Spanky. I do not know the details. I did not inquire as to any royalties that might be due Oz (he did perform after all). To me, if anyone got anything I would be happy for them since they had gotten so little previously....Oh yes I could get a lawyer and try to show that if Oz had been getting residuals or mechanicals over the years that he might still be alive today. But what would that accomplish? It won't bring him back. Oz's and my daughter, Belinda, died last year. She was uninsurable due to 'preexisting conditions.' I mortgaged my house to try to provide her with as much as I could but lost her anyway. No amount of money will ever bring her back. I do sometimes wonder what life might have been like had Oz been compensated over the years for the marvelous work he did with Spanky and Our Gang...."

Perhaps the most cantankerous of all the old entertainers I contacted was John Claude Gummoe, lead singer and songwriter for The Cascades, who hit it big with 1962's *Rhythm of the Rain*. In a January 14, 2009 email, Gummoe advised me, "'Rhythm of the Rain' as you know is one of the most popular songs in the world. BMI, at the close of the last century named it the 9th most performed song of the last century. That being said, I should say, yes, your questions are intrusive and frankly, none of your business. Suffice it to say that through the years, my song has attained a 'life of it's own' and it's been very good to me. It's been covered by 100's of artists, most of them versions that I've never seen a penny from. At least three versions in Mandarin Chinese. I've heard it in French, Dutch, Tagalog, and many, many more. I once heard a waitress in Sedona, Arizona sing it to me in Porteugese. Probably, spelled that wrong, but you get the picture. Strangely enough, it's been used in very few motion pictures. Most commercials it's been used in have been foreign. So that's what you get from me. Good Luck..............John Claude Gummoe." A few years later, Gummoe appeared to have forgotten my intrusive questions, and sent me an invitation to connect on Linkedin. We are also friends on Facebook.

When I resumed work on this book in 2016, I tried to contact more of these entertainers. Jerry Mathers, forever ensconced in every Baby Boomer's memory as Theodore "Beaver" Cleaver, replied to me personally, but politely stated, "Thank you for your interest regarding the Leave it to Beaver residual payments. However, I don't wish to participate with this project." Melanie Chartoff, who was a cast member of the late night show *Fridays* and went on to provide the voice of Didi Pickles in the popular 1990s Nicktoon *The Rugrats,* exchanged a few interesting emails with me in May 2017. Melanie wrote, "I've lots of dark experiences, some black comic, some just black, and a few in the red where I was stiffed out of payment. I may not have known about many underpayments--SAG can't always be counted on to track things that are sold as electronic downloads in other countries." An assistant to Ronnie Spector replied to my email on May 30, 2017 with: "Thanks for your interest in Ronnie Spector. After speaking with Ronnie about your request, I can tell you she will certainly purchase a copy of your book when it comes out--but as someone who lived through the darker side of show business, it's nothing she wants to speak about anymore." I had read Ronnie's book *Be My Baby: How I Survived Mascara, Miniskirts, and Madness* years earlier, and couldn't really blame her. She'd been held a veritable prisoner in her home by her husband, legendary music producer and later convicted murderer Phil Spector. Jerry Burgan, one of the co-founders of the folk-rock group The We Five, who recorded the huge 1965 hit *You Were on my Mind,* generally referred me to his own book for specific details, but declared, "...I suspect you could get broad spectrum of responses from the surviving members ranging from 'we were screwed,' to 'I was educated, positioned for success, and when we delivered, compensated for the experience.' I wrote a book on the subject called 'Wounds to Bind - A Memoir of the Folk Rock Revolution' It's been well reviewed and gives my view on what happened. Fingers are pointed where appropriate and I did not get rich--but it was a very brief window and I still get royalties."

Carl Giammerese of the Buckinghams, who scored with a slew of hits in the 1960s like *Kind of a Drag* and *Mercy, Mercy, Mercy*, responded to me thusly; "The Buckinghams like so many from our genre didn't get what they deserved. We have had a relationship with Sony for many years and receive our royalties twice yearly." Frank Allen, who joined the long-running, successful band The Searchers in 1964, sent me a lengthy email reply on March 29, 2018. It read, "As with almost everyone from our era, with the exception of Dave Clark who was incredibly astute in making his own masters and leasing them for much higher rewards, not to mention retaining all publishing rights, we were on the usual low royalty rates. Nobody knew any better. It was a learning curve. The rate in the original PYE Records contract was for two per cent on eighty five percent of sales. I believe the remaining fifteen percent were for promotion copies and breakages...The royalty rate outside the UK was halved due to distribution arrangements necessary with foreign companies. The contract included four yearly options on the company's side. For the second year there was an increase of a half a percent. Should all the options be taken up the final rate would reach four per cent on domestic sales. In the light of the greater rates these days (twenty per cent plus is very normal and can be significantly higher for the biggest artistes) it was on reflection a derisive amount... I was with Cliff Bennett and The Rebel Rousers for the three years prior to joining The Searchers in 1964. During that time we made six singles none of which achieved any chart position but EMI Parlophone kept faith until the success came (as it happens immediately after I departed the group). There are people I know who are still very bitter about the poor remuneration for their efforts and maybe they have a legitimate grouse but that's the way things were then. For me I looked on it as the price of an education. It does you no good to hold on to bitterness."

Jonathan King, who wrote and sang the huge 1969 song, *Everyone's Gone to the Moon*, sounded feisty in a March 20, 2018 email, "I was on two percent as singer which was the acceptable royalty at the time; and bloody grateful too. My producers were Joe Roncoroni and Ken Jones - I was sent to them by the mighty Tony Hall (still with us, just) who chose them from my list of admired producers (they produced the Zombies) because they were straight, decent and honest and would not "rip me off". The moment it was a hit they formed a 50/50 publishing partnership with me (JonJo Music) which is still my publisher today. Yes it was tiny (I sold 5 million) but I made loads more as writer and composer. Enough to buy my little house for £18,650 which I still own today. I then became a producer (Hedgehoppers Anonymous, Genesis) and paid my artistes a tiny royalty (all now raised to 50% after digital began). I never resented it. They invested the thousands needed to hire orchestras, studio etc. All I did was sing. And Ken's arrangement, slowing it down and adding soaring strings, was a major reason for its success. Like the silly drama now (pay women more) - why not moan because people with brown eyes get more than blue? Stupid. Do your job. Accept the current going rate. And be bloody grateful."

I was thrilled to speak to one of my musical favorites, Graham Parker, in a lengthy Skype conversation on April 12, 2018. Parker joked about someone tweeting him regarding his being worth $5 million, according to Celebrity Net Worth, "I wish!" He told me that he'd "be happy with a million. That would be all I need." I checked online after speaking with him, and sure enough, Parker is listed as having $5 million by Celebrity Net Worth. Parker did better than a lot of his contemporaries, because he wrote all his own material. He was also fortunate in that he had a private pension set up, and his taxes were paid. Artists like Willie Nelson found out the hard way how a neglected tax bill can add up to millions with penalties accrued. Parker was a huge celebrity to me personally, but like many artists whose songs earned heavy rotation on progressive radio stations in the 1970s and 1980s, he didn't have any hit singles. As he told me, his highest selling album reached #11 on the UK charts. In those days, the record companies would sometimes take chances, and invest money, in talented artists like Parker if their executives admired them. "I always had fans in the record companies, who thought I'd make it big," he stated. In spite of never quite cracking the top ten in sales, Parker said that artists like him still actually made more money than some performers today with bigger hit records. While Parker's contracts were pretty generous, they had an "in perpetuity" clause, which he explained meant that the artist had to pay many of the personal expenses associated with his act (tour bus, crew, band members, etc.). Parker also reiterated what I'd already learned, that "after our day in the sun," as he put it, some of the members of his band The Rumour had to "get day jobs." While Graham Parker still loves to play and record, his tours, in his late sixties, are to help him make "a modest living." In fact, when he plays with a band like The Rumour, he told me he is lucky to break even. The solo tours may earn him a small profit. When Parker toured the Washington, D.C. area later in 2018 and then in 2019, he left me tickets, and I was delighted to meet and speak with him personally.

Donna Loren was the "Dr. Pepper" girl in a series of popular 1960s commercials, a featured singer on the television series *Shindig*, and appeared in many other shows and movies, including the "Beach Blanket Bikini" series of films. Loren sent me the following private message response on Facebook on May 15, 2018: "Hi Donald, My career was kind of an anomaly in that I signed a 7 year contract w/ Dr Pepper as their spokesperson. Whatever else I did was a bonus. It's true that because I didn't publish and write all the songs I recorded, royalties were insignificant. Thanx." Danny O'Keefe, an underrated singer-songwriter who had a Top Ten hit in 1972 with *Good Time Charlie's Got the Blues,* replied to me on June 13, 2018. "Don- I'm not sure that I can offer anything of value. I haven't been with a major record label since 1980 and the business has changed considerably since then," O'Keefe stated. "I still record and release my own music but it's largely for my own benefit as a writer. I think the biggest concern is the way the streaming entities like Spotify, Pandora, Google Music, etc. have access to recordings but the artists, publishers and writers have very little say in the deals. Looking at the structures of the deals that allow the companies who own the recording masters to allow the streaming companies access for what is an insignificant royalty rate should probably be a key focus of your book. It has made the greatest change in the music business over more than twenty years starting with Napster. The accounting in the record business, and other arts, has always been 'creative' and it's probably no different than many businesses. Having a good lawyer and accountant is always the key to maintaining fairness. I wish you the best of luck with your project."

Arch Hall, Jr., who starred in a handful of B-movie cult classics like *Eegah* (which later experienced a resurgence of interest when it was riffed on *Mystery Science Theater 3000*) in the early 1960s, sent me a long email response on April 23, 2018. "I was legally permitted to work in my first film THE CHOPPERS (a Union film in 1959) not being affiliated with the Screen Actors Guild or SAG because of provisions of the Taft-Hartley Act of 1947," Hall wrote. "Subsequent films working for my father's production company (Fairway International Films) were all non Union productions. Therefore, I had no expectations of ever seeing any residuals. My years of working in films, while great fun it also taught me many unpleasant things about the business which led me to recognize that it really did not appeal to me enough to make it my life's work. This probably best self describes my participation in the "family business" more as an apprentice or intern actor than a professional career actor and thus explains best why I made the decision to pursue other endeavors. Although all the Fairway films were sold and continue to live on in syndication, I understand the new legal owner failed to renew their legal copyright, thus allowing the entire Fairway catalog to fall permanently into public domain."

Peter Staples, a member of the Troggs, whose 1960s hits included *Wild Thing* and *Love is All Around*, emailed me on June 12, 2018. He wrote, "Thank you for your e mail. Your new project sounds very interesting and I don't know if you've read my recently published book 'Wild Thing – A Rocky Road' in which I have outlined some of the difficulties we had with contracts and 'lost' money; these details I'd be happy to expand on if you needed further information." He never replied to my follow up emails. I exchanged several emails and spoke on the phone with Tracy, the daughter of the late Larry Ramos, former lead singer of the Association. She was extremely helpful, and wrote in a June 11, 2018 email: "My Dad was Larry Ramos (of The Association and New Christy Minstrels.) I happen to know royalties were never given to NCM members, they were salary only. I bet interviewing some of the old members of that group would be very enlightening. (Everyone except Randy Sparks who I believe received all the royalties for the group.) I can reach out to the members I know (Barry McGuire & Art Podell) to see if there is any interest from them." I never heard back from any members of either the New Christy Minstrels or the Association.

I exchanged a series of emails with George Tomsco, lead guitarist for the Fireballs, who had a number one hit in 1963 with *Sugar Shack*. On June 23, 2018, Tomsco replied to my initial email, saying, "Interesting subject you have going here. Yes, I've got some 'good' stories, and some 'bad' stories on *compensation*. I've forwarded your email to some other may be 'interested' parties - that could also contribute to your book." I never heard from any of these "interested parties," and we didn't communicate again until almost a year later. After he asked about being compensated for an interview (something I hadn't done with anyone), Tomsco emailed me on April 3, 2019, and noted dramatically, "Just thinking about the last email I sent you, …the information I have experienced – if some of those people are still living and found out I'm *'talking'* it *could be* a life threatening situation to me. Know what I mean?" I exchanged emails with Guy Catalano, aka Guy Williams, Jr., regarding the family's battle to obtain back royalties for his father's work on *Zorro* and *Lost in Space*. On June 26, 2018, Catalano wrote, "I would be interested in discussing further, however right now I am in the middle of moving, and will be out of the country the month of July. Perhaps you might remind me sometime mid-August at this email address." Catalano never replied to my subsequent emails. I heard back from a representative for La La Brooks, the second lead singer of the girl group the Crystals, who sang on their memorable 1963 hits *Then He Kissed Me* and *Da Doo Ron Ron*. On June 12, 2018, he wrote, "I'll talk to La La about this. I suspect she'll do it and will have a lot to say about it. You're right - the record companies and producers got all the money." He never responded to my follow up emails.

I am friends on Facebook with Linda Jones Clough, daughter of legendary Warner Brothers cartoon director Chuck Jones. On October 30, 2018 we had an interesting exchange via personal message on Facebook. "My father was work for hire his whole career. He felt fortunate to be paid for what he loved doing," Linda told me. "He did not get paid residuals for the compilations. He did get residuals from the Seuss films and the Cricket and Kipling specials, which his company owns. No, I did not feel rich or privileged growing up. We were comfortable and had a good, solid life style. My understanding is that Mel Blanc got (and his family still gets) residuals from the cartoons he voiced, but I don't know that as a fact." Correspondingly, Jones reportedly died with a respectable net worth of $6 million, but Blanc did much better, with a $25 million fortune.

Billy Gray, who starred as Bud Anderson on the iconic Fifties sitcom *Father Knows Best,* was one of the greatest child actors who ever lived, in my estimation. I was honored to have a nice phone conversation with him on May 22, 2018. I knew how Gray felt about his role from the following quote I'd read from him, "I think we were all well motivated, but what we did was run a hoax. *Father Knows Best* purported to be a reasonable facsimile of life. And the bad thing is that the model is so deceitful. ... If I could say anything to make up for all the years I lent myself to that kind of bullshit, it would be: *You know best."* Indeed, that seems to have become his personal signature, as Gray ended his email reply to me with "You know best." He noted how the original radio show had a question mark after *Father Knows Best,* which represented Robert Young's perspective; he never meant it to be a declarative statement. Gray's political radicalism was evident in his remark that sponsor Kent Cigarettes, "those murderers," had demanded that the question mark be removed. Gray noted, as so many had, that they had all been "ripped off, I believe is the term." They were paid for six reruns, on a sliding downward scale, so that all six payments added up to about the minimum weekly salary in the industry at the time, which he thought was $250. Robert Young, as co-producer and owner of the show, obviously fared very well in comparison to the others. Like so many other television actors, after the show ended, Gray was typecast as the quintessential Fifties teenager Bud Anderson, and was initially low-balled for the 1977 TV movie *The Father Knows Best Reunion.* However, he called them on their threat to "go in another direction," and "they wound up paying me decently." I asked him about the story I'd heard that he at one time was living in a cave. He laughed and explained that there was a cave adjacent to his home, which was where that particular rumor probably started. Billy Gray is just as he appears in interviews: outspoken, but affable and a very down to earth person.

Shortly after our first conversation, Billy Gray emailed me, "When you have time - I'll tell you how FKB fucked me out of about $80,000." Naturally intrigued by this, I spoke again to Gray on May 30, 2018. Gray revealed that he'd been paid a decent $300 weekly during the filming of the 1951 sci-fi classic *The Day the Earth Stood Still.* "As you went along in the business, your salary went up," he told me. He was being paid a solid $500 each week for *Father Knows Best,* but explained that at a certain point in the show, they talked him into filming two episodes each week, but kept paying him the same, effectively cutting his salary in half. "They realized this resulted in a loss of quality," Gray stated, so they returned to shooting once weekly. The only problem was they kept him at his new rate of $250 per show. Gray calculated that losing half his salary for the remainder of the seven years of the program added up to about $80,000. Apparently, the other cast members, including his two on screen siblings, had different, better arrangements, so they weren't shortchanged in the same way financially. Lauren Chapin, who played his little sister Kathy "Kitten" on the show, experienced a tumultuous adulthood after being sexually assaulted by her own father and his friend as a child, which led to drug addiction, a suicide attempt, a stay in a mental institution and jail time for check forgery. Oddly, despite having her acting career grind to a halt following the end of *Father Knows Best,* which forced Chapin to take such jobs as dog groomer, insurance claims examiner, carhop and cocktail waitress, she is said to be worth a pretty impressive $6 million. Gray, meanwhile, is reported to have a $1.5 million net worth.

I spoke with Kathy Garver, who starred as Cissy on the 1960s television show *Family Affair,* on May 24, 2018. Kathy did not feel "ripped off" during her five-year run of the series, and explained that while the children were paid the industry minimum, it was increased each year and was totally negotiable. Adult stars Brian Keith and Sebastian Cabot were given a piece of the show, and obviously fared better financially. Kathy was still perturbed, however, over Melissa Gilbert's actions as President of the Screen Actors Guild; during her tenure, a new contract regarding residuals was signed, which excluded those whose shows began prior to 1974. "Guess what year *Little House on the Prairie* started?" Kathy exclaimed. "1974!" Kathy also spoke of how co-star Johnnie Whitaker, who came from a devout Mormon family, had almost nothing left of his childhood earnings when he became an adult. Kathy Garver was just as classy, polite and friendly as I expected her to be.

On June 7, 2018, I had a pleasant phone conversation with Bobby Rydell, who enjoyed huge hits like *Wild One* and *Do the Cha-Cha-Cha* in the early '60s, and appeared in films like 1963's *Bye Bye Birdie*. Rydell was apparently one of the more fortunate entertainers of his era; he told me that his royalty rate per record was five cents, significantly higher than what most of his peers were paid. He spoke of still getting hefty royalty checks, and was grateful to the Washington, D.C. based Sound Exchange, who filed a lawsuit with Pandora and iTunes and other newer outlets, regarding paying artists for their hits prior to 1971. In fact, Rydell told me his wife had actually called that company the previous year to verify that the check he had received was really for $50,000. As Rydell put it, "I lead a comfortable life." While he still gets paid well for his old hit songs, Rydell's manager made the mistake of taking a lump salary (he recalled it was either $20,000 or $25,000) for *Bye Bye Birdie*, instead of asking for a percentage of the very robust profits from the film. As a result, he gets tiny royalty checks from Columbia (usually $1 and change, the largest he remembered was $3) for rebroadcasts. This brought to mind how horror icon Vincent Price accepted a $20,000 fee in lieu of a percentage of album sales, for Michael Jackson's famous *Thriller* video. The album, of course, went on to become the biggest seller of all time, leading a bitter Price to later remark, in the midst of all the allegations of sexual improprieties with children against Jackson: "All I can say is that Michael Jackson fucked me - and I didn't get paid for it." Rydell has teamed with fellow teen idols Frankie Avalon and Fabian since 1985 in regular tours as "The Golden Boys." He seemed justifiably proud that the shows continue to be very popular.

On June 21, 2018, I had a delightful conversation with Don Wilson, guitarist and last surviving member of the original Ventures. The band was noted for their mostly instrumental tunes, which included the 1960 smash hit *Walk, Don't Run*, and the theme song for the long-running television series *Hawaii Five O*. Wilson sounded spry and energetic at eighty-five, and was full of mostly happy recollections.

He was understandably proud of legendary guitarists like Jimmy Page, George Harrison, and Eric Clapton having admitted to being influenced by his band. He recalled how Billy Joel told him, prior to the band's introduction into the Rock and Roll Hall of Fame, how *Walk, Don't Run* had been one of the first songs he'd learned on the piano. The good-natured Wilson echoed the comments of so many others, however, when he declared that the music industry "cheats you any way they can." It was, and still is acknowledged, for instance, that *Walk, Don't Run* sold over a million copies, but Wilson said the record company told the members of the Ventures that there were only 650,000 sales. They were on a royalty rate that paid them each one percent. The Ventures hired an outside auditor at one point, and it was determined that they had been shortchanged some $600,000 in royalties. The record company countered with an offer to pay them $6,000, and never even paid that. Much as John Claude Gummoe and the Cascades struck it big in the Philippines, the Ventures sold forty-five million records in Japan, and Wilson said he was still getting royalties from there. Wilson's biggest payday came from the inclusion of their song *Surf Rider* in the soundtrack of the 1994 film *Pulp Fiction*. I found Wilson to be unfailingly open and cordial.

On June 25, 2018, I had an interesting phone conversation with Joyce Moore, wife of Sam Moore from the soul duo Sam and Dave. I was aware of the fact that Sam Moore had sued The Weinstein Co. (headed by Harvey Weinstein) over the 2008 film *Soul Men*. Moore's lawsuit was dismissed, and he lost an appeal in 2013. In 1994, Sam Moore and the estate of Dave Prater (Dave unfortunately died in a 1988 car crash), joined with other big acts like the Coasters, the Chambers Brothers, and the Young Rascals, in suing a slew of record companies, producers and distributors, over an alleged shortage of close to $750 million in pension funds and $500 million in health benefits. My discussion with Joyce was rather rushed; she spoke fast and was dealing with a physical injury that had temporarily confined her to a wheelchair. She told me that the monthly amount the fund wanted to pay Sam was a mere $63.67. I wondered about the 1978 hit film *The Blues Brothers*, starring John Belushi and Dan Aykroyd. The comic duo had become recording artists in their own right while still working on *Saturday Night Live*, with one of their seminal numbers being Sam and Dave's old hit *Soul Man*. While many older R & B musicians appeared in *The Blues Brothers* movie, Sam and Dave didn't. "The manager screwed it up," Joyce said. Sam and Dave received nothing from the film. Joyce held former record company executive Henry Stone especially responsible for screwing over her husband financially. As his August 10, 2014 obituary in the *Miami New Times* described it, Stone was "an acute businessman who always made sure that contracts and publishing agreements were written in his favor."

I was intrigued by the fact that Frank Cady, who played Sam Drucker on three different rural comedies in the 1960s: *Petticoat Junction*, *Green Acres*, and *The Beverly Hillbillies*, was initially reported to have been laid to rest in Meridian United Church in Wilsonville, Oregon. Online references, however, now state he was cremated and his ashes buried at California's Los Osos Valley Memorial Park, in the same plot with his wife. I spoke to Frank Cady's daughter Catherine Turk on July 19, 2018, to see if she could clarify things. She told me she hadn't heard anything about her father being buried in Oregon, and verified that his ashes lay in Los Osos Valley Memorial Park. She said that she had managed her father's money during the later part of his life, and while he continued to get residuals, "they never amounted to more than a couple hundred dollars a year." I was fascinated when Turk told me she hadn't really watched her father's work as an adult, although "of course we all watched them as kids." In fact, she declared that she hadn't had a television set for many years. She did, however, proudly note that her father was the only actor to ever play the same character in three different television series. While she acknowledged that their family had lived a good life, we both laughed when I commented that she obviously hadn't inherited "the great Cady fortune."

On July 19, 2018, I spoke with Bob Cowsill. I was familiar with the sad story of the Cowsills, the large family musical act that the television show *The Partridge Family* was based on. Bob told me how after their few years of fleeting fame, he discovered he had some $21,000 in tax debt to show for it. I had read an earlier interview with Bob on the Classic Bands website where he stated, "I was living in Los Angeles in 1969 with the number one song in the country, 'Hair' and by 1970, I had a job sweeping a garage." Bob didn't speak much about his father, who mismanaged the group, but went into some detail about the Cowsills' eight-year long legal battle with Universal Music Group. Bob had signed the band's original 1967contract without reading the fine print, like so many of his peers in the business had. While he'd sworn to being twenty-one in so doing, he was actually only seventeen. The suit was finally settled, to everyone's satisfaction, with a lump sum of $100,000 to each member of the band as what was surely only partial compensation for past royalties. The group negotiated a buyout and a new royalty rate that, in Bob's words, was one that "anyone can dream about." Bob shared a telling anecdote that I found especially moving, describing his daughter hearing their huge hit *The Rain, the Park, and Other Things* playing as she sat in the theater watching the 1994 film *Dumb and Dumber* (for which, of course, the Cowsills received no remuneration). I could only wonder how many children of other entertainers had been through the same experience. Bob Cowsill remains upbeat, and noted that their lawsuit proved that things "can be resolved successfully with no hard feelings." Still touring regularly, Bob left our conversation to get ready for another show.

I've had the pleasure of making connections with many entertainers from my youth on Facebook. One of the most rewarding has been Susan Olsen, who played Cindy on *The Brady Bunch*. Susan and I clicked personally and politically, and I was honored to appear as a guest several times on her LA Talk Radio show. I told Susan about this book, and she was the first person to read a working copy of it. We talked some about her career on July 28, 2018. She remarked on how gratifying it was to meet people who considered her a part of their childhood, but also felt that there is a "double edge sword" element to the attention. It probably is frustrating to be known and lauded for what you did as a very young child, as if you hadn't achieved anything else noteworthy in the ensuing decades. Susan is still in contact with the other child actors from the show, and is especially close to Mike Lookinland, who portrayed Bobby Brady. In fact they make public appearances together. In 2019, all the Brady children reunited for Home and Garden TV's series *A Very Brady Renovation.*

Another friend I've made through Facebook is Lorin Hart, the granddaughter of Golden Age screen icon John Gilbert. Lorin emailed me on October 18, 2018. "Well, my beautiful mom was so scarred by her experience in Hollywood as the child of stars that she never mentioned it…we were raised in a near blanket of silence regarding who John Gilbert was," Lorin explained. "And to be fair, my mother sort of assumed the rumors about her dad were true, that he was a failure, had a bad voice, drank himself to death… and so, although we heard stories from my grandmother, Leatrice Joy, that I enjoyed and that she took on the road all over New England in shows to ladies clubs and the like, regaling them with tales of 'Hollywood's Golden Era', we really didn't give John Gilbert much attention." Lorin was understandably proud of her mother Leatrice Gilbert Fountain's 1985 book *Dark Star: The Untold Story of the Meteoric Rise and Fall of Legendary Silent Screen Star John Gilbert*, and generously offered to mail me a copy. Lorin noted that her mother "single handedly restored her father to his well deserved place in the minds of serious film buffs at least. Here in Los Angeles people who read her book treat me like 'Hollywood Royalty' … and I appreciate it in his honor …I remain proud of him, even though I know he drank and womanized …

with his looks and charm and calling, he could hardly have been otherwise."

I had actually touched base with Leatrice Gilbert Fountain first. She replied to my introductory message on Facebook on January 29, 2010, writing, "I quite agree, Donald. It probably helped end his career, but It must have been a great satisfaction to find his hated boss groveling on a bathroom floor. It's nice to see him restored to his proper place as a silent mega star. Thanks for you message, Leatrice." She was referring to my mentioning Gilbert punching Louis B. Mayer. We exchanged a few more Facebook messages. On August 31, 2010, she stated, "Hello Donald. I was happy to read your message. Isn't it amazing that seventy odd years after he died, firmly convinced that he had been a complete failure, my father's name is hotter than ever, and for all the right reasons. I liked 'Phantom' too. I had never seen it before but the good reviews that came out at the time hinted that it was a decent picture. Most of the little talkies they pushed him into, trying to wear out his contact with trash, were just that, with a few good Gilbert moments shining through. He had a sharp, steep decline and he was physically not up to it. Well, if vindication is a reward, he has it in full. Thanks for writing, Leatrice." Leatrice died in 2015 at the age of ninety.

Lorin recalled how her mother was astonished at "the way the press treated her after her parents were no longer 'Top Stars' crushed her and spurred her to flee Hollywood for New York." I had a pleasant phone conversation with Lorin Hart later in the evening on October 18, 2018. She told me that Gilbert had done extremely well financially, making some $10,000 weekly, and had left "a huge estate." Unfortunately, none of that estate went to her mother, even though Gilbert's will expressly left the bulk of it to his daughter. Apparently, his fourth wife, actress Virginia Bruce, destroyed it and prevented her mother from getting anything. As Lorin had explained in her email, Leatrice's "principles led her to refuse to challenge Virginia Bruce's destruction of Gilbert's final will leaving a lot to my mother. I can't complain as I would not be here had it gone differently, of course, but I find it interesting that both my mom and I suffered financially at the hands of 'wicked stepmothers.'" Lorin Hart is an accomplished musician, well known in the folk music community, but as she noted, has never been able to earn enough money to make it a full time occupation.

I had a long, fascinating phone conversation with Ernest Henry Raft, grand-nephew of Golden Age actor George Raft on December 18, 2018. I came across him on Facebook while reading a thread about the JFK assassination, a subject which has long interested him as well. Raft spoke of how his illustrious ancestor had been one of Bugsy Siegel's first investors in the fledgling Las Vegas, and went on to co-own casinos and clubs in both pre-Castro Cuba and the United Kingdom. Raft and other capitalists were thrown out of Cuba after Castro took power, and the Raft family was forbidden by Scotland Yard to reenter the United Kingdom. Raft described his grand-uncle as definitely having connections to the mob, which was understandable in that many gangsters, like Bugsy Siegel himself, grew up in the same neighborhood. Touching upon one of my favorite areas of research, it was illuminating to learn that George Raft was still shaken by the JFK assassination years later, and never believed Lee Harvey Oswald was responsible. One colorful story related by Ernest Raft concerned a drunken Anthony Quinn nearly breaking his five-year-old arm, at a birthday party for his grand-uncle. Evidently, young Raft wasn't twirling his spaghetti skillfully enough for Quinn. Ernest Raft called Quinn "a piece of crap" and a "rotten bastard." He also told me that his grand-uncle thought Gary Cooper was a "prick" after he sang before the House Un-American Activities Committee. Regarding any Raft fortune, Ernest told me all that he received from his grand-uncle "fit in a couple of suitcases." Ernest Raft was kind enough to send me George Raft's FBI file, which ran to 111 pages. Other than including news articles like the one that reported Raft had helped get his "old pal" Al Capone out of jail, and incorrectly describing the actor as Italian (he was actually Jewish), the file is littered with blacked out redactions, which is all too typical with publicly released government documents. Raft died without a will, and left behind an estate of just $10,000 and some furniture. He'd been subsisting on $800 monthly from Social Security and his pension. Raft's remaining personal effects were sold for a paltry $800 in 1981.[148]

Marta Kristen-Kane, who played Judy Robinson on the classic 1960s television series *Lost in Space,* sent me a lengthy Facebook message on April 10, 2019. "Yes, it is not fair that corporations are making money from our work, but we are not." Making the same point Kathy Garver had, Marta wrote, "I believe it wasn't until the early 70s that residuals for actors became what is known as 'in perpetuity.' That new rule should have been retroactive to cover actors in shows prior to the SAG change. Unfortunately, our union was not truly actor-centered prior to the 70s, otherwise the new rule would have been on the books years before. There are advertisers who pay various cable channels showing the classic shows. Some of that revenue should go to the artists. It is only fair. Many of these actors are scratching to make a living, while the studios are raking in the money. This is a corporate world, and unless you also have the power and the funding to make a change, they have you in their greedy grasp. My philosophy professor father would call this 'moneyed malice.' Unfortunately, it seems we see more and more of this now than ever before. It would be a dream to start a class action lawsuit about this unfair practice, but it has been tried, and little came of it. I guess the companies figure that sooner or later we will all die off! Thanks for your interest in this matter. You are a shining knight!"

On August 1, 2019, I had a long conversation with Paul Rapp, now a successful attorney but in the early '80s better known as Lee Harvey Blotto, drummer for Blotto, one of my favorite bands at the time. Rapp spoke about being "fucking broke" after the band split up in 1984. Blotto, despite getting strong airplay on alternative rock stations like WHFS, in my own Washington, D.C. area, never got a major label to sign them. One prominent executive rejected them by saying they were "going in another direction" and then followed that up by informing them that "Blotto is my kid's favorite band." They were one of those bands that came agonizingly close to the big time, once touring as the opening act for Blue Oyster Cult. I was curious about the origin of the band's name, having always assumed it might have been a tip of the hat to the old Laurel & Hardy short *Blotto*. Rapp told me that the name derived instead from the name of author Horne Smith's dog. Smith wrote many books, the most famous being *Topper,* which was made into a major motion picture in 1937 starring Cary Grant. Evidently, Broadway Blotto, the group's primary songwriter and nominal leader, was a big fan of Smith's work. An interesting anecdote was the fact that Rapp became a licensed lifeguard at the age of sixty, which was incredibly ironic considering that the band's most popular song was *I Wanna Be a Lifeguard.* The video was popular enough to be played by MTV during its first day on the air in 1981. Their entertaining comedic style lent itself naturally to music videos.

On August 14, 2019, I spoke with Mike Farrell, best remembered for his role as B.J. Hunnicutt in the long running television series M*A*S*H. Farrell confessed in an August 7, 2019 email response that, "I'm not aware of any difficulties in payments, so I'm not sure I can be helpful." During our relatively brief conversation, he reiterated that he had nothing to offer in terms of being shortchanged by the business. He did mention that his wife, actress and singer Shelley Fabares, "didn't make a dime" initially from her huge hit single *Johnny Angel.* Fortunately, a lawyer later managed to arrange royalty payments from the song, which she is still receiving. He also noted that Fabares, like almost all young actors in the early years of television, didn't make much money from her role on the hit series *The Donna Reed Show.* Farrell pointed out that it was Tony Owen, producer of the show and husband of star Donna Reed, who got rich from Fabares' hit song. Celebrity Net Worth claims Shelley Fabares is worth a modest $1.5 million, while Farrell has $10 million.

On October 1, 2019, I spoke with Karolyn Grimes, beloved to classic film lovers as little Zuzu in Frank Capra's iconic 1946 movie *It's a Wonderful Life*. Karolyn was bubbly, upbeat, with a much younger voice than her 79 years, and a lovely, infectious laugh. I knew from reading about her that she'd experienced more than her share of tragedies, including losing both of her parents by the age of fifteen. Sent to Missouri, she lived in what she termed a "bad home," and she was effectively shut off from any remaining contacts in Hollywood. Karolyn left the film industry behind her, and established a career as a medical technologist, which she described to me as especially rewarding. She told me how she'd made $3000 less than the minimum qualification for a pension from her film work. She married and raised children, and was hired, along with the other child actors in the film, by Target in 1993, as part of an advertising campaign featuring the grown up Bailey kids. She recounted how James Stewart had a secretary track her down as an adult, which resulted in her thereafter being close friends with him for the rest of his life. She marveled at what a moral, kind soul Stewart was, apparently very much like all the wonderful onscreen characters he portrayed. She didn't stay in contact with Donna Reed or any other adult actors from the film, and regretted not trying to communicate with director Frank Capra, although she became friends with his late son, his daughter, and especially his granddaughter Monica Capra Hodges. Even when describing a personal or professional loss, Karolyn laughed and said you "have to move forward." Now involved for three months every year with conventions that celebrate her Zuzu character, Karolyn called it a "blessing" to meet so many countless people who are brought to tears, as they recount how much the film meant in their lives.

I was thrilled to talk with Brad Server, the grandson of Curly Howard, who in the view of most (including me) *was* the Three Stooges, on November 14, 2019. He has an act that celebrates his grandfather's work, and goes by the professional name of Curly G. His voice sounds a lot like Curly's, and he does a nice impression of him. Brad intimated that the families of all the Stooges weren't terribly close. As he explained, his mother (Curly's daughter) was only four when her father died, and she never really knew him. He said they really didn't discuss the Stooges much, because she didn't want to have that overshadow the relationship with her second husband. I was particularly interested in a video on Brad's You Tube channel, which featured the attractive young great-granddaughter of Shemp Howard, Curly and Moe's real-life brother, who took Curly's place in the shorts when his (Curly's) health problems made it impossible for him to continue. Brad explained that he'd only met her in recent years. He also revealed that the family of Curly Joe DeRita, a mediocre talent who appeared in the early Sixties films, controls the rights to the images of the Three Stooges, and are the only ones who've grown rich off of their work.

There were many others that I emailed who never replied. However, a pattern emerged from nearly all the responses I did get, which demonstrated clearly that most of these performers felt they'd been ripped off or shortchanged in some way by the entertainment industry.

Chapter Three

Death In The Entertainment Industry

"But show business has always been like that - any kind of show business. If these people didn't live intense and rather disordered lives, if their emotions didn't ride them too hard— well, they wouldn't be able to catch those emotions in flight and imprint them on a few feet of celluloid or project them across the footlights."

- Raymond Chandler

ON THE EVE of his death, living all alone in a cheap hotel, D.W. Griffith lamented, "I thought I was a great genius." Seven years earlier, the already forgotten film legend was asked what he thought of young Orson Welles' *Citizen Kane*. Griffith replied that he "particularly loved the ideas he took from me."

The list of personal tragedies in show business is far, far longer than any recounting of rags to riches success stories. John Harron, best remembered as the romantic lead in 1932's horror classic

White Zombie, was the brother of silent screen star Robert Harron, whose own "accidental" shooting death in 1920 rocked the film colony. The younger Harron died quite suddenly in 1939 at only thirty-six, from spinal meningitis. Harron's precipitous career decline was as perplexing as his death; the promising young leading man was an uncredited player by 1936. He appeared in countless solely uncredited roles from that point on. Keystone Kops comedian Fred Mace died from a stroke at only thirty-nine-years-old, which was apparently brought on from stress over being unemployed. Actor Joe Donahue had some juicy roles during his mysteriously brief film career. His screen credits abruptly ended in 1932, when he was only thirty-three. Eleven years later, Donahue died in his home state of Massachusetts on his forty- forth birthday of undisclosed causes. One of Donahue's handful of parts was opposite the incredibly star-crossed Marilyn Miller, in 1930's *Sunny.* Miller was a Broadway legend, who made only three motion pictures before succumbing to, believe it or not, chronic sinus infections, at the tender age of thirty-seven. One of her husbands was the similarly ill-fated Jack Pickford, brother of America's Sweetheart, who died at thirty-six after multiple bouts of syphilis and years of excessive drinking. Another of Pickford's wives was gorgeous Olive Thomas, who died under suspicious circumstances at just twenty-one in a Paris hotel room. The official narrative went that she reached for sleeping pills and accidentally grabbed a convenient bottle of bichloride of mercury instead. Trouble seemed to follow Jack Pickford everywhere. He also became embroiled in a scandal involving wealthy young men bribing military officers in exchange for soft positions far from the fields of battle during the World War I era. He was saved from a dishonorable discharge thanks to the intercession of his famous sister. Mary Pickford's other sibling, Lottie, was a society partyer like her brother, and died of a supposed heart attack (attributed in large part to her excessive drinking) at just forty-three.[149]

The great Barrymore acting family experienced a little known strange, early death when John Drew died at only thirty-four on May 21, 1862 after tripping and hitting his head during a birthday party for his daughter. The Eskimo who was showcased in Robert Flaherty's classic 1922 documentary *Nanook of the North* died of starvation two years after it completed filming. The first actress to appear nude onscreen, Audrey Munson, led about as tragic a life as one can lead, while still living to be an astonishing 104-years-old. Munson's celebrated nudity occurred in 1915's *Inspiration*. She went on to be the model for several statues in New York, and was known by names like "Miss Manhattan" and "American Venus." The owner of a boarding house Munson was living in with her mother fell in love with her, which prompted him to murder his wife. The man, Dr. Walter Wilkins, would be convicted but hung himself before he could be executed. Her career over because of the scandal, and financially devastated, Munson attempted suicide herself and was subsequently institutionalized in the St. Lawrence Hospital for the Insane, where she spent the last sixty-five years of her life.[150] One of Barbara La Marr's many memorable quotes, "Life is too short to waste on sleep" (she reportedly only slept two hours a night), seemed to epitomize the mindset of the wild, Roaring Twenties. Not merely an actress, the talented La Marr had signed what was termed a "lucrative writing contract" with 20th Century-Fox in 1920. Married five times during her short, meteoric career, the creative La Marr often engineered her own publicity. This would culminate in her "adoption" of a baby boy in 1922, who eventually was shown to be her biological child. The boy would come to believe his father was actually the doomed Paul Bern (married to the equally star-crossed Jean Harlow), and would be adopted by La Marr's best friend, quirky actress Zasu Pitts. Her addiction to heroin eventually took its toll, and "The Girl Too Beautiful to Live," as the newspapers referred to her, died suddenly of tuberculosis at only twenty-nine.[151]

At just twenty-one, Susan Peters became one of the youngest Academy Award nominees in history, for Best Supporting Actress in her first substantial screen role, in 1942's *Random Harvest*. On New Year's Day, 1945, Peters was paralyzed from the waist down in a freak hunting accident. Her career effectively over, although MGM rather shockingly continued to pay her salary, Peters went into a downward spiral. Understandably deeply depressed, she eventually stopped eating and died in 1952, at only thirty-one years of age, of kidney failure and starvation. She left behind an estate of only $6,000.[152] Beautiful Gail Russell seemed to have a scintillating screen career ahead of her, starring in 1944's *The Uninvited* and other big-budget films. In the aforementioned film, the popular song *Stella by Starlight* was introduced, in homage to her character. However, she couldn't control her drinking, resulting in charges of public drunkenness and later driving under the influence. On August 26, 1961, Russell was found dead in her small Brentwood apartment, from not only the effects of years of alcohol abuse, but also malnutrition. She was only thirty six.[153] Maggie McNamara's inexplicable fall from the limelight could not be easily attributed to some tragic accident or alcoholism. Nominated for an Academy Award for her performance in 1953's *The Moon is Blue*, she unfathomably made only three more feature films, then finished her fledgling career with a handful of television guest starring roles. For the last fifteen years of her life, she worked temporary jobs as a typist to support herself. She was found dead at forty-eight of an overdose in her New York City apartment on February 18, 1978, with a suicide note left on the piano.[154] Elizabeth Hartman went from the youngest Best Actress nominee in Hollywood history, for 1965's *A Patch of Blue*, and other memorable roles in films like 1973's *Walking Tall*, to tumbling into such obscurity that she moved to Pittsburgh and was forced to work at a museum and get by with government and family assistance. Allegedly paranoid and suffering from agoraphobia, she jumped from her apartment window on June 10, 1987. "That initial success beat me down," Hartman told an interviewer. "I was not ready for that."[155] Statuesque Susanne Cramer guest-starred on 1960s television shows like *The Man From U.N.C.L.E.*, *Perry Mason*, *My Favorite Martian*, *Get Smart*, and many others. She led a tumultuous personal life, which included two unsuccessful suicide attempts. She went to Munich, Germany in late 1966 to visit her friend and fellow actress, Renate Ewert. On December 10, Cramer found Ewert's body; she'd evidently taken her own life a week or so before. Compounding the tragedy on an almost incomprehensible scale, Ewert's parents were so grief-stricken by their daughter's suicide they poisoned themselves shortly afterwards. Cramer died in a private Hollywood clinic, aged only thirty-two, on January 7, 1969. IMDb informs us that "there were reports of a medical malpractice." Wikipedia attributes her death to pneumonia.

Danny Cedrone, a member of Bill Haley and the Comets, died at only thirty-three when he fell down a flight of stairs and broke his neck. Innovative rocker Eddie Cochran died in a car crash at only twenty-one; involved in the same wreck were singer Gene Vincent (who suffered severe injuries and would go on to die himself at only thirty-six from a stomach ulcer - he was so destitute that the city of Los Angeles had to bury him, because his family couldn't afford it) and songwriter Sharon Sheeley (Cochran's fiancée whose most notable song was Ricky Nelson's 1958 #1 hit *Poor Little Fool*). Johnny Horton died in a car wreck as well at thirty-five. Patsy Cline was just one of numerous musical artists to die in a plane crash, at only thirty-years-old. Dinah Washington died at thirty-nine of an accidental overdose. Twenty-seven-year-old Rudy Lewis, of the Drifters, choked to death in his sleep. Sam Cooke was shot and killed by a motel manager at thirty-three. Folk music artist and novelist Richard Farina, who was married to Joan Baez's sister Mimi, died in a motorcycle accident at only twenty-nine. Few probably realize that Beatles manager Brian Epstein was just thirty-two-years-old when he died of a supposedly accidental overdose on August 27, 1967.

Otis Redding was another plane crash victim, at just twenty-six. His biggest hit, the 1968 #1 smash *Dock of the Bay,* became the first posthumously released song to top the charts in the United States. Frankie Lymon died from a heroin overdose at twenty-five, after being treated so unfairly by the music business. Malcolm Hale of Spanky and Our Gang died at twenty-seven from accidental carbon monoxide poisoning. Rock legends Jimi Hendrix and Janis Joplin died unnaturally within a few weeks of each other in 1970, both at age twenty-seven. Joplin is alleged to have reacted to Hendrix's death by exclaiming, "God damn it! He beat me to it." Brian Cole of The Association was one of countless musicians to die from a drug overdose, at age twenty-nine. Dan Hamilton, of the group Hamilton, Joe Frank & Reynolds, who scored with the huge 1971 hit *Don't Pull Your Love,* but left the group before its biggest song, 1975's *Fallin' In Love,* died at only forty-eight. According to Wikipedia, he became "seriously and mysteriously ill, and was eventually diagnosed as suffering from Cushing's Syndrome," a rare disease associated with prolonged exposure to cortisol. Hamilton had co-written *Fallin' In Love,* and in 2012 a jury awarded his widow over $560,000 in back compensation.[156]

There are some intriguing questions that still swirl around the plane crash that took the lives of iconic young rock pioneer Buddy Holly, along with singers Richie Valens and J.P. "the Big Bopper" Richardson. One rumor held that a shot or shots had been fired on the plane. These rumors were significant enough that Richardson's son Jay Perry had his father's body exhumed in 2007. No indications of foul play on the body were found. Bill Griggs, editor and publisher of *Rockin' 50s* magazine, interviewed Jerry Dwyer, the owner of the plane Holly leased, and asked him about his curious secrecy regarding the wreckage, which he had rather oddly kept. A more specific offshoot of the rumor regarding the gun shots claimed that there was a bullet hole in the back of the pilot's seat. In an interview with Gary James on the Classic Bands web site, Griggs stated, "No outsider to my knowledge, has ever seen that wreck-age. As for Jerry Dwyer, I did give him the opportunity to answer questions. He refused. I have no idea why his secrecy, if there is a secret at all." A gun owned by Holly was supposedly found in the same Iowa cornfield with the wreckage, with two rounds empty. In recent years, there were reports that the National Transportation Safety Board was looking into re-opening the investigation into the crash, but in April, 2015, it was announced there would be no new inquiry.[157] Both of Holly's surviving brothers had curiously opposed such efforts, with Travis Holley (Buddy had changed the spelling of his last name) stating, "I don't think they need to be looking into it again."[158] An urban legend holds that there is a "curse" associated with Buddy Holly, who also supposedly foretold his own death in dreams. Many people don't know that at the time of the crash, Buddy Holly had just broken up with his band the Crickets (it's said that John Lennon was inspired by his admiration for Holly to come up with the name the Beatles). Another oddity known to few is the fact that the singer hired to replace Holly for the remainder of the Winter Dance Party tour, Ronnie Smith, hung himself three years later, at a hospital where he'd been committed for his drug addiction. Also, young David Box was brought in by the Crickets as their new lead singer, and he too would die in a plane crash in 1964, like Holly at just twenty-two-years-old. Perhaps strangest of all, recording engineer and producer Joe Meek would warn Holly in 1958 about a message he'd received at a Tarot meeting, which read, "February third, Buddy Holly, dies." Holly paid no heed, and would in fact perish on that date the following year (1959). Meek produced a slew of hits in the early 1960s, including *Telstar* by the Tornadoes, but later became financially insolvent. On February 3, 1967, the eighth anniversary of the Holly plane crash, Meek shot and killed his landlady then turned the gun on himself.[159]

Buddy Holly was a unique personality. He proposed to Maria Elena Santiago, who was four years his senior, on their first date;

not exactly the kind of move expected from a budding young rock star. Peggy Sue Gerron, the girl that inspired Holly's huge smash *Peggy Sue,* would go on to marry Jerry Allison, the Crickets' drummer. However, in her 2008 memoirs, Gerron claimed that Holly was actually a Casanova who was about to leave his wife for her at the time of his death. Gerron, colorfully described as "a twice-divorced exhibitionist," called Holly's widow, who tried to legally stop publication of the book, a "bully."[160] Holly never lacked for self-confidence. He got in LaVern Baker's face when she derided the Crickets during an often contentious tour with several black artists. When Ed Sullivan told them they couldn't perform their latest hit, the raucous *Oh Boy,* Holly refused to go onstage until the proud variety host relented. Later, when the band was at its peak, Sullivan tried to book them at double the previous rate, but Holly turned him down.[161] Holly's producer Norman Petty, who also gave himself undeserved songwriting credits on many of his biggest hits, was suspected by the Crickets of "creative" bookkeeping. In fact, Holly was planning to confront Petty over what he thought was the theft of his earnings, and fire him as his manager and producer. In a lamentable footnote that happens all too often in show business, when Buddy Holly died, he had all of $73.34 in the bank.[162] A February 3, 2009 *Denver Post* article headlined, "Buddy Holly, a Victim of Rock 'n Roll Economics," provided details of Holly's recording contract, although it also stated that his royalty rate was actually "quite favorable for the day." The singer-songwriter ironically had to pay for the rental plane he died in out of his own pocket.

Rory Storm, vocalist for another Liverpool band that was popular during the same time as the Beatles, Rory Storm and the Hurricanes, died very strangely at only thirty-four. Both he and his mother's bodies were found at her Liverpool home. Police concluded that Storm had not taken enough sleeping pills to overdose, and exhibiting typical flawed logic held that his mother had killed herself upon finding his body (after he died from the effects of a chest infection). Storm had gone from being a wildly popular live act in Liverpool and Hamburg, Germany (albeit with little success as a recording artist) to working as a disc jockey at an ice rink. In another connection to the Beatles, Ringo Starr was the Hurricanes' drummer before going on to rock immortality.[163] The drummer Ringo replaced, Pete Best, attempted suicide and then worked for twenty years as a civil servant before starting his own band. Best is one of the saddest stories in entertainment history; literally weeks away from being part of a cultural phenomenon the likes of which the world had never seen before. The Beatles were not exactly apologetic about firing Best when they were on the cusp of superstardom. As Best put it in his autobiography; when he subsequently tried to make it with his new band, "The Beatles themselves certainly never held out a helping hand and only contributed to the destruction with their readily printed gossip that I had never really been a Beatle, that I didn't smile, that I was unsociable and definitely not a good mixer. There was not a single friendly word from any one of them."[164] Best would later successfully sue Ringo Starr, over his own disparaging comments. John Lennon would eventually admit that "We were cowards when we sacked him. We made Brian do it." Another drummer, Jimmie Nichol, briefly experienced the apex of fame as a replacement for the temporarily ill Ringo Starr at the height of Beatlemania on their 1964 tour. Naturally thinking this would look pretty good on his resume, his Beatles' association didn't help his career at all, and he declared bankruptcy in 1965.

Bobby Fuller, leader of the Bobby Fuller Four, who hit it big with *I Fought the Law* in 1966, died very mysteriously only a few months after the song reached the Top Ten, at the age of twenty-three. He was found dead in an automobile parked outside his Hollywood apartment on July 18, 1966. According to author Dave McGowan, Fuller "was found dead in his car near Grauman's Chinese Theater on July 18, 1966, after being lured away from his home by a mysterious 2:00-3:00 AM phone call of unknown origin...There were multiple cuts and bruises on his face, chest and shoulders, dried blood around his mouth, and a hairline fracture to his right hand. He had been thoroughly doused with gasoline, including in his mouth and throat. The inside of the car was doused as well, and an open book of matches lay on the seat. It was perfectly obvious that Fuller's killer (or killers) had planned to torch the car, destroying all evidence, but likely got scared away. The LAPD, nevertheless, ruled Fuller's death a suicide – despite the coroner's conclusion that the gas had been poured after Bobby's death. Police later decided that it wasn't a suicide after all, but rather an accident. They didn't bother to explain how Fuller had accidentally doused himself with gasoline after accidentally killing himself."[165] In an interesting side-light, Bobby's half-brother Jack Leflar had been "murdered, left to die in the desert" in 1961. The 2015 book *I Fought the Law: The Life and Strange Death of Bobby Fuller* by former Cramps drummer and Fuller fan Miriam Linna, reexamined this mysterious case.[166]

Twenty-seven-year-old Christa Helm had worked in a low-budget film and had a few television roles, but was mainly known in Hollywood for being quite the "party" girl. On February 12, 1977, she was stabbed twenty-two times and bludgeoned to death outside her agent's West Hollywood home.[167] Rumors swirled that Helm had kept a diary and even recordings of her trysts with numerous celebrities. In another curious twist, actor Sal Mineo had been murdered in the same neighborhood exactly one year earlier. Mineo was one of Hollywood's "conspiracy theorists," having called the Warren Report on JFK's assassination "totally bullshit" and was set to play Sirhan Sirhan in Orson Welles' aborted film about the assassination of RFK.[168] Mineo was associated with what has been called the *Rebel Without a Cause* "curse," joining cast mates James Dean (who died at only 24 in a 1955 car crash) and later drowning victim Natalie Wood. Christa Helm's murder was never solved, and her diary and recordings have not been found. Twenty-nine-year-old David Bacon had just played the title role in *The Masked Marvel* serial, when he died under very suspicious circumstances on September 13, 1943. Bacon emerged from his car after driving it off the road, clad only in a bathing suit, and died shortly thereafter from a knife wound to the back. A camera found in the car contained a photograph of Bacon nude on the beach. Bacon's widow alleged that her husband was gay, and had been having an affair with Howard Hughes.[169] Promising early talkies' lead actor Ross Alexander shot himself a year after his wife committed suicide.[170] His second wife, stunning actress Anne Nagel, whose own career went into an inexplicable downward spiral, died at only fifty. Her death was attributed to heavy drinking, and she was virtually penniless when she left this world, with no children or surviving relatives. Nagel had filed a particularly strange lawsuit in December, 1947, against noted Hollywood Dr. Franklyn Thorpe (ex-husband of actress Mary Astor), which alleged that during an appendectomy he'd performed a decade earlier, he had removed other organs without her consent, leaving her unable to bear children.[171] Nagel is yet another celebrity who was buried in an unmarked grave.

Singer-songwriter Phil Ochs was an even more radical anti-establishment figure than Bob Dylan. In 1973, Ochs was assaulted, and his vocal chords were permanently damaged. Three years later, he took his own life at just thirty-six. Folk singer Jim Glover (half of the recording duo Jim and Jean) knew Ochs well (and even taught him how to play the guitar), and I established an online relationship with him through our common interest in the JFK assassination. Glover claims that Ochs was keenly interested in the assassination, and was in fact in Dealey Plaza on November 22, 1963. He even was allegedly caught in some photos at the scene. Glover had some interesting connections himself. In an August 2, 2018 email to me, he wrote, "Around 1947 Club Foot Allen Dulles called me down the stairs to watch my dad toss CPUSA membership records in the furnace and told me, 'Jim, never forget this.'" Glover mentioned several curious aspects of Ochs's life, including an alleged trip to

Chile shortly before the CIA overthrew Salvador Allende. He also said that Ochs claimed to be working with the Fair Play for Cuba Committee (the pro-communist front group that was tied to Lee Harvey Oswald and his intelligence work), as well as "a domestic National Security deal like CIA." Lisa Howard started out as an actress, with numerous television appearances as well as roles in films like *The Man Who Cheated Himself* and *Donovan's Brain*. She made the highly unusual transition to radical left-wing journalist, and became the first woman to host her own television news show. She was the crucial intermediary between President John F. Kennedy and Cuban leader Fidel Castro, as part of JFK's little-publicized efforts at opening a dialogue between the two nations. Ultimately, Castro and Howard developed a romantic liaison. After JFK's assassination, Howard hosted two television specials about Cuba under Castro. President Lyndon Johnson had quickly cancelled the rapprochement talks with Castro.[172] JFK assassination researchers like me weren't shocked by Howard's death, allegedly by her own hand, on July 4, 1965, at just thirty-five. Howard was also close friends with Mary Meyer, wife of high-ranking CIA official Cord Meyer, who allegedly had an affair with President John F. Kennedy and would be murdered under extremely suspicious circumstances on October 12, 1964.

Sonny Bono, who shot to fame with Sonny and Cher, and went on to become a United States congressman, died in a skiing incident that remains wrapped in mystery. On January 5, 1998 (ironically, less than a week after Robert F. Kennedy's son Michael was killed in the exact same highly unusual manner), Bono died from injuries received from striking a tree while skiing in Nevada. Bono's fourth wife Mary, who would go on to take his place in Congress, rather oddly told *TV Guide* that her husband had been addicted to prescription drugs, which she claimed had caused the accident. This was contradicted by the coroner finding no drugs or alcohol in Bono's system. Sonny Bono left a remarkably modest estate of under

$2 million, which was contested for years because he didn't have a will. This is even more mystifying considering that Bono wrote several of the duo's huge hit records, like *The Beat Goes On* and *I Got You Babe,* as well as songs like *Needles and Pins,* which were hits for other artists, and had been earning a not unsubstantial congressional salary. His famous ex-wife Cher, despite being worth an incredible $320 million herself, nevertheless sued his estate for $1.6 million in back alimony. Some people found it difficult to accept the official story of Bono's death. Ted Gunderson, former head of the Los Angeles FBI office, said, "It's nonsense for anyone to now try to suggest that Bono died after crashing into a tree…There's zero evidence in this autopsy report to show such an accident happened…."[173] Gunderson and internet researcher David "DC Dave" Martin focused attention on the curious injuries found at Bono's autopsy, which included a black eye, bloody nose, bruised jaw and two knocked out teeth, which all would seem to suggest an assault of some kind. Martin claimed that Rep. Bono was looking into U.S. military and government officials being involved in arms and drug deals in Central America and Southeast Asia. Bono had aggressively questioned Attorney General Janet Reno about the deaths at Waco during Congressional hearings, and was said to be deeply troubled about what happened there.

Eleven years later, on March 18, 2009, forty-five-year-old actress Natasha Richardson died after a similarly bizarre skiing accident. At first, it appeared her injuries were minor and she casually refused medical care, thinking she was just fine. She talked to her husband, actor Liam Neeson, on the phone afterwards, telling him "Oh darling, I've taken a tumble in the snow." Evidently the damage was a lot more severe than first thought – Richardson had suffered a serious head injury. By the time she got to the hospital, it was too late. Neeson would report that his last words to his wife were "You've banged your head. It's– I don't know if you can hear me, but that's– this is what's gone down. And we're bringing ya back to

New York. All your family and friends will come." Neeson honored Richardson's wishes by pulling the plug on any extraordinary measures to keep her alive. Some found it inexplicable that Richardson could have suffered such a deadly blow when taking a simple fall on a beginner's "bunny" slope. Even mainstream outlets questioned this, and some suggested that her death either aggravated a previous unknown or undisclosed injury, or even was unrelated to the fall.[174] Dana Reeve remained remarkably loyal to her *Superman* star husband Christopher, lovingly caring for him for years after his tragic May 1995 accident, which left him paralyzed from the neck down. After Reeve's death from a reaction to an antibiotic in October 2004, Dana died very quickly herself of lung cancer, at just forty-four, in March 2006. This seemed all the more strange since Dana had never been a smoker. *Sesame Street* actor Northern James Calloway was apparently beset by mental problems, which culminated in his death at only forty-one years of age. One incident involved him stealing a youngster's backpack and fleeing the scene clad only in a Superman tee shirt, while shouting, "Help! I'm David from Sesame Street and they're trying to kill me!"[175] Calloway went into cardiac arrest after a violent altercation with a physician at a New York psychiatric facility. The cause of his January 9, 1990 death was determined to be from Excited Delirium Syndrome, although a web site specializing in tabulating the deaths of black performers noted, "Despite the official death claim, it's been alleged that the Medical Examiner couldn't determine the cause of death."[176]

In 2004, while singer Teena Marie was sleeping in a hotel room, a large picture frame fell and struck her on the head. The blow caused some surprisingly serious damage, leaving her with periodic seizures for the rest of her life. On the afternoon of December 26, 2010, an unresponsive Teena Marie was discovered by her daughter, Alia Rose, at her home in Pasadena, California, and the fifty-four-year-old was pronounced dead by paramedics at the scene. An autopsy performed by the Los Angeles County coroner found no signs of apparent trauma or any discernible cause of death, and resorted to the default conclusion in these cases, when there is no logical explanation, that she had died from "natural causes."[177] Vickie Lynn Hogan Marshall, better known as Anna Nicole Smith, died at only thirty-nine on February 8, 2007, in her Hollywood, Florida hotel room, from a prescription drug overdose. Smith, perhaps the perfect definition of a classic "gold digger," was evidently prevented from receiving any proceeds from her ninety-year-old husband's estate by his son. Her last months were filled with sadness, as Smith mourned the loss of her own son Daniel, who had died quite oddly on September 10, 2006 at only twenty, while visiting his mother and new-born half-sister in a Bahamas hospital room. When the coroner cryptically labeled Daniel's death as "reserved," Anna hired renowned forensic pathologist Cyril Wecht to perform a second autopsy, which concluded he had accidentally overdosed on Zoloft and two other drugs.[178] Nineteen-year-old promising singer-song-writer Taylor Mitchell became only the second known person in North America to be killed by coyotes, as she was attacked in 2009 while hiking through a Canadian national park. Dana Hill starred in numerous '80s television series and films, including *National Lampoon's European Vacation*. She was diagnosed with Type 1 diabetes at age ten, which stunted her growth and eventually caused her tragic early death at just thirty-two.

Marlon Brando was beset by family tragedy. His daughter Tarita Cheyenne Brando, was injured when she crashed the jeep of her boyfriend, leaving her with a scar on her face that ended her modeling career. Cheyenne's mother was a Tahitian actress, and she resented Brando's absence in her life, stating in a 1990 interview, "I have come to despise my father for the way he ignored me when I was a child. He came to the island maybe once a year but really didn't seem to care whether he saw me or not. He wanted us but he didn't want us."[179] In 1990, Cheyenne claimed that her boyfriend and father of her unborn child, Dag Drollet, was abusing her, which led to her half-brother Christian Brando shooting and killing Drollet. Cheyenne was sent back to Tahiti for medical treatment, which prevented her being issued a subpoena to testify at Christian's trial. Cheyenne would hang herself on April 16, 1995, at only twenty-five years of age. Marlon Brando and half-brother Christian were not able to attend her funeral. Christian Brando pled guilty to manslaughter in the Drollet case, and was released from prison in 1996. He subsequently became involved with Bonnie Lee Bakley, who would be murdered on May 4, 2001; her new husband actor Robert Blake would be charged, but found not guilty of killing her. Blake claimed to have gone back into the restaurant where they'd just eaten, to retrieve a gun he'd left there, and returned to find Bakley had been shot fatally in the head while sitting in their car. There was testimony from someone who claimed Blake had tried to hire him to kill his wife, but "reasonable doubt" has quite a different meaning when the defendant is a celebrity. Blake, incidentally, was Bakley's *tenth* husband. Christian Brando died of pneumonia on January 26, 2008 at the premature age of forty-nine.[180]

Jack Nance, the star of David Lynch's cult classic *Eraserhead*, died alone at fifty-three in his apartment in South Pasadena, California on December 30, 1996 under mysterious circumstances. Nance had told friends the previous day that he'd been punched in the head during a fight with two men at a donut shop. His death was attributed to a subdural hematoma caused by blunt force trauma. But because Nance was also legally drunk at the time, some believed that he had injured himself. It was a fitting ending to a bizarre life. Nance had been a regular in David Lynch's projects. In 1991 his porn star wife, Kelly Jean Van Dyke, daughter of actor Jerry Van Dyke, had committed suicide. Adding a surreal twist to this was the fact that Lisa Loring, who played little Wednesday on the '60s television show *The Addams Family*, was the one who found Kelly Jean's body.[181] Loring herself led as tumultuous a life off-screen as any entertainer ever has. Her mother died of alcoholism when Loring was just sixteen, and already a mother herself. The third of her four marriages was to a porn star. She was a heroin addict for years, and was forced to work for a time as a bartender. Not surprisingly, her net worth is currently said to be just $500,000. Cult favorite New Wave figure Peter Ivers, who recorded several albums and hosted a television variety show, wrote the song "In Heaven" for *Eraserhead*. He was found bludgeoned to death in his apartment at only thirty-six, on March 3, 1983. Mary Ann Ganser of the Shangri-Las' death at only twenty-two has been variously attributed to encephalitis, a seizure and a drug overdose.[182] The Rolling Stones' Brian Jones drowned suspiciously in a swimming pool at only twenty-seven. He coined the band's name, competed with Mick Jagger for the alpha male role in the group, and had been unceremoniously dumped from the group less than a month before. A friend of mine who'd been a session drummer for many years, with some of the biggest names in the industry, once told me that it was common knowledge in the business that "Mick Jagger offed Brian Jones." Recently, investigative journalist Scott Jones alleged that Jones had been murdered by Frank Thorogood, a builder who'd been working on the house, and that the police had instituted a cover-up.[183] It is unclear just why police would cover up for a builder who'd murdered a rock star. On the fiftieth anniversary of his death, Jones' daughter Barbara Marion told *Sky News,* "I think he was murdered and I think the police did not investigate it the way they should have." She also expressed frustration that Jones had never received due credit for his influential role in the band, declaring, "He chose every member, he got them their gigs. If it weren't for my father, Mick Jagger would be an accountant somewhere."[184]

The death of pop superstar Michael Jackson on June 25, 2009 remains cloaked in controversy. Jackson was only fifty, and his death shocked the entertainment world. The official narrative held that the singer had been found unresponsive at home by his personal physician Dr. Conrad Murray, who said he had administered

CPR to no avail. A few months later, the LA County Coroner's office would conclude that Jackson had been the victim of a homicide. Jackson had been administered a trio of prescription anti-anxiety drugs prior to his death. In 2011, Dr. Murray was convicted of involuntary manslaughter and served a two-year prison sentence. The night before his death, at a rehearsal performance, Jackson was said to have looked good, and was visibly energetic. Sister LaToya Jackson would speak of "a shadowy entourage" that she inferred might have administered the fatal dosage of drugs to him, and a year later in 2010 declared that her brother had been "murdered for his music catalogue." She also called Dr. Murray a "fall guy" and claimed her brother had told her he feared he'd be killed for his music catalogue. Father Joe Jackson echoed these sentiments, and used the exact same "fall guy" term in doing so. Jackson's daughter Paris was even bolder, in an interview with *Rolling Stone* magazine. In regards to her father being murdered, Paris stated, "All arrows point to that. It sounds like a total conspiracy theory and it sounds like bullshit, but all real fans and everybody in the family knows it. It was a setup. It was bullshit." When asked who she thought would have wanted her father dead, Paris replied, "A lot of people."[185] Some in the conspiracy world have claimed Jackson knew about the Illuminati, and was silenced by them. *The Sun* reported that a shocking note written by Jackson, just weeks before his death, had stated "They are trying to murder me," and confessed that he was "scared about my life."[186] In a May, 2017 interview with Daphne Barak on the Australian television show *Sunday Night,* Jackson's German businessman friend Michael Jacobshagen revealed that the entertainer had been in an "emotional meltdown" shortly before his death, and told him, "They are going to murder me."[187]

Few remember Van Louis Martin, a strident anti-war writer who wound up in Hollywood. His family, who hadn't heard from him in years, was informed of his sudden death on December 10, 1935 at forty-four, from meningitis, after he'd already been cremated and buried. His sister, Juanita, worked for the FBI and insisted a "hit" had been ordered on him for his anti-war sentiments.[188] Largely forgotten singer Johnny Burnette, best remembered for his 1960 hit *You're Sixteen,* died in a bizarre boating accident at only thirty. His son, Rocky, who later became a recording star himself, described how "When Dad died we lost our home, our car and all our Hollywood friends." An exception to this was Glen Campbell, who assisted the family financially and hired Burnette's widow as his secretary.[189] Singer Jeff Buckley drowned in only a slightly less strange incident at only twenty-nine, and his mother claimed that he was far too good a swimmer for the official story to be believable.[190] Keith Reif, lead singer of the Yardbirds, was electrocuted to death by an improperly grounded guitar. Another musician, Stone the Crows' guitarist Les Harvey, was electrocuted in front of 1,000 fans while warming up for a concert in Wales. Johnny Thunders, an original member of the New York Dolls, was found dead under mysterious circumstances in New Orleans on April 23, 1991. Thunders' body was found underneath a coffee table in a very unusual position, and rigor mortis had already set in, indicating it had been there for some time. Witnesses claimed the body was bent "like a pretzel." The official cause of death was assumed to be drug-related, but the autopsy revealed no fatal amount of drugs in his system. Thunders' manager Mick Webster would state, in a 1994 interview with *Melody Maker*: "We keep asking the New Orleans police to re-investigate, but they haven't been particularly friendly."[191] Dee Dee Ramone would write in his autobiography, *Lobotomy: Surviving the Ramones,* "Johnny had gotten mixed up with some bastards … who ripped him off for his methadone supply. They had given him LSD and then murdered him."[192] Ramone himself would die of a heroin overdose at age fifty. "Rape rock" artist Eldon Hoke, better known as El Duce, was found dead on the train tracks on April 19, 1997 at age thirty-nine, only two days after he declared in an interview that Courtney Love had asked him to kill Kurt Cobain. Linda

S. Stein managed the likes of the Ramones and Steve Forbert, and went on to become a "real estate agent to the stars." She was found dead in her Manhattan apartment at age sixty-two, on October 30, 2007, from blunt trauma to the head and neck. Her former assistant would be tried and convicted of the crime.[193]

Overlapping into the corrupt world of politics, a subject I explored in my 2014 book *Hidden History,* is the case of screenwriter Gary Devore. Devore had finished a script which alleged a nefarious purpose behind the U.S. invasion of Panama, and was said to be on his way to deliver it when he vanished mysteriously. A year after he disappeared in June, 1997, his body was found strapped into his vehicle in the California Aqueduct. In a truly macabre twist, his hands were missing. It is unclear from news reports, but evidently these hands were retrieved separately. The coroner would later report that the hands were found at the autopsy to be in fact some two-hundred-years-old. No one attempted a logical explanation for *that*. Devore was well-known in Hollywood for his screenwriting on films like *Dogs of War* and *Time Cop*. His script about Panama was for his directorial debut, to be called *The Big Steal*. Devore promised friends, who included the likes of Arnold Schwarzenegger and Tommy Lee Jones (he had served as Jones' best man at his wedding), that it would be "the hardest hitting film studios have ever seen." His widow was only one of those who claimed Devore had worked with the CIA. "'When we first married he told me he got a lot of calls from government agencies. He told me to ignore it, so I did….We had a few at first, then not very many. Then in the last month one man was calling all the time." Wendy Devore stated. "He was dealing in things that you're not necessarily supposed to deal in. I found out a lot of people in Hollywood had these connections with the CIA and knew things that will never be made public. After he disappeared, things just didn't add up. It's very easy to sound like a conspiracy theorist, but when you're married to someone you know little things about them that seem insignificant but are actually crucial. I know there are things that don't add up."[194] A 2014 documentary, *The Writer with No Hands,* explored the case.

Another screenwriter, twenty-nine-year-old David Crowley, was alleged to have killed his wife and five-year-old child, then turned the gun on himself when the bodies of all three were found in their suburban Minnesota home in January, 2015. Crowley had been working on a suitably conspiratorial film (titled *Gray State*) about the Federal Emergency Management Agency taking over the country by force, which naturally led to "conspiracy theories" about the deaths. Predictably, the local police chief concluded that Crowley had simply "snapped" and claimed there was no evidence of foul play. Found at the scene were the words "Allah Akbar," written in his wife's blood on a wall. Crowley's wife had been raised as a Muslim in Pakistan before converting to Christianity.[195] Another oddity was the fact a neighbor discovered the bodies when he saw presents on the porch, a month after Christmas. There was no extended family that had tried to contact them, even during the holiday season? How did the gifts remain out in the open like that for so long, without anyone noticing? All three bodies were also located strangely near the front door. There were few details provided about the relatively early and sudden death of director and stunt man David R. Ellis, whose body was found in a South African hotel room in January, 2013, as he was filming the animated feature *Kite*. It was postulated that he'd had a heart attack, but no official cause of death was released.[196] If it was ever announced, I could find no source for it. Ellis directed the underrated 2004 film *Cellular,* one of Hollywood's rare productions that focused on police corruption.

The tale of screenwriter Pierre Collings is a sad one, even for Hollywood. He suffered a nervous breakdown upon completing the screenplay for the 1936 film *The Story of Louis Pasteur.* He was thus unable to attend the Academy Awards ceremony, where he won two Oscars. Inexplicably spurned by the industry despite his success, Collings' excessive drinking led him into poverty. His death from pneumonia, at the age of thirty-six, was described by the *Los Angeles Times* as being fueled by "heartache and despair."[197] On top of all that, both of Collings' Academy Awards' trophies have disappeared. Sidney Howard, who wrote the screenplay for one of the biggest movies ever made, 1939's *Gone with the Wind,* was crushed to death the same year, in a freak accident involving his tractor. He became an early posthumous recipient of an Oscar, for best adapted screenplay. The first known posthumous Oscar winner was Gerald Duffy, who won the Best Writing award for *The Private Life of Helen of Troy* in 1928. Few details are known about his early death at age thirty-two, other than it happened in Hollywood while he was "dictating a script."[198] The following year, actress Jeanne Eagels, whose substance abuse problems included a heroin addiction, became one of the few human beings to ever die of "alcoholic psychosis," whatever that is, at just thirty-nine years of age. She was then posthumously awarded the Best Actress Oscar for *The Letter.*

George Reeves was one of the most remembered stars of early television, playing the title role in the 1950s show *The Adventures of Superman.* Reeves, like so many entertainers, suffered financial problems once the series ended and was perhaps television's first notable casualty of typecasting. On June 16, 1959, somewhere between 1:30 and 2 a.m., Reeves reportedly shot himself in the head in the bedroom of his Los Angeles home, while his fiancée, playwright Leonore Lemmon, and some friends were partying downstairs. Initial police reports indicated that the forty-five-year-old Reeves was depressed because he wasn't getting any acting roles. His mother, Helen Bessolo, refused to accept that Reeves had killed himself. An enormous amount of speculation has swirled around this case. There are valid reasons to suspect Reeves was murdered, possibly over his relationship with married ex-showgirl Toni Mannix, wife of MGM's intimidating powerhouse Eddie Mannix.[199] The 2006 Ben Affleck film *Hollywoodland* explored that angle in some detail, but ultimately drew no clear conclusions. I recall seeing an interview with Jack Larson, who portrayed Jimmy Olsen on the show, in which he rather unpersuasively, in my view, insisted that Reeves had taken his own life. The cast of *Superman* was woefully underpaid; even Reeves started at a salary of just $1,000 per episode, and wound up making $5,000 for each show. Noel Neill, who portrayed Lois Lane in all but the first season, made a measly $225 each episode.[200]

Thirty-two-year-old martial arts legend Bruce Lee is another actor whose death remains shrouded in mystery. Many believe that Lee was murdered by jealous "Chinese martial arts lords" for revealing trade secrets in his films. Lee met with producer Raymond Chow on July 20, 1973, days before the release of the film *Enter the Dragon,* to discuss his new project, *Game of Death.* The two then drove to the home of Taiwanese actress Betty Ting Pei. When Lee complained of a headache, Pei allegedly gave him an Equagesic—a combination aspirin and muscle relaxant. Lee reportedly decided to take a nap, but never woke up. The only substance found in the actor's blood during the autopsy was Equagesic. It would be claimed that he died due to a hypersensitivity to the muscle relaxant in the drug. It is difficult to accept that such a young man, who was in better physical condition than most human beings will ever be, simply died so easily. A safely non-conspiratorial theory was postulated in Matthew Polly's 2018 book *Bruce Lee: A Life.* Polly claimed that the martial arts legend died of heatstroke, after he'd had sweat glands surgically removed from his armpits.[201] Lee's son, Brandon would die suspiciously as well, when he was accidentally shot and killed at just twenty-eight, by a gun that was supposed to be filled with blanks during the filming of *The Crow* in 1993. On March 16, 2019, rising country music star Justin Carter was killed under similar, but even stranger circumstances, after a gun in his pocket supposedly went off accidentally during a video chat session.[202]

John Denver was one of the most successful musical artists of the 1970s. He was born Henry John Deutschendorf, Jr., the son of an Air Force officer, interestingly enough in Roswell, New Mexico. Denver was heavily into politics, and had kind of an early "new age" aura about him. One of his little reported statements was, "I can do anything. One of these days I'll be so complete I won't be human. I'll be a god."[203] In December, 1979, the FBI notified Denver that a series of threatening phone calls, from a woman speaking both German and English, had been received daily in Los Angeles. The woman claimed that her mother's boyfriend was going to kill Denver. Denver was also a huge fan of the space program, and supposedly passed NASA's rigorous testing, just missing out on being selected for the doomed January, 1986 *Challenger* space shuttle flight. On October 12, 1997, Denver's privately flown plane plunged into California's Monterey Bay. His body was so badly mangled that he could only be identified by his fingerprints. Denver's license to fly had been revoked because of his series of drunk driving arrests, although an autopsy would find no alcohol or drugs in his system.[204] A gun had been found under Denver's pilot seat, leading to speculation that he was either suicidal or feared for his life. In April, 2017, the Reelz television network series *Collision Course* intimated that someone caused Denver's death, and noted that there were others who had threatened Denver's life for unclear reasons.

The November 29, 1981 death of actress Natalie Wood is yet another Hollywood case that left more questions than answers. Wood was on a yacht off Catalina Island, with her husband Robert Wagner and actor Christopher Walken, her co-star in *Brainstorm*, which had nearly finished filming. After a night of heavy partying, Wagner and Walken got into an argument on the boat, and Wood went to bed. According to Wagner, when he went to say goodnight to his wife, she was missing. Hours later, the forty-three-year-old actress was found floating dead in the water. Although her death was ruled an accidental drowning, police reopened the case in November 2011 after the boat captain, Dennis Davern, told NBC News that the fight between Wagner and Walken had actually led to her death. After an underpublicized nine month investigation, Wood's cause of death was officially changed from accidental drowning to "drowning and other undetermined factors." The LA County Coroner's office would later announce that some bruises on Woods' body might have been inflicted before she went into the water.[205] Natalie's sister, actress Lana Wood, remains skeptical about the official explanation, and had a heated filmed encounter with Wagner at an airport in early 2016. In early February 2018, Robert Wagner was suddenly announced as a "person of interest" in the case, and CBS broadcast a probing new look into Natalie's death on *48 Hours*, which featured significant interview excerpts with Lana Wood.

I spoke with Lana Wood in September, 2019. She agreed to appear on my radio show "I Protest" on September 6, 2019. We had a great conversation; Lana is an unassuming, very cordial lady. You would never know she'd been in countless television shows and movies, working alongside the biggest names in the business. In recounting her show business career, Lana described being crudely propositioned at age fourteen by actor Maximilian Schell, the Academy Award-winning actor, director and producer who was sixteen years her senior. Most of our conversation concerned the mysterious death of her sister. Lana has been a one woman crusader for the truth in this case, to the point of alienating much of her family, including her mother, who she described as being "Hollywoodized," and unwilling to consider suspicions directed at her famous son-in-law Robert Wagner. Lana remains as dubious as ever over the accidental drowning theory. As she noted, "Natalie would never have gone out that night in her nightgown. She never even left the house without all her makeup on."

Philip Taylor Kramer went from being a member of the band Iron Butterfly (best known for their 1968 hit *In-A-Gadda-Da-Vida*) to a career in aerospace engineering. He founded the multimedia company Total Multimedia Inc., and by all accounts, his life was happy. In February of 1995, right after having made what some claim was an important discovery, a math formula "for transmissions at 'faster than light' speed," the forty-three year-old Kramer left his home to pick up a business associate at LAX Airport. He never arrived. Kramer's final phone calls were eerie. He called former musician friends, stating that he loved them, and then his wife, telling her, "Whatever happens, I'll always be with you." His last call was to 911, in which he told the dispatcher, "This is Philip Taylor Kramer, and I am going to kill myself." Kramer was said to be worth over a million dollars, but disappeared with only forty cents in his pocket.[206] A massive search was launched, but years went by with no trace of him found. The case was featured on *Unsolved Mysteries* and other shows. In May of 1999, skeletal remains found inside a minivan in Decker Canyon, just outside of Malibu, California, were positively identified as those of Philip Taylor Kramer. Given his 911 call just before he vanished, his death was ruled a probable suicide by police, but Kramer's family still disputes this.

More than one member associated with the Coasters band met tragic ends. King Curtis, a session musician who played on some of the band's biggest hits, was stabbed to death by two junkies in 1971. Cornelius Gunter was shot to death while sitting in a Las Vegas parking garage.[207] One of the members of an offshoot Coasters group, Nate Wilson, was murdered and his body dismembered in 1980, with the band's manager Patrick Cavanaugh convicted of the heinous crime. Christine Cavanaugh, who is remembered for providing the voices of the title character in the 1995 movie *Babe*, the original Dexter in *Dexter's Laboratory*, and as Chuckie Finster in *Rugrats*, left showbiz in 2003 to return to her native Utah. According to reports, this was to "be closer to her family," although she was divorced and had no children. Her early death, at age fifty-one, on December 22, 2014, seems even stranger considering that there is no cause listed anywhere that I could find. One obituary disclosed that the cause was "unclear, with the results of an autopsy expected to take up to eight weeks."[208] The results of that autopsy, whatever they were, have yet to be made public. In a similar case, fifty-two-year-old Suzanne Crough, who was one of the kids on *The Partridge Family* but had only a few acting roles after the series ended, died suddenly on April 27, 2015, of undisclosed causes. At the time of her death, she was working as a manager of an OfficeMax store in Arizona. Las Vegas police helpfully reported that her death was "not suspicious," and the county coroner attributed it to a rare heart disorder.[209] Later reports spoke of a bankruptcy and a slew of tax liens which had been filed against her. John David Carson's acting career started off promisingly, with a lead role in 1971's *Pretty Maids All in a Row*, but he wound up working guest roles on television shows before retiring in 1990. He died in 2009 at only fifty-seven, and again there is no listed cause of death that I could find. In one of those curious connections, Carson was briefly married to the ill-fated Vicki Morgan, who was the powerful Alfred Bloomingdale's mistress and was brutally murdered in 1983 at just thirty-years-old, in an unconvincing scenario by a gay friend infatuated with her. The alleged perpetrator, Marvin Pancoast, would conveniently die in prison at forty-two, of AIDS-related complications.[210] In June 2012, Erica Kennedy, singer, fashion journalist, and author of the acclaimed 2004 novel, *Bling,* was found dead at her home in Miami Beach at only forty-two. While her family confirmed the death to the *Associated Press,* neither the cause nor the precise date Ms. Kennedy died was provided. Some speculated it was suicide[211], but there was no funeral or memorial service, and as of early 2021, no cause of death has ever been reported. Stories a week or so after her death noted that, as is typical, police declared there were no signs of foul play, and that it was being classified as "a death investigation pending toxicology results." The police politely noted that such results normally take four to six weeks.[212] That was in 2012.

One of the first movie stars to die under suspicious circumstances was Florence LaBadie, one of the biggest names of the silent era. LaBadie died as a result of injuries suffered in a 1917 car wreck, at only twenty-nine. A notable conspiracy theory developed in this case, as it was alleged by some that LaBadie had been having an affair with President Woodrow Wilson. Under this theory, Wilson ordered that her car brakes be cut (the accident supposedly was the result of brake failure), in order to squelch public knowledge of the affair, which was rumored to have resulted in a pregnancy. Several online sites have debunked this theory, in typical knee jerk fashion, but intriguing questions remain nonetheless. Why did LaBadie's adoptive mother mysteriously skip the funeral? LaBadie was from a wealthy Catholic family, yet she was buried in a nonsectarian cemetery in Brooklyn, in an unmarked grave like an astonishing number of celebrities. Oddly, LaBadie's biological mother had signed an affidavit just five days before her death, authorizing the burial of her daughter in another plot that had been purchased by her late grandmother. The Wilson conspiracy theory was widely promulgated in Charles Foster's 2000 book *Stardust and Shadows: Canadians in Early Hollywood.* In a fantastic intertwining connection, LaBadie's passenger in the car, her fiancee Daniel Carson Goodman (who survived with only a broken leg) would seven years later be aboard William Randolph Hearst's yacht when producer Thomas Ince died under very questionable circumstances. Goodman's obituary would strangely omit any mention of either LaBadie or Ince.[213]

Sons of Anarchy star Johnny Lewis died under very odd circumstances on September 26, 2012, at age twenty-eight, after either jumping or falling from the roof of the home where he rented a room. Inside the residence, his eighty-one-year-old landlord was found murdered and a cat was discovered to have been beaten to death. *Sons of Anarchy* creator Kurt Sutter pretty much threw Lewis under the bus, stating that he was "deeply sorry that an innocent life had to be thrown into his destructive path."[214] One wonders why so unstable an actor would have been employed in the first place, but Tinseltown is full of such stories. Another actor on *Sons of Anarchy*, forty-seven-year-old Alan O'Neill, was found lifeless in the hallway of his apartment by his girlfriend on June 6, 2018. According to TMZ, the actor had a history of heart problems, was a heavy smoker, and drank excessively. Not surprisingly, officials quickly ruled out any kind of foul play.[215] R & B singer Ephraim Lewis' death was nearly as strange. Lewis had been marketed as a British Michael Jackson. The twenty-six-year-old died on March 18, 1994, when police were called to the scene of his small apartment in Hollywood, because of "a naked man acting crazy," and the naked Lewis either jumped or fell to his death after they arrived.[216] His funeral a month later was full of tension between record executives and Lewis' family, who angrily kept asking, "How did Ephraim really die?"

Gilbert Gottfried's favorite actor, Skelton Knaggs, supplanted the great Dwight Frye in memorable character roles in some of the classic horror films of the 1940s. However, like Frye, Knaggs died all too young, succumbing to cirrhosis of the liver at just forty-three on May 1, 1955. David Ruffin, lead singer for the Temptations on most of their biggest hit records, died at only fifty on June 1, 1991, in a Philadelphia hospital, allegedly from an adverse reaction to cocaine. Ruffin had led a troubled life, fueled by drug abuse, which resulted in his being fired from the Temptations and even a stint in prison. Ruffin's family and friends disputed the cause of death, citing the fact that the proceeds from his current tour, amounting to some $300,000, were nowhere to be found on him.[217] A miniseries on the Temptations would portray Ruffin's death in a more sinister light, depicting him being beaten and left in the street in front of the hospital, and his body lying unclaimed in a morgue for a week. Another original member of the Temptations, Paul Williams, was found dead at just thirty-four. The death was ruled a suicide, although his family disputed this, as the coroner claimed that Williams, in JFK assassination witness-style, had shot himself with his right hand in the left side of his head. The gun was also found to have fired two shots. After Williams' son Kenneth strangled his great-aunt with a telephone cord in 1989, he asked his sister to save his share of royalty checks for him. When he exited prison after serving a surprisingly light twenty year sentence, Williams found the estimated $200,000 had already been spent by his sister. According to news reports, Williams' heirs had been splitting about $80,000 a year in royalties. Adjusting quickly to life outside prison, he filed a lawsuit against her.[218] The many troubles of the group were covered in the 2010 book *Ain't Too Proud to Beg: The Troubled Lives and Enduring Soul of the Temptations* by Mark Ribowsky.

Marion Aye, a WAMPAS Baby Star of 1922, and one of Mack Sennett's bathing beauties, never made the transition to sound, and finally succeeded after several suicide attempts, in taking her own life at the age of forty-eight. Aspiring actress Dorothy Hale only had two small appearances in films, but she hobnobbed with high society due to the connections of her rich husband, Gardner Hale. After her husband's car went over a cliff in late 1931, Hale eventually had to rely on financial benefactors like Bernard Baruch and her good friend Clare Booth Luce., who would later remark, in her customary blunt fashion, "Dorothy had very little talent and no luck." After the "farewell party" she gave herself on October 21, 1938, (among the guests was R. Buckminster Fuller), she attended the theater with J.P. Morgan and his wife. She then returned to her high-rise apartment and leaped to her death, dying at only thirty-three.[219] Her suicide would later be immortalized by artist Frida Kahlo, in a painting commissioned by Clare Boothe Luce. The previous year, Hale had been involved in a torrid affair with President Franklin D. Roosevelt's Works Project Administration Administrator Harry Hopkins, which Hopkins had coldly ended under pressure from powerful forces. Ona Munson, early on a leading lady but best remembered for her supporting role in 1939's *Gone with the Wind,* overdosed intentionally on February 11, 1955, at the age of fifty-one. Clara Bandick, "Auntie Em" in the classic 1939 film *The Wizard of Oz,* came home from Palm Sunday services on April 15, 1962, displayed her favorite photos and memorabilia in prominent places, and set up a collection of press clippings from her lengthy career. She proceeded to take an overdose of sleeping pills. "Auntie Em" left the following note: "I am now about to make the great adventure. I cannot endure this agonizing pain any longer. It is all over my body. Neither can I face the impending blindness. I pray the Lord my soul to take. Amen."[220]

Tom Graeff is best remembered for directing, writing, and acting in the kitschy 1959 film *Teenagers from Outer Space.* The openly gay Graeff became despondent when the movie earned him no money, thanks to a cheap deal with Warner Brothers, who quickly peddled the film off to drive-in theaters. Graeff appears to have become mentally unstable over this, and eventually took out ads in the *Los Angeles Times,* proclaiming himself to be the second coming of Jesus Christ. Unable to launch his new project, a sci-fi adaptation of the L. Frank Baum classic, which he called *The Wizard of Mars,* Graeff took his own life on December 19, 1970.[221] British actor Lee Quigley, whose sole claim to fame was playing the infant Kal-El in 1978's *Superman,* died at only fourteen, from inhalation of drugs. Charles Butterworth was one of the busier character actors in early talkies. An intellectual who graduated from Notre Dame with a law degree, he participated in the legendary "Algonquin Roundtable" discussions and was close friends with Robert Benchley. Inconsolable over Benchley's death, Butterworth is thought to have killed himself by intentionally crashing his car, on June 14, 1946, although there is no way of knowing this for certain. At the time of his death, he was romantically involved with a young Natalie Schafer, later to achieve Baby Boomer immortality as "Lovey" Howell on *Gilligan's Island.* Jean Seberg was harassed relentlessly by the FBI for her supposed ties to the Black Panthers. In a very sad end to a promising film career, the forty-year-old Seberg's decomposing body was found in the back seat of her car, wrapped in a blanket, on September 8, 1979. It was said to have been there for at least a week. [222] Seberg was rumored to have become increasingly paranoid in her final days, even believing that her refrigerator had been spying on her. Chester Morris, a leading man in the early talkie era, and an Oscar nominee for 1929's *Alibi,* overdosed intentionally on drugs at age sixty-nine, without leaving a suicide note. Urbane actor George Sanders took an overdose of drugs as well, and left behind one of the more memorable suicide notes, which read, "Dear World, I am leaving because I am bored. I feel I have lived long enough. I am leaving you with your worries in this sweet cesspool. Good luck."[223] On October 19, 1978, Oscar winner Gig Young shot and killed his fifth wife, who was half his age, before turning the gun on himself. He left the bulk of his estate (including his Oscar) to his agent, and just $10 to his teenage daughter, who was his only child. Young, who was once married to *Bewitched* star Elizabeth Montgomery, was buried in Waynesville, North Carolina, alongside several family members, under his birth name of Byron Barr.[224]

Bella Darvi was briefly a leading lady in three big-budget 1950s films, but quickly fizzled out and committed suicide at age forty-four. Her body had apparently lain in her apartment for a week before being discovered. In her obituary, it was noted that Darvi was "a long-time friend of the film producer Daryl F. Zanuck."[225] Laurie Bird, whose last of her three film appearances was in Woody Allen's 1977 classic *Annie Hall,* and was Art Garfunkel's live-in girlfriend, ended her own life two years later at age twenty-five. Trent Lehman, child star of the television series *Nanny and the Professor,* who found little work in the industry after it was cancelled, chose to hang himself on the grounds of his old elementary school at age twenty, on January 18, 1982. Lehman went from making a surprisingly substantial $1200 a week (and again, compare that to the much lower salaries other child stars, with bigger roles, received) at ten-years-old to being unable to find lowly paid jobs as a young adult. His mother stated that it had broken her heart to see how unwanted the once popular child star felt.[226] Twenty-four-year-old Yugoslavian actor Milos Milos, who had appeared in just two films, murdered Mickey Rooney's estranged wife Carolyn Mitchell and then shot himself, on January 31, 1966. Erin Fleming, Groucho Marx's companion in his later years, would shoot herself in 2003, while homeless and in poverty. She had been center stage during the battle over Groucho's estimated $2.6 million estate in 1977. Squaring off against his three grown children, Fleming was able to get the likes of Carroll O'Connor and George Burns to testify in her behalf. Perhaps the most colorful part of the proceedings was the revelation that Fleming regularly paraded around the house naked, and whether that constituted cruelty or kindness to the eighty-six-year-old comedian.[227] Jim Carrey's much younger girlfriend, Cathriona White, took her own life at age thirty. A wrongful death lawsuit filed against Carrey by White's family was dismissed in early 2018.[228] The third of William Shatner's four wives died under mysterious circumstances. Forty- year-old Nerine Shatner's nude body was found at the bottom of their swimming pool on August 9, 1999. Autopsy results revealed a high blood alcohol content (0.27 percent) as well as the fact she'd taken sleeping pills. There were facial bruises and two cracked vertebrae in her neck as well. Why someone would take sleeping pills, and discard their clothing, before deciding to go swimming is something only those who reflexively conclude "no foul play" can explain. In one of those endless fascinating connections, Nerine was close pals with Suzanne Gregard, former wife of Dodi Fayed, who died in Paris along with his lover Princess Diana a few years earlier.[229] Paul Lynde's "traveling companion" James "Bing" Davidson plunged to his death from a San Francisco hotel balcony in 1965. A couple of police officers, rather strangely in my view, claimed to have witnessed the whole thing from street level, and immediately supported Lynde's accidental fall explanation. The gay Lynde was a hopeless alcoholic with a nasty disposition. Former *SCTV* star Andrea Martin, in her book *Lady Parts,* matter-of-factly states, "the brilliant comedian Paul Lynde was not apprehended on a Southwest flight when he said to the mother of a screaming child, "You shut that kid up, or I'll fuck it."[230]

Jerry Lee Lewis notoriously married his thirteen-year-old cousin; that was the third of his seven marriages. Years later, his much younger fifth wife Shawn Michelle Lewis was found dead under highly questionable circumstances in their home on August 24, 1983, at just twenty-five. The marriage had been troubled from the start. Shawn's sister claimed that Jerry Lee had once warned her, "You scared of me? You should be. Why do you think they call me the Killer?" Early reports indicated Jerry Lee had bloodstains on his bathrobe and a cut wrist, and exhibited slurred speech when investigators arrived on the scene. There were no visible causes of death, and clearly "the Killer" should have been scrutinized thoroughly. An expensive private autopsy was arranged, paid for by Lewis, and performed by Dr. J.T. Francisco, who years earlier had conveniently reported that heart problems killed Elvis Presley. There were several strange elements to the crime scene inside the Lewis home; investigators found barred doors and windows, bloody clothes in the master bedroom, and bullet holes in the walls and windows. In the words of mortician Danny Philips: "I'd like to see it investigated. I just can't believe that girl just lay down and died." The man who signed the death certificate never saw the body. During the contentious phone conversation afterward between Jerry Lee and Shawn's mother, "the Killer" snarled at one point, "Well, she's dead. And I'm alive." There were other notorious incidents in Lewis's background. He'd once shot his bass player in the chest, and on another occasion drunkenly tried to crash the gates of Graceland, all the while waving a pistol and threatening Elvis Presley. Lewis also lost a three-year-old son to drowning. Another son became a drug addict before dying in a car crash at nineteen. And astoundingly, this was not the first wife of Jerry Lee Lewis to die unnaturally. That honor belonged to fourth wife Jaren Gunn Lewis, who was found at the bottom of a Memphis swimming pool on June 8, 1982, just before her final divorce settlement.[231]

Barbara Bennett - the far less successful sister of fellow actresses Joan and Constance, and mother of Morton Downey, Jr., only succeeded on her fifth suicide attempt. Not only did Art Linkletter's daughter Diane commit suicide; a few weeks before that, his son-in-law John Zwyer put a bullet in his head. Pepi Lederer was the niece of Marion Davies and spent much of her youth at William Randolph Hearst's Castle. Pepi was a lesbian, and her aunt and Hearst had her committed to a mental institution, where she summarily jumped out of one of the windows. One of the all-time great character actors, James Gleason, had a son who was also an actor. Sergeant Russell Gleason either jumped or accidentally fell from the fourth floor of New York's Hotel Sutton on Christmas Day, 1945. Jazz legend Chet Baker plummeted, accidentally or otherwise, from an Amsterdam hotel room at age fifty-eight. Frankie Valli of Four Seasons fame lost two children; his stepdaughter Celia fell off a fire escape in 1980, and six months later a drug overdose took the life of his youngest daughter Francine. Perhaps oddest of all, Linda Christian (better known as Tyrone Power's wife than for her own film career) had a beloved dog that became so distraught over the constant parade of bullfighter boyfriends at her Rome penthouse he flung himself off the terrace. Well, actually George Zucco's story was probably even odder. The distinguished character actor seemingly went mad, believing that he was indeed one of the crazed villains he portrayed in numerous films for Monogram Studios. Urban legend holds that his concerned wife and daughter went to the lengths of moving into the mental asylum with him, in hopes they could jolt him back to normal. Adding an almost incomprehensible postscript, on the following midnight after his death, his grieving wife and daughter supposedly decided to join him by taking their own lives. On the Forteana website of the Charles Fort Institute, a prolific poster claimed that "Zucco is said to have died from 'sheer fright' while screaming that Cthulhu and others of writer H. P. Lovecraft's (fictional) demon-deities were coming to devour him." While this is an enticing tale, it appears to be one of Kenneth Anger's more fanciful inventions. Mainstream sources attribute Zucco's death to pneumonia and report that his widow lived to be 99.[232] An "impoverished and forgotten" Zucco apparently did, however, take to the streets of Los Angeles in the costume he had worn and saved from *Voodoo Man,* "calling on his old pal Ramboona," which led to him being institutionalized.[233] Eddy Howard was a popular singer and bandleader at the tail end of the big band era, best remembered for his 1946 #1 hit *To Each His Own.* Howard died at only forty-eight of a cerebral hemorrhage, after ceding the rights to the Eddy Howard Orchestra name to his sometime saxophonist and vocalist Norman Lee. Lee and his wife were murdered fifteen years after Howard's death, on December 6, 1978, by one of the band's former trumpet players.[234] Lee also played with Lawrence Welk's orchestra, and co-wrote *Champagne Polka* with him.

Joseph Brooks, best known for composing the syrupy song *You Light Up My Life,* killed himself in 2011, apparently despondent over upcoming charges of rape. Tony Scott, high profile director known for *Top Gun, Beverly Hills Cop II, Enemy of the State* and many other successful films, jumped off a bridge to his death at the unlikely age of sixty-eight. Sawyer Sweetin, child star of *Everybody Loves Raymond,* shot himself in the head at only nineteen. His real life brother and series co-star, Sullivan Sweetin, hasn't had a film credit since the series ended. Lee Thompson Young, who starred as *The Famous Jett Jackson,* and was in *Friday Night Lights* and other television shows, took his own life at twenty-nine. Don Cornelius, creator and host of *Soul Train,* shot himself in 2012. Comedian Richard Jeni took his own life in 2007. Comedian Greg Giraldo overdosed on prescription meds on September 25, 2010. Dana Plato, the lovely teen known almost exclusively for playing Kimberly on *Diff'rent Strokes,* died at the age of thirty- four from a drug overdose. Almost eleven years later to the day, Plato's son Tyler Lambert died at age twenty-five from a self-inflicted gunshot wound to the head in Tulsa,

Oklahoma.[235] One of England's most promising directors, Michael Reeves, overdosed on sleeping pills in 1969. He was just twenty-five. *Family Feud* host Ray Combs somehow managed to hang himself, while being on seventy-two-hour observation in a psychiatric ward. Combs was notable for having six children with his wife, which constituted an extremely rare large Hollywood family. After his death, it was discovered that Combs had been deeply in debt. The family home was foreclosed on, and his wife was forced to sell much of the memorabilia from his career.[236]

Brad Delp, lead singer of the band Boston, took his own life in 2007. As MTV put it at the time, the former factory worker "died virtually anonymous." Boston's lead guitarist and songwriter Tom Scholz sued the *Boston Herald* later, over what he claimed were defamatory articles that intimated he had driven Delp to suicide. Former band mates testified that Delp "didn't like Tom and didn't trust Tom. He felt that Tom had taken advantage of him financially, especially." Delp apparently wasn't able to stand up to Scholz. In 2015, Scholz was ordered to pay the newspaper $171,529 in court costs and interest.[237] Scholz could afford it, having a $100 million net worth. Delp's wife, meanwhile, auctioned off his grand piano, record collection, and other personal items, perhaps indicating that he didn't leave behind a large fortune.[238] Keith Emerson, keyboardist of Emerson, Lake and Palmer, killed himself on March 10, 2016. Crowded House drummer Paul Hester hanged himself in a park in 2005. Country music singer Mindy McCready shot herself in 2013. Bob Welch, originally with Fleetwood Mac and then a successful solo artist, shot himself in 2012. Well known fashion designer L'Wren Scott, Mick Jagger's longtime girlfriend, hanged herself in 2014. Doug Hopkins, lead guitarist and songwriter for the Gin Blossoms, shot himself at only thirty-two. He reportedly had taken his gold record for the song *Hey Jealousy* off the wall and smashed it only days before. Hopkins had serious issues with alcohol, and the financially strapped guitarist had been pressured by his bandmates (who had already booted him from the group) and the record label to sign over half of his publishing royalties, in exchange for a one-time payment of $15,000.[239] Soul singer Donny Hathaway took his own life at thirty-three. Nirvana's Kurt Cobain supposedly shot himself in the head at age twenty-seven in 1994, although many conspiracy theories have been postulated. Tom Grant, a private investigator hired by Cobain's wife Courtney Love, believed he was murdered, and railed about the "lies, contradictions in logic, and countless inconsistencies. Motivated by profit over truth as well as a web of business deals and personal career considerations, Courtney Love, her lawyers, and many of Courtney's industry supporters have engaged in an effort to keep the public from learning the real facts of this case."[240]

Peter Ham, singer-songwriter for the group Badfinger, took his own life a few days before his twenty-eighth birthday, despondent over his financial and personal circumstances. Later, band mate Tom Evans, who sang lead on songs like *Come and Get It,* would follow suit. Badfinger had been promoted by Apple Records as the next Beatles, but their experiences with Apple, Warner Brothers Records, and their management would add up to what one fellow musician termed a "rock and roll rip-off." Ham and Evans also co-wrote the song *Without You,* which Harry Nilsson (whose legendary drinking exploits contributed to the heart attack that killed him at fifty-two) took to the top of the charts. Both men were despondent over their inability to get royalties from either Apple or Warner Brothers Records.[241] Wendy O. Williams, the outrageous leader of the punk bank the Plasmatics, shot herself to death at age forty-eight. Thirty-seven-year-old INXS lead singer Michael Hutchence was found dead in an Australian hotel room on November 22, 1997, ruled to be a suicide from a combination of alcohol and drugs. Hutchence was involved with Boomtown Rats front man and Live Aid organizer Bob Geldof's wife Paula Yates. Yates would claim that Geldof had threatened them; at one point proclaiming, "Don't forget, I am above the law."[242] Yates would die unnaturally as well, of a supposed accidental heroin overdose, on September 17, 2000. In yet a third tragedy connected to Geldof, he and Yates's daughter, Peaches Geldof, died at only twenty-five of another accidental drug overdose.[243] Peaches was an interesting character, and several conspiracy theories tying her to the occult have been promoted online.

One prominent musician who didn't kill himself was Jim Gordon, perhaps the most highly regarded session drummer of the 1970s, who also co-wrote (along with band leader Eric Clapton) Derek and the Dominoes' iconic rock song *Layla*. Gordon worked with the biggest names in the industry, but began to exhibit signs of schizophrenia in the early 1970s; in one infamous incident, he severely beat his then girlfriend, singer Rita Coolidge, while touring with Joe Cocker. It was alleged by some that Gordon stole the piano piece used on *Layla* from Coolidge, without crediting her. On June 3, 1983, he attacked his elderly mother with a hammer, then finished her off with a butcher knife. While he was sentenced to a typically generous celebrity term of sixteen years to life, and was actually first eligible for parole in only eight years, Gordon sabotaged his chances by first claiming his mother was still alive, and then refusing to even attend his own parole hearing.[244] Gordon is serving his time at the notorious psychiatric prison in Vacaville, California. Another rock murderer was Sid Vicious, bassist for the Sex Pistols, who was charged with killing his girlfriend Nancy Spungen, but died of an overdose before he could go to trial. Claudine Longet, the sultry, much younger wife of singer Andy Williams, was charged with the 1976 murder of her boyfriend, Olympic skier Spider Sabich, but in a typical "celebrity special," was convicted only of negligent homicide and served merely thirty days in jail. Like other reclusive celebrities before her, Longet went into such seclusion that there have been no photos publicly available of her in decades. One of the sons of Lincoln Perry, known popularly as Steppin Fetchit, was alleged to have opened fire on the Pennsylvania Turnpike in April, 1969, wounding sixteen people and killing his wife and three others, before turning the weapon on himself. Fetchit, although he'd only met his son two years previously, came to believe that his child had been framed, as part of his involvement with the Black Power movement and the FBI's notorious COINTELPRO program.[245]

From 2005-2013, fourteen stars of "Reality Shows" on television killed themselves.[246] In November, 2016, Valerie Dowden Wells, who starred in the 2012 reality series *Bayou Billionaires,* was killed in a bizarre murder-suicide as she sat in a car outside a Shreveport, Louisiana McDonald's.[247] Like an alarming number of true adult film stars, Janet Banzet, star of sexploitation films in the late '60s and early '70s, took her own life on July 29, 1971. The life expectancy of a porn star is not very long, and they tend to die unnaturally. Among the many examples: Jon Dough, who hanged himself in 2006, the beautiful twenty-three-year-old known as Savannah, who shot herself in 1994, and Tera Wray, who took a drug overdose in 2016. The internet has spawned several new kinds of celebrities, who achieved their fame primarily through videos on You Tube. One of these young stars, Caleb Brataley, died suddenly at age thirteen on October 1, 2015. His premature death certainly raised some eyebrows. The official cause of death was reported to be an undetected heart condition. Originally, Caleb's family had reported he died from "natural" causes. Perhaps fittingly, his family broadcast Caleb's memorial service live on Facebook. It was viewed more than 116,000 times in just the first hour.[248] Popular You Tuber Yoteslaya was killed while allegedly trying to outrun a train. Bodybuilder and healthcare guru, You Tube star Greg Plitt, died in the exact same, incomprehensible way. "Style vlogger" Tamisha Ridge was murdered by her ex-boyfriend.

According to studies by the Center for Suicide Research, musicians kill themselves at three times the national average. The director of the organization, Steve Stack, explained, "As an occupational group, artists are more likely than others to experience labor market strains…Some work at menial jobs by day and do art at night." Generally speaking, artists of all types have not only higher suicide rates, but higher rates of mental illnesses.[249] As *The Atlantic* reported, on October 19, 2012, writers are twice as likely to end their own lives as the general population, with Ernest Hemmingway, Virginia Woolf and Jack London among the most notable examples. In Hollywood, it's always been the onscreen performers who have this curious propensity to end it all. As Kenneth Anger wrote, "Few aging editors, wrinkled sound men, arthritic script girls, senescent makeup artists, or grips unlucky-in-love reached for sleeping pills or revolvers."[250] Tabulating the history of suicides in the entertainment industry is a daunting task. What follows is an incomplete, but illuminating list, of entertainers who chose to end it all themselves:

Joyce Jameson, one of the "Fun Girls" in a handful of memorable *Andy Griffith Show* episodes; Kitty McHugh, best remembered for her numerous roles in Three Stooges shorts; Big Band leader Ben Pollack; Eve Miller, veteran of more than 40 films and plenty of guest-starring television roles; Robin Stille, who had prominent roles in '80s schlock films *The Slumber Party Massacre* and *Sorority Babes in the Slimeball Bowl-O-Rama;* Rose Stradner, an actress who was married for nineteen years to renowned director Joseph L. Mankiewicz; Debbie Weems, a regular on *Captain Kangaroo* in the mid-1970s; Mary Kay Bergman, who voiced nearly all the female characters during the first three seasons of *South Park*; child actor Chet Allen; David Arkin, regular supporting player in Robert Altman's films; Todd Armstrong, who could never turn his lead role in *Jason and the Argonauts* into a productive film career; Hooper Atchley, veteran of 214 films between 1929 and 1943; Charles Avery, one of the original Keystone Kops; long-time Western character actor Don "Red" Barry; prolific character and voice actor Herman Bing (who left an unforgivably stark suicide note for his daughter, which read, "Dear Ellen. Such insomnia. I had to commit suicide. Your Daddy."); teen heartthrob Jonathan Brandis; rising young '70s actor

Barry Brown (whose sister, actress Marilyn Brown, would later kill herself, too); prolific silent and early talkie character actor Arthur Edmund Carewe; firefighter turned actor John Costelloe; long time *Today* show host Dave Garroway; two time Academy Award nominee Claude Gillingwater; actor and writer Spalding Gray; veteran actor Jonathan Hale - yet another figure whose grave was unmarked for over forty years, until a gravestone was erected thanks to the "Dearly Departed" fan group; Rusty Hamer, child star of *Make Room For Daddy*, who never made the transition to adult roles and was living in a trailer when he killed himself, while there was no memorial service held for him; "Captain Video" Judd Holdgren; child actor Tim Hovey; Rick Jason, who ended it all for unclear reasons and left no suicide note, just one week after a reunion of the cast from the television series *Combat!*; *Family Affair* star Brian Keith, who took his own life two months after his daughter did; *Porky's* star Wyatt Knight; Andrew Koenig, actor and son of *Star Trek's* Walter Koenig; Alan Lake, husband of Diana Dors; yet another Our Gang actor we neglected to mention earlier-Kendall "Breezy Brisbane" McComas; Paul McCullough, half of the comedy duo Clark and McCullough, who abruptly grabbed the razor from his barber during a shave and slit his own throat and wrists; dwarf actor David Rappaport; Will Rogers, Jr. (at the age of eighty one); Another eighty-one-year-old, prolific actor Walter Slezak; soap star actor Nick Santino, who was despondent over having "betrayed" his dog; Academy Award-winning producer Pete Smith, who remarkably jumped off the roof of a nursing home at age eighty-six; *McHale's Navy* star Gary Vinson; and *Wonderful World of Disney* announcer Dick Wesson.

Glenn Quinn, who played Mark on *Roseanne*, and had parts in other television shows, died at only thirty-two of an accidental heroin overdose. Evidently, he didn't have a great deal of money, considering that his *Rosanne* co-star Michael Fishman set up a memorial fund for him. Amanda Peterson will always be remembered as the quintessential blonde cheerleader in 1987's *Can't Buy Me Love*. Her career fizzled out by the '90s, and she died at just forty-three of an accidental drug overdose. A stranger death was that of actress Sunny Johnson, whose career was just blossoming in the early 1980s when she was found unconscious in her home. After being rushed to the hospital, she remained on life support for a day before her parents had her taken off the respirator. Most sources attribute her death to a burst blood vessel in the brain. She was only thirty-years-old. Actress Holly Lewis, probably best known for several high-profile commercials, died at only forty-six in 2012. There is no information about what took her life, and the official obituary page simply stated "There will be no visitation." Although a Catholic, she was cremated and the family, rather strangely in my view, asked that donations be made to the cemetery or "the donor's choice." Lisa Robin Kelly, who starred on the television series *That '70s Show*, was a chronic drug addict who died at only forty-three after multiple run-ins with the law. Muppets creator Jim Henson's sudden death at only fifty-three was attributed to toxic shock syndrome. Henson's son John would die at an even younger age, succumbing to a heart attack at forty-eight while playing in the snow with his daughter. That was almost as sad as when comedian Tracey Ullman's father died of a heart attack while reading to her (she was only six). When Charlize Theron was fifteen, she witnessed her mother shoot her abusive father in self-defense. Many people have heard the strange, sad tale of how Jack Nicholson didn't learn his "sister" was actually his mother until he was thirty-seven-years-old, eleven years after she died. Singer Bobby Darin, who died from heart disease at only thirty-seven, went through the exact same kind of bizarre situation. Nicholson is a literal enigma; in the words of Dave McGowan: "It is said that Nicholson was born at St. Vincent's Hospital in New York City, but there is no record of such a birth either at the hospital or in the city's archives. As it turns out, Jack Nicholson has no birth certificate. Until 1954, by which time he was nearly an adult, he did not officially exist. Even today, the closest thing he has to a birth certificate is a 'Certificate of a Delayed Report of Birth' that was filed on May 24, 1954. The document lists John and Ethel Nicholson as the parents and identifies the location of the birth as the Nicholsons' home address in Neptune, New Jersey. It appears then that there is no way to determine who Jack Nicholson really is. He has told journalists that he has no interest in identifying who his father was..."[251]

Rita Coolidge's sister was killed by her husband in a murder-suicide in 2014. Actor Kelsey Grammar experienced not only the bizarre murder of his father, when an unknown assailant set fire to his car, but also the murder of his sister. For good measure, his two half-brothers died in a scuba diving accident. That's almost Kennedy-esque. Connie Francis was one of the most successful recording artists of the late '50s and early '60s. She not only was raped and almost killed by a still unidentified assailant in 1974, her brother was murdered in a 1981 mafia hit. Singer Shania Twain's poverty-stricken childhood was augmented by the deaths of her mother and stepfather in a car crash. Actor Dylan McDermott's thug father was shot to death when his son was only eleven, six years after he murdered Dylan's mother. Sofia Vergara's brother was kidnapped and murdered. In an unimaginable tragedy, Jennifer Hudson's mother, brother and nephew were all murdered by her sister's estranged husband in 2008. Bill Cosby's only son was shot and killed while changing a flat tire. Mark Ruffalo's brother was shot to death in his Beverly Hills Condo in 2008. It was described by police as an "execution-style" killing.[252] Both of Patrick Duffy's parents were murdered during a 1986 robbery of their Montana bar. Dave Navarro, founder of the band Jane's Addiction, lost his mother in 1983 when she and a female friend were shot and killed in her Los Angeles apartment. *Glee* star Charice Pempengco's father was stabbed to death in 2011, during a fight at a grocery store. Omarosa Manigault, who achieved her fifteen minutes of fame on Donald Trump's show *The Apprentice*, experienced the separate murders of her father (when she was only seven) and her brother. Duane

Allman's father was killed by a hitchhiker. Legendary radio broadcaster Paul Harvey lost his father at the tender age of three, to a truly bizarre robbery-turned-murder while hunting. Wanda Young, lead singer of the Marvellettes, witnessed the separate shooting deaths of her sister, and her daughter, both of which took place at her Inkster, Michigan home. No wonder she struggled with drugs and alcohol. Veteran British actress Margaret Rutherford's father bludgeoned her grandfather to death after being released from a lunatic asylum. He received an astonishingly light sentence, and was released from the mental health facility just seven years later and reunited with his wife, who had just as amazingly waited for him. Two years later, Margaret was born. Compounding things unfathomably, Rutherford's mother hung herself from a tree while pregnant with her second child, when the future actress was just three.[253]

Jodie Sweetin, the child actress who played Stephanie on *Full House,* was adopted at nine months old. She later found out that her biological mother was a drug addict, and that her father had been killed in a prison riot. Sweetin began abusing drugs and engaging in promiscuous sex at an early age, and subsequently had three failed marriages. Her acting career was revived with the 2016 Netflix series *Fuller House,* where she portrayed the adult Stephanie Tanner. Pioneering black actress Dorothy Dandridge was sexually abused by her mother's lover, and was forced to care alone for her brain-damaged daughter. After losing some $150,000 to those entrusted to handle her finances, Dorothy had to move into a small apartment in West Hollywood, where she was found naked and dead at only forty-two years of age. The cause of death was either an accidental drug overdose or an extremely rare embolism, depending upon the source. Linda Darnell was swindled out of her earnings as well, and died in 1965 at only forty-one from a fire at a friend's home, after they'd watched one of Darnell's old movies, *Star Dust,* on television. In one of those Tinseltown ironic coincidences, it was reported that Darnell had always had a deathly fear of fire. Darnell was saddled with a domineering stage mother who eventually would be banned from the studio lot, a manager who defrauded her, and a husband who extorted some $125,000 from her - practically her entire worth at the time. Her modest Hollywood home had been foreclosed upon in 1962. Dominican actress Maria Montez was found dead in her bathtub at only thirty-nine; the official cause was said to be from a heart attack, but the circumstances remain mysterious. On October 14, 1980, Mary Tyler Moore's son Richie died from an accidental self-inflicted gunshot wound, shooting himself in the head while handling a sawed-off shotgun. Just before his death, Moore had secured a job for him in the CBS mailroom. In a macabre twist, at the time of his death, Moore was busy promoting her new film, *Ordinary People,* which dealt with the very same subject. Two years earlier, Mary had lost her much younger sister Elizabeth to an overdose at only eighteen. Now forgotten, but once very popular 1950s actress Joan Davis starred in the television series *I Married Joan,* opposite Jim Backus and Beverly Wills, her real life daughter who played her sister on the show. Davis died suddenly of a heart attack at only forty-eight, and two years later a fire claimed the lives of her mother, daughter and two grandsons. Jeanne Deckers, the "Singing Nun" who had the smash hit single *Dominique* in 1963, and was later portrayed on screen by Debbie Reynolds, saw little if any money from her song (although her religious order received at least $100,000 in royalties) and subsequently left the convent. She and her lesbian lover would end their lives together (Deckers was just fifty-one), primarily over financial reasons. In their suicide note, the lovers requested a church funeral, and reiterated that they had not lost their faith.[254]

An early Hollywood curious death involved Jean Harlow's husband Paul Bern. Bern's supposed suicide has conventionally been attributed to his frustration over being sexually impotent. However, author Dave McGowan noted, "Bern's death was, needless to say, written off as a suicide. His newlywed wife, strangely enough, was never called as a witness at the inquest. Bern's *other* wife – which is to say, his common-law wife, Dorothy Millette – reportedly boarded a Sacramento riverboat on September 6, 1932, the day after Paul's death. She was next seen floating belly-up in the Sacramento River. Her death, as would be expected, was also ruled a suicide. Less than five years later, Harlow herself dropped dead at the ripe old age of twenty-six. At the time, authorities opted not to divulge the cause of death, though it was later claimed that bad kidneys had done her in. During her brief stay on this planet, Harlow had cycled through three turbulent marriages and yet still found time to serve as God-mother to Bugsy Siegel's daughter, Millicent."[255] Paul Bern's mother had previously killed herself, reputedly because he had married a gentile. Inside Hollywood gossip held that both MGM executives and Howard Hughes suspected that Harlow had shot Bern, and conducted a clean-up of the crime scene. Samuel Marx, an MGM story editor, would claim he found Irving Thalberg interrogating the servants when he arrived at the scene. Louis B. Mayer himself showed up later. An unidentified man who was friends with MGM security chief Whitey Hendry told Marx that Hendry claimed to have accompanied Mayer to Bern's house and that he had personally planted the gun in Bern's hand. He also stated that the suicide note was a forgery. In 1990, Marx wrote a book about the case, *Deadly Illusions: Jean Harlow and the Murder of Paul Bern*.[256]

Thelma Todd was a popular actress, who starred in comedies with the likes of the Marx Brothers, Laurel and Hardy, Patsy Kelly and Zasu Pitts. She was only twenty-nine when her body was found behind the wheel of her car, parked in the Malibu garage of pro-ducer and director Roland West. Todd owned a posh restaurant that bore her name, and attracted the biggest stars of the day, as well as a slew of gangsters. Todd was allegedly involved romanti-cally with mobsters like Lucky Luciano and Pat DiCicco, an agent with underworld connections whom she married. DiCicco would go on to marry Gloria Vanderbilt and regularly beat her, too. The official cause of Todd's death was ludicrously determined to be accidental and/or suicide, even though she had a broken nose, bruises on her throat and two cracked ribs. Presumably she beat herself to death, much as her thuggish lovers had been known to beat her. Hal Roach's studio abused her in a similar manner to the way Judy Garland was treated by MGM. They had something called a "potato clause" in her contract, which stipulated that a weight gain of a mere five pounds would result in her being fired. Thus, she turned to diet pills much as Garland would.[257] The *Los Angeles Times,* in a December 17, 1935 story that was never followed up, noted that Todd "within the past few months had been the recipient of several extortion notes threatening her with death unless she paid $10,000." Todd's business partner was silent film actress Jewell Carmen, who had been married to Roland West. Carmen's career strangely ended before the talkies, and she lived in such obscurity afterwards that her death in 1986 didn't even garner an obituary in *Variety,* an honor customarily given to virtually all entertainers. The blonde who replaced Todd in Hal Roach's comedies with Patsy Kelly was Lyda Roberti, who had starred in several films that showcased her unique accent and singing style. Roberti died of a heart attack at just thirty-one-years-old, on March 12, 1938. Precocious Virginia Weidler, one of the most talented child actors in the history of the business, never transitioned to adult roles, and died of a heart attack at just forty-one. Virginia's longtime husband Lionel Krisel noted that she "would always change the subject as quickly as possible without being rude. She never watched her old movies or replied to requests for interviews. Although she was never one to criticize, I think our boys got the impression that their mother didn't think very much of the motion picture industry."[258]

On Saturday evening, February 1, 1941, twenty-nine-year-old dancer and showgirl Dolores Delmar died under circumstances strangely similar to those on the night Natalie Wood would die forty years later. Dolores was with a group of people that included wealthy

California department store scion Arthur Hamburger. Also aboard the yacht were actor Robert Tracy and Dolores' roommate, dancer Alice Dere. The quartet had been to various Hollywood night spots before Hamburger suggested a sail on his yacht, El Con-A-Dee. According to Dere, Dolores dove into the water at some point with all her clothes on. Dere pulled Delmar out of the water, and Dolores removed her wet clothes and went to a cabin to warm up. Dere went to get Dolores a robe, but when she returned, Dolores was gone. Running to the deck, Dere heard a splash, and saw bubbles in the water. Apparently, Dolores had plunged into the water wearing only a bra and panties. Dolores' body was found after a brief search. Both Hamburger and Tracy would claim to have been asleep and stated they saw or heard nothing. Police believed the death was accidental, but coroner Frank Nance found Dolores' desire to swim in the cold and dirty water baffling, despite the fact she'd been drinking.[259] It is difficult to find any information beyond that, in regards to what the ultimate findings about her death were. Dolores Delmar's father, Berhardt Rohn of Detroit, did state that he did not believe his daughter drowned accidentally because she was a good swimmer. Broadway singer and actress Evelyn Hoey was found shot to death in an upstairs bedroom of oil heir Henry H. Rogers III's Pennsylvania house on September 11, 1935. Rogers was the son of a late Standard Oil executive. Hoey had been a guest at the home for a week. At a coroner's inquest, Rogers would testify that he was seated in the living room with another individual when they heard a shot. Their testimony was supported by three other witnesses. District Attorney William E. Parke disputed the verdict of a coroner's jury that Hoey had shot herself, and requested that a grand jury investigate her fatal shooting.[260] Parke was also concerned about the conduct of the coroner's jury members, and wanted to explore their association with certain journalists who had covered the inquest. After a week's investigation, the grand jury concluded that Hoey committed suicide, but did acknowledge that members of the coroner's jury were too intimately associated with reporters. They denied there was any criminal interference involved. [261]

The list of unnatural deaths of not only entertainers, but those connected to them in some way is very, very long. Christine Hinton, leader of the Byrds' fan club and David Crosby's girlfriend, was killed in a car crash on September 30, 1969. Twenty-year-old Amy Gossage, girlfriend of Crosby's later band mate Graham Nash, was stabbed nearly fifty times and bludgeoned to death in her San Francisco home on February 13, 1975. According to Dave McGowan, a year following Jimi Hendrix's death from an alleged overdose of barbiturates, the underage prostitute he'd been with the day before his death, Devon Wilson, jumped out of a window at New York's Chelsea Hotel. Hendrix's former manager Michael Jeffery was killed in a 1973 mid-air plane collision. After his death, it was found that Jeffery had been funneling much of Hendrix's money into offshore bank accounts linked to drug trafficking. Hendrix's girlfriend Monika Danneman, who found Hendrix's body, would allegedly take her own life in 1996.[262] Jim Morrison's death - purportedly from a heart attack at the extremely early age of twenty-seven - has always been shrouded in mystery. It allegedly occurred two years to the day after Brian Jones of the Rolling Stones drowned under suspicious circumstances. Fueling speculation that Morrison staged his own death was the fact the doctor who signed the death certificate has never been identified, there was no autopsy, and only two people saw the body.[263] His girlfriend, Pamela Courson, died of an alleged heroin overdose a few years later. Eric Clapton's four-year-old son, Conor, plunged tragically to his death from a Manhattan high rise on March 20, 1991. Clapton would write the emotionally powerful song *Tears in Heaven* in response. Roy Orbison, whose magnificent voice was compared to an opera singer by Bob Dylan and others in the industry, was beset with unimaginable tragedy. His first wife, Claudette Frady, was killed in a motorcycle accident; Orbison had written the Everly Brothers 1958 hit *Claudette* for her, and his own smash *Pretty Woman* was inspired by her as well. Industry legend has it that Claudette slept around notoriously, while her luckless rock star husband was far better behaved in this regard. Two years after the death of his wife, Orbison's two eldest sons died in a house fire. Orbison died of a heart attack at only fifty-two, just as his musical comeback was hitting full stride, with the release of the Traveling Wilburys' first album, featuring band mates Jeff Lynne of the Electric Light Orchestra, Tom Petty, George Harrison, and Bob Dylan.[264] Author John Kruth, in his book *Rhapsody in Black: The Life and Music of Roy Orbison,* recounted how only days before his death, Orbison had told journalist Kristina Adolfsson, "My life is a never-ending dream…." And, as noted earlier, Orbison is one of countless celebrities who were buried in unmarked graves. Otis Williams, the last surviving member of the original Temptations, lost a son to a construction accident in 1983. The fact that the young son of a member of such an iconic music group was employed as a Detroit construction worker, probably tells us a great deal about how wealthy Williams had grown from all those hit records.

Brandon DeWilde was a high-profile actor, best remembered for his role as the hero-worshipping Joey in the classic Western *Shane*, who became entrenched in the Laurel Canyon crowd in the 1960s. He was close friends with the ill-fated Gram Parsons and David Crosby. DeWilde was killed at only thirty in a freak automobile accident. The very young Christine Frka, housekeeper and governess to Frank Zappa's daughter Moon Unit, died of a reported overdose on November 5, 1972, although Dave McGowan claimed, "friends suspected foul play." Hours after being fired by Neil Young from his Crazy Horse band, guitarist and songwriter Danny Whitten died of a supposed overdose at only twenty-nine. Bruce Berry, a roadie for Crosby, Stills, Nash & Young and brother of Jan and Dean's Jan Berry, died of an alleged heroin overdose, shortly after, according to Dave McGowan, flying "out to Maui to deliver a shipment of cocaine to Stephen Stills…" The Byrds' Clarence White was struck and killed by a drunk driver, who was subsequently given an incredibly lenient one-year suspended sentence.[265] Punk singer Stiv Bators was hit by a taxi while walking in Paris, France in 1990. Seemingly not seriously injured, he went to a hospital but became impatient over the long wait and went home, where he died in his sleep from a concussion at just forty years of age. Bob Marley and his band the Wailers were about as cursed as any group could be. Not only did Marley die at thirty-six of an extremely strange cancer (which originated under one of his toenails), drummer Carlton "Carly" Barrett was murdered by a hit man hired by his wife and her lover (for which she oddly only served a year in prison), and Peter Tosh, who would become famous in his own right, was shot and killed by intruders in his Jamaica home.

The death of twenty-seven-year-old actor Anton Yelchin probably tops them all. Yelchin was best known for playing "Chekov" in the latest reboot of *Star Trek*. Yelchin's death was weird beyond belief; he was crushed when his SUV rolled down his driveway and trapped him against a brick pillar outside his home on June 19, 2016. Many questioned the extremely bizarre circumstances. In an August 3, 2016 comment on the World Mysteries blog, one Tray Caladan claimed that "I received this email the other day from director David Silva: 'Hi Tray. Thanks for sending. I worked with Anton Yelchin, amazing/curious/smart kid. Mom was also nice not like typical stage Moms. I'm so sorry he has passed. He was a genuinely good person and I thought he was a good actor as well. I know in the Hollywood hills everything is steep, but still find his "accident" implausible. Haven't read anything yet about his death other than crushed by own car when his car slipped from park to something else, pinned him and killed him?! He was a good guy, a kid…I worked on a feature with him called 'Delivering Milo.' I was 2nd Assistant director, shot in 1999.'" As usual, the authorities were quick to dismiss any notion of "foul play." It was reported that Yelchin exited his vehicle at around one a.m. and it thereafter rolled back down the steep incline of his driveway and crushed him. Trying to picture this is difficult; did Yelchin leave the driver's seat and then immediately run back behind the car? How else could he have been in position to have it roll into him? Why didn't he simply step out of the way? Also, stories indicated he was on his way to rehearsal at the time of the freak accident, and when he didn't show up, his friends became worried and were the ones to discover his body. Rehearsal at one a.m.? And how do we reconcile his getting ready to leave for rehearsal with him getting out of the vehicle just before it rolled back into him? The LAPD simply stated, "It appeared he had momentarily exited his car leaving it in the driveway."[266] As happens in so many of the political stories I cover, there was an early report that thereafter disappeared down the memory role, from a Detective William Bustos, that stated the crash was at least partially filmed by a surveillance camera, and he was working with the security company on this. There were also numerous reports that Yelchin had been in the process of getting his mail, but the mailbox was located in a completely different brick pillar. Most disturbingly, the few pictures available online of Yelchin's driveway don't show any incline, "steep" or otherwise. Friend and *Star Trek* co-star Simon Pegg accurately noted the "circumstances that defy explanation."[267] The troubling questions were obvious, but journalists displayed their typical lack of curiosity. Yelchin's parents reached a settlement with the makers of Jeep Grand Cherokee in 2018.[268]

Clarence White's fellow Byrds' band mate, legendary Flying Burrito Brothers' founder Gram Parsons, supposedly overdosed at a motel at just twenty-six-years-old on September 19, 1973. This was a decidedly odd conclusion, since his blood was found to contain no traces of barbiturates. His death had some very strange elements to it. Only two months previously, Parsons' house had burned down. As David McGowan has pointed out, celebrity homes burning down are a strangely common occurrence. After his death, his body was abducted by his band's manager Phil Kaufman, who then conducted a ritual burning of it. Kaufman was one of many in Laurel Canyon who knew Charles Manson well, and had even been a fellow inmate with him at Terminal Island. Kaufman boasted of sleeping with all of the high profile girls in Manson's "family" and would become road manager for the Rolling Stones during their notorious 1969 tour, which culminated in a free concert at Altamont speedway, where four people died while the Stones' played *Sympathy for the Devil*, trusting their Hell's Angels security force to maintain control. In another of those unfathomable connections, one of the young cameramen for the documentary of the Stones' tour *Gimme Shelter*, was future industry icon George Lucas. As David McGowan revealed, that documentary was purposefully deceptive on several counts. The member of Hell's Angels who was prosecuted for stabbing concertgoer Meredith Hunter to death, Alan David Passaro, was inexplicably acquitted, and later found floating dead in a reservoir in 1985, with $10,000 in his pocket.[269] Parsons' father, career military officer Ingram Cecil "Coon Dog" Connor, Jr., had seemingly killed himself in 1958, although no suicide note was left behind. Gram's mother remarried, to Robert Parsons, who was connected to anti-Castro Cuban exiles in Florida. Parsons' mother died very suddenly in 1965, the day after being admitted to the hospital. Parsons' sister would die at forty-one in 1993, along with her daughter, in a Virginia boating accident.[270] Parsons, like his similarly star-crossed friend and musical peer, Gene Clark, had a keen interest in UFOs.

Both Mama Cass Elliott and Who drummer Keith Moon died in the same room in the London home of hard-drinking singer Harry Nilsson, four years apart. Whether Elliott died of a heart attack or from choking on a ham sandwich, McGowan sarcastically called it "knowing where too many of the bodies were buried."[271] Tim Buckley, a singer-songwriter whose aforementioned son Jeff would later drown under strange circumstances, died of an alleged drug overdose on June 29, 1975. Jackson Browne's wife Phyllis Major died of a supposed overdose on March 25, 1976. Not only Duane Allman, but Allman Brothers Band mate Berry Oakley died in separate motorcycle accidents. Oakley was killed a year after Duane, in 1972, at a spot located only three blocks away.[272] Yet a third member of the Allman Brothers Band, drummer Butch Trucks, would shoot and kill himself at age sixty-nine, in front of his wife.[273] Singer Johnny Ace died at only twenty-five while playing Russian Roulette. Terry Kath, a founding member of the band Chicago, was another victim of Russian Roulette. Nikki Bacharach, the daughter of songwriter Burt Bacharach and actress Angie Dickinson, died in January 2007 from using helium combined with a plastic bag. She had Asperger's syndrome, an autism spectrum disorder, which may have contributed to her bizarre death.

On January 2, 2009, John Travolta's autistic son Jett died at only sixteen, allegedly after a seizure caused him to hit his head on a bathtub. Prominent Toronto neurologist Dr. Peter Carlen was only one of many to question the strange circumstances of the teenager's death. Carlen noted that Jett, who was autistic to the point of supposedly not being able to talk, was not on medication, a byproduct of the Church of Scientology's distrust of pharmaceuticals (Travolta is one of the most high profile Scientologists), and claimed that "is one of the risk factors for sudden unexplained death from epilepsy."[274] Jett required constant care, to the extent that the Travoltas had hired two nannies to look after him full-time. It is difficult to envision how such an accident could have occurred, when at least one of them was always in close proximity. On the ten-year anniversary of their son's death, Travolta and wife Kelly Preston praised Scientology in an interview with *US Weekly,* with the actor maintaining that "the church never left our sides for two years. I don't know if I would have made it through without their support." For years, it has been alleged that one of the reasons Travolta remains loyal to Scientology is the long-time rumor that he is gay, to the point of the church helping him handle the allegations of assault or harassment that have been lodged against him by multiple males. This was covered in more detail in Lawrence Wright's 2013 book *Going Clear: Scientology, Hollywood, and the Prison of Belief*. "The church hierarchy was desperately concerned that their most valuable member would be revealed as gay," Wright wrote, "at the same time, the hierarchy was prepared to use that against him."[275] Kelly Preston died from cancer in 2020 at fifty-seven. Led Zeppelin's drummer Jon Bonham overdosed on alcohol, as did AC/DC's lead singer Bon Scott. Sixty-two-year-old Mike Edwards, one of the founding members of the Electric Light Orchestra, died when a huge bale of hay rolled down a hill and landed on his passing van in Devon, England, on September 3, 2010.

In one of Tinseltown's great ironic tragedies, long-forgotten silent film star Charles Emmett Mack was killed in an automobile accident while driving to the track to film a racing scene in 1927's *The First Auto*. The Band T-Rex's lead singer, Marc Bolan, had a fear of cars, which made his death in an automobile accident just before he turned thirty as strange as Linda Darnell, who feared fire, dying in a fire, or Natalie Wood, who feared the water, drowning. Bolan's band mate Steve Currie died in a car crash four years later. Playwright Tennessee Williams died when he accidently swallowed the cap to a bottle of eye drops. In a truly "Believe it or Not" entry, legendary dancer Isadora Duncan was strangled when her scarf somehow became wrapped around one of the wheels of the car she was riding in. Actor Leslie Howard was presumed dead after his civilian plane was allegedly shot down by the German Luftwaffe on June 1, 1943, but the body was lost at sea. Howard's main role in the war effort was at disseminating propaganda, like many other celebrities. Howard was not reticent about what he was doing, once declaring, "To hell with whether what I say is propaganda or not, I've never stopped to figure it out and I don't think it matters anymore."[276] *My Sister Sam* star Rebecca Schaffer became the most tragic victim of celebrity stalking, when she was shot to death in her apartment doorway by obsessed fan Robert John Bardo on July 18, 1989, at only twenty-one years of age. *Hogan's Heroes* star Bob Crane was brutally murdered by a still unknown assailant or assailants on June 29, 1978. Crane's son Robert would later write the sensational book *Crane: Sex, Celebrity, and my Father's Unsolved Murder,* which revealed the actor's addiction to wild and kinky sex. Early leading man Ramon Novarro choked to death on a dildo, which was thrust down his throat by two hustling punks. The dildo had been given to him by Rudolph Valentino, nearly half a century earlier. You couldn't make that one up.[277] Gwili Andre, a Danish actress who'd been dubbed "the highest priced model in America," ended her life in fitting Tinseltown fashion by surrounding herself with publicity stills and other paraphernalia from her brief film career and setting them ablaze, along with herself, in her apartment.[278] Albert Dekker, perhaps best known as the lead in *Dr. Cyclops,* had one of the most tabloid-like deaths imaginable. On May 5, 1968, his naked body was discovered by his fiancée, in a kneeling position in the bathtub, tied and bound, with a horse bit in his mouth, and crude sexual terms written on his body in lipstick. Despite the fact he also had two hypothermic needles inserted into him, and his hands were cuffed, the coroner would laughably rule Dekker's death an "accident."[279] Dekker's sixteen –year-old-son Jan had been found shot to death the previous year, a supposed suicide.

Dr. Haing Somnang Ngor won the 1985 Academy Award for Best Supporting Actor in his debut film, *The Killing Fields.* He was shot and killed outside his Los Angeles Chinatown home, on February 25, 1996, by members of an Asian gang. Forty-nine-year-old Vanessa Marquez, who was a regular on the hit series *ER* during the 1990s, was shot and killed by a police officer performing a welfare check at her residence on August 30, 2018. Marquez had been troubled for quite some time, and had made allegations the previous year about being blacklisted by the show's star George Clooney, after she'd reported being racially and sexually harassed on the set.[280] The actor who played Andy Hardy's father, Lewis Stone, died of a heart attack while chasing a gang of youths who were throwing rocks at his house. Boris Sagal was a well-known director and the father of Katey Sagal, who starred on *Married with Children*, as well as twins Liz and Jean Sagal, who were the stars of the short-lived television series *Double Trouble.* Boris died in as unfathomable a fashion as anyone in the history of Hollywood. While filming the miniseries *World War III,* he somehow accidentally walked into the rotor blades of a helicopter in an Oregon parking lot. The deaths of veteran character actor Albert Salmi and his wife in 1990 were quickly declared to be a murder-suicide. It was never adequately explained why Salmi allegedly used two different weapons, one on his wife and the other on himself.[281] Salmi famously turned down an Academy Award nomination, apparently because his preference for stage work led him to hate working in films. Actress Romy Schneider evidently never recovered from the tragic death of her fourteen-year-old son, who was killed while trying to climb a spiked fence in 1981. Schneider either took her own life a year later, or succumbed to a heart attack, although the circumstances surrounding her death remain unclear. This was largely due to the Paris coroner refusing to order an autopsy. Schneider's daughter was incensed over the 2018 biopic of her mother, *3 Days in Quiberon.* Her complaints seemed to center around the film's allegations that Schneider was a problem drinker.[282] Elvis Presley was said to be so distraught over the death of his *Jailhouse Rock* co-star Judy Tyler in a 1957 car accident, only a few weeks after the film had completed shooting, that he could never bring himself to watch it. The now forgotten Tyler was a rising twenty-four-year-old star. Steve Cochran was a macho womanizer, in real life as well as onscreen. His death was exceedingly weird, even by the standards of the industry. In 1965, Cochran hired an all-female crew to accompany him on a perusal of potential locations for an upcoming film he was producing. His schooner was found drifting near Guatemala, with his frightened crew (one of the girls was only fourteen) and the forty-eight-year-old Cochran's body on board. It was estimated he'd been dead for nearly a week. Cochran's former flame Merle Oberon attempted unsuccessfully to push the authorities to further investigate the very strange circumstances. It would be officially determined that Cochran died of a lung infection, which somehow caused paralysis.[283]

Henry Fonda's onscreen image belied the reality of a personal life littered with too many unnatural deaths. To quote the great, late Dave McGowan: "We can begin, I suppose, by noting that Hank served as a decorated US Naval Intelligence officer during World War II, thus sparing Peter the stigma of being the only member of the Laurel Canyon in-crowd to have not been spawned by a member of the military/intelligence community. Not too many years after the war, Hank's wife, Francis Ford Seymour, was found with her throat slashed open with a straight razor. Peter was just ten-years-old at the time of his mother's, *uhmm*, suicide on April 14, 1950. When Seymour had met and married Hank, she was the widow of George Brokaw, who had, curiously enough, previously been married to prominent CIA asset Claire Booth Luce.....I should probably mention that Hank's first wife, Margaret Sullavan – who was yet another child of Norfolk, Virginia – also allegedly committed suicide, on New Year's Day, 1960." Nine months later, her daughter Bridget followed suit.[284] McGowan continued, "Frank Sinatra was also a client of hairdresser-to-the-stars Jay Sebring, as was Henry Fonda, who also at one time, strangely enough, lived in the guesthouse at 10050 Cielo Drive." Sebring was one of the victims of the Manson gang murders that took the life of actress Sharon Tate, in her 10050 Cielo Drive home.[285]

The death of Phil Hartman has always mystified me. Something about it just never seemed quite "right." In fact, it was through an online search for information about his death that I first came upon the fascinating work of Dave McGowan. McGowan wrote the following about the death of Phil Hartman: "As everyone likely remembers, *Saturday Night Live* alumnus Hartman was murdered in his Encino home on May 28, 1998. That much is not in dispute. Decidedly less clear is the answer to the question of who it was that actually shot and killed Hartman. The official story, of course, holds that it was his wife Brynn, who shortly thereafter shot herself – with a different gun, naturally, and reportedly after she had left the house and then returned with a friend, and *after* the LAPD had arrived at the home. There is a very strong possibility, however, that both Phil and his wife were murdered, with the true motive for the crime covered up by trotting out the tired but ever-popular murder/suicide scenario."[286] According to the official narrative, Brynn went to a friend's house after shooting Hartman in his sleep, and confessed. He didn't believe her, and they returned to the scene of the crime. When he realized she was telling the truth, he called 911. Once the police arrived, they attended to the Hartmans' understandably hysterical young son. But they inexplicably left the confessed murderer free to walk back into the bedroom where her husband's body lay, and shoot herself. Why wouldn't they have immediately handcuffed her? According to a poster on the alternet forums, actor Steve Guttenberg more than once in interviews pleaded with the public not to inquire into what had actually happened to his friend Phil Hartman. Joe Rogan spoke on his podcast about the lawsuit against Pfizer, makers of the dangerous drug Zoloft, which Brynn Hartman was taking at the time of the tragedy, which apparently led to their children receiving a financial settlement. Supposedly Hartman's *Saturday Night Live* compatriot Jon Lovitz was incensed at unstable actor Andy Dick, whom he blamed for re-introducing cocaine to Hartman's wife. Hartman left behind a very modest estate of $1.2 million.

1980 Playmate of the Year Dorothy Stratten was murdered by her abusive, psychotic husband Paul Snider on August 14, 1980. Snider killed himself, too, but only after having sex with his wife's corpse. Stratten was just twenty, and had been having an affair with director

Peter Bogdanovich at the time. In a perverse footnote, Bogdanovich would marry Dorothy's younger sister Louise four years later, after paying for her private education and modeling classes.[287] Actor Vic Morrow was the victim in perhaps the most celebrated death on a movie set, as he was decapitated by a burning helicopter during filming of John Landis' *Twilight Zone: The Movie* on July 23, 1982. Two young children died in the incident as well. Landis and others were acquitted of involuntary manslaughter charges, although the parents of the children and Morrow's children received an undisclosed settlement. Alan J. Pakula, director of the conspiracy-tinged 1974 film *The Parallax View* and many others, died in a bizarre car accident on November 19, 1998, when a driver in front of him on the Long Island Expressway struck a metal pipe, which flew back through Pakula's windshield and struck him, causing him to swerve off the road and be killed instantly. Bob Clark, director of the 1983 holiday favorite *A Christmas Story,* was killed along with his twenty-two-year-old son when a vehicle being driven by a drunk illegal immigrant crossed the median and struck his car, on April 4, 2007.

Busty blonde Carol Wayne, perhaps best remembered for her regular appearances as Johnny Carson's ditzy foil on *The Tonight Show,* drowned under very mysterious circumstances on January 13, 1985.[288] Ironically, she'd once quipped that, "With this chest, this lady will never drown." While on vacation in Mexico, Carol and her male friend, Edward Durston, supposedly had a quarrel, which led to her going for a walk on the beach. Durston would subsequently leave Mexico without Carol. Two days later her body was discovered by fishermen in the water. Her death was ruled "accidental." Mexican authorities were understandably puzzled by how Carol could have drowned in water only four feet deep, fully clothed. There were no abrasions or other signs of trauma on her body, casting doubt on any accidental fall theory. She also tested negative for drugs and alcohol. Carol's ex-husband Barry Feinstein, a well-known photographer, arrived on the scene to claim the body and collected on a double indemnity insurance policy. Carol's sister Nina Wayne, who was once married into the Barrymore family, protested that she had no say in the matter. Nina's daughter Jessica Barrymore, half-sister to Drew, was found dead in her car, surrounded by pills, just before her forty-eighth birthday on July 29, 2014. I exchanged a few emails with John Blyth Barrymore, son of John Drew Barrymore and also half-brother to actress Drew Barrymore. I hoped he might be able to shed some family insight on the very suspicious death of Carol Wayne. "I didn't know much about Carol's death beyond the obvious; 'accidental drowning' of an expert swimmer and rumors that she was involved with some cartel guy down there and couldn't keep her mouth shut," Barrymore told me in a November 1, 2018 email. Barrymore had gone homeless in 2012, and qualified for food stamps. During this period, he became fond of wearing a shirt that read, "I'm Drew Barrymore's brother." After his sister Jessica Barrymore was found dead in her vehicle, John had publicly lashed out at Drew for turning her back on both of her less successful half-siblings. He suggested I contact some of his relatives, specifically advising that "Dorothy Steinbeck should not only know how to reach them, she can probably fill you in on Carol's death. Dorothy was the person Jessica adopted as a surrogate mother because Nina wasn't exactly the most maternal woman on the planet." I asked him to give Dorothy my email, but I never heard back from either of them.

An online article on tvparty.com alleged that "In 1984, a thin, pale Carol Wayne declared bankruptcy due in large part to a cocaine and alcohol problem. It was said the entertainer was reduced to being an occasional escort for wealthy businessmen in order to make a living." In contradiction to John Blythe Barrymore's contention to me that Carol was an "expert swimmer," most accounts of the incident reported that she didn't know how to swim. This article quoted U.S. Consular William LaCoque as saying in 1990 that "Carol Wayne's death is unsolved, certainly, but I don't think it was a drowning. A drowning, yes, of course, but there is much more to it than that." Incredibly, Edward Durston had also been at the scene of an earlier strange death, that of Diane Linkletter, daughter of famed television personality Art Linkletter, on October 4, 1969. After baking cookies together that morning, Durston claimed that a "despondent and depressed" Diane suddenly walked into the kitchen and jumped out of the window. Remarkably, Durston was not named as a suspect in either case. Other than the fact he died in 2007, there is virtually no further information about Durston on the internet. Art Linkletter would publicly castigate the drug culture and blame his daughter's death on LSD. The problem with that theory is that an autopsy on Diane revealed no presence of alcohol or drugs.[289] Durston was also friends with Abigail Folger, another one of the victims of the Manson-Tate murders, and was rumored to be a well-known drug dealer in Hollywood. Mary Jennifer Selznick, daughter of actress Jennifer Jones and film mogul David O. Selznick, died similarly, plunging to her death from a twentieth-floor Los Angeles window at just twenty-two-years-old.

Walter Scott, lead singer for Bob Kuban and The In-Men, who struck it big with the 1966 song *The Cheater*, died under industry-standard unnatural circumstances. Scott simply vanished on December 27, 1983. It wasn't until four years later that his decomposed body, hog-tied and shot in the back, was found floating in a small reservoir. Evidently, Scott's wife had been, with incalculable irony, cheating on him with one James Williams, who went on to murder both Scott and his own wife, Sharon Williams.[290] The circumstances of Grace Kelly's death remain questionable as well. Did the fifty-two-year-old actress, still in marvelous shape, really suffer an unlikely stroke while driving her car in Monaco, which resulted in her death the following day, on November 14, 1982? Or was her young daughter Stephanie, who emerged from the crash with no serious injuries, actually at the wheel? Twenty years later, a frustrated Stephanie would break her silence and deny all the rumors that she'd been behind the wheel, even though she was too young to be legally driving.[291] The inevitable conspiracy theories emerged, suggesting that Grace had been murdered, but her husband Prince Rainier dismissed them as "tabloid fodder."

John Belushi's tragically early death has always left many questions in my mind. I have tried to follow up, without success, on what appears to have been his keen interest in the JFK assassination. I became intrigued by Dan Aykroyd's comment in *Live From New York: The Complete, Uncensored History of Saturday Night Live,* that "He counted among his friends Lauren Bacall and Judge Jim Garrison, and he was a student of American politics." There would seemingly be no other logical reason for the actor to be friends with the much older former New Orleans district attorney whose name was so intertwined with the Kennedy assassination. Cathy Evelyn Smith (a thirty-three-year-old backup singer for Gordon Lightfoot, and also connected to the similarly ill-fated Gene Clark) certainly appeared to be guilty of *something* in relation to Belushi's sudden death, supposedly from a massive amount of drugs, on March 5, 1982, but she served only fifteen months in prison for injecting Belushi with what was referred to as a "speedball." Afterwards, the familiar mantra of an out-of-control drug addict, spinning inexorably towards an early death, was cemented in the public mind by an endless series of news reports. Dissatisfied with the official findings regarding his death, Belushi's widow Judy Jacklin hired famed Watergate reporter Bob Woodward to investigate the case. Eventually, Woodward would write the controversial book *Wired: The Short Life and Fast Times of John Belushi* in 1984. The thirty-three-year-old Belushi had, interestingly enough, purchased a home in Martha's Vineyard recently, from none other than Robert McNamara, JFK's Secretary of Defense who would later be instrumental in LBJ's disastrous buildup of U.S. forces in Vietnam. I asked one of my Facebook friends, Judith Dagley Flaherty, ex-wife of *SCTV* star Joe Flaherty, if she'd broach the subject of the JFK assassination to Belushi's widow, who she is friends with. In an October 21, 2013 personal message on Facebook, Flaherty told me, "Judy did not have anything to offer (or that she chose to offer, who knows) when I asked on your behalf quite awhile ago."

One truly inexplicable death was that of twelve-year-old Heather O'Rourke, still remembered for uttering the eerie line, "They're *here*," utilized to great effect in promoting the *Poltergeist* movies, all three of which she starred in. The child actress died on the operating table, officially from an undetected bowel obstruction, complicated by septic shock, which had been initially misdiagnosed as Crohn's disease. Subsequent reports mentioned cardiac arrest, brought on by intestinal stenosis. Later in the same year, following her daughter's February 1, 1988 death, Heather's mother Kathleen O'Rourke Peele filed a lawsuit against the Kaiser Foundation Hospital and the Southern California Permanente Medical Group.[292] The case eventually was settled out of court. Several doctors expressed their astonishment. "I would have expected a lot of (digestive) difficulties throughout her life and not just to have developed a problem all of a sudden," said Dr. Daniel Hollander, head of gastroenterology at University of California, Irvine, Medical Center. Southern California pediatrician Dr. Carlo DiLorenzo declared, "I cannot understand what precipitated the death because it's usually clear when they're born they have an important disease." According to USC gastroenterologist Dr. Hartley Cohen, "It just doesn't seem to quite make sense." O'Rourke's manager and lawyer Mike Meyer stated, "It's weird. She was completely healthy Saturday, they thought she had the flu on Sunday and she was dead on Monday."[293] Some in the conspiracy world have postulated that O'Rourke was in fact a victim of powerful pedophiles, and her death was sexually related. O'Rourke's *Poltergeist* co-star, Dominque Dunne, was attacked by her crazed boyfriend John Thomas Sweeney, and her family removed her from life support on November 4, 1982, just before her twenty-third birthday. The jury's controversial verdict resulted in her murderer receiving only a six-year prison sentence. After serving less than four years, Sweeney became the head chef at a trendy Santa Monica restaurant.[294] A lesser known child actress, Judith Barsi, was earning more than $100,000 annually by the age of seven, primarily through her extensive work in commercials, and as a voice actor in hit films like *All Dogs Go to Heaven* and *The Land Before Time*. In a surprisingly under reported tragedy, she was shot and killed by her alcoholic father, who also killed her mother and then himself, on July 25, 1988. She was barely ten years old.

Hollywood has always lived by different rules. When Anthony Perkins married Berinthia "Berry" Berenson on Cape Cod in 1973, his pet collie, Murray served as best man. Berenson would later become one of the more notable victims of 9/11, as a passenger on board American Airlines Flight 11. Silent film character actress Margaret Campbell died about as tragically as one can: she was bludgeoned to death by her own son at age fifty-six. People remember Phil Spector, the legendary record producer who was convicted of murder, but the victim, forty-year- old actress Lana Clarkson, remains anonymous. Barbara Colby was a busy television actress in the 1970s, appearing on numerous programs like *The Mary Tyler Moore Show*. On July 24, 1975, she was shot and killed at just thirty-six-years of age, along with fellow actor James Kiernan, as they walked through a Los Angeles parking lot. There was no robbery or any other apparent motive. Karyn Kupcinet had a very brief acting career in the early Sixties. Her naked body was discovered by future *Lost in Space* actor Mark Goddard and his wife only days after the assassination of President Kennedy. Some researchers have claimed that Karyn had tried to warn of the impending assassination in a distraught phone call. Plentiful drugs were found in Karyn's apartment, along with what could reasonably be interpreted as a suicide note. The problem was, she'd been strangled, and thus her death was officially ruled a homicide. Despite the evidence of strangulation, renowned crime writer James Ellroy would nonsensically speculate that her death had been accidental, in his book *Crime Wave.*

Crooner Russ Columbo was accidentally shot and killed by his longtime friend, Lansing Brown, on September 2, 1934, at just twenty-six. Brown provided a suitable Tinseltown-style explanation, claiming that he had lit a match too near an old-fashioned dueling pistol, causing it to discharge. Columbo was a child prodigy as a musician and an accomplished songwriter, as well, and at the time of his death was linked romantically to actress Carole Lombard. Jane Dornacker was a postal worker who transitioned to show business with a role in 1984's *The Right Stuff,* and as a member of the bands The Tubes and Leila and the Snakes. She also was a traffic reporter for radio stations in San Francisco and New York, and died in a helicopter crash at just thirty-nine while doing a traffic report in New York City. Jeffrey Hunter starred as Jesus Christ in *King of Kings* and appeared in many other films and television shows. He died at just forty-two, from either the effects of a stroke or from hitting his head during a fall from a short flight of steps, depending upon the source. In yet another of the endless ironic deaths in the history of show business, director, writer and producer Kenneth Hawks, brother of legendary director Howard Hawks, was killed in a plane crash along with nine others on January 2, 1930, while filming the aerial scenes for *Such Men are Dangerous.* He was married to up and coming actress Mary Astor and was just thirty-one.

High profile Hollywood publicist Ronni Chasen, who worked with numerous A-list stars, was shot and killed in her car on November 16, 2010 in Beverly Hills. There are numerous questions left unanswered about her death, as is the case all too often in the entertainment world. Documentary filmmaker Ryan Katzenbach was one of the few seeking answers to these questions. There appeared to be no rationale for the murder; her life was squeaky clean and nothing was stolen from her. The police eventually settled on a random act of violence committed by one Harold Smith, who went on to shoot himself in the head when authorities attempted to question him. Katzenbach tried in vain to obtain the surveillance video of Smith's alleged suicide, which took place in the lobby of his apartment building, but it was curiously being withheld. Just one of the many inexplicable mysteries here is how Chasen continued to drive after being shot. "This woman who had a shattered humorous bone here and was losing massive blood through artery supply and had another bullet that ended up in her bicep here, turned a car and drove a quarter of a mile down the street before losing control," stated Katzenbach. A local news station received the following comment from the Beverly Hills Police Department: "At this point we are not releasing the crime report. We are in the process of reviewing the requests that we have received and will be making a decision soon as to release of information. I will keep you updated as to the progress of your request." This statement came *five years* after the murder of Chasen.[295]

Forgotten actress Rhea Mitchell, who appeared in over 100 films during her long career, was strangled by a disgruntled tenant and possible lover, on September 16, 1957. Forty-year-old Adrienne Shelly's body was found hanging in her shower on November 1, 2006. Eventually, an illegal immigrant from Ecuador confessed to murdering her and staging it as a suicide, and received a surprisingly light twenty-five-year sentence. Shelly had starred in, written and directed some well-received independent films, including *Waitress*, which was released after her death and won five awards. Young Sixties actress Katherine Walsh, who appeared in several films and television shows, including her last role, in Jack Nicholson's 1967 film *The Trip*, was found dead in her London flat on October 7, 1970. There is curiously little information about her unnatural death at age twenty-three. She lived in an expensive area, which should seemingly have protected her from the threat of random crime. Her death was ruled a homicide, but to quote Wikipedia: "no details have ever been known to be released, and the case remains unsolved." Sandra Edwards, who appeared in several episodes of various television series in the 1960s, shot and killed her estranged husband and fellow Sixties actor Tom Gilson on October 6, 1962. It was ruled justifiable homicide, but the incident ended her acting career. Silent and early talkie star Madge Bellamy fired three shots at her lumber tycoon lover in 1942. The tycoon was unharmed, and Bellamy received the typical light celebrity sentence.

Dick Kallam, best remembered for playing the title character in the short-lived 1965-66 television series *Hank,* was shot and killed on February 22, 1980 during a robbery at his New York apartment. In a truly mind-boggling coincidence, two different eighty-eight-year-old actors, Charles Waggenheim and Victor Kilian, were beaten to death in separate March, 1979 robberies, only five days apart. What made it incomprehensibly eerie was that both elderly men had just appeared in the same *All in the Family* episode. Rob Knox, who played the role of Marcus Belby in *Harry Potter and the Half-Blood Prince,* was stabbed to death outside a London bar on May 24, 2008, at only eighteen years of age. Veteran English actor George Rose was beaten to death by his adopted son and three others, including the boy's biological father. He was buried in an unmarked grave in the Dominican Republic. Nick Adams, best known for playing the lead character in the short-lived series *The Rebel,* was found dead of a supposed suicide on February 7, 1968, but according to author David Kulcyzk, Adams was murdered because he was writing a titillating expose about the sexual secrets of Hollywood. Adams may have taken his best-known role on screen to heart; his son was named Jeb Stuart. Actor Forrest Tucker is supposed to have declared, "All of Hollywood knows Nick Adams was knocked off." According to author David McGowan, "Nick's relatives reportedly received numerous hang-up calls on the day of his death, and his tape recorder, journals and various other papers and personal effects were conspicuously missing from his home."[296] His lifeless body, sitting upright in a chair, was discovered by his attorney, Ervin 'Tip'

Roeder. On June 10, 1981, Roeder and his wife, actress Jenny Maxwell, who appeared in plenty of films and television series during her short life, but is probably best remembered for being spanked by Elvis Presley in the 1961 movie *Blue Hawaii*, were shot and killed in the lobby of their Beverly Hills condo, during a supposed robbery. Barry Sadler, remembered for his 1966 hit record *Ballad of the Green Berets,* was shot in the head in Guatemala City while sitting in a cab. It was never determined whether Sadler somehow shot himself accidentally, or was the victim of an assassin. Flown back to the United States on a private jet owned by *Soldier of Fortune* magazine publisher Bob Brown, Sadler lingered for nearly a year, during which his family reported him being missing at one point, prior to a contentious court battle regarding his competency, before dying at age forty-nine.[297] Eleven years earlier, in 1978, Sadler had been convicted of shooting and killing a country music songwriter, and was sentenced to an incredibly lenient thirty days in the county workhouse.[298]

Clarine Seymour, a rising young silent screen star, died at only twenty-one on April 25, 1920 of "strangulation of the intestines." She had just signed a four year, two million dollar contract. James Murray, so memorable as the lead in King Vidor's bleak and powerful 1928 classic *The Crowd,* didn't handle stardom well and was relegated to panhandling only a few years later (one of those he begged, ironically, was Vidor). On July 11, 1936, at only thirty-five, he either jumped or fell into the Hudson River. Well known silent actor Max Linder talked his wife into a suicide pact in 1925. He was only forty-two. British actress Patricia Cutts, perhaps best remembered for her role in one of William Castle's schlocky horror films, 1959's *The Tingler,* took her own life at forty-eight. In November, 1958, she'd probably been a beneficiary of the last vestiges of Hollywood's studio protection system; after being arrested for a hit and run accident, the charges were subsequently dismissed when the other driver suddenly couldn't remember seeing or talking to her.

The story of silent screen star Wallace Reid's early death by over-dose is well known, but few recall the popular actress he was hav-ing an affair with, Evelyn Nelson. Nelson followed Reid's untimely death by killing herself at only twenty-three years of age, leaving two suicide notes behind, one of which mentioned her desire to "be with my friend Wally." Another silent star, Mack Sennett Bathing Beauty Marvel Rea, killed herself at only thirty-seven by swallowing ant paste. John Bowers was a popular leading man in the early silent films. Like many, he didn't transition successfully to sound pictures. On November 17, 1936, Bowers rented a sail boat and traveled to the island where his old friend, director Henry Hathaway, was making a film featuring Gary Cooper. Bowers hoped to land some kind of part in the picture, but after evidently being rejected, legend holds that he simply walked into the ocean and ended his life. The fifty-year old actor's body eventually washed up on the Santa Mon-ica shore.

Those who don't actually kill themselves often drink themselves to death in the entertainment industry. Peggie Castle was a tall, sul-try blonde who was seen regularly on the big screen in the 1950s. After at least one unsuccessful suicide attempt, she died from cir-rhosis of the liver at only forty-five years of age. Her then boyfriend, the similarly ill-fated war hero turned movie star Audie Murphy, had been instrumental in getting her into the business.[299] Legend-ary singer Billie Holliday drank herself to an early death at just for-ty-four. Whether or not the legend that she had only *70 cents* in the bank when she died (sometimes embellished with $750 taped to her leg) is true, she is known to have left behind a pathetic estate of $1,000.[300] The Great Profile, John Barrymore, was fortunate to make it to sixty considering his hard drinking lifestyle. Actor and director John Cassavettes died at only fifty-nine from cirrhosis of the liver. Urbane actor Tom Conway's heavy drinking caused his brother George Sanders to break off all contact with him and to leave him in financial straits. Conway died at only sixty-two from his alcoholism, and brother George took his own life five years later. Actress and singer Cass Daley died in bizarre fashion, by falling onto a glass coffee table, probably while drunk. Rock impresario Alan Freed died from cirrhosis of the liver at only forty-three. Tommy James, in his memoir *Me, The Mob, and the Music,* claimed that Freed was "near penniless" at the time of his death, his drinking exacerbated by his involvement in the payola scandals.[301] Clyde McPhatter of the Drifters struggled with alcoholism and died at just thirty-nine; as Jay Warner described it in his book *On This Day in Music History,* "broke and despondent over a mismanaged career that made him a legend but hardly a success."[302] Danny Rapp, front man for Danny & the Juniors, best remembered for their 1958 hit *At the Hop,* shot himself just short of his forty-second birthday, after a round of heavy drinking. Forgotten actor Wendell Corey died at only fifty-four from heavy drinking. Abigail Adams was a struggling actress, with mostly uncredited roles on her resume. She was married very briefly to Lyle Talbot, who had a long, robust career as an actor, and had a stormy relationship with George Jessel. A well-known party girl, Adams was found dead from the effects of alcohol and barbiturates in her low-rent apartment on the Sunset Strip, at just thirty-three. Luana Walters was a very pretty B-movie actress who is probably best remembered for her leading role in one of Bela Lugosi's Poverty Row features, *The Corpse Vanishes.* She died at only fifty from her heavy drinking. Walters apparently never recovered from the sudden death of her only husband, bit role actor Max Hoffman, Jr., whom she found collapsed in his New York hotel room. Hoffman, Jr. died a few hours later at just forty-two from unknown causes.

Edward Furlong was a busy actor, in big films like *Terminator 2* and *American History X.* Thanks to years of heaving drinking and drug abuse, Furlong currently has a net worth of only $100,000. Humphrey Bogart was a high functioning alcoholic whose death at fifty-seven was certainly acerbated by his chain smoking and nonstop drinking. Bogie once quipped that he'd spent "the worst afternoon of my life" in that one brief time he went off the wagon. It was actually Bogart who started the first edition of the Rat Pack, but his cohort Frank Sinatra loved his alcohol, too. Sinatra spiked Jack Daniels' sales by referring to his favorite liquor brand regularly while on stage. The signal for the beginning of drinking time at Sinatra's Twin Palms compound was the hoisting of a Jack Daniels flag. Robert Mitchum in real life was just what he portrayed onscreen; a hard drinking brawler of a man. He described working with other notable alcoholic actors Frank Sinatra, Broderick Crawford, and Lee Marvin on 1955's *Not as a Stranger* as "not so much a cast as it was a brewery." During the wild parties at night, the cast regularly trashed their hotel rooms, and on one notable occasion Crawford was thrown off a hotel balcony. Ann-Margret (born Ann-Margret Olsson) became such an alcoholic that she admitted to being incapable of "separating fantasy from reality."[303] She would confess in her autobiography that, "I'd drink a fifth of scotch, pass out, wake up, drink some more, and pass out again." Montgomery Clift's legendary drinking was colorfully described by his acting coach as "the longest suicide in Hollywood history."[304] Clift nearly ruined his career after crashing his car and suffering serious facial injuries. Marilyn Monroe said that Clift was "the only person I know who is in even worse shape than I am." Clift's death at just forty-five was long anticipated in the film colony, and clearly was a result of his chronic alcohol and drug usage. Tallulah Bankhead loved the drunken sophisticates (Dorothy Parker, Robert Benchley, George S. Kauffman and the like) that formed the legendary Algonquin Roundtable so much that she moved into the Algonquin Hotel. Her alcohol-inspired behavior became so notorious that hotel owner Frank Case declared, "I can either run this hotel or look after Tallulah Bankhead. I can't do both."[305] She drank so much it enlarged her head, causing her hats to fall off. It was amazing she lived to be sixty-six, as she spent her last years consuming more than a quart of bourbon each day, and combined that with a slew of legal and illegal pills and a generous share of cocaine. Her last words were reportedly, "Codeine. Bourbon."

The marvelously talented musician Bix Biederbecke died at only twenty-eight, largely from his excessive drinking. A similar musical prodigy, trumpeter Bunny Berigan, met an identical tragic end, dying at only thirty-three because of drinking. John Bonham, Led Zeppelin's drummer, made it only to thirty-two because of his inebriated lifestyle. Richard Burton's death at fifty-eight could be largely attributed to his chronic alcoholism. Legend has it that when he died, Burton's spine was discovered to be coated with crystalized alcohol from top to bottom. W.C. Fields, as associated with heavy drinking as much any entertainer in history, was fortunate to live to be sixty-six years of age. One of Fields' many memorable quips was, "I have never imbibed while sleeping, and I drink nothing stronger than gin before breakfast."[306] Errol Flynn's nonstop partying left him looking old and haggard far beyond his years when he died at just fifty. Flynn's Malibu bachelor pad, which he shared with actor David Niven, was charmingly nicknamed "Cirrhosis-By-The-Sea." Clyde Bruckman was a writer and director who worked with some of the industry's all-time greats, including Buster Keaton, W.C. Fields, Laurel and Hardy, and the Three Stooges. After he resold some gags he'd originally written for Harold Lloyd, the multi-millionaire Lloyd sued Universal and was awarded more millions in damages, causing Bruckman's alcoholism to grow more severe. He became a pathetic figure in Hollywood, seen stumbling around the streets with a bottle protruding from his pocket. In 1955, he borrowed Keaton's pistol, left a note to his wife thoughtfully explaining that he didn't want to mess up the living room, and blew his brains out in a pay phone booth. Bruckman once waxed nostalgic about his salad days, stating, "I often wish that I were back there with Buster and the gang, in *that* Hollywood."[307] Jean Hagen was never happy playing Danny Thomas's wife on the television series *Make*

Room for Daddy, even though she had a sweeter deal than most of those appearing in 1950s-era television, with a contract giving her seven percent of the show's profits.[308] Hagen supposedly caused discord within the cast, and her character was killed off after three seasons. Sherry Jackson, who played the oldest daughter on the sit-com, seemed to counter this, when she told an interviewer that "She was my only friend from the 'Make Room for Daddy' cast." Hagen's personal life unraveled thereafter, due largely to her serious drinking problem, and she died at only fifty-four.

One of the Big Band era's most popular singers, Dick Haymes, would later admit, "By the early Sixties I was a desperate alcoholic. I had been forced into bankruptcy with a half million dollars in debts and no assets."[309] According to the Associated Press, there were "no friends or relatives at his side" when Haymes died at only sixty-one in 1980. This was especially sad considering Haymes, who also acted in a number of films, had six children by his six wives. Singer Johnnie Ray not only has unfairly drifted into historical obscurity, he inexplicably started down this road at the height of his fame. Ray's unique, histrionic style was all the rage just prior to the advent of rock and roll, with 1952's hit single *Cry* and later, in 1958, with *Just Walkin' in the Rain.* Ray's alcoholism was exacerbated by his strange career plunge; for no obvious reason, his music was unavailable for sale, and he didn't appear on American television, during the first half of the 1960s. Ray only made one motion picture. When later questioned about this, Ray simply responded, "I was never asked." Ringo Starr was quoted in a May 22, 1981 story in *The New York Times* as admitting that the three singers the Beatles listened to the most in their early days were Chuck Berry, Little Richard, and Johnnie Ray. In that same story, it was noted, "The fact that Mr. Ray, in the years since his first blush of success, has been seen and heard so infrequently in the United States is somewhat ironic because it was his rhythm and blues style of singing that help lay the groundwork for the rock-and-roll that turned Mr. Ray's entertainment world around." Tony Bennett would call Ray "the father of rock and roll." The original drummer of the Byrds, Michael Clarke, died at just forty-seven due to decades of heavy drinking. Another shocking slide to obscurity precipitated largely by alcoholism concerned actor, screenwriter and director King Baggot. Baggot has a star on the Hollywood Walk of Fame, but his name is completely unknown to most these days. He was so big in silent films that he's often given credit for being the first individually publicized leading man. After drinking derailed his career, Baggot actually wound up working as a background extra.[310] Art Acord was another popular silent film star who couldn't make the transition to sound, thanks largely to heavy drinking. Acord was forced into mining and rodeo work, and died mysteriously at just forty in Mexico, allegedly from suicide.[311] However, some believed he was murdered because of his affair with a powerful Mexican politician's wife.

Songwriter Lorenz Hart died from the effects of alcoholism at only forty-eight. Actor William Holden drank himself to death at sixty-three, when he fell while drunk and hit his head on a table, evoking memories of songwriter Stephen Foster's unusual exit from this world over a hundred years previously. His body wasn't found until four days later.[312] No funeral or memorial service was held, according to his wishes. Holden had previously killed another motorist while driving drunk. British actor Oliver Reed's persistent urge to prove himself was fueled by enormous amounts of alcohol, leading to his death at sixty-one. Singer Amy Winehouse died of alcohol poisoning at just twenty-seven. Legendary country music songwriter and performer Hank Williams drank himself to death at the tender age of twenty-nine. Elizabeth Pena, best known for films like *La Bamba,* died from cirrhosis of the liver at only fifty-five. Whitney Houston drowned in a bathtub at just forty-nine because of excessive alcohol and drug consumption. *Glee* star Corey Monteith died at thirty-one, from a heroin and alcohol overdose. Comedian Chris Farley's death at thirty-two was almost entirely precipitated by alcohol and drug consumption. Former teen phenomenon and *The Partridge Family* star David Cassidy struggled with alcoholism for much of his adult life, resulting in several DWI arrests. He filed for bankruptcy in 2015, and his waterfront home was sold in a foreclosure auction on September 9 that year, the same day he was involved in a hit and run accident that resulted in a number of criminal charges.[313] His arthritis was so bad he could barely play the guitar near the end of his life, and then he announced that he could no longer perform due to the early onset of dementia. On March 18, 2016, *Radar Online* reported that Cassidy was claiming to have only $478 in the bank. Cassidy certainly had a lot of bad luck and seemed plagued by more physical maladies than most sixty-seven year olds, when he died of multiple organ failure on November 21, 2017. The former teen heartthrob left behind an estate originally reported to be just $500,000.[314] However, nearly a year later, stories broke that his only son had received the bulk of Cassidy's estate, at "upwards of $1.68 million."[315] David's father, actor Jack Cassidy, had died at only forty-nine in a house fire. In another of those endless Hollywood intertwined connections, Jack Cassidy was married for eighteen years to Shirley Jones, the actress who played David's mother on *The Partridge Family*. Jack Cassidy was known to be irrationally jealous of his son's success. He apparently physically and emotionally abused David, and left him out of his will. Stepmother Shirley Jones noted, "When David was nine or so, I'd often see him crying in the corner because of something Jack had said or done to him."[316]

Some deaths in show business are just weird beyond belief. Redd Foxx's most famous line on *Sanford and Son* was "This is the big one," referring to a heart attack, and when he collapsed during rehearsals on a television set from a real one, everyone naturally assumed it was just part of the act.[317] Dick Shawn went out the same way - dropping dead from a heart attack during a live show, leaving the audience thinking it was just an elaborate joke. Nelson Eddy suffered a stroke while performing on stage, and died the following day. Singer Jackie Wilson collapsed on stage from a stroke and never regained consciousness, although he didn't die until eight years later. At the time of his death, there was a court case pending alleging that Wilson had been defrauded of at least $1 million in royalties. *Rawhide* star Eric Fleming drowned in the Amazon while filming a movie. John Glasscock, a member of the band Jethro Tull, died from a heart infection caused by an abscessed tooth. Character actor Butterfly McQueen died from burns received while lighting a kerosene heater in her apartment. Beach Boy Dennis Wilson, ironically the only true surfer in the band, drowned after diving off his yacht. Wilson had been a heavy drug user and drinker for years, and almost certainly wasn't sober at the time. At the time of his death, Wilson was said to be homeless and effectively estranged from the other members of the band, telling an interviewer that if "there wasn't the Beach Boys and there wasn't music, I would not even talk to them."[318] Director F.W. Murnau was killed in a car crash, while being given a blow job by a fourteen-year-old Filipino boy, according to legend. Tommy Dorsey choked to death in his sleep after eating a heavy meal. Singer and bandleader Skinnay Ennis choked to death while eating at a Hollywood restaurant. Ennis got his start singing with Hal Kemp's orchestra. Kemp himself died at only thirty-six from the aftereffects of a car accident. Comedian Sam Kinison, a loud critic of religion, died strangely in a car crash at only thirty-eight. He appeared relatively uninjured after exiting his car, and then lay down, while witnesses reported he engaged someone or something unseen, in a soft, peaceful conversation. Another truly cutting-edge comedian, Bill Hicks, died suspiciously young (at only thirty-two) of pancreatic cancer which had already spread to his liver when it was diagnosed. Hicks is the only high-profile comedian I know of that made criticism of the Warren Report (as well as similar subjects like the official narrative about Waco) part of his standup act. Fellow stand-up comic Denis Leary stole much of Hicks' act, which resulted in an end to their friendship.[319] Coincidentally or not, one part of Hicks' routine that Leary didn't pilfer was the persistent references to the JFK assassination. He also didn't die of cancer at an incredibly young age, and continues to pile up the credits on IMDb. Hicks has become a cultural icon in the conspiracy world, where a significant number of devoted fans believe that he faked his death and actually became talk show host Alex Jones.

The October 2, 2017 death of rock icon Tom Petty really shook me. Petty was a key component of the soundtrack of my youth, and always fueled memories of when I first met my wife Jeanne, who introduced me to his music. As is usually the case with me, I immediately began investigating reports of Petty's death, which happened very suddenly, at just sixty-six years of age. Sometimes I feel like W.C. Fields, who is rumored to have been discovered reading the Bible near the end of his life, despite being a noted nonbeliever. Fields allegedly responded to the shock this elicited by proclaiming, "Just looking for loopholes." That's what I seem to be doing in much of my research; looking for loopholes. At any rate, there were certainly odd elements here. For one thing, the death was announced prematurely several times, and then retracted, resulting in an angry social media post from Petty's daughter. Despite an autopsy, on October 4, the Los Angeles coroner's office stated that the cause of death remained to be determined, and an investigation was ongoing. A few days later, *TMZ* and other outlets would report that the cause of death had been "deferred," subject to extensive additional testing. Finally, in January, 2018, a report from the medical examiner was released, which found that Tom Petty had died of an accidental overdose of multiple medications. Most of these medications were for pain, as Petty was suffering from a fractured hip, as well as emphysema and coronary disease.[320]

On January 15, 2018, Dolores O'Riordan, lead singer of the Irish rock band the Cranberries, died very suddenly at only forty-six. O'Riordan was reportedly found unresponsive in her London hotel room, but the Metropolitan police quickly determined that her death was "non-suspicious." A few days later, stories broke that, for unclear reasons, the coroner's office was awaiting the results of the autopsy, and a hearing had been set for April 3, to rule on when to release the findings.[321] Adding to the intrigue, as April 3rd neared, it was announced that the inquest into her death had been "removed from the schedule," with no new inquest date set. It wasn't until September 2018 that it was reported O'Riordan had died from accidental drowning in a bathtub, while having a deadly blood alcohol content of 0.33%. [322] Actress Lisa Sheridan, a star of the television series *Halt and Catch Fire,* was found dead in her New Orleans apartment on February 25, 2019. The cause of death for the forty-four-year-old was not immediately announced, but her family stated that it was not a suicide. Sheridan had also starred in an intriguing show I regularly watched, *Invasion,* which was cancelled after a single season. "I am devastated by this loss. I had just spoken with her and everything seemed great and she seemed happy and in good spirits," said actress and friend Donna D'Errico. "We are waiting on a coroner's report on cause of death," Sheridan's manager Mitch Clem stated. In early May, 2019, it was disclosed that Sheridan died from "complications of chronic alcoholism," although somehow this was labeled as "natural." It was also revealed that the still young actress had "hyperinflated lungs," a cyst on one of her ovaries, and had suffered a "remote brain injury" from an unspecified fall. In addition to all this, the troubled Sheridan had a "reported history of benzodiazepine abuse."[323]

Stage and television actor and dancer Jack Burns was found dead in his Scotland home on December 1, 2019, at the tender age of fourteen. As happens all too frequently in show business, no cause of death was initially announced, although police were quick to state that there was no foul play suspected. Rather oddly, Burns' death wasn't announced until ten days later, on December 11. As a December 12, 2019 story on the Pop Culture web site, put it, "*In Plain Sight* actor Jack Burns' death is still shrouded in mystery." *E! News* reported that a Scotland police spokesman told them, "Around 3:30 pm on Sunday, December 1, police were called following the death of a 14 year-old boy to a house in the Esplanade area of Greenock. Inquiries are ongoing to establish the cause of death but police are not treating it as suspicious. A report has been submitted." While many suspected it might have been a suicide, a family representative would attribute the youngster's death to pneumonia in short order. How pneumonia could take the life of a previously healthy fourteen-year-old so suddenly, and why it wasn't initially mentioned, wasn't explained.[324] Later that month, it was disclosed that young Burns, who was referred to without elaboration as having been bullied, hanged himself. One Facebook friend did note that Burns "did not deserve the stuff he went through," presumably referring to bullying.[325]

Unnatural deaths are a tragic tradition in the entertainment world. Few people know that the death of one of the world's greatest composers, Pyotr Tchaikovsky, remains unexplained. His sudden demise at only fifty-three is usually attributed to cholera from drinking un-boiled water. Others have speculated that he committed suicide. Regardless, there should be no mystery surrounding the death of a person of such fame. Or any celebrity, for that matter. How many of us would be satisfied with such unsettled conclusions about the death of any of our loved ones?

The more of these cases I research, the more I think Randy Quaid's "star whackers" theory may have something to it. Murder, suicide, and unexplained deaths are strangely prevalent in show business, and the unwillingness to recognize this is just as strange.

Chapter Four

The Residuals Of Fame

You hear entertainers all the time, saying, 'If I couldn't get paid for this, I'd do it for free.' When's the last time you ever heard a business person say, 'If I couldn't get paid for being chairman of British Petroleum, I'd do it for free'?

Dick Gregory

ROBERT WOOLSEY IS now mostly forgotten, but in the 1920s and 1930s, he was half of the comedy team Wheeler and Woolsey, a top-drawing act for RKO studios. Woolsey's comedic persona revolved around constant wisecracks, delivered behind an exaggerated set of horn-rimmed glasses. He had a style and an appearance that was an amalgamation of Groucho Marx and George Burns. During the filming of the comedy duo's 1929 feature *Rio Rita* (later to be remade under the same title by Abbott and Costello), he fell ten feet during a carelessly staged bit, landing on a wooden sawhorse. The studio infirmary claimed he only had minor injuries, and failed to even take any x-rays. Woolsey had in fact suffered severe internal damage to his kidney, and it plagued him for the rest of his life, which ended far too prematurely at age fifty in 1938.[326]

Upon Woolsey's death, the Screen Actors Guild passed two emergency resolutions. The first awarded a lifetime pension to Woolsey's widow, and the second threatened an immediate strike if the studios didn't institute health and safety reforms, including the disability and worker's compensation benefits required by California state law. Yvonne DeCarlo, star of numerous films but best remembered as Lily on *The Munsters,* married stunt man Robert Morgan, who lost a leg after being run over by a train during filming on *How the West was Won* in 1962.[327] MGM claimed no responsibility for the accident, and the couple sued them for $1.4 million.

As several of those entertainers adversely impacted by it informed me, no one could have foreseen the explosion of old material recycled on television, some twenty to thirty years after movies and short subjects had initially been released, and TV series at this point still rerunning strong fifty or even sixty years after they were recorded. Baby Boomers like me grew up watching Three Stooges, Little Rascals and East Side Kids material that had been filmed decades earlier. Television made the stars of these old theatrical productions much more famous and beloved than they ever were in their prime. The Screen Actors Guild fought for years to try and get financial compensation for old movie stars, whose films were also being rerun continuously now on television, as well as to establish a health and pension fund. The studios argued against the very concept of residuals, insisting that it was tantamount to paying someone multiple times for the same job. One distraught studio head allegedly broke down in tears during negotiations. At the time of the 1960 SAG strike (led by guild president Ronald Reagan), 69 percent of guild members were making less than $4,000 annually. A compromise settlement in 1960 resulted in residual payments for all theatrical releases in 1960 and afterward. In lieu of residuals for the older films, SAG was given $2.25 million to establish a health and pension plan. Things didn't improve for the acting rank and file; the Screen Actors Guild reported that more than 85 percent of its members earned less than $5,000 annually in 1996.[328]

Shirley Temple was commanding $10,000 weekly at the peak of her prepubescent acting career. When she turned eighteen, however, she was shocked to discover a mere $44,000 waiting for her, instead of the $3.2 million she'd earned, thanks to her parents using it for bills and their own investments.[329] The Coogan Law was passed to protect future Shirley Temples and Jackie Coogans. Later to be endeared to Baby Boomers for his role as Uncle Fester on *The Addams Family,* Coogan had been a prolific child star, but found out his estimated $4 million fortune had been squandered by his mother and stepfather. Coogan's stepfather bluntly told *Life* magazine, "Every dollar a kid earns before he is 21 belongs to his parents. Jackie will not get a cent of his earnings." Coogan's mother coldly claimed, "No promises were ever made to give Jackie anything" and further called him "a bad boy."[330] Coogan had lost his biological father, along with three others, including rising nineteen-year-old actor Junior Durkin, in a 1935 car crash which he alone survived. Later, when Coogan was a down and out adult, he asked Charlie Chaplin, with whom he co-starred in the 1921 silent film *The Kid,* for help, and was given a generous $1,000. Mimi Gibson was a later day child actor, whose substantial earnings were frittered away by her mother, leaving her without funds for college tuition. The California Child Actor's Bill, enacted in 1939, stipulated that 15 percent of a minor's earnings must be placed in a trust. That didn't seem to help all child actors; *Diff'rent Strokes* child star Gary Coleman's tragic adult life was preceded by his parents and a financial advisor spending his multi-million dollar fortune. Another diminutive child actor, Emmanuel Lewis, who starred on the television series *Webster,* is said to presently be worth just $500,000. Actress Patty Duke, who was ultimately diagnosed with bipolar disorder, had an unstable mother who permitted exploitative talent managers John and Ethel Ross to run her career. As a teenager at the height of her fame, Patty was miserable. The Rosses allegedly encouraged her to take alcohol and prescription drugs starting when she was only thirteen years old. At any rate, Duke seems not to have been ripped off financially, since she left a $10 million estate when she died in 2016.

Dick Clark made a fortune with his "Cavalcade of Stars" tours in the late Fifties through the early 1960s. The performers didn't fare as well financially. While the top names could earn around $1,200 for fourteen shows a week, most of the "stars" earned less than half that. As Clark himself described it, "It didn't matter if there were twelve people in the band…Once they got their $500 or $600 they divided the money among themselves, took off 10 percent for their agent, 10 percent for their manager, put some aside to pay their taxes, paid for their room and board on the tour - they were lucky if they had $20 a week to play with."[331] Jimi Hendrix was the highest paid act at Woodstock, at $18,000 plus expenses, while Blood, Sweat & Tears earned $15,000, Creedence Clearwater Revival and Joan Baez $10,000 each, Jefferson Airplane, The Band, and Janis Joplin were each paid $7,500, The Grateful Dead $7,500, Richie Havens, Sly and the Family Stone, and The Who were paid between $6-7,000, Alro Guthrie and Crosby, Stills, Nash & Young $5,000, The Lovin' Spoonful's lead singer and songwriter John Sebastian just $1,000, and Santana a shockingly low $750.[332] Some sources, in fact, claim that Hendrix was actually paid $30,000.[333] The odd disparity of Hendrix's much larger fee, juxtaposed against the significantly smaller amounts for comparably celebrated acts, seems par for the course in the entertainment industry.

The October 16, 2007 *Los Angeles Times* ran a story about writer Marc Cherry, who fell into obscurity after hitting it big with *The Golden Girls*. He was forced to sell his home and moved back in with his mother. Eventually, he struck more gold with the *Desperate Housewives* series, but continued to receive nice pocket change from *Golden Girls* royalties; when the show was sold to the Lifetime

Channel, he was paid $75,000 in residuals one year. The Writers Guild went on strike in 2007, over residual fees paid to actors, writers and directors, as well as earnings from home video, DVD sales and foreign markets. At the time, writers were being paid 4 cents for every DVD sold. In the same *LA Times* article, Nick Counter, president of the Alliance of Motion Picture and Television Producers, was quoted as saying, "It is simply no longer tenable to be paying residuals on losses as we have for three decades. We must adapt to the realities of the marketplace, the new demands from our audiences and new technologies, or suffer the fate of those who deny change or don't adapt fast enough." The residual payment system still in use dated back to the early days of radio. Hollywood studios had begrudgingly begun offering TV residuals in 1952. "You tell me you're going to cut back on my residuals, you might as well put a gun to my head," the article quoted veteran television and film actor Vic Polizos. "That's my lifeblood. It's my kids' lifeblood." Polizos is one of those "character" actors Hollywood has always depended upon, even if audiences rarely recall their names. As the article notes, "Despite his large body of work, Polizos lives modestly in a middle-class neighborhood in Reseda. He earns about $75,000 to $100,000 a year and as much as $35,000 more from residuals." Polizos admitted, "I don't know what I would have done without the residuals." The article went on to describe how health insurance benefits for guild members are tied to minimum earnings.

Veteran actor James Best, memorable as Sheriff Roscoe P. Coltrane on *The Dukes of Hazzard,* unsuccessfully sued Warner Brothers over merchandising royalties in 2012. Former *Happy Days* stars Marion Ross, Donny Most, Erin Moran and Anson Williams, along with the estate of Tom Bosley, filed a $10 million lawsuit against CBS in 2011, over unpaid merchandising revenue. The case was later settled out of court, with each actor receiving $65,000.[334] In 2012, stories broke about the long troubled Erin Moran being financially destitute and homeless. Moran had supposedly been booted from her trailer park, and was said to be living as a recluse in an Indiana hotel, where she was reported to be working on her autobiography. Moran last worked regularly on the 2008 edition of *Celebrity Fit Club*.[335] In a sad postscript, Erin Moran died at only fifty-six in April, 2017. In an interview with *The Sun*, Moran's brother Tony said, "Erin was a tortured soul who never recovered after Happy Days. Hollywood chewed her up and spat her out." Moran wanted no funeral, and at the time of her death was back living in the same trailer park, married to a Walmart employee.[336] Incidentally, IMDb reports that Donny "Ralph Malph" Most earned $12,500 for each episode of *Happy Days*. Most is presently said to be worth $2 million, slightly more than Anson "Potsie" Williams, who has $1.8 million according to Celebrity Net Worth. They lag far behind Marion Ross, at some $10 million, Henry Winkler at $30 million, and of course Ron Howard, who is worth an incredible $160 million. Tom Bosley left behind a $5 million estate.

Mike Connors, who starred as the title character in the long running television series *Mannix*, launched a lawsuit in 2011, claiming that he'd *never* received any royalties from CBS and Paramount Studios. This seems exceedingly strange, given that another television detective from the same era, Dennis Weaver (who starred as *McCloud*), negotiated a contract provision for all actors, which provided him with handsome royalties for the rest of this life, as president of the Screen Actors Guild in the mid-1970s.[337] Veteran Hollywood screenwriter, film critic, and *Real People* co-host and creator John Barbour told me, in an April, 2018 phone conversation, that his friend James Garner was bitter over not getting royalties from the hit television series *The Rockford Files*. "It broke his heart," Barbour recounted. Garner in fact battled Universal Studios for years, fighting the company's absurd contention that the popular show had somehow lost millions of dollars during its six year run.[338] As probably shouldn't surprise anyone at this point, Dennis Weaver left behind a $16 million estate, while at his death Garner was actually said to be worth more, at \$20 million. Barbour, who I was fortunate enough to meet and become good friends with through our mutual interest in the JFK assassination, also recounted how Tom Laughlin didn't "make a cent" initially from 1971's *Billy Jack*, despite the fact it was a box office smash. Edd Byrnes, who starred as teen heartthrob "Kookie" on the hit television show *77 Sunset Strip*, remarked in a 1969 interview that he had made more in the previous year (when his acting career had seemingly fizzled out) than he made during the entire series run with Warner Brothers Studios.[339]

In 2008, the surviving members of the Allman Brothers Band sued Universal Music for \$13 million in unpaid digital royalties. The lawsuit, filed in Manhattan federal court, declared that Universal "refuses to pay Plaintiffs at the correct royalty rate for its digital exploitation of the Capricorn Masters," including from CDs, digital downloads and ringtones. Universal, which bought out Polygram Records, with whom the Allman Brothers signed a 1985 agreement, had only paid the band a small fraction of what was agreed upon in the original contract, which stipulated that they would be paid fully half of the profits accrued through any other commercial usage.[340] The prolific songwriting team of Holland-Dozier-Holland had to sue Motown for \$22 million in unpaid royalties.[341] A documentary entitled, "Who Got the Rollers' Millions?" explored just what happened to the supposed financial fortune the Bay City Rollers, probably the first true "boy band," generated. There were the customary accusations that the band members were defrauded by their management and/or their record company. Despite varying sales estimates of anywhere from 70 to 300 million records worldwide, the band members themselves appear to have earned very little. In March 2007, six former members of the group launched a lawsuit against Arista Records, claiming they were owed "tens of millions of dollars" in unpaid royalties. The lawsuit was finally settled out of court in 2016, with each member getting a disappointing, just over \$87,000.[342] The surviving members of the band Cornelius Brothers and Sister Rose filed a multimillion dollar lawsuit against Capitol Records in 2001, which was dismissed three years later when the plaintiffs oddly decided not to pursue it.

Aretha Franklin never received any radio royalties for her huge hit *Respect*. Neither did any of the jazz musicians who backed her up on the recording. Aretha prospered quite nicely, nonetheless, leaving behind an $80 million fortune.[343] Rosalie "Rosie" Hamlin of the group Rosie and the Originals, actually wrote the band's smash hit *Angel Baby* when she was only fifteen years old. However, she received no songwriting credit and therefore was unable to collect the royalties she was due. She eventually obtained the copyright, but there were decades of court battles. John Lennon was a huge fan; during the introduction to his cover of *Angel Baby*, which wasn't included on the released version of his album *Rock N' Roll*, he declared, "This here is one of my all-time favorite songs. Send my love to Rosie, wherever she may be." Hamlin would die at seventy-one after suffering from fibromyalgia for a number of years.[344] Phil Spector was sued by three of his girl groups for unpaid royalties. It has been routinely reported that the members of the iconic punk band The Sex Pistols made very little money after they burst upon the scene in the late 1970s. After lead singer Johnny Rotten (John Lydon) continued his success afterwards with the band Public Image Limited, he found that he still owed Virgin Records money a decade later. Even the Rolling Stones never made really big money until they formed their own record label in the 1970s. The Stones' original royalty rate, like the Beatles, was an unfathomably miniscule less than a penny per record. You can go online and still see a photocopy of a royalty check singer-songwriter Janis Ian, best remembered for her huge 1975 hit *At Seventeen*, received in 2014 for $0.01. Maybe she swapped it for a free drink; supposedly there is a Studio City bar that will do that if the residual check is less than a dollar. Lester Chambers, lead singer of the Chambers Brothers, claimed to have never received a single penny in royalties from 1967 to 1994, despite the band's *ten* albums, which all sold well, and their 1968 psychedelic hit *Time Has Come Today*. Even when compared to their likewise trusting young musical peers of the day, Eric Burdon and the Animals still made an astonishingly small amount of money, considering the popularity of *House of the Rising Sun* and their other hits. According to original bass player Bryan "Chas" Chandler, the band's business affairs "were in a total shambles."[345]

Fred Parris, who wrote the classic 1950s hit *In the Still of the Night*, like many black composers and artists, was naïve and trusting enough to accept a one-time payment of $783 as a "fee" for other artists covering the song, instead of the estimated $100,000 he should have earned based on sales. Ahmet Ertegun, who founded Atlantic Records, claimed that a Columbia Records executive had once told him that they never paid their black artists any royalties. Pat Boone was one of the white artists who re-recorded hits by black groups and made far more money from them than the original performers ever did. An unapologetic Boone told Tavis Smiley in a May 2015 interview, "Guilty? No….There were lots of rhythm and blues artists and they were doing well in their genre and they were famous and they had the charts and everything. (But) the only ones anybody knows today are the ones that were covered by the Beatles, by Elvis, by me and by many artists." Boone pointed out that when legendary disc jockey Alan Freed asked his audience which version of *Ain't That a Shame* they'd rather hear - the original by Fats Domino or Boone's remake, they chose Boone's. Because many of these black artists wrote their own material, Boone maintained that "They made more money from my records than they did from their own." This seems like a contradiction in logic. So these artists were strangely paid songwriting royalties for cover versions of their work, but not their own recordings? Boone certainly did better financially than most of his black peers; he is presently worth some $50 million according to Celebrity Net Worth.

On the other hand, as of 2013, Don McLean was said to still be earning some $300,000 annually off of his 1971 monster hit, *American Pie*. "American Pie is probably worth 10 or 15 hit records," McLean told the UK's *Telegraph* in 2015. McLean stated that his classic song was still being played an average of five hundred times each day by radio stations, and that he earned a royalty each time. That same year, McLean sold the original handwritten lyrics to his iconic song at auction for $1.2 million.[346] Cat Stevens, one of the biggest artists of the 1970s, before morphing into Yusef Islam, admitted that "The royalties from my albums continue to support my charity work." Singer-songwriter John Stewart, who wrote the smash hit *Daydream Believer* for the Monkees, and had a Top Ten hit of his own in 1979 with *Gold,* once claimed that the first song he ever sold, to the Kingston Trio, paid him more on the initial royalty payment than his racetrack trainer father earned in a year.[347] Although he died in 2011, Gerry Rafferty's estate was still earning some $100,000 off of his 1978 hit *Baker Street* in 2014. Members of the Swedish super group Abba continue to accumulate millions in royalties each year for their slew of hit singles in the 1970s-1980s. Roy Orbison and Bill Dees earned an impressive $19.75 million for composing Orbison's smash hit *Pretty Woman*. Ben E. King, Jerry Lieber and Mike Stoller earned an astounding $27 million for their song *Stand by Me*. Barry Mann, Cynthia Weil and Phil Spector made some $34 million for co-writing the Righteous Brothers' unforgettable hit *You've Lost That Lovin' Feelin'*. Nobody knows much about the Hill sisters, but they wrote *Happy Birthday* and earned approximately $50 million from it. Later, giant Warner Music would purchase the copyright and charge a hefty fee every time it was used in a film or television show. This is why you so seldom see *Happy Birthday* sung onscreen. George Cory and Douglass Cross co-wrote Tony Bennett's signature tune, *I Left My Heart in San Francisco,* and claimed to have earned $5 million each from residuals.[348] We see here again how inconsistent the process is, how some performers earn an incomprehensible amount of wealth, while others who are equally successful struggle financially. This seems to be a strange, ironclad pattern in show business.

On May 4, 2004, several major record label and music publishers agreed to pay an estimated $50 million in unpaid royalties to thousands of recording artists. The settlement was in response to a New York State Attorney General's investigation. Huge stars, such as David Bowie, Billy Idol, Tom Jones, Dolly Parton and Luciano Pavarotti, Gloria Estefan and Dave Matthews, along with the estates of Elvis Presley and Frank Sinatra, were included on the list of under-compensated performers, along with lots of relative unknowns. The largest payout went to 1950s singer Tommy Edwards, best remembered for his 1958 hit *It's All in the Game,* who received $230,000. New York Attorney General Eliot Spitzer stated, "We have this misperception that artists have all gained enormous wealth. But there are many artists who struggle, who have one successful song, and they depend on these royalties."[349] The record companies used absurd excuses to defend their lack of royalty payments; for example, they claimed that some artists or their heirs couldn't be located. The families of Elvis Presley and Frank Sinatra couldn't be found? Under the agreement, unclaimed royalties automatically reverted to the state. In January 2002, Universal Music agreed to set up a $4.75 million fund to compensate artists or their heirs for "accounting irregularities" stretching back over several decades. That case was originally brought by singer Peggy Lee, and settled just a few days before her death. Artists whose estates benefited from the agreement included Louis Armstrong, Pearl Bailey, Patsy Cline, Ella Fitzgerald, and Billie Holiday.[350]

If the biggest stars in the music industry can be screwed over routinely by record companies, imagine how the session musicians fare. The 2002 documentary film *Standing in the Shadows of Motown* exposed how shortchanged the musicians who created the classic Motown sound of the 1960s were. Those particular musicians, collectively dubbed the Funk Brothers, eventually got their due acknowledgement; because of the film's success, they toured nationwide to packed houses. An even more famous group of studio musicians, who became known as The Wrecking Crew, played the actual instruments on most of the huge hit singles of the 1960s that didn't come from Motown. One of the Wrecking Crew, guitarist Glen Campbell, went on to establish a significant career of his own later, but most remained anonymous to the public. Dick Clark probably expressed the view of most in the industry when he commented on The Wrecking Crew's distinctive sound in an interview with, "Who created it? Who cared?" Beach Boys' leader Brian Wilson would acknowledge, "I mainly worked in the studio with the Wrecking Crew to achieve what I wanted." Members of the Wrecking Crew worked in television, too; Tommy Tedesco, for instance, played the signature guitar riffs on the theme songs for *The Twilight Zone, Green Acres, Bonanza* and *Batman*.[351] Leon Russell was another Wrecking Crew member who would carve out a successful solo career. One of the Wrecking Crew's drummers, Hal Blaine, played on countless albums for the biggest artists in the business, and on forty number one singles, as well as 150 top ten songs. The classic opening drumbeats to the Ronettes' *Be My Baby* were the work of Blaine, who also is credited with naming the group the Wrecking Crew.[352] Supposedly, the Association, who scored with mega 1960s' hits like *Windy* and *Cherish,* "played virtually not a single note" on their recordings. The band is alleged to have told one of the Wrecking Crew, in explanation for not crediting them as musicians, "We don't want kids to know we didn't play on the record."[353] The 2008 documentary *The Wrecking Crew* was directed by Tedesco's son Denny. "This is going to break your heart, but much of the music you heard in the Sixties and early Seventies wasn't recorded by the people you saw on the album covers. It was done by me and the musicians you see on these walls... Many of these kids didn't have the chops and were little more than garage bands..." Hal Blaine, the Wrecking Crew's drummer, was quoted as saying in the March 23, 2011 edition of the *Wall Street Journal,* "At concerts, people hear with their eyes. Teens cut groups slack in concert, but not when they bought their records."

Because of the fact the Wrecking Crew has achieved notoriety in recent years, critics have tended to dismiss the famous bands they played anonymously for. Some artists from that era have taken umbrage at this. The Grass Roots were just one of the many popular acts who were frustrated over not being allowed to play their instruments on their own recordings. Floyd Marcus, the drummer for the late Sixties bubblegum powerhouse the 1910 Fruitgum Company, known for huge hits like *Simon Says* and *1,2,3, Red Light,* stated, "There were bands out there that were totally fabricated, but we were not one of them."[354] In an interview with Song Facts, Gary Lewis was adamant on the subject. "We went in the studio, myself and the Playboys played on every single track we ever did. I mean, we were the track band," Lewis explained. "And so many people say Gary Lewis and the Playboys never played on anything. I've even read write-ups that said Gary Lewis didn't even sing on his records. All that is just such bull. The Playboys and I played on absolutely everything we ever did, album tunes, everything. And since we were so young and inexperienced, that's when the Wrecking Crew came in to do overdubs and solos..." In the mid-1980s at least, Mickey Dolenz and Peter Tork (of the Monkees, generally the foremost band accused of not playing their own instruments) were competently playing drums and guitar, respectively, when I saw them during a comeback tour. Michael Nesmith of the group was definitely a real musician and songwriter; Linda Ronstadt began her musical career with the Stone Poneys, whose big 1967 hit single was Nesmith's composition *Different Drum.* John Lennon of all people defended the Monkees, saying, "They've got their own scene, and I won't send them down for it. You try a weekly television show and see if you can manage one half as good!" The cynical

Beatle told Mike Nesmith in 1967: "I think you're the greatest comic talents since the Marx Brothers. I've never missed one of your programs." At that same nostalgic concert I attended, Herman's Hermits (minus Peter "Herman" Noone) also performed; their original lead guitarist and the rest of the surviving members were on stage and playing their own instruments. While the elite session musicians appear to have been paid well, that doesn't seem to have been the case with the unsung backup singers who provided harmony on many of these same hit records. Their story was chronicled in the 2013 documentary *Twenty Feet from Stardom*.

Contestants on *American Idol* are required to sign a restrictive contract which grants 100 percent control over merchandising, touring, movie deals, etc., to the show's production company. This was nothing new, of course; rock 'n roll icon Richard "Little Richard" Penniman wrote in his autobiography *The Life and Times of Little Richard* that record sales for the early black artists were irrelevant, because the record labels owned all the publishing rights. In 1984, Little Richard launched a $115 million federal lawsuit against three music companies, alleging that he hadn't been paid royalties for his hit songs like *Tutti Frutti* since 1955. The suit was settled out of court for an undisclosed sum in 1986. Michael Jackson came into possession of Little Richard's music catalog, and various sources claim that he either gave back the rights, offered him a job that he didn't accept, or kept the rights to himself. At any rate, Little Richard appeared to have come out of it all pretty well, as at the time of his death in May 2020, he had accumulated a $40 million fortune, according to Celebrity Net Worth. Bad Boy Records, a company that came along later, earned a reputation for signing artists to unfair contracts. When Salt-N-Pepa signed with Next Plateau Records in 1985, they naively agreed to half the standard royalty rate of one cent per album. Even after three platinum albums, the women were receiving $100,000 a year, while their management made millions. One of the group's members, DJ Spinderella, would launch a lawsuit in 2019, alleging that her band mates owed her a significant amount of unpaid royalties.[355] The well-respected '90s band The Posies continues to earn a living through their music, but they hardly lead a glamorous existence. A 2009 story about them reported that they still owed mega-mogul David Geffen money, and were hawking their own CDs behind a merchandising table before their shows.[356] The '80s teen group New Edition signed a disastrous contract and received checks for a laughable $1.87 after their first big tour.[357] They switched to major label MCA, whose complex relationship with a production company forced them to borrow money from the record company, leaving them in debt and unhappily tied to MCA for seventeen years. We hear about artists borrowing money from their record companies quite a bit. The Beach Boys were betrayed by Murray Wilson, their manager and father of the three brothers in the band. In the late '60s, he sold the publishing rights to their catalog for a mere $750,000.[358] It would later be estimated that the catalog was worth some $40 million. A 2010 report, published on multiple web sites, claimed that for every $1,000 in sales, the average musician gets $23.40. More mainstream, conservative estimates cite a still shameful statistic that musical performers only get 12 percent of music revenue.[359]

The following comes from an open letter written by Courtney Love in 2001, which was widely disseminated online: "Corrupt recording agreements forced the heirs of Jimi Hendrix ('Purple Haze,' 'All Along the Watchtower' and 'Stone Free') to work menial jobs while his catalog generated millions of dollars each year for Universal Music. Florence Ballard from the Supremes ('Where Did Our Love Go,' 'Stop in the Name of Love' and 'You Keep Me Hangin' On' are just 3 of the 10 #1 hits she sang on) was on welfare when she died. Merle Haggard ('I Threw Away the Rose,' 'Sing Me Back Home' and 'Today I Started Loving You Again') enjoyed a string of 37 top-ten country singles (including 23 #1 hits) in the 60s and 70s. Yet he never received a record royalty check until last year when he released an album on the indie punk-rock label Epitaph." In an earlier, June 14, 2000 article published by *Salon,* Love broke down the costs every band incurs, and concluded, "the band may as well be working at a 7-Eleven." Love went on to say, "Of course, they had fun. Hearing yourself on the radio, selling records, getting new fans and being on TV is great, but now the band doesn't have enough money to pay the rent and nobody has any credit. Worst of all, after all this, the band owns none of its work ... When you look at the legal line on a CD, it says copyright 1976 Atlantic Records or copyright 1996 RCA Records. When you look at a book, though, it'll say something like copyright 1999 Susan Faludi, or David Foster Wallace. Authors own their books and license them to publishers. When the contract runs out, writers get their books back. But record companies own our copyrights forever. The system's set up so almost nobody gets paid."

In 1986, Congress held hearings on the issue of unpaid royalties to performers. Rep. John Conyers told witness Ruth Brown that, "Your record 'Teardrops in My Eyes' woke me up for years in the service. Nobody could change the radio station without peril to his life." Brown and her attorney Robert Liotta recounted her 16-year battle with Atlantic Records, over what they claimed was at least $60,000 in unpaid royalties. The only way Brown was financially able to sue Atlantic was through a racketeering law that lets individuals seek civil damages from corporations. Brown described how Atlantic and other record companies had cheated countless black performers like Clyde McPhatter, Joe Turner, Frankie Lymon, Dee Clark, Etta James, Brook Benton, Dinah Washington, the Clovers, the Platters, the Drifters, the Five Keys and the Moonglows. Brown noted that the survivors of deceased entertainers cannot afford to legally confront corporate giants like Atlantic Records. Attorney Liotta accused Atlantic and other record companies of not reporting royalties or sending "intentionally false" royalty statements to performers as far back as the 1950s, which "effectively cheated them out of possibly hundreds of thousands of dollars." The song Conyers had mentioned, for instance, "Teardrops in My Eyes," sold a million copies, but Brown's royalty statement only reported sales of 200,000. Brown testified that she'd seen her records being sold in Europe recently, without receiving any royalties for them, and that the price being asked for them in Paris was "very exorbitant."[360]

Even very successful musical acts in today's world struggle to approach the status of the "rock stars" of the 1970s classic era. A widely disseminated 2014 online article, headlined, "Loads of UK Rock Bands Still Have Day Jobs," described how award-winning groups, who once filled impressive sized venues and made the UK rock charts, still weren't making enough money to rely on that income. To quote from the article, "This year, you can probably count the UK bands comfortably out of the 9-5 grind on one or two hands." A more mainstream article in *The Guardian* focused on the same subject a few years later.[361] Jack Conte of the band Pomplamoose (who is also the co-founder of Patreon) wrote a detailed description of touring expenses vs. income, and reported that they'd actually lost nearly $12,000 during the 2014 tour in question.[362]

Digital downloads from ITunes, Spotify, You Tube and the like pay peanuts to the artists. To understand just how little even the biggest stars make on streaming music, consider that the highest estimate for Taylor Swift's take for 46.3 million plays of her hit *Shake if Off* was $390,000.[363] Needless to say, the Taylor Swifts are extremely rare in the modern music world. Considering what comparable musical icons were earning in the 1970s and 1980s, that's not a lot of money for such astronomical record sales. The major labels continue to report record revenues from streaming music, led by Universal Music Group's incredible $4.7 billion for just the first nine months of 2018. While David Crosby's dubious claim that a million streaming plays results in the artist receiving all of $5 appears to be wrong, independent studies have shown that the artist in such cases is paid just over $7,800 by Apple Music, and a paltry $3,970 on

Spotify.[364] According to another source, a million plays on Pandora pays even less - $1,650.[365] I've tried to contact some newer musical artists, to find out exactly how they are faring financially these days, with little success. The lovely young MonaLisa Twins have a nice cult following; when I messaged them on Facebook last year, they did answer back (and even called me "groovy"), referring me to their manager, who never replied to my email.

Deborah Dozier Potter, daughter of William Dozier, producer of the campy *Batman* 1960s television series, launched a lawsuit against 20th Century-Fox in 2006, alleging that she was defrauded out of some $4.4 million. "I wish it could have been avoided," Potter said. "Nobody likes litigation."[366] Online posters claim that Vicki Lawrence has reported her residuals for *Mama's Family* were something like $100 per month. Actor Kevin Hagen (best known as Doc Baker on *Little House on the Prairie*) disclosed that he only received about $8 per week in residuals, and bitterly reflected on his contract, which prevented him from earning well over $1 million after the show left the air. Hagen was extremely candid in a 2005 interview with the *National Enquirer,* with inferences that series star and creator Michael Landon had fared much better financially than the rest of the cast. Hagen would subsequently express feelings of remorse about the interview in a conversation with his series co-star Alison Arngrim. When Arngrim told him that everyone (except Landon, whom Hagen felt the *Enquirer* had inaccurately portrayed as greedy in the article), was woefully underpaid on the show, Hagen told her he wished he'd been even more forceful in his comments. *Little House* co-star Melissa Sue Anderson threatened to sue Arngrim after she noted that Anderson had moved to Canada and "renounced her citizenship." Arngrim also intimated that Anderson was a stuck up diva on set.[367] Little known Alex Anderson, Jr. was a boyhood friend and later collaborator with Jay Ward, who struck it big in the cartoon world with *Crusader Rabbit* and especially *Rocky and Bullwinkle.* Anderson had to sue Ward's heirs in order to receive financial compensation for creating the original versions of the characters Rocky, Bullwinkle and Dudley Do-Right.[368] Ted Key, creator of the comic strip *Hazel* (which became a successful television series) also had to sue Ward's estate over his creation of the Mr. Peabody and Sherman characters. Nancy Avery-Arkley, daughter of legendary animator Tex Avery, bitterly commented, on a Cartoon Brew article about the film *Who Framed Roger Rabbit*, "My name is Nancy and I am the daughter of the late Tex Avery. He created Roger Rabbit. Richard Williams watched my fathers MGM 1952 cartoon, 'Magical Maestro' That was the rabbit that he copied, and even the clothes."

Some more fortunate entertainers did very well with residuals. Jack Klugman and Tony Randall both earned much more from reruns than from the original episodes of *The Odd Couple*. Werner "Col. Klink" Klemperer enjoyed the same experience. Unfortunately, his *Hogan's Heroes* cohort, series star Bob Crane, was strapped financially at the time of his brutal murder, but had he lived a few more years he'd have earned millions in residuals. In just one of a lifelong series of bad business decisions, Redd Foxx signed over his residuals to *Sanford & Son* in a divorce settlement rather than pay his wife something like $800,000. As a result, he died broke while his ex-wife raked in lucrative royalties. In the 1990s Audrey Meadows was still receiving residuals from the original, classic thirty-nine episodes of *The Honeymooners*. She was the only member of the cast to have shrewdly demanded them during contract negotiations. Joyce Randolph, who played Trixie Norton on the show, did receive residuals later when the "lost" episodes from Jackie Gleason's variety show were released. However, again, finances in the entertainment world rarely make sense; while Meadows left behind a $3 million estate, Randolph is said to have a $10 million net worth (the same amount her legendary co-star Jackie Gleason had at his death - Art Carney left behind $16 million), despite having only a few minor credits since her last appearance as Trixie Norton for Gleason in 1957. Dawn Wells, the lovely Mary Ann from *Gilligan's*

Island, was reportedly paid $1,200 per week under her original con-
tract. In an interview, Wells claimed that she never made "a bit"
of money beyond the standard first five runs of each episode. In
fact, Wells revealed just how much the producers of these shows
can make, when she told a New York talk show in 2012 that Sher-
wood Schwartz "made $90 million on the re-runs of 'Gilligan's
Island' alone, but we didn't get any of it." Wells also guessed that
the cast "made $50,000 (per season), I don't know."[369] Wells would
reveal on Vicki Lawrence's show *Vicki!* that her cast mate Natalie
Schafer, who portrayed "Lovie" Howell on the series, had lived with
her for the last years of her life. Some sources state that Schafer,
who'd become wealthy through investments, left most of her estate
to Wells. According to Celebrity Net Worth, Wells accumulated a $7
million fortune.

Evidently, that alleged $7 million didn't keep Dawn Wells from
struggling financially. Wells told Fox News and other outlets, in a
September 2018 interview, that a loved one had set up a GoFundMe
page to "help her overcome her financial woes." Earlier in the
month, Wells' publicist had told Fox News, "Although Dawn won't
deny that she is indeed having a rough time, she has been keeping
her wits about herself and like so many others is doing her best
to overcome difficult times." Wells herself was quoted as saying, "I
thought I was taking all the proper steps to ensure my golden years.
Now, here I am, no family, no husband, no kids and no money."
The actress was supposedly "desperate" for the funds following an
"unexpected accident that required hospitalization for two months,"
according to a previous report by TMZ. TMZ had disclosed that the
actress wanted to be moved to a smaller living facility that special-
izes in assisting those in the film and television industry, but she was
denied due to her debt.[370] According to statements from her friend
and hairstylist, who set up the GoFundMe page for her, Wells owed
nearly $200,000 in back taxes to the IRS. TMZ, however, attributed
the trouble primarily to medical bills from a broken knee and a

previous surgery, and the fact she lost "almost everything" during the 2008 banking crisis. They also reported that Wells had already lost her home.[371] Sadly, in late December 2020, eighty-two-year-old Dawn Wells died in a Los Angeles nursing home. The only survivor listed was a stepsister.[372]

A poster on the Straight Dope message board claimed that his theatre professor told him she'd made enough money from playing a mom in a 1980s McDonald's commercial to pay for graduate work and provide a substantial nest egg, which he put at "well into the high 5 figures." In his obituary, it was mentioned that singer-song-writer Warren Zevon made royalties from the song *Like the Seasons,* which was the B-side of the Turtles huge 1967 hit *Happy Together* "that paid his rent for years."[373] As should be obvious, there really is no consistency in the way entertainers are compensated. After leaving the hit show *Two and a Half Men,* it was estimated that former series star Charlie Sheen still stood to make some $100 million in future residuals.[374] Sheen was the highest paid television series performer in history prior to that, netting an incredible $1.8 million *per episode.* Numerous stars of recent shows have been paid $500,000 and up per episode. You can bet they have much more lucrative residuals than the old television performers did as well. A show that is little remembered today, even though it ran for seven seasons in the 1990s, *Mad About You,* paid its two stars, Paul Reiser and Helen Hunt, $1 million for each episode. The amount that stars from hit shows like *Seinfeld* and *Friends* earn from reruns is probably incalculable. As of 2015, *Big Bang Theory* star Jim Parsons was the highest paid performer on television, earning $29 million yearly, two million more than series co-star Johnny Galecki.[375] An online poster claimed that Garcelle Beauvais, hardly a major star, who appeared on *The Jamie Foxx Show* in the late 1990s, reportedly receives an incredible $700,000 plus every year in royalties.

On the big screen, Zack Ward, who played the bully in the 1983 film *A Christmas Story*, reportedly receives just a modest $1,800 in

Canadian currency every two years in royalties, as of 2017.[376] The film was given a small budget, and director Bob Clark was so eager to make it he put up $150,000 of his own money and waived his director's fee.[377] It is still shown continuously on television during Christmas season. Judy Garland, always underpaid by MGM, only earned $500 per week for 1939's classic *The Wizard of Oz*. There has long been an urban legend that Garland was even paid less than the dog that portrayed Toto, but this appears to be untrue. For the record, Terry, the Cairn Terrier who played the iconic animal, was paid $125 weekly. All the Munchkins, however, were paid less than Terry the dog, at just $50.[378] In an all too familiar injustice, her adult co-stars Ray Bolger and Jack Haley made far more than young Judy, at approximately $3,000 per week.[379] Director Victor Fleming also apparently felt comfortable in slapping the young actress whenever he felt her behavior on the set warranted it.

Fay Wray was paid $10,000 for her portrayal of Ann Darrow in the timeless original 1933 version of *King Kong*. Producer Merian C. Cooper supposedly prepared her for her most remembered role by declaring, "You're going to have the tallest, darkest leading man in Hollywood." Wray, like so many other entertainers, experienced her share of personal tragedy, despite living to the ripe old age of ninety-six. Her brother, J. Vivian Wray, escaped from a mental institution in 1928 and took his own life by throwing himself in front of a Stockton, California streetcar. Although she grew to love her legendary role, Wray claimed to have only seen *King Kong* four times during her lengthy life.[380] This conjured up comparisons to another long-lived actor associated with a classic horror film, David Manners. Near the end of his near century of life (he lived to be ninety-seven), Manners revealed that he had never seen the 1931 film *Dracula,* for which he is chiefly remembered. Oddly embarrassed about his connection with such a beloved movie, Manners specifically requested that fans not send him any videos of *Dracula,* and flatly stated he had no interest in viewing it. Maybe he felt guilty about being paid so much more than the film's star, Bela Lugosi. Manners had no love for either Lugosi or *Dracula* director Tod Browning. He called Lugosi "a pain in the ass from start to finish. He would pace around the sound-stage between scenes, velvet cape wrapped around him, posing in front of a full-length mirror while he intoned with sepulchral emphasis, 'I am Dracula . . . I am Dracula!'" Asked about Browning, Manners said, "The only directing I saw was done by Kurt Freund, the cinematographer."[381] Donna Reed's daughter Mary Owen revealed that *It's a Wonderful Life* was not shown in their home, and in fact she didn't see it until she was a young adult, at a Los Angeles theater. Even more remarkably, Karolyn Grimes, who played George and Mary Bailey's youngest child Zuzu in the classic film, claimed she never watched it until 1980.[382]

Industry awards, like royalties, are usually baffling and often unfair. Jerry Seinfeld was nominated for five Emmys, but never won. Steve Carell was nominated six times for his iconic lead role on *The Office,* without bringing home a single Emmy. The great Andy Griffith was never even nominated for playing the kind-hearted sheriff without a gun in perhaps the greatest television series of all time, although strangely he did win a Grammy for a country LP in 1997. Irene Ryan was nominated twice for her iconic role of Granny Clampett in *The Beverly Hillbillies,* but didn't win either time. Cast mate Max Baer, Jr. was never even nominated for his hilarious character Jethro Bodine. The '60s classic series *Green Acres* never garnered a single nomination for best comedy show, or for any of its marvelous writers or performers. Redd Foxx was nominated three times for the lead role in *Sanford and Son,* without winning. During his lengthy television career, Jackie Gleason only received two Emmy nominations (one for playing Ralph Kramden in the classic *The Honeymooners*), but never won. Meanwhile, Tyne Daly has won six Emmys (and been nominated an incredible sixteen times). As for the Academy Awards, while Matthew McConaughey and Jamie Foxx have won Oscars, Johnny Depp, Bill Murray, Tom Cruise,

Samuel L. Jackson, Edward Norton, Hugh Jackman, Gary Oldman and Jim Carrey haven't. Histrionic artists Katharine Hepburn and Meryl Streep won four and three Oscars respectively. Streep has been nominated an absurd eighteen times. Gail Patrick, an undervalued actress who shone in classics like 1936's *My Man Godfrey,* and later produced the long-running *Perry Mason* television series, disparagingly referred to Hepburn as "Great Kate," blasted her for her consistently pretentious airs, and claimed that Ginger Rogers was a much better actress. In her fittingly acerbic style, Dorothy Parker denigrated Hepburn for "running the gamut of emotions from A to B." Performers with ordinary acting chops have been rewarded time and again, like Ingrid Bergman (with three Oscars), Sean Penn (with two) and Tom Hanks (with two). Meanwhile, Alfred Hitchcock never won an Academy Award. Well, at least not a real one; like other overlooked legends, he was belatedly issued an honorary Oscar in 1968. In my view, perhaps the two greatest actresses of all time were Barbara Stanwyck and Jean Arthur. Stanwyck never won an Oscar, while being nominated four times. Arthur was only nominated a single time, without winning. The ultimate smooth and polished performer, Cary Grant, was nominated twice without a win. Another classy and superb actor, William Powell, was nominated three times without winning an Oscar. Edward G. Robinson was never even nominated. More recently, the great Donald Sutherland has yet to receive a nomination in his long and distinguished career. Other modern actors who surprisingly haven't been nominated include Jim Carrey, Ray Liotta, John Cusack, and Kevin Bacon.

How to explain why, for instance, Mike Altman, the son of famed director Robert Altman, made far more money from the lyrics to the *M.A.S.H.* television series theme song, "Suicide is Painless," which were never used, than his father did in directing the iconic film the series was based on? Ian Hunter is an underappreciated rock legend, from his days fronting Mott the Hoople to a solid solo career. When pop star Barry Manilow recorded his song "Ships" in 1979, it became a hit and, by Hunter's own admission, earned him more in royalties than he'd made in his entire lengthy career. Manilow was noted as much for the advertising jingles and pop songs he wrote as for being an entertainer, but one of his biggest hits - *I Write the Songs* - was written by Bruce Johnston. Johnston probably made more money from that hit song than he did in all his years as a member of the Beach Boys. In a clear reflection upon the relative value of industry awards, Johnston became the first member of the Beach Boys to win a Grammy when *I Write the Songs* won Song of the Year in 1977. Think about that - Bruce Johnston won a Grammy twenty-eight years before Beach Boys' legend Brian Wilson was even nominated (Wilson did actually win a Grammy in 2005). The Grammys are perhaps even more ridiculous than the Oscars in terms of rewarding merit. Groups like the Kinks and the Talking Heads were never even nominated for an award. Neither was Chuck Berry. One of the greatest singer-songwriters of the modern era, Chantal Kreviazuk, has never been nominated. The Who was nominated twice without winning. Creedence Clearwater Revival, Jackson Browne, Dusty Springfield, Sam Cooke, Bob Marley, Jimi Hendrix, Janis Joplin, Buddy Holly and Queen are among the artists who've never been honored with a Grammy. One of the most popular and accomplished modern bands, Blink 182, has only been nominated once, without winning. The brilliant band Vertical Horizon has never received a nomination. Perhaps the greatest modern artist of the post-disco era, Elvis Costello, has only one Grammy award. Meanwhile, the likes of DJ Jazzy Jeff and the Fresh Prince, not to mention Barack Obama, have won Grammys. The much lampooned Michael Bolton was awarded two Grammys.

The Rock and Roll Hall of Fame, like the Major League Baseball and Pro Football Halls of Fame, has specialized in inducting unworthy honorees, while leaving more deserving performers out in the cold. Jethro Tull, one of the greatest progressive rock bands of the 1970s, isn't in the Hall of Fame. Neither is Roxy Music, one of the very best groups of all time in my estimation. Willie Nelson isn't there. But Bobby Darin is. The comparatively unimpressive resumes of Curtis Mayfield and Isaac Hayes somehow got them into the Hall. Lou Reed, Deep Purple, AC/DC, Madonna, The Beastie Boys, Kiss, Guns N' Roses, The Red Hot Chili Peppers, N.W.A. and Public Enemy are in, but Gram Parsons and Warren Zevon aren't? Why the Jackson 5 but not Emerson, Lake and Palmer? James Brown? Okay, but did they have to separately induct his backup singers as well? And why was Brown among the first batch of inductees, while the Beatles and Bob Dylan had to wait until the third group to be inducted? Tommy James and the Shondells was one of the biggest groups of the 1960s, but they aren't in the Hall of Fame. Meanwhile, Joan Jett, a much less successful artist who remade James and co.'s smash *Crimson and Clover,* was inducted into the Hall in 2015. Another act that garnered seven Top Ten hits in the '60s, Gary Lewis and the Playboys, remains outside the Hall as well. Dean Torrance, half of the huge '60s duo Jan and Dean, bitterly commented on the fact that they were being snubbed from induction in a 2012 interview with historian David Beard: "We have the scoreboard if you just want to compare number of hits and musical projects done. We beat 75-percent of the people in there. So what else is it?" Many of these artists who have been inexplicably inducted weren't even playing rock 'n roll, let alone producing Hall of Fame caliber rock 'n roll. These are just some examples of the unfairness and inconsistency associated with all these kinds of honors.

Sometimes, a single tune can be extraordinarily lucrative. Merv Griffin came up with the catchy theme song to the television show *Jeopardy* in what he later estimated was less than a minute. Griffin claimed that the royalties from this simple tune had earned him between $70 and $80 million. Songwriter Vic Mizzy wrote two of the catchiest theme songs in the history of television, for *The Addams Family* and *Green Acres.* He must have done pretty well financially by them, as he declared in a 2008 interview, "Two finger snaps and you live in Bel-Air."[383] According to Paul Anka's blog, he received royalty payments every time the theme song he wrote for *The Tonight Show* was played, and this amounted to some 1.4 million times over the thirty-year run of the show. *60 Minutes* reported in 2003 that Police lead singer and songwriter Sting was making $2,000 per day just from the hit song *Every Breath You Take,* which at last count had added up to over $20 million. Legendary composer Johnny Mercer was supposedly given the idea for the hit 1962 song *I Wanna Be Around* by a housewife named Sadie Vimmerstedt. In an unusually generous gesture, Mercer gave her co-credit for writing the song, and she supposedly made enough to live off this for the rest of her life. Don McLean used to respond to questions about what his huge hit *American Pie* meant, by answering: "It means I never have to work again." Mel Torme was a highly successful songwriter, and he earned some $19 million alone from the seasonal favorite *The Christmas Song.* The little remembered songwriting duo Haven Gillespie and J. Fred Coots made a cool $25 million for *Santa Claus is Comin' to Town.*[384] Totally unremembered musician Dieter Meier wrote the techno tune *Oh Yeah* for the blockbuster 1986 film *Ferris Bueller's Day Off.* Through shrewd investments, Meier turned the money he made from the song into a $175 million fortune.[385] Doug Fieger, who wrote and sang The Knack's huge 1979 hit *My Sharona,* declared in a 2009 interview, one year before his premature death, "I continue to get very, very sizable royalty checks to this day" and admitted to being "by anybody's reckoning am very well off."[386]

Probably the greatest one-hit wonder of all time was 1969's *In the Year 2525,* by Zager and Evans. Rick Evans wrote the huge hit, and apparently did quite well by it in terms of royalties. Decades later, a You Tube video of a bitter Denny Zager was produced, claiming it was "MY song," and intimating he'd never been compensated adequately. A defiant Evans, who'd chosen to lead a quiet life in New Mexico, granted an interview to a blogger in 2013, in which Evans charged that Zager had "contributed next to nothing" and "didn't even need to be there" for the recording of the song. Perhaps the greatest one-album band of all time was Thunderclap Newman. The band's 1970 LP *Hollywood Dream* included the smash hit single *Something in the Air.* The band evidently never got along, and broke up after their one, highly successful record. All three primary band members died before their time, including guitarist Jimmy McCullough, who would go on to play in Paul McCartney's Wings, and passed away at only twenty-six of a heroin overdose, and primary songwriter and vocalist Speedy Keen (who was Pete Townshend's chauffeur - Townshend produced their record and played bass on it under a pseudonym), left the business in discouragement and after suffering for years from arthritis died at only fifty-six in 2002.[387] One hit wonder, James "Shep" Sheppard of the group Shep and the Limelites, scored big with 1961's *Daddy's Home,* but found no follow up success. Sheppard was murdered in his car during a robbery at age thirty-five. After hitting it big with *Pretty Little Angel Eyes* in 1961, Curtis Lee's career fizzled out and he eventually went back to working construction with his father.[388]

Rolf Harris had one smash hit, 1963's *Tie Me Kangeroo Down, Sport,* but didn't make the headlines again until 2014, when he was imprisoned for a slew of sexual offenses from decades earlier, some with underage girls.[389] John Frank Wilson's band J. Frank Wilson and the Cavaliers, struck it big in 1964 with *Last Kiss.* In one of those ironies which the entertainment world is strangely renowned for, Wilson was in a terrible car crash himself after the recording of this song, whose lyrics revolved around an auto accident. Wilson's manager died in the crash, and he was severely injured.[390] Wilson plugged on without any further musical success, and was forced to supplement his income by working in oil fields off the Gulf of Mexico, before dying from alcoholism at only forty-nine. One hit wonder Robert Knight, who charted big with 1967's *Everlasting Love,* went on to work as a groundskeeper, a lab technician and a chemistry teacher.[391] James Curtis, one of the original members of the legendary doo-wop group The Five Satins, best known for the classic 1956 song *In the Still of the Night,* later worked in the University of New Haven's cafeteria, according to Wikipedia. Largely forgotten singer and songwriter Arthur Alexander, whose work was recorded by the early Beatles, the Rolling Stones, and Bob Dylan, among others, never made much money in the business, even after Elvis Presley scored a #2 hit in 1972 with his composition *Burning Love.* By the 1980s, Alexander abandoned his music career and worked as a bus driver.[392] He died of a heart attack at only fifty-three, shortly after he had resumed performing. Margaret Battavio, as Little Peggy March, scored a number one hit with *I Will Follow Him* in 1963, but found no follow-up success. March actually suffered from the Coogan Law, because her parents were prevented from managing her money, and her manager squandered away all her earnings except for $500. Another young one-hit wonder was Marcia Blank, who under the name Marcie Blane recorded the #3 smash *Bobby's Girl* in 1962. Blane would leave the business after a few more songs failed to chart well, and went into the educational field. She refused all requests for interviews but one, which appeared in *Goldmine* magazine on December 30, 1988. She told the interviewer: "I decided not to continue…It was too difficult…It's taken all these years to be able to enjoy what there was."

When some entertainers do receive royalty checks, as noted earlier in the case of Janis Ian, they are often so small it's hardly worth the effort to cash them. A February 8, 1998 story in the *Los Angeles Times* recounted how Pat Morita, who played Arnold on *Happy Days,* had just been paid $14.18 for twenty-eight reruns of the long-running television series. At the other extreme, the financial radio program Marketplace estimated that Lisa Kudrow, one of the stars of the '90s show *Friends,* had earned an incredible $2,360,000 in residuals from reruns, as of 2014. The inconsistent nature of the business is especially stark in regards to royalties.

While the lead star of the television show *Punky Brewster,* Soleil Moon Frye, reportedly gets only $1 to $2 for each rerun of her show, actor Bob Gunton, who played a relatively minor role in the film *The Shawshack Redemption,* admitted that his royalties from the movie, even ten years after it was released, were close to six figures. Gunton termed it a "very substantial income," and admitted that, "I suspect my daughter, years from now, will still be getting checks."[393] And again, compare that to what the bully from *A Christmas Story* gets, for a similar role in a similarly successful film. It must be incredibly frustrating for those on the unfortunate side of such an inconsistent and unfair spectrum; in a November 2, 2019 Facebook post responding to the question "Do you still get residual pay when American Graffiti is on TV?," Paul Le Mat, one of the film's lead actors, replied, "Maybe. But miniscule. It diminished over time. That's how they work things." In an October 25, 2020 Facebook post, Le Mat addressed the subject of residuals from movies again, stating, "Yes but it isn't much, maybe $100, or $50 a year. It starts out okay for the first few times it shows on TV but diminishes (residuals) after that. The DVDs provide a bit."

As a writer, while figures vary some, I'm well aware of the fact that, according to a 2006 report from *Publishers Weekly,* the average published book sells only about three thousand copies. However, by 2012, the average nonfiction book was now said to be selling less than a paltry 250 copies per year.[394] A 1995 report found that the average LP from a major label sold 9.134 thousand copies.[395] By 2009, Nielsen Research showed that just 2.1 percent of the albums released that year sold even 5,000 copies. Just as one must factor in the Stephen Kings and J.K. Rowlings, which dramatically inflate the average book sales numbers, one must also factor in the huge music stars when tabulating album sales. Most writers, therefore, like most musical artists, actually sell even less of their creations than these already depressing numbers indicate. Given the struggles the fortunate few in the entertainment industry confront in trying to get their royalties, imagine the situation many far less successful people encounter, and the dismal proceeds they receive, when they are actually paid.

In 1940, the Motion Picture Relief Fund purchased forty-eight acres in the San Fernando Valley, to be used for a Motion Picture Country House. Many old actors had fallen on hard times financially, and this was the industry's way of providing them with shelter and a decent retirement. The House was dedicated on September 27, 1942. In 1948, a Motion Picture Hospital was added to the grounds. Later, the facility was opened up to those who'd worked in the television industry as well, and the new names, Motion Picture & Television Country House and Hospital, reflected that. While some notables were able to pay their own way, others (especially those who'd primarily worked behind the scenes) resided there for free, as everything was based upon an ability to pay. The majority of those who have resided there have been the anonymous people at the end of the credits, the bit actors, costume designers, grips, makeup artists and best boys; or actual examples like Sam Peckinpah's secretary, Bob Hope's publicist and the like. Still, a lot of surprisingly big names have found their way there as well.

The number of well-known performers who resided at the Motion Picture & Television Country House and Hospital is too lengthy to list. To cite just some examples of those who ended their days there: Bud Abbott, Eddie "Rochester" Anderson, Mary Astor, Whit Bissell, Eileen Brennan, Johnny Mack Brown, Virginia Bruce, Bruce Cabot, Mae Clarke, Ellen Corby, Robert Cummings, Yvonne DeCarlo, "Curly" Joe DeRita, Brian Donlevy, Norman Fell, Stepin Fetchit, Larry Fine, Max Fleischer, Annette Funicello, Peggy Ann Garner, Hoot Gibson, James Gleason, Virginia Grey, Edmund Gwenn, Curly Howard, DeForest Kelley, Patsy Kelly, Edgar Kennedy, Stanley Kramer, Elsa Lanchester, Joel McCrea, Hattie McDaniel, Virginia O'Brien, Donald O'Connor, Louella Parsons, Hank Patterson, Blossom Rock, Mack Sennett, Norma Shearer, Jay Silver-heels, Hal Smith, Hope Summers, Regis Toomey, Forrest Tucker, H.B. Warner and Johnny Weissmuller. While this is perhaps the world's most renowned nursing home, it is still a nursing home, and it's shocking to me that it has always been so "popular."

A lesser known place, the Percy Williams Home for aged and destitute actors, in East Islip, NY, was the final residence of prolific early talkie actor Guy Kibbee. Another lower profile place, the Lillian Booth Actors Home in Englewood, New Jersey, was where actress Sheila MacRae died at age ninety-two.[396] Melody Patterson, the lovely young star of television's *F Troop*, died in a Missouri nursing home at only sixty-six.[397] Onslow Stevens was a busy actor, from the pre-code talkies to the early years of television. He ended his days in a Van Nuys nursing home, after breaking his hip "under unclear circumstances," to quote IMDB. A coroner's inquest would mysteriously conclude that the injury had occurred "at the hands of another, not an accident."[398] Stevens was married to his fifth wife at the time of his death (but like so many others in Hollywood, he had no children), and she understandably tried to take the nursing home to task for mistreatment, but the case was eventually dropped. Stevens was buried in an unmarked grave, again like so many other entertainers. Perhaps strangest of all, Oscar winner Gloria Grahame went from being a popular leading lady to living in a Liverpool boarding house, where she met a boyfriend thirty years younger than her, Peter Turner. Turner's account of their relationship was turned into the movie *Film Stars Don't Die in Liverpool*. Grahame must have been financially strapped to be living in a boarding house, and Turner spoke of her hitting him up for money shortly after they first met. Press accounts also reported that the couple would often fly back and forth to the actress's apartment she still held in Manhattan Plaza, once notorious as part of the "Hell's Kitchen" section of New York City, which was an unusual Section 8 housing project, with occupancy limited to residents who were presently, or had once been, engaged in the performing arts.[399] After the actress actually moved in with Turner's parents and siblings, two of Grahame's children took her back to New York City, where she quickly died of her reoccurring cancer at only fifty-seven.

My friend John Barbour has talked about living in a California boarding house circa 1949, where one of his fellow residents was "a tall elegant former star of silent films. He had a wonderful head of long grey hair, a low rumbling voice that should have made him successful in talkies. But didn't. His last name was Kirkwood. I never tired of asking him about those days and those stars. And he never tired of telling me."[400] He was referring to James Kirkwood, who had played the lead in many of D.W. Griffith's early films. Kirkwood worked behind the camera as well, and was known to be Mary Pickford's favorite director. In one of those all too frequent Six Degrees of Kevin Bacon kind of connections; his son, actor and writer James Kirkwood, Jr., was personal friends with the notorious Clay Shaw, tried for the murder of John F. Kennedy by Jim Garrison, with whom Barbour later was associated. Barbour produced two excellent documentaries about Garrison's work: 1992's *The Jim Garrison Tapes* and 2017's brilliant *The American Media & the Second Assassination of President John F. Kennedy*.

As was made clear in the case of Natalie Wood's sister Lana, many close relatives of the rich and famous don't share in their success. Despite having one of the most famous sisters in the world, for example, Anthony Ciccone recently revealed that he was homeless and living on the streets in Michigan. "You think I haven't answered this kind of question a bazillion times -- why my sister is a multibazillionaire and I'm homeless on the street?" Madonna's older brother told the *Michigan Messenger*.[401] Julia Roberts' half-sister Nancy Motes took her own life in 2014 at just thirty-seven, and in her suicide note specifically accused Julia of not helping her, of being so cruel she "drove me into the deepest depression I've ever been in" and specifically requested that all of her very modest estate go to her fiancée John Dilbeck and not her family. At last report, Roberts, worth an astronomical $250 million, and her family were still engaged in a contentious legal battle with Dilbeck over the estate. In one of a series of earlier tweets, Motes had proclaimed, "Just so you all know, America's Sweetheart is a bitch." Dilbeck called Roberts a "monster" in an appearance on the television show *Inside Edition*.[402] For what it's worth, Roberts and especially Madonna have very poor reputations in their private interactions with the common riff-raff. Another entertainer with a horrible track record in dealing with fans, Mariah Carey has been estranged from her sister Allison, who had turned to prostitution and drugs, since the early 1990s, and has not seen fit to use any of her estimated $500 million fortune to help her.[403] Years ago, Laurence Fishburne's mother appeared on a talk show, basically pleading for her famous son to help her. In 2015, eighty-year-old Hattie Fishbourne told a reporter that, after emptying her retirement savings to finance her son's climb to stardom, she'd been unable to pay her rent for months, and was now facing eviction. "For 20 years, I funded my son's career. He promised me he would take care of me…To this day, I have not got a Christmas present or a 'Thank you, Mama' present. He hasn't given me a penny," Hattie claimed.[404] Halle Berry's half-sister was a food service worker in Alabama at last report.[405] Actress Meg Ryan didn't even invite her own mother, from whom she was estranged for unclear reasons, to her wedding to Dennis Quaid. Actress Heather Graham hasn't involved her family in her life since hitting it big in Hollywood.

Sondra Locke was estranged from her family to such an extent that her brother remarked, at the time of her death in 2018, that she'd only visited twice in fifty years. Her mother worked at a box factory, and was known to burst into tears at the mention of Sondra's name; the other employees were counseled not to even ask about her famous daughter. In a 1989 interview, Pauline Locke declared that she hadn't seen her daughter in fifteen years, and bitterly remarked, "One of those children Clint made her abort could've been the grandson I've always wanted." Locke was married for over fifty years to a gay man (the marriage was apparently never consummated), but had an open affair with Clint Eastwood from 1975-1989 and starred in six films with him. In their acrimonious split, Locke alleged that Eastwood had tapped her phone, was notoriously unfaithful, and eventually threw her belongings out on the lawn. Locke claimed she was blacklisted in Hollywood following her breakup with Eastwood.[406] Indeed, post- Eastwood, Locke had only two roles in 2000, and one curtain call in 2017.

George Harrison's much older sister Louise has spoken out in recent years, revealing that her brother had set up a modest $2,000 monthly pension for her in 1980. However, a year after Harrison's death in 2001, his widow Olivia stopped payments to the pension, leaving her in dire financial straits. The ex-Beatle left a $300 million estate behind, but stories with headlines like "Beatle George's Sister, 86, Broke Alone and in Missouri" focused on Louise "struggling to eke out an existence, living in a pre-fabricated home."[407] Louise's memoir, *My Kid Brother's Band a.k.a. The Beatles!* was published in 2014. Although she didn't see her famous brother for twenty years during the height of his fame, and was left entirely out of his substantial will, Louise maintained a stereotypical British stiff upper lip. "I have enough abilities that I can earn a living," she declared, "so don't worry about that. Obviously somebody needed the $2,000 a month more than I did. It's only money. As far as I'm concerned, I'm wealthy, because I have really good friends." Louise's income derives primarily from managing the Liverpool Legends, one of the better Beatles tribute bands.[408]

Academy Award-winning siblings Olivia de Havilland and Joan Fontaine had perhaps the most intense feud in the history of show business. Shockingly immature in their pettiness and envy towards one another, the sisters barely spoke to each other for decades. Olivia's press agent, Henry Rogers, provided a suitably nonsensical explanation for the vicious animosity, stating, "This goes back for years and years, ever since they were kids — a case of two sisters who don't have a great deal in common."[409] Considering how they each defied all actuarial odds in becoming famous, Oscar award-winning actresses, it would seem they had a great deal in common. The Andrews Sisters, the most successful female recording group in pop music history, feuded constantly with each other. Strong-willed brothers Jimmy and Tommy Dorsey had a decade long feud, but later reunited into a second version of the Dorsey Brothers band. Kinks' brothers Ray and Dave Davies were notorious for their feuds and fist fights. In 1996, Ray ruined his younger brother Dave's fiftieth birthday party by jumping on top of the cake, and proclaiming what a genius he was. The brothers have not performed together since then. Phil Everly abruptly walked off the stage in the middle of a 1973 Everly Brothers concert, leaving brother Don to tell the audience that the duo was finished. They broke off communication for a decade until a 1983 reunion concert. Brothers Robert and Richard Sherman wrote the scores for many Disney films, including the unforgettable soundtrack for *Mary Poppins,* and composed other popular songs such as *It's a Small World After All.* For unclear reasons, they had a very strained personal relationship, and their families didn't speak to each other for forty years. When they attended movie premieres, they sat on opposite sides of the theater with their respective families. When their father died, each brother held a separate ceremony.[410]

Cousins and Beach Boys' band mates Brian Wilson and Mike Love have had a contentious relationship for decades. Non-relatives Paul Simon and Art Garfunkel had constant troubles, too. When Garfunkel took the high road during the duo's induction into the Rock and Roll Hall of Fame ceremony by praising Simon's songwriting skills, Simon responded by declaring, "Arthur and I agree about almost nothing, but it's true, I have enriched his life quite a bit."[411] Agnetha Faltskog, the blonde singer in Abba who was widely promoted as a sex symbol, went into virtual seclusion for twenty-five years after the group broke up. The four band members attended the Swedish film premiere of *Mama Mia!* in 2008, but residual bitterness prevented them from even posing for a photograph together. Agnetha's spokesman explained, "They do not socialize with each other. They just happened to come to the same premiere."[412] While the cast members of one of my favorite television shows, *SCTV*, certainly seem to have gotten along well, I was still a bit shocked when reading Andrea Martin's 2014 memoir *Lady Parts*. Martin recounted how she'd emailed all of her former co-stars, to ask for their personal remembrances to include in her book. Evidently, she never heard from Joe Flaherty, but wasn't very surprised about it, describing him as extremely talented but eccentric. She didn't quote email responses from Rick Moranis or Dave Thomas, either, leading me to believe they didn't reply to her. That's just unfathomable to me. I guess I shouldn't complain about these veteran celebrities not answering *my* emails.

George Raft and Edward G. Robinson were not only rivals for the same kinds of roles, they despised each other off-screen. Robinson also hated the difficult and temperamental Miriam Hopkins. Hopkins had a legendary feud with another difficult star, Bette Davis. Davis allegedly slapped practical jokester and Golden Age stud Errol Flynn, with a hand full of heavy period rings, on the set of *The Private Lives of Elizabeth and Essex*. Just one of Flynn's "jokes" consisted of placing a dead snake in Olivia de Havilland's underwear. The even more celebrated battle between Davis and Joan Crawford probably added to the overall appeal of their film *Whatever Happened to Baby Jane?* Another classic A-list feud was between W.C. Fields and Mae West. Not only did Joan Fontaine have a strained relationship, to put it mildly, with her famous sister, she also couldn't stand Cary Grant. Jack Warner didn't even attend his brother Harry's funeral, after they'd worked together for fifty years. Greer Garson and Clark Gable detested working with each other, and Vivien Leigh loathed kissing Gable, claiming that his dentures produced some extremely bad breath. The very respectable Leigh (who nevertheless began her torrid romance with Laurence Olivier while both were married to others) also found young Marlon Brando crude and repulsive. Lee Marvin was so perturbed by *Paint Your Wagon* director Josh Logan that he urinated on his shoes. It's rumored that Lawrence Olivier whispered obscenities in Joan Fontaine's ear throughout the filming of Alfred Hitchcock's classic *Rebecca*. Competing combative personalities Frank Sinatra and Marlon Brando reportedly wouldn't even exchange greetings on the set of *Guys and Dolls*.

Martin and Lewis rivaled Abbott and Costello as the top comedy duo of the 1950s. Their breakup was almost as epic as Lucy and Ricky's divorce. Jerry Lewis tended to blame things on Dean Martin, once explaining, "I loved Dean almost as much as my wife and kids. I worked twenty four hours a day to keep him liking me… But he was never as warm and outgoing as I hoped he'd be." Plenty of anecdotal evidence, however, suggests Lewis was a difficult person to work with. Norman Lear, who started out in the biz writing for Martin and Lewis, claimed that Lewis couldn't stand it when the naturally funny Martin got the laughs, and would respond like a child, sulking in the corner. When Dean walked out on the act, he told Lewis, "You can talk all you want about love. To me, you're just a dollar sign."[413] Lou Costello would leave Bud Abbott in a similar way, apparently fed up with carrying the act. In contrast to his lovable screen persona, Costello was a melancholy drunk in real life, his alcoholism understandably exacerbated after his small son died tragically. In 1958, Abbott sued Costello for some $222,000 in unpaid royalties[414], a year before his portly ex-partner died suddenly of a heart attack only a few days prior to his fifty-third birthday. Abbott lost whatever money he had, and lived off of his $180 monthly Social Security benefit in his sad final years. The heirs of Abbott and Costello sued a Broadway play in 2015, claiming copyright infringement of the duo's famous "Who's on first?" routine.[415]

Two comics who were never a team, Jackie Gleason and Milton Berle, despised each other.

Some entertainers have such a terrible reputation that it is impossible for the industry to hide it. One of show business's all-time bastards was Arthur Godfrey. It would probably be difficult for anyone to top what Godfrey did to young, up-and-coming singer Julius LaRosa, during an October 19, 1953 live broadcast of *Arthur Godfrey and Friends*. Godfrey shocked the young crooner by firing him on air. The notoriously cheap Godfrey had been paying LaRosa $191 weekly, which was industry scale, but the exposure was indispensable for his huge record sales. Incredibly, it was for all intents and purposes the end of a highly promising career. Except for a stint as a disc jockey in New York and sporadic nightclub appearances, LaRosa was essentially finished in show business.[416] Godfrey wasn't exactly popular in the entertainment world. "That folksy shit of Godfrey's," Ed Sullivan once said, "just hides the fact that he's downright ignorant." There were plenty of nasty real-life personalities in the early days of television. Milton Berle was an incorrigible comedy plagiarist, and Red Buttons bullied and abused his staff so thoroughly that no one wanted to work with him.

The other cast members of *The Beverly Hillbillies* found working with Raymond Bailey (who played banker Milburn Drysdale) to be very difficult. Maybe they were bitter over the fact legend has it that they were all (except star Buddy Ebsen) being paid barely above union scale. Ebsen was a hard-line Republican conservative, and when Nancy Kulp (Jane Hathaway) ran for Congress as a liberal Democrat, even though he didn't live in her district, Ebsen campaigned openly for her opponent, who was victorious. Max "Jethro Bodine" Baer, Jr. didn't become rich from the show, but he made quite a bit of money later from producing and writing the extremely low budget (only $110,000) 1974 film *Macon County Line*, which earned nearly $25 million at the box office. Baer's net worth is said to be an impressive $50 million. Tina Louise, who played the pretentious movie star Ginger on *Gilligan's Island*, was apparently very much like her character in real life. Dawn Wells recounted how Louise would order mink eyelashes from New York, which were $50 a pair, and "was glamorous all the time."[417] Barbara Eden reported, in her 2011 memoir *Jeannie Out of the Bottle* that when she won an early role on Ann Sothern's television program, the star was so jealous of her good looks she forced wardrobe to make the young beauty look less attractive when they did scenes together. Eden also recounted how Lucille Ball was constantly arguing with her unfaithful husband Desi Arnaz. Interestingly, Eden claimed to have rebuffed the advances of many, including legendary ladies men John F. Kennedy, Elvis Presley, and Warren Beatty. She revealed that *I Dream of Jeannie* co-star Larry Hagman, who was known to abuse alcohol and drugs and was very demanding with the crew, once urinated on the set and on another occasion swung an axe at some visiting nuns. According to Eden, Hagman was paid a very generous for the time $150,000 yearly. Another of her revelations was that guest star Groucho Marx refused a fee because he didn't want to pay taxes on it, and instead accepted a new television set as payment. Like so many others in show business, Eden experienced personal tragedy when her son overdosed on heroin at age thirty-five. Co-star Bill Daily and director Gene Nelson both recounted how difficult it was to work with Hagman. Nelson, echoing one of Eden's claims, stated that "When Larry got really mad, he'd go down to the set and piss all over the set. I understand that, eventually, NBC had to hire an on-the-set psychiatrist to be with him every day."[418]

Considering that he starred not only in *I Dream of Jeannie*, but the later super successful *Dallas*, Hagman's estate of $15 million was pretty modest. Especially when considering that his onscreen wife in *Dallas*, Linda Gray, is worth nearly as much, at $12 million, despite doing not a whole lot before or after the series. That's show business for you.

Chapter Five

Show Business Crime And Corruption

It's interesting that these themes of crime and political corruption are always relevant.

Martin Scorsese

ACTOR WOODY HARRELSON once remarked, "Every [acting] business I ever entered into in New York seemed to have a casting couch....I've seen so many people sleep with people they loathe in order to further their ambition."[419] Actress Jenny McCarthy similarly acknowledged that "L.A. [Los Angeles] is the worst place in the world to try to feel secure. The girls that moved out there at the same time as me, I watched them fizzle and turn into walking on the streets at night. You see that in the movies and hear about casting couches---which I thought were just big fluffy couches---but you don't know till you experience it how corrupt it is. I was the only girl in my clique who wasn't sleeping with someone to get a job."[420]

Chris Hanley, producer of films like *American Psycho, The Virgin Suicides* and others, discussed the Hollywood casting process at his class reunion at Amherst College. "Almost every leading actress in all of my 24 films has slept with a director or producer or a leading actor to get the part that launched her career," he declared.[421] The explosive revelations concerning Hollywood magnate Harvey Weinstein and others which burst into the headlines in 2017, verified what many fans had long suspected. It isn't who you know, it's who you blow, and all that. Rose McGowan was one of many actresses accusing Weinstein of improprieties. McGowan's former manager Jill Messick, who'd been caught in the crossfire, took her own life on February 7, 2018. Messick's family issued a statement referring to her as "collateral damage in an already horrific story."[422] Two women alleged that *Ren and Stimpy* creator John Kricfalusi regularly hit on teenage girls during the 1990s, when he was in his thirties. One girl claimed that he'd first started talking to her when she was just thirteen. She would later move in with him as his underage girlfriend. More than one of his young female friends accused him of possessing child pornography.[423] Actress Candy Clark, best remembered as the unattainable blonde, Debby, in *American Graffiti,* answered my question if she knew Weinstein on Facebook in an October 26, 2019 post, saying, "I'm too old for him. Donald, I have met him in the past but I do not know him. Gawd, he is an ugly man. In every way. He had to expect this would happen. Pariah, now."

Sadly, it isn't just adults who are steered toward the casting couch. Actor Corey Feldman, himself a survivor of childhood sexual abuse by largely unnamed Hollywood power brokers, "unflinchingly warned of the world of pedophiles who are drawn to the entertainment industry," to quote from a December 5, 2011 Fox News story that would be updated on April 8, 2016. "I can tell you that the No. 1 problem in Hollywood was, is, and always will be pedophilia." Feldman declared. A child star from an earlier era, Paul Petersen of *The*

Donna Reed Show, echoed Feldman's claims. "When I watched that interview, a whole series of names and faces from my history went zooming through my head," Petersen said. "Some of these people, who I know very well, are still in the game....The casting couch is a real thing, and sometimes just getting an appointment makes people do desperate things (like prostitute themselves)." According to actress Alison Arngrim, best remembered for her role in *Little House on the Prairie,* "This has been going on for a very long time.... It was the gossip back in the '80s. People said, 'Oh yeah, the Coreys [Corey Feldman and actor Corey Haim], everyone's had them.' People talked about it like it was not a big deal....I literally heard that they were 'passed around'....The word was that they were given drugs and being used for sex....There were all sorts of stories about everyone from their, quote, 'set guardians' on down that these two had been sexually abused and were totally being corrupted in every possible way."[424] Elijah Wood echoed Feldman's claims, and stated that while his mother had protected him, other child actors had been "preyed upon" by "vipers" in Hollywood. In 2014, Stephen Collins, star of the television series *Seventh Heaven,* confessed to molesting at least one underage girl years before. When a reunion of the show was being discussed in early 2017, his onscreen wife Catherine Hicks reversed her early position that Collins "would have to be dead" for the cast to come together again, and said she had forgiven him and would participate.[425]

Isaac Kappy was an actor who had bit roles in movies like 2011's *Thor* and 2009's *Terminator Salvation.* Kappy gained notoriety in 2018 when he released videos alleging that multiple Hollywood figures, such as *Family Guy* voice actor Seth Green, were part of an insidious network of pedophiles, prompting an investigation by the Los Angeles Police Department. Adding a suitable exclamation point to his controversial allegations was Kappy's supposed suicide on May 13, 2019. The forty-two-year-old was said to have jumped from a bridge in Bellemont, Arizona.[426] Like others linked to political corruption (for example, Deborah Jeane Palfrey, the so-called "D.C. Madam"), Kappy had publicly declared that he would never kill himself. After his allegations were "investigated" by the LAPD, Kappy himself became the focus of police attention, and supposedly had threatened a shootout with them. He was also accused of choking Michael Jackson's daughter Paris, and stalking Seth Green and his wife. In July, 2018, Kappy tweeted out, "In light of the interesting traffic happening around my house I want to make something CRYSTAL CLEAR: while I am a VERY strong advocate of peaceful disclosure, make no mistake, assets are in place and if you kill me or even try, it will rain .50 cals in the Hollywood Hills."[427] Was Kappy merely mentally unbalanced? Or another silenced whistleblower? One big name Kappy fingered was Steven Spielberg, whom some in the conspiracy world have connected to the earlier discussed, very strange death of young Heather O'Rourke, who achieved her greatest renown in the *Poltergeist* films, which he produced and co-wrote. In 2017, stories broke that Spielberg had also actually been the initial 1982 film's uncredited director.

The myriad of sordid #MeToo revelations that broke concerning not only Harvey Weinstein, but seemingly much of Hollywood, thrust Corey Feldman and his claims back into the headlines in late 2017. Feldman was frustratingly slow about revealing any big names, but did charge that Charlie Sheen had raped then fourteen-year-old Corey Haim. The show business industry exploded with allegations of sexual improprieties, including those leveled against numerous entertainers, like Ben Affleck, Dustin Hoffman, Louis CK and Kevin Spacey. The most shocking claim, at least to me, concerned former *Smallville* star Allison Mack. The quintessential "girl next door"-type, Mack was exposed as being second-in-command of a surreal sex cult, under the auspices of a "self-help" group called NXIVM DOS. The secretive organization was accused of beating and branding women and blackmailing them into sexual slavery. The controversial group was founded in 1998 by Keith Raniere.

DOS allegedly stands for Dominus Obsequious Sororium, Latin for "Master over the slave women." Mack was supposedly totally subservient to Raniere, agreeing to run some forty miles a week and maintain a strict diet regimen in order to stay as thin as possible. The group's former publicist was quoted as saying that Mack, like the girls she dominated, had been "brainwashed" by Raniere.[428] Former *Dynasty* star Catherine Oxenberg was one of those who came forward to allege that her daughter had been abused by the cult. A March 28, 2018 story in *Rolling Stone* disclosed that Mack's *Smallville* co-star Kristen Kreuk had also been involved, but had left before becoming as deeply entwined with the cult as Mack. Raniere was finally arrested in Mexico, and a disturbingly emaciated looking Allison Mack was photographed at the scene. Mack and the other women in the group were absolutely submissive to Raniere, as the rules dictated that he could enjoy multiple lovers, while they must all remain monogamous. Apparently, Raniere had used incriminating personal information to blackmail his slaves into servitude. Further updates mentioned that the group had even been tied to child pornography.[429]

The group allegedly had numerous celebrated connections, to the likes of the Clinton Foundation, veteran political strategist Roger Stone, and Doug Rutnik, wealthy father of U.S. Senator and Democratic Party presidential candidate Kirsten Gillibrand.[430] In April, 2019, a notably unrepentant Mack (she declared that "Through it all, I believed Keith Raniere's intentions were to help people. I was wrong.") pleaded guilty to reduced charges. [431] A few months later, in June, Keith Raniere was convicted on all counts of sex-trafficking and coercing women into sex. He was ultimately sentenced to 120 years in prison.[432] Criminal defense attorney Silva Megerditchian told Yahoo Entertainment that "Allison Mack is facing a total of 40 years maximum confinement time in the two charges she plead guilty to in federal court," but expected a legal defense that stressed her lack of a previous criminal record, remorse, and attempted to portray her as a victim.[433] Shortly thereafter, Mack's lawyers argued that she shouldn't be considered guilty of "forced labor" if the Church of Scientology isn't. They cited a 2009 case where a couple unsuccessfully sued the Church of Scientology for forced labor.[434] In late 2020, a documentary miniseries on the cult appeared on both Starz and HBO.

The Tragic Case of Patricia Douglas

The dual standard of justice in America is ironclad, as is the anti-whistleblower mentality. Thus, sexual assault and rape often go unpunished in the entertainment world. Those who've been victimized by someone powerful within the industry will almost inexorably be ostracized for going public. An aspiring actress named Patricia Douglas, for instance, was a background dancer in Hollywood musicals. In 1937, Douglas responded to an MGM casting call for more than one hundred female dancers, to act as hostesses at a sales convention. On May 5, the convention concluded with a wild party at the Hal Roach Studios ranch. During this party, the women were sexually harassed by intoxicated guests. At one point, actor Wallace Beery supposedly beat up a couple of men to protect one of the hostesses. Douglas was force fed alcohol by a salesman named David Ross, who then dragged her out to his car and raped her. Douglas was treated at a nearby hospital, but no police report was filed. Douglas decided to file a complaint herself against MGM. The studio responded by smearing Douglas' name in the media. A grand jury subsequently failed to indict Ross. Douglas attempted to file a lawsuit against Ross and prominent film executives like Hal Roach and Eddie Mannix. The court dismissed her case and Douglas was, not coincidentally, blacklisted by Hollywood. The eighty-six-year-old Douglas was tracked down in 2003, shortly before her death, and her story appeared in the April 2003 *Vanity Fair* magazine. It was then turned into the documentary *Girl 27*.

Before her rape and subsequent exile from the film world, Douglas had hobnobbed with a variety of big stars, including Bing Crosby, Dick Powell, and George Raft, whom she reported had cried on her very young shoulder about his sexual impotence. She memorably described eating with Larry Fine of the Three Stooges, about whom she said, "What a blue tongue! Even at the dinner table, you should've heard him: 'Pass the fucking potatoes!'" Douglas had to count on the integrity of then district attorney Buron Fitts, who had recently been indicted for perjury in a rape case involving a sixteen-year-old girl. One of Fitts' close friends was MGM head Louis B. Mayer, whose studio had been the largest contributor to Fitts' campaign. Budd Schulberg, son of Mayer's partner B.P. Schulberg, bluntly stated, "Buron Fitts was completely in the pocket of the producers. The power MGM had is unimaginable today. They owned everyone—the D.A., the L.A.P.D. They ran this place." MGM hired the Pinkerton Detective Agency to warn every other "dancer" at the party where Douglas was raped to toe the party line. Some of them portrayed the tee-totaling Douglas as a heavy drinker, and one internal Roach Studios memo declared, "Douglas must have attempted to proposition men. Many of them must have turned her down but can testify to her solicitation." Hal Roach himself attempted to force urologist Dr. Wirt Dakin to falsely claim that an innocent cyst on Douglas' bladder had actually been gonorrhea. Only two of the 120 dancers at the party testified for Douglas at a sham grand-jury hearing on June 16, 1937. One of them had been defended by Wallace Beery, as noted previously, but the actor now denied this in a studio-scripted statement. Douglas had to endure the defense attorney pointing at her in scorn and exclaiming to the jury, "Look at her. Who would want her?" The daughters of a parking lot attendant who initially identified salesman David Ross fleeing from a disheveled, distraught Douglas but changed his testimony, revealed decades later that MGM had offered him "any job he wanted" in return for his perjury.

Douglas continued to fight for justice, filing a lawsuit in Los Angeles Superior Court against Ross, Mannix, Roach and others. An internal MGM memo from Roach Studios attorney Victor Fred Collins essentially confessed to more payouts for perjured testimony, stating, "I just had another talk with [bit player and gossip-monger] Bobby Tracy, one of our star witnesses in the Douglas case. He seems badly in need of work, and was very much in the hopes that somebody could phone Mr. Mannix direct about him getting a few days at M-G-M…. It is highly imperative that we keep these people in good humor, and get them some kind of work. May I again say—it is really important!" On February 9, 1938, a superior court judge predictably dismissed the case. Still battling, Douglas immediately filed a suit in U.S. District Court. This case was dismissed as well, when Douglas' own defense attorney sabotaged her. Buron Fitts would later become yet another of Hollywood's plentiful suicides, when he shot himself a week after his seventy-eighth birthday. Eddie Mannix candidly admitted shortly before his own death in 1963, that "We had her killed." Another anonymous interviewee would later echo this, telling reporter David Stenn, who wrote the story in *Vanity Fair* and wrote and directed the *Girl 27* documentary, "They had her killed." Although this was only in a figurative sense, Douglas would declare, at age eighty-six, that "It absolutely ruined my life." Believing herself to be a "tramp," Douglas began acting like one after all her legal efforts failed. She wound up marrying three times in five years, and then, at the tender age of thirty-seven, swore off relationships and sex for the rest of her life. An interesting footnote to the Douglas story is the fact that Jacqueline Kennedy Onassis was David Stenn's editor. Stenn described how she'd asked, "What are we going to do next?" following their collaboration on *Bombshell: The Life and Death of Jean Harlow*.

Actress Janis Paige, still alive at age ninety-eight as I write this, was a lot luckier than Patricia Douglas. In the wake of the slew of disclosures coming out in 2017 against Harvey Weinstein and other powerful figures in Hollywood, Paige decided to break her silence and say "Me, too." Paige described being set up on a date with Alfred Bloomingdale, heir to the department store fortune. Bloomingdale was a sordid character who was bestowed with the dubious honor of being "the father of the credit card." As I described in detail in my earlier book *Hidden History*, decades later Bloomingdale would make headlines for being involved in a sadomasochistic affair with the much younger Vicki Morgan, who would go on to be murdered under highly questionable circumstances. Paige reluctantly went out with Bloomingdale, whom she was not remotely attracted to, and was taken to Hollywood's distinctive Romanoff's restaurant. After luring her inside his apartment, Paige described what happened: "Dutifully, I followed him into the elevator and up to his apartment. He opened the door, and as I stepped inside, I heard it slam. Without a word, he suddenly reached around me and tore my blouse open. I could feel his hands, not only on my breasts, but seemingly everywhere. He was big and strong, and I began to fight, kick, bite and scream. When he put his hand over my mouth, I couldn't breathe and thought I was going to die. I bit him as hard as I could and opened the door. I ran down about six flights of stairs, hysterical and sobbing to Sunset Boulevard…." Paige remained silent for all those decades, because she feared for her job, and didn't think anyone would believe her.[435]

Joan Bennett, perhaps the most famous of the acting sisters, began an affair with her agent, Jennings Lang, while she was married to high-profile producer Walter Wanger. On December 13, 1951, Wanger fired two shots at Lang, which caused superficial wounds. When Wanger was indicted for assault with attempt to commit murder, his attorneys argued a defense of temporary insanity, maintaining that he was under considerable stress due to financial difficulties. In a true "celebrity special," Wanger was sentenced to four months at the Wayside Honor Farm, an institution clearly catering to wealthy offenders, and then successfully resumed his career. Oddly, it was Joan Bennett's career that was seriously impacted, and for a period of time she was practically blacklisted. Despite the scandal, Wanger and Bennett remained married until 1965.[436] Tough guy actor Paul Kelly lived up to his screen image by inflicting a severe beating on vaudeville performer Ray Raymond on April 16, 1927. Kelly had been having an affair with Raymond's wife, Dorothy Mackaye, who'd appeared uncredited in one 1917 film and would later write a play that would be turned into the 1933 Barbara Stanwyck vehicle *Ladies They Talk About*. Raymond died a few days after being beaten by Kelly, who was imprisoned for only two years at San Quentin. Mackaye herself served two months in prison for helping to cover up the crime. After he was released, Kelly and Mackaye were married, and remained a couple until she was killed at just forty in a one-car automobile accident. The scandal hardly hindered Kelly's career, and he flourished in the same tough-guy roles until his death in 1956.[437]

Donnell "Spade" Cooley was country music's first superstar. During the 1940s, Cooley often performed in Hollywood Westerns. Cooley married Ella Mae Evans, a singer in his band. A very jealous man, Cooley murdered his wife in a fit of rage on April 3, 1961 over her confession that she'd had an affair with his frequent co-star Roy Rogers, and had in fact been part of an early-day sex "cult." Cooley even forced his fourteen-year-old daughter to watch him beat and then shoot her mother.[438] Cooley was sentenced to life in prison, and was a model prisoner at Vacaville. In 1969, he learned he was going to be paroled, thanks to the influence of his longtime friend, California governor Ronald Reagan. On November 23, he was granted a three day furlough to play at a benefit concert in Oakland. After the performance, the fifty-eight- year-old died of a heart attack backstage. Spade Cooley is the only convicted murderer to have a star on the Hollywood Walk of Fame. Busy actress Lila Lee, perhaps best recalled for her role in the remake of *The Unholy Three,* Lon Chaney's last film and only talking picture, somehow avoided a nasty scandal when her boyfriend, Reid Russell, was shot to death in 1936 while on the garden swing at a friend's cottage. Authorities couldn't determine if it was a case of murder or suicide.[439]

One actress who combined crime with an astonishing descent into obscurity is the now completely forgotten Constance Smith. The Irish-born Smith starred in some big-budget films in the 1950s, and was a presenter at the 1952 Academy Awards ceremony. Smith became one of the many actresses forced to undergo an abortion by the studios, and her fiery temperament didn't endear her to the studio bosses. Falling inexorably for the allure of drugs and alcohol, Smith was sentenced to three months in prison for stabbing her filmmaker boyfriend Paul Rotha in 1962.[440] She stabbed Rotha again in 1968 and was charged with attempted murder. Despite all this, Rotha married her in 1974. Smith also attempted suicide multiple times and was in and out of hospitals during the later part of her life. Whatever earnings she made in Hollywood long gone, Smith eventually was forced to work as a cleaner.[441] Joey Heatherton's story is almost as tragic. A voluptuous sex symbol of the 1960s-70s era, Heatherton married pro football star Lance Rentzel, who would go on to expose himself to a ten-year-old-girl. As Heatherton's career began to wane, her personal troubles escalated. In July, 1985, she was arrested twice; first for theft of services regarding an unpaid hotel bill, and then for disturbing the peace and interfering with the duties of a government agent at Manhattan's U.S. Passport Agency Office. In 1986, she stabbed her ex- boyfriend and manager in the hand during an argument. She was charged with assault and misdemeanor drug possession.[442] That same year, she was charged with income tax evasion by the IRS. The former star has had two minor screen credits in the past thirty years, and posed nude for Playboy in 1997, still sexy at age fifty-three. Heatherton was plagued by substance abuse and eating disorder problems. In a trivial historical tidbit, Joey Heatherton was the "mystery guest" on the game show *What's My Line* on November 7, 1965. Only a few hours later, longtime panelist Dorothy Kilgallen would be found dead under very suspicious circumstances, which some suspect was connected to her investigation into the assassination of John F. Kennedy. Former Mouseketeer Darleen Gillespie became a nurse after her brief fame on *The Mickey Mouse Club* ended, but made headlines in 1997 when she and her husband were arrested for petty theft, and served three months in prison for a 1998 conviction for check kiting and fraud. In 2005, she was indicted along with her husband on multiple charges, which were later dropped.[443]

English actress Sarah Miles, who'd been nominated for an Academy Award in *Ryan's Daughter* a few years previously, was starring alongside huge box office attraction Burt Reynolds in 1973's *The Man Who Loved Cat Dancing*. With the married Miles on the set was her twenty-six-year-old business manager and apparent lover, David Whiting. On the evening of February 11, Miles went to Reynolds' motel room after a party and stayed until the early morning hours. When Miles returned to her own room, an enraged Whiting physically attacked her. Reynolds came to Miles' rescue and took her back to the safety of his room. When Miles returned to her room in the morning, Whiting was lying dead on the bathroom floor, in a huge pool of blood and with an empty vial in his hand, while pills lay scattered across the floor. Miles would change her story, and Reynolds admitted removing the vial from Whiting's hand, but couldn't recall what he did with it. The initial cause of death was reported to be a drug overdose, but a pharmacologist hired by Whiting's family found that there wasn't a lethal amount of drugs in his system. Whiting also had a cut on the back of his head, unexplained scratches on his body, and there were blood traces throughout the room. There was understandable speculation at the time that Reynolds and/or Miles had been involved in Whiting's death. An investigation inexplicably concluded, however, that despite the non-lethal amount of drugs in his system, and the mysterious injuries on his head and body, that

Whiting had taken his own life. Miles later commented: "It went on for six months. Murder? Suicide? Murder! Suicide! Murder! Suicide! And, gradually, the truth came out, which I'm not going to speak about, but it certainly wasn't me. I had actually saved the man from three suicide attempts so why would I want to murder him? I really can't imagine."[444] Miles, whose last screen credit was in 2004, boasts of the health benefits she has incurred from drinking her own urine for years. According to the book *With Love and Laughter, John Ritter* by Amy Yasbeck, the star of *Three's Company* was noted for shocking nearby patrons in restaurants by slamming his hands down upon the table and declaring, "And *that*, kids, is how Burt Reynolds got away with murder." Reynolds was also the last known person to see actress Inger Stevens before she allegedly killed herself, after having an argument with him on the evening of April 29, 1970.

Lenny Bruce, over fifty years after his death, remains perhaps the most controversial comedian of all time. As one writer put it, Bruce was "a public figure who could seldom work in public." After he was found naked on August 3, 1966, with a needle in his arm, dead at only forty, *Time* magazine, a bastion of the establishment he regularly excoriated, labeled him "the Elvis of comedy." One of those who prosecuted Bruce for indecency was quoted in the comedian's defense attorney Martin Garbus's 1971 book *Ready for the Defense* as admitting, "I feel terrible about Bruce. We drove him into poverty and bankruptcy and then murdered him...."[445] According to John Barbour, who knew Lenny Bruce; his mother Sally Marr, with whom he had a very close relationship, "was convinced that the LAPD had set him up by selling him treated cocaine, and that as a warning and an example to America, staged the gruesome death photo, sticking the needle in his arms. She also wondered aloud, when Bill Hicks, who reminded her of her son, started to fill auditoriums attacking the government, if maybe they, too, had something to do with his getting cancer at such a young age."[446]

What Happened to Brittany Murphy?

The death of thirty-two-year-old actress Brittany Murphy is another truly baffling case. Brittany was a typically slim film star who, we are told, died of "natural causes" in the prime of her life. The official narrative is that the young actress was discovered lying on her bathroom floor on December 20, 2009 by her mother Sharon Murphy, who lived with her along with Brittany's husband Simon Monjack. The L.A. County Coroner would state that Brittany's mother's 911 call was "10 minutes too late." She was subsequently declared dead at Cedars-Sinai Medical Center. Brittany's father Angelo Bertolotti was very critical of the autopsy findings, which concluded his daughter had died from a combination of "community acquired pneumonia," iron deficiency anemia and multiple drug intoxication, which ludicrously added up to "natural causes." Bertolotti declared that his daughter's case was "opened and closed on the same day" without factoring in any toxicology results from hair and tissue samples, which he would charge were never completed. Bertolotti would in fact sue both the LAPD and the L.A. coroner, in an effort to obtain samples to independently test.[447] To cite just one example of the incomplete nature of the autopsy, Brittany Murphy's nails were not examined. Like too many entertainers, Brittany was taking an absurd number of medications, and was also evidently suffering from chronic anxiety. It remains unclear just how many of these drugs were being taken by Brittany, and how many were actually for her mother and husband, who both were on a number of pharmaceuticals as well. Reports indicated that Brittany was purchasing between 200-400 pills every month at a local drug store.

Brittany Murphy, for a seemingly fit woman in her early thirties, seemed to have some serious medical issues. She was diabetic, and was taking medicine for high blood pressure. According to the autopsy report, she'd been complaining of shortness of breath and abdominal pains in the week leading up to her death. However, the same report stated that "There is no history of alcohol or drug abuse." While a litany of prescriptions and over-the-counter drugs are listed as being used by Brittany, it is glaringly odd that her mother had told the 911 dispatcher, more than once, that her daughter had not been taking any medications.[448] Brittany's forty-year-old husband Simon Monjack, who suspiciously tried to prevent an autopsy after his wife's sudden, inexplicable death, would die himself under eerily similar circumstances just five months later. Monjack's autopsy would disclose that he'd suffered a mild heart attack the month before, and report that Sharon Murphy had waited at least forty-five minutes before calling 911, even though Monjack was unresponsive. The coroner determined that Monjack could in fact have been dead for hours before help was summoned.[449] There was a redacted reference in the report to Monjack and Sharon Murphy sleeping together. Simon's mother would later allege that she had pleaded with Sharon over the phone to get her son some medical help, to no avail.

Angelo Bertolotti, who had previously served time in prison for his apparent organized crime activities, nevertheless was seemingly the only one pursuing the truth about his daughter's death. "I've been attacked and slandered for my attempts to expose the truth about the way my daughter and son-in-law were treated before and after their deaths," Bertolotti declared. "Justice will no longer be obstructed through name-calling and media cover-up. The day of accountability is near....Years after my daughter's untimely death, toxicology testing on her hair still has not been completed. Office of the Los Angeles Coroner and the Los Angeles Police Department admitted that such tests were not done and refused to conduct them. At this point, I am asking the court to intervene and allow me to get the specimens independently tested. Brittany's hair and tissues were about to be destroyed, but I've paid to have them preserved, so that they could finally be examined. I'm not going to rest until my daughter's untimely demise is properly investigated, which hasn't happened so far. Her case deserves more than a superficial glance."[450] Bertolotti paid for two independent tests, both of which found that there were unsafe levels of metals and toxins in Brittany's body. This, of course, strongly suggests poisoning. Bertolotti blasted the way the media inaccurately reported his daughter's death, and admitted, "I expected to be attacked for embarrassing the L.A. Coroner....There is nothing natural in the way Brittany and Simon died." Sharon Murphy would respond angrily to Bertolotti's claims, in an open letter published by the *Hollywood Reporter* on November 25, 2013. She alleged that Bertolotti had never been there for Brittany as a father during her life, called it "madness" to suggest their daughter had been murdered, and dismissed any theories of foul play.

Bertolotti's suspicions about his daughter's death were stoked by Julia Davis, formerly a Customs and Border Protection Officer with Homeland Security. Davis was one of those pesky whistleblowers, who alleged that the Department of Homeland Security had not adequately investigated her charges that dangerous terrorists were being allowed to enter the country. In typical fashion, Davis herself was instead investigated a multitude of times. Through a strange coincidence involving Davis's superior's daughter crossing paths with Brittany Murphy, the actress became a scheduled witness for Davis during her trial for whistleblowing. However, Brittany's sudden death prevented her from testifying. Those of us accustomed to chasing down these rabbit holes understand that the most significant crime scenes are often destroyed. Thus, it wasn't a surprise to learn that Brittany's home was demolished after Simon Monjack's death, when Sharon Murphy sold it. Julia Davis worked with Bertolotti in trying to reopen the investigation into Brittany's death, and declared, "We believe that she was poisoned by somebody." She charged that both Brittany and Monjack had been targeted by Homeland Security.[451] According to the documentary, *Top Priority: The Terror Within*, there were other unexplained deaths and false imprisonments connected to Davis's case.

Alex Ben Block, a friend of Brittany and her family, would talk with Simon Monjack shortly after Brittany's death. "Simon…was convinced — before the autopsy report on Brittany came back — that she had literally died of a broken heart caused by the shoddy way she had been treated in Hollywood." Block stated. "He wanted to expose the studios, producers and talent reps he believed had used rumor and innuendo — about her alleged lateness, inability to remember lines, drug use and partying — to destroy her career…. Simon believed there had been a conspiracy against her among former agents and managers." Block reported that Murphy had been diagnosed with a heart murmur as a youngster, and thus was afraid to use stimulant drugs even if she'd wanted to. Some of Brittany's friends and family members apparently believed that Simon used this kind of paranoia to maintain control over Brittany, According to Block, Monjack told him their house was "under surveillance by helicopters and their phone was bugged."[452] Angelo Berolotti would tell *The Examiner* that, "Brittany and Simon were ridiculed by *The Hollywood Reporter* when they complained of being under surveillance and in fear for their lives." Berolotti reacted to the predictably inaccurate, tabloid movie about his daughter which aired on the *Lifetime* network by saying, "I am disgusted and outraged that Lifetime decided to produce such a trashy project, defiling the memory of my beautiful, talented daughter, Brittany Murphy…Frankly, I am amazed at their audacity of calling it 'a true story,' without conducting any research or consulting with any members of the family. 'The Brittany Murphy Story' is an affront to everything my daughter was in real life. It's hideous, unauthorized and completely untrue."[453]

After Angelo Bertolotti died in January 2019 at the age of ninety-two, his son (and Brittany's half-brother) Tony Bertolotti picked up the mantle. Revealing that he'd been investigating the case behind the scenes, Tony proclaimed "sometimes an actress is worth more dead than alive." He admitted to going over all the "conspiracy theories," and simply concluded that her death could not have been accidental. Tony's primary suspect was Simon Monjack, who was said to be saddled with debts, and facing lawsuits and potential deportation. "If you look at it from a distance, it's like here's this young lady, a fairly healthy girl, she's home with her supposed husband and mother, and she died. How absurd is it?" Tony Bertolotti stated. "It's only in Hollywood that it's considered another day at the zoo. No one takes her to a hospital, which is just four miles away. I spent years looking at this, suppressing my own anger. I think Brittany was taken out. Who killed Brittany? She didn't die of natural causes." The outspoken half-sibling declared, "You've got to look at who's collecting the money now? I don't know. Every time the movie comes on, someone is getting paid. Whoever's got the money knows the truth. There was a group of at least 15 to 30 people around Brittany, and you tell me that no one knows nothing? Are you kidding? If I had the money to properly investigate her death, I'd go round all of them, but they wouldn't speak to me. My father was up to it like a hound dog, but then got sick and had a stroke. 'Til his dying day he was obsessed with finding out what happened. He went up to a bunch of these people, but no one would talk to him. We couldn't find out anything. What's it all tell you? The thing is locked down." Tony expressed his belief that Monjack was actually dating Brittany's mother Sharon, and they were engaged in a marriage of convenience. In this article, it was also noted that Sharon "disappeared just a few months after Monjack died and hasn't been seen since although Bertolotti says he has credible information that she's back in Hollywood."[454]

Who Killed Marilyn Monroe?

The death of Hollywood icon Marilyn Monroe is perhaps the greatest mystery in the history of Tinseltown. The medical examiner penciled in "probable" suicide from an overdose of drugs in his report, but there are very strong reasons to doubt this. On August

5, 1962, the thirty- six-year-old actress was discovered dead in her bed, and there was a curious, unexplained lapse of some six hours before help was called. No trace of any tablets were found in her stomach or intestines, but she had enough Nembutal and Chloral Hydrate ("knockout drops") in her bloodstream "to kill an elephant," to quote from Richard Belzer and David Wayne's book *Dead Wrong*, which probably presents the most convincing argument that Monroe was murdered. As Stanley Weinberg, the Chief Medical Examiner of Suffolk County, New York, put it, "It would have been impossible for her to have taken the barbiturates orally and not have some residue turn up in the stomach. The evidence points to all the classic features of a homicide...."[455] When coroner to the stars Thomas Noguchi requested Monroe's organs for testing, he was told they couldn't be located! Shades of JFK's missing brain. Author Donald Wolfe quoted an unnamed Deputy District Attorney in his book *The Last Days of Marilyn Monroe* as saying, "In the entire history of the L.A. County Coroner's Office there has never been a previous instance of organ samples vanishing." Noguchi found that Monroe's stomach was not only missing any evidence of drug intake, but also food or alcohol. In fact, her stomach was basically empty. Since there were no needle marks found on her body, it is reasonable to speculate that she might have been given a drug-induced enema. There seems no other way for the barbiturates to have entered her system. John Miner, who worked in the Los Angeles District Attorney's office and attended Monroe's autopsy, verified this with the statement, "Noguchi and I were convinced this was absolutely the route (enema) of admitting the fatal dose." Noguchi would call in vain for a new official investigation into Monroe's death. [456]

The first officer to arrive at Monroe's home, Sergeant Jack Clemmons, directly stated that the death scene had been cleaned up by someone, and concluded the actress had been murdered. Clemmons told author Anthony Summers, who wrote the 1985 book *Goddess:*

The Secret Life of Marilyn Monroe, "It was the most obviously staged death scene I have ever seen."[457] As noted, there was a telling gap of six hours between the time of death and the time police were contacted. Clemmons noticed that maid Eunice Murray was already doing a third load of laundry at 4:45 am. Clemmons found both this and her agitated and nervous demeanor to be extremely odd. The fact that such a dramatic person would not leave a suicide note was also suspicious. Monroe's filing cabinet, which held her most important papers, had been broken into on the night she died. Not only Monroe's organs, but the original autopsy report and original police report are alleged to be missing. The FBI seized Monroe's telephone records for the days just preceding her death and they too disappeared.[458] Monroe, of course, has been widely reported to have had affairs with both President John F. Kennedy and his brother, then Attorney General Robert F. Kennedy. She also had ties to high profile mafia figures, through her friendship (and seeming affair) with Frank Sinatra. When Clemmons arrived at Monroe's house, both her private physician, Dr. Hyman Engelberg, and her psychiatrist Dr. Ralph Greenson, were present with her body in the bedroom. Both doctors quickly informed Clemmons that Monroe had taken her own life, and pointed to an empty bottle of Nembutal on the nightstand. Clemmons noticed that the body was in a peculiar, unnatural position, and there was no trace of the common vomit found in such overdose cases. Clemmons found the attitudes of both doctors puzzling. He told author Donald Wolfe that Greenson "was cocky - almost challenging me to accuse him of something." Murray strangely had called Dr. Greenson first, about four hours before the police were notified. Greenson found Monroe's bedroom door locked, so he went outside and broke her bedroom window.[459] Murray, in addition to her other bizarre behavior, had called someone right away, in the middle of the night, to repair the window. The doctors explained to Clemmons that the police hadn't been immediately notified, because they had to contact Monroe's studio first and get their permission.

The list of oddities in Monroe's death is endless. Clemmons noticed no water glass near the empty bottle of Nembutal, for instance, when he first examined the scene, but found that one had been placed there later on. There were fresh bruises on Monroe's body, indicating that a struggle had taken place. Police investigative files remain unreleased. Eunice Murray was the most important potential witness to any investigation, but she was allowed to leave for an extended trip to Europe. Peter Lawford, who was Marilyn's connection to the Kennedys, never gave a statement to police until 1973. In 1985, a grand jury foreman announced his request for a special prosecutor to reopen the Monroe case, but was replaced in his position by a Superior Court judge in the midst of his press conference.[460] It has been alleged that both the mafia and the FBI had bugged Monroe's home, but those tapes have never been found. It has also been alleged that Robert Kennedy visited Monroe on the day she died. In his book *How Did Marilyn Monroe Die?* Tony Plant concluded that "to reach the drug levels present, she must have ingested the contents of not less than seventy-seven and not more than eighty-eight pills: sixty to seventy Nembutal and seventeen to eighteen Chloral Hydrate."[461] This stands in stark contrast to the known fact that Monroe had prescription access at the time to no more than twenty-five Nembutal capsules. On the November 5, 1988 edition of Fox TV's *The Reporters*, former Deputy District Attorney John Miner claimed that his own report was missing from the DA's office. As Thomas Noguchi wrote in his 1983 book *Coroner*, "No one has been able to explain why Marilyn was 'laughing happily with Joe DiMaggio, Jr.' and then 'dying only thirty minutes later.'" Indeed, everyone who spoke to Marilyn that day reported she was in extremely good spirits. Noguchi noted that "friends and associates said that her career, which had been in a decline, was now on an upswing." Marilyn's last phone call was allegedly with former boyfriend (Monroe's inner circle disputed that he was ever anything more than an escort) Jose Bolanos, who claimed that a perfectly normal sounding Monroe had reported, in mid-conversation, hearing some kind of disturbance, and put the phone down without ever coming back. When Monroe's body was discovered, the bedroom phone was supposedly found off the hook. Bolanos told Anthony Summers that Monroe had also revealed, "something that will one day shock the whole world," but refused to elaborate.[462] Bolanos took this secret to his grave, dying in Mexico City at only fifty-eight in 1994 of undisclosed causes. A 1982 case review of Monroe's death by the LA District Attorney's Office did admit that FBI files on the actress were "heavily censored," but predictably found no evidence of foul play.[463]

One of those who have investigated the Monroe case in depth is William Matson Law, a renowned JFK assassination researcher and author of books like *In the Eye of History: Disclosures in the JFK Assassination Medical Evidence*. During the course of his investigation, Law flew to Hollywood to talk with actress Natalie Trundy, a busy guest star on numerous 1960s' television programs who also appeared in the *Planet of the Apes* series of films. Trundy was the wife of Arthur Jacobs, one time publicist of Marilyn Monroe. Trundy claimed that she and Jacobs were at a Hollywood Bowl concert when someone came and tapped him on the shoulder and whispered something to him. Telling Trundy "It's Marilyn," Jacobs left and was not seen by her for three days. This was in the late evening of August 4, 1962, hours before her body was reportedly discovered. Although Law went to the time and expense of making such a trip, when he arrived at Trundy's door, she refused to see him. Law came back again two or three days later, and her boyfriend, who answered, responded to the offer of a book on Marilyn written by Law's friend and researcher Matthew Smith by saying, "Natalie doesn't want it," and closed the door. Matthew Smith would tell Law about setting up an interview with Pat Newcomb, who also worked as Marilyn's publicist under Jacobs. As Law recounted in a March 4, 2021 email to me, "He said that he had talked to Pat Newcomb and she okayed him to come out and see her. He went to 'a rather posh hotel' where she kept him waiting for an hour and then when she got there she looked him up-and-down and said 'no' and walked out." Jacobs died of a sudden heart attack at only fifty-one, after producing several hit movies, including the aforementioned, original *Planet of the Apes* series. William Law also told me that he tracked down a woman who'd been a little girl when her family moved into Marilyn Monroe's home after her death. He asked her if she'd ever heard her parents talking about indications of bugging devices being found in the house. She replied, "I know the answer, and I don't want to answer." Veronica Hamel, who would go on to star in the television series *Hill Street Blues*, purchased Monroe's home with her husband in the early 1970s. During remodeling of the house, contractors "discovered and removed a sophisticated, government grade eavesdropping and telephone tapping system that extended into every room of the house."[464]

Marilyn Monroe left most of her estate to her acting coach Lee Strasberg. Former husband and baseball legend Joe DiMaggio was inconsolable at her funeral, weeping uncontrollably and constantly uttering, "I love you." The bereaved DiMaggio had spent the entire night beside her body in the Chapel of Palms reposing room. The Yankee Clipper would go on to place an order of "Six fresh long-stemmed red roses," to be delivered to her crypt "three times a week....forever." Former husband Arthur Miller didn't attend her funeral, and his belatedly released diary revealed an excerpt which charged, "Let the public mourners finish the mockery... Most of them there destroyed her." Miller's biographer Christopher Bigsby would compare the treatment Monroe experienced in Hollywood to the recent allegations of sexual abuse directed at Harvey Weinstein and others. Bigsby said that Monroe was "passed around as a kind of product when she was in Hollywood."[465] There were only thirty-one mourners at Marilyn Monroe's funeral. Joe DiMaggio, who took charge of everything, specifically banned his old friend

Frank Sinatra from attending.[466] The likes of Sammy Davis, Jr., Peter Lawford, and Dean Martin were turned away at the funeral home gates. DiMaggio in fact forbade any movie stars, producers, agents or reporters at the ceremony, with the exception of his personal friend Walter Winchell. Marilyn's mother, who had been confined to a sanitarium for years, wasn't even informed of her daughter's death. Marilyn had rarely visited her, and some speculated that her mother no longer even knew who Norma Jean (Marilyn's birth name was Norma Jean Baker) was. And the devoted DiMaggio reportedly returned to the dark and deserted cemetery that night, to sit some more beside the love of his life. In yet another of those intriguing connections, Marilyn's publicist Patricia Newcomb was the daughter of a powerful lobbyist for a corporation owned by the father of Ethel Skakel, wife of Robert F. Kennedy.

The Strange Death of Elvis Presley

Suzanna Leigh was an English actress who appeared in many films and television shows from the 1950s through the 1970s. Perhaps her most memorable role was opposite Elvis Presley in the 1966 movie *Paradise, Hawaiian Style.* She became friends with Elvis, and also dated actors like Richard Harris, Steve McQueen and Michael Caine. Leigh always questioned the circumstances of Elvis Presley's death, and was eventually moved to share her thoughts, in a lengthy article in the September 30, 2011 *UK Daily Mail.* The article was excerpted from her book *Paradise, Suzanna Style.* "As soon as I saw photos of the aftermath of Elvis's death, alarm bells went off in my head," Leigh related. "There was a picture of a woman, who was close to Elvis, standing in the doorway at Graceland in the middle of the night, just hours after his death. She looked immaculate, her make-up perfect. What was wrong with this? Well, if the love of my life had just been found dead, I would have looked like the Witch of Endor, mascara streaming down my face." In 2003, Leigh went to work as a VIP tour guide at Presley's Graceland estate. "It was there that I first heard rumours from people on the estate that Elvis had been murdered," Leigh wrote. "And when I went to the library to find out more, I discovered that many reputable people believed his death — from apparent heart failure, compounded by drug abuse — was not straightforward."

The article continued, "One book pointed the finger at Elvis's doctor, 'Nick' Nichopoulos, who prescribed scores of pills for his hypochondriac patient, although it's hard to believe he would kill his paymaster. The most interesting theory was by British journalist John Parker, who claimed there was a Mafia connection. Then there's the fact that the post-mortem report will not be available until 2027. Why would the Federal Bureau of Investigation lock documents away if there was nothing to hide? I soon learned Elvis had in fact been part of one of the largest FBI investigations of the Seventies, codenamed Fountain Pen. Apparently, he had been the innocent victim in a Mafia fraud case involving billions of dollars. Scores of federal agents worldwide had investigated it, and Elvis was due to give evidence. The FBI was meant to be protecting Elvis when he died. Despite this, Elvis's death has never been officially investigated." Elvis's lawyer, Beecher Smith, told Leigh that in fact Elvis and his father were scheduled to testify before a grand jury on August 16, 1977, the very day of his death. Another old friend of Elvis's, George Klein, told Leigh that Presley had fired half his staff, including the infamous Colonel Tom Parker, just prior to his death. Elvis felt it necessary to hire a new team of ex-police officers for security, headed by Dick Grob. Grob would disclose to Leigh the interesting tidbit that Vernon Presley had always believed his son was murdered. Grob further claimed that someone had phoned a newspaper from Graceland at 1 a.m. to alert them about a big story coming up, an hour before emergency personnel were contacted. "Elvis died of a massive codeine overdose," Grob told her. "It doesn't matter what other things they say he died of — that is what he really died of." Leigh was aware that Elvis was allergic to codeine.

As happens so often in these cases, the scene of Presley's death was hopelessly corrupted. Someone cleaned the carpet before police arrived. Other sources on the internet claim that syringes without needles were planted there in order to emphasize the drug angle. Grob revealed, "so much stuff was walking out the door. A lot of things disappeared that night and were sold later." Perhaps the person who most benefited from Presley's death was the one who'd already benefited the most from his career; the redoubtable Colonel Tom Parker, Elvis's long-time manager. Beecher Smith disclosed that the day after Elvis's death, the Colonel persuaded Vernon Presley to sign over fifty percent of his son's posthumous earnings to him. Although perhaps a logical suspect himself, Parker wasn't at Graceland the night Elvis died. Parker had a shadowy past, which included being discharged from the military as a psychopath, and even inferences by some that he fled his home country the Netherlands after murdering a woman.[467]

Grob suspected the mafia. As Leigh recounted, "He told me they did not want Elvis or his father to appear in court because of all the media interest it would create, so they must have got someone inside the house. 'That's what Vernon believed all along,' said Dick. 'Someone from inside let the killer into the house.'" Leigh began experiencing some strange things herself. A wheel came off her truck while she was driving, and a mechanic found that the nuts on the other wheels were loosened as well. Leigh continued, "Then, one night as I was walking my dog, I stood like a rabbit in the headlights while a young black girl, not more than 20, stuck her arm out of the window of a passing car and fired at least five very loud shots from a handgun, which hit some trees above me. On another occasion, someone broke into my car, then someone tried to break into my house and stabbed one of my other dogs." It certainly sounds as if *someone* didn't want her looking into the case. Leigh died from liver cancer in December 2017 at the age of seventy-two. A GoFundMe page had been set up to help with medical expenses.[468]

The Assassination of John Lennon

John Lennon was not only the most politically active Beatle, he was one of the most radical activists of his era. Jaded from my extensive research into the JFK, MLK and RFK assassinations, I instantly questioned the pat, lone-nut explanation for his December 8, 1980 shooting death. Lennon had been targeted by the government for a long time. In just one instance, undercover FBI agents had recorded remarks made by the ex-Beatle and others during a December, 1971 rally at the University of Michigan.[469] Fenton Bresler wrote the 1989 book *Who Killed John Lennon?*, which raised a number of troubling questions. Bresler obtained government files through the Freedom of Information Act, which revealed that Lennon was under nearly constant government surveillance, especially from 1971-1972. In an April 10, 1972 memo from J. Edgar Hoover to the FBI's New York office, Hoover instructed his agents to "...promptly initiate discrete efforts to locate subject [Lennon] and remain aware of his activities and movements. Handle inquiries only through established sources... Careful attention should be given to reports that subject is heavy narcotics user and any information developed in this regard should be furnished to narcotics authorities and immediately furnished to bureau in form suitable for dissemination." Lennon was perfectly aware of what was going on. In December 1975 he told an interviewer, "We knew we were being wire-tapped... there was a helluva lot of guys coming in to fix the phones." In 1968, Lennon had been arrested in England and charged with possession of marijuana.[470] The U.S. government used this prior arrest as a means of threatening Lennon with deportation.

Fenton Bresler interviewed Arthur O'Connor, the commanding officer of the twentieth precinct of the New York police that dealt with Lennon's murder. O'Connor told him that Chapman "looked like he could have been programmed," and even more boldly declared, "As far as you are trying to build up some kind of conspiracy, I would support you in that line. Like I said originally over the phone, if this gentleman [Chapman] wanted to get away with it, he could have got away with it. There was the subway across the road and no one around to stop him." Instead, of course, "lone nut" Mark David Chapman calmly sat and waited for police to come after shooting Lennon, while reading his cherished copy of *Catcher in the Rye* by J.D. Salinger. Chapman's trial had a circus atmosphere to it; Chapman based his defense upon following "voices" who ordered him to kill Lennon. Three eminent psychiatrists were enlisted, to provide their opinions on Chapman's mental competence. One of these psychiatrists was Dr. Milton Kline, an authority on hypnosis who'd also been a consultant to the CIA on the topic of programmed assassins. Kline had once boasted that he could create such a "Manchurian Candidate" in a matter of months.[471] Another was Dr. Bernard Diamond, a mind control expert who'd worked with Robert Kennedy's alleged assassin Sirhan Sirhan. Sirhan had complained to another psychologist that "Whatever strange behavior I showed in court was the result of my outrage over Dr. Diamond's and other doctors' testimony. They were saying things about me that were grossly untrue, nor did I give them permission to testify [on] my behalf in court."[472] The third psychiatrist was Dr. Daniel Schwartz, who'd examined David "Son of Sam" Berkowitz, and concluded that the accused serial killer believed he'd been commanded by "demons" to kill. Schwartz would testify that Chapman's "voices" were similar to Berkowitz's "demons." He declared that Chapman "continued to operate under this primitive kind of thinking, in which he believed or believes that forces outside of him, supernatural or otherwise, determined his behavior." On the other hand, defense consultant Dr. Dorothy Lewis hinted at

Chapman being under some form of mind control, stating that he may have acted in response to a "command hallucination."[473]

As we find so often, Mark David Chapman had some interesting connections. He had supposedly graduated from fundamentalism to devil-worship. Months before the murder, he visited Satanist and filmmaker Kenneth Anger, also renowned for writing the sensational best- seller *Hollywood Babylon,* at a screening in Hawaii. Chapman shook hands with Anger and handed him two .38 caliber bullets, telling him, "These are for John Lennon."[474] Some researchers have alleged that Hawaii was notorious for its mind control programs, sponsored by the U.S. military. Chapman shared a connection with Ronald Reagan's attempted assassin John Hinckley, whose father sat on the Board of Directors for the evangelical charity World Vision. Chapman assisted Vietnamese refugees at a resettlement camp in Arkansas, while working for World Vision. World Vision has supposed ties to the CIA as well. Chapman was quite the world traveler for a young man, and although a strident anti-communist, had oddly requested to be sent to the Soviet Union after he joined the YMCA's International Camp Counselor Program. For whatever reason, Chapman's personality changed dramatically at a young age, as he went from a happy, hard-working Christian to a deeply depressed Satanist who attempted suicide, which resulted in a 1977 hospital stay. Chapman would later oddly be hired by the same hospital, and was rapidly promoted to the customer relations office. He spontaneously quit the job and embarked upon a world tour.

By August, 1980, Chapman was writing cryptically of a "mission" in New York, in a letter he attempted to mail that was returned undelivered, and sat in the dead-letter file for three years until it was given to Yoko Ono, who merely glanced at it before dropping it into her "Deranged" collection. Ono's security chief Dan Mahoney would open the letter in June, 1983, but before he could inform Yoko of its contents, which he felt strongly suggested premeditation and/

or conspiracy, the letter disappeared. It would even more strangely suddenly reappear on Yoko Ono's kitchen table, in a slightly altered form, with a new postmark of 1981. The slight alteration was tremendously significant; the "mission" reference was gone. Lennon's friend and publicist Elliot Mintz would allege that Lennon's personal assistant Fred Seaman, author of *The Last Days of John Lennon: A Personal Memoir,* had helped orchestrate a bizarre plot along with psychiatrist Bob Rosen, and "decided to engage in this 'Project Walrus' conspiracy. [This] involved setting up an apartment as well as a warehouse in Manhattan, have Fred steal as many things as he could — not just the journals, although the journals were the most important things — and for these four guys to 1. sell the materials privately, because this was right after John's death and obviously the sky was the limit in terms of what one could charge for those kinds of things; and 2. write a book that would corner the gossip market on John Lennon … and Yoko."[475] Rosen threw Mintz and other conspirators under the bus after entire filing cabinets of material were discovered missing. Rosen received full immunity, but revealed to Yoko Ono that he was in fear of his life. One of these conspirators was Aerosmith guitarist Rod Dufay. Lennon's diary was among the items never recovered.

Elliot Mintz remarked, "Some of Yoko's bodyguards were at the time New York City police officers. This is not unusual because New York has the Sullivan Law, which is the strictest anti-gun law in the United States. In New York City, it is very difficult for a private citizen to [legally] possess a weapon and keep it on his or her person secretly. The people who are allowed to do it are off-duty New York City police officers. So it's not unusual for a number of very well-known celebrities in New York to have this [bodyguard] arrangement. Naturally, some of the off-duty officers who were protecting Yoko and Sean at the time were aware of things that were disappearing. You would go someplace to look for a file and the contents of whole file cabinets would be missing."[476] Fred Seaman claimed that, in Mintz's words, "one or both of the officers physically assaulted him, beat him up, held a gun to his head, took him for a ride, parked under a bridge somewhere and made clear threats, then brought him to the police station where he was booked, mug shots were taken and he confessed on videotape. I'm here to tell you that one of the people who he names as a police officer who arrested him ... was never part of Fred's arrest, was never there that night ..."[477] This frightening conspiracy went far beyond the theft of Lennon's journals. According to Mintz, Project Walrus was a surveillance, assassination and psychological operations program. Mahoney would find listening devices planted at the Lennons' Dakota apartment in March 1983. Bringing to mind all the JFK assassination witnesses who reported receiving threats, Yoko would get a call from an unidentified man in Los Angeles on December 9, 1980, the day after Lennon was shot, who told her he was flying to New York to "finish the job that Chapman started." A man was subsequently arrested at the Los Angeles airport, after he swore to "get" Yoko, and punched a police officer. In February, 1983, Yoko received a letter warning her, "I am going to kill you. You were not supposed to have survived." Evidently two brothers were found to be responsible, and one was arrested outside the Dakota. Although he freely admitted that he meant to "get" Yoko, the authorities released him. A little while later, during a trip to San Francisco, Yoko was notified by police that they'd arrested a sniper a mile away, confiscating 700 rounds of ammunition and a collection of books about John and Yoko. Lennon's son Sean is probably the best known "conspiracy theorist" in this case, maintaining there was a "government" conspiracy behind his father's death and referring to those who believe the official narrative as naïve at best. Albert Goldman's sleazy book *The Lives of John Lennon* was said to be largely sourced upon the Project Walrus Conspiracy.[478]

The Chapman letter wasn't the only material mysteriously lost or found. In the March 1984 *Playboy*, authors David and Victoria

Sheff recounted a series of "unexplained events" that took place at the Dakota: "Passports are found to be missing and then turn up days later on the kitchen table; lyrics to new songs disappear and then just as mysteriously reappear; collages by Lennon disappear and then reappear in unexpected places. It is beginning to sound like the movie Gaslight, in which a woman is made to feel she is going crazy." Apparently, there was also a continuous stream of death threats via mail and phone. Fred Seaman was sentenced to five months' probation in May 1983. He is alleged to having continued to "discredit Ono at all costs," leaving messages for her at the Dakota about being 'useless,' and inferring she had Paul McCartney arrested in Japan for marijuana possession, among other claims.[479] Along with Goldman's negative portrayal of Lennon, truly absurd conspiracy theories emerged, the foremost being one postulated by a Steven Lightfoot, who insisted that Lennon had actually been killed by author Stephen King.

In 2010, author Phil Strongman claimed, in his book *John Lennon — Life, Times and Assassination,* that Lennon had been assassinated by the CIA, while Chapman was a mere patsy. Strongman contradicted many of the accepted facts in the Lennon case, including the much ballyhooed claim that Chapman was an obsessed Beatles' fan. He stated that, until the weekend before Lennon's shooting, "Chapman, the supposed Lennon 'obsessive' and 'fan of fans," did not own one Lennon single, book or album." Of the alleged fourteen hours of Lennon songs Chapman was said to have on tapes, Strongman declared, "They have never been photographed or produced for the simple reason that they do not exist." Strongman logically questioned the "fame seeking" assumption regarding Chapman, by noting that, "If he was an attention-seeker, then why did he turn down the chance of what would have been the trial of the century? By pleading guilty, Chapman missed all of the attention he was supposedly seeking." Chapman's incredibly calm demeanor after the shooting certainly fits the profile of a hypnotized, programmed killer. Strongman mentioned another of Chapman's curious travel destinations; the young man had landed in Beirut at a time when it was rumored to be a hub of CIA activities. Chapman's extensive travels must have been expensive, and the funding for them has never been adequately explained. In 1975 alone, Chapman went to Japan, the United Kingdom, India, Korea, Vietnam and China. Regarding Chapman's fascination with *Catcher in the Rye,* Strongman insisted it "was part of Chapman's hypnotic programming, a trigger that could be 'fired' at him by a few simple keywords, via a cassette tape message, telex or telegram or even a mere telephone call." Strongman was even skeptical that Chapman fired the shots that killed Lennon. "Put simply," Strongman said, "the authorities' investigation, or lack of it, into the assassination was shockingly slack and beggars belief." As Strongman noted, "Chapman was standing on Lennon's right and, as the autopsy report and death certificate later made clear, all Lennon's wounds were in the left side of his body." Strongman went on, "His bizarre post-killing calm was not questioned, his behaviour was not checked with a drugs test, his 'programmed' state [a word used about him by more than one police officer] was not investigated, his previous movements were not thoroughly looked into."[480] I interviewed Phil Strongman on my weekly radio show in January, 2020.

One under-publicized and extremely odd aspect to this case is the fact that Chapman's wife, Gloria Hiroko Chapman, has remained shockingly loyal to her husband. In 2018, she even admitted to knowing that her husband was planning to kill Lennon. "He came home scared, telling me that to make a name for himself he had planned to kill Lennon. But he said my love had saved him," Gloria stated. She visits him regularly; the couple is allowed forty-four hours together every year. According to a news report, "they spend their time making pizzas, watching 'Wheel of Fortune' and having sex in a caravan on the grounds of the Wende Correctional Facility in Alden, New York." Gloria seemed to revel in her role as

"Mrs. Mark David Chapman, the wife of a murderer and not just any murderer but one whose victim was known and loved by millions around the world."[481]

John Lennon was always one of my personal favorites; I idolized him as a teenager and consider him to be one of the very top musical figures of the twentieth century. Considering his radical political stances, it's likely in my view that he was silenced by powerful forces. However, he was a complex and flawed man. He had a strained relationship with Julian, his son by his first wife Cynthia. "I've never really wanted to know the truth about how dad was with me. There was some very negative stuff talked about me ... like when he said I'd come out of a whisky bottle on a Saturday night..." Julian stated in a January 1981 *Playboy* magazine interview. "You think, where's the love in that? Paul and I used to hang about quite a bit ... more than Dad and I did. We had a great friendship going and there seems to be far more pictures of me and Paul playing together at that age than there are pictures of me and my dad." Julian was miffed about his father's public stance as an advocate for peace, declaring, "I have to say that, from my point of view, I felt he was a hypocrite. Dad could talk about peace and love out loud to the world but he could never show it to the people who supposedly meant the most to him: his wife and son. How can you talk about peace and love and have a family in bits and pieces—no communication, adultery, divorce?"[482] Julian was excluded from his father's will, but shared a very modest trust fund with his half-brother Sean. Julian later sued his father's estate and in 1996 reached a settlement agreement worth a reported twenty-six million. Paul McCartney is said to have written the huge Beatles hit *Hey Jude* for Julian, to comfort him during his parents' breakup.

The Death of Kirsty MacColl

Kirsty MacColl recorded many memorable songs in the 1980s, such as *See That Girl, Alcoholic Teenager in Love,* and *There's a Guy Works*

Down the Chip Shop Swears He's Elvis, to name just a few. She gravitated to show business naturally; her father Ewan MacColl was a prominent singer-songwriter in Great Britain. His song *The First Time Ever I Saw Your Face* was a huge hit for Roberta Flack in 1972. On December 18, 2000, Kirsty MacColl died tragically in a boating accident that is still shrouded in mystery. Forty-one-year-old MacColl was vacationing in Cozumel, Mexico with her two sons and partner James Knight. They decided to go diving in an area where boats were prohibited from entering. As they came up from a dive, MacColl saw a speedboat racing into the restricted waters, and pushed her son to safety before the boat struck and killed her. On board the boat with his family was the owner, Guillermo Gonzalez Nova, one of the wealthiest men in Mexico. One of Nova's employees admitted to driving the boat, but eyewitnesses claimed that it was Nova himself who was driving so recklessly. The patsy employee was convicted and received a sweetheart fine of $90.

Celebrities including U-2 front man Bono (born Paul David Hewson) joined a "Justice for Kirsty MacColl" campaign. The Mexican government promised to reopen the case but never did. The committee formed to seek justice for MacColl was disbanded in 2009, and released a statement that spoke of being "successful in achieving most of its aims," and admitting "it is unlikely that any more could be achieved." Jean MacColl, Kirsty's then eighty-six-year-old mother, bitterly remarked that "And when I hear those words: 'You scumbag, you maggot,'" referring to lyrics from the Christmas song Kirsty collaborated on with the Pogues, *Fairytale of New York,* "I'll think of that man." Having finally exhausted all legal avenues to bring Guillermo González Nova to justice, Jean reluctantly abandoned the Justice for Kirsty campaign. "But it felt dishonest to go on, to keep asking for money, when we don't feel we've got a chance," Jean MacColl stated. The campaign had helped her deal with grief she felt over the horrible incident, which traumatized Kirsty's then thirteen and fifteen-year-old sons, who were left with nightmares of "swimming in Mummy's blood." The Justice for Kirsty campaign had claimed that Jose Cen Yam had drunkenly told friends he took the rap with the understanding that he'd be paid off with a house on Cozumel, where González Nova owned a vacation home, and where Yam was reportedly living in a small building.[483]

In a more recent report, Jean MacColl, still irate at ninety-one, declared, "All I wanted was the truth. I didn't want his money, it's dirty. I just wanted him to tell me the truth but he didn't have the nerve or the courage. I even wrote him a letter saying I just wanted the truth but he never replied." Jean explained why the campaign for justice was disbanded: "The only reason I gave up was that we were told by someone who is quite high up in our legal system that we would not get justice because the system is so corrupt."[484] "It's a tough battle to fight a multi-billionaire in what is effectively a Third World country..." added Kirsty's son Louis Lillywhite.[485] Jose Cen Yam proved to be elusive, as Jean MacColl stated, "I don't know if he's bought a new house because I can't find him."[486] At one point, the Mexican government responded to subpoenas issued by the Mac-Coll family for Gonzalez Nova and his daughter in law, Norma Haggas, by claiming that they "could not be found." A local on Cozumel Island told Jean, "Oh, he`s the don. His name is law around here. I have to be careful. I have a family to keep." I tried contacting Jean MacColl twice via her website, but never received a reply. She passed away in 2017, the day after her ninety-fourth birthday.

The September 13, 1996 death of rapper Tupac Shakur, at the tender age of twenty-five, fueled almost as much speculation, and conspiracy theories, as the death of Elvis Presley. Suspicion was immediately focused on powerful rap impresarios Suge Knight and Sean "Puffy" Combs. The fact that Knight was in the car with Shakur when he was shot on the night of September 7th (he would remain alive for six days in the hospital, until his mother removed life support) hasn't quelled these suspicions. Perhaps more significantly, FBI files released in 2011 revealed that Shakur had received death threats from the violent Jewish Defense League.[487] When rival rapper Biggie "The Notorious B.I.G." was gunned down a year later, even more theories emerged. Some posited that the two had been murdered by the government, in an effort to end the long-standing rap battle between the east and west coasts. Interestingly, the FBI files on Smalls' death produced explosive information about the rare ammunition used in the shooting being found in the home of LAPD police officer David Mack. Mack had been moonlighting as a bodyguard for Suge Knight, and would be arrested for bank robbery later in 1997. In 2001, Mack would suffer a nonfatal stabbing in prison.[488] Suge Knight's name was raised in this case as well, as having ordered Mack and others to "hit" Smalls. A wrongful death suit lodged against Mack by Smalls' family was dismissed in 2005. Perhaps the most prevalent theory, however, is that Tupac faked his own death, with the claim that he left behind several "clues" to this effect in songs, evoking comparisons to the "Paul is dead" notions about the real Paul McCartney actually dying in 1966 and being replaced by a lookalike.

Cliff Robertson won an Academy Award in 1968 for his role as the title character in *Charly*. A decade later, Robertson was essentially blacklisted by Hollywood. In 1977, the IRS informed Robertson that he had not declared a $10,000 payment from Columbia Pictures. The confused actor was certain that he'd never received the money in question. Robertson would subsequently discover a $10,000 check from Columbia, with his forged signature on it. When Robertson confronted Columbia head David Begelman about the matter, he blamed it on an underling. Robertson did not believe this, and alerted the authorities. An investigation disclosed that it was Begelman who'd forged Robertson's signature, as part of a scheme to embezzle thousands of dollars from the studio. Begelman was fired and charged with grand theft, but received the usual "celebrity special" punishment of community service. Columbia was desperate to avoid the negative publicity from the scandal, and pressured Robertson to keep quiet. A defiant Robertson responded by going public. In retaliation, the actor found very little work in Hollywood for years thereafter. Eventually, the scandal was covered in the *Wall Street Journal* and a best-selling book, and Robertson was able to finally resume his career. Begelman managed to recover and somehow become head of MGM studios, but wound up embroiled in more scandals. After going bankrupt, Begelman joined the lengthy list of Hollywood suicides in 1995. Begelman had a sordid reputation throughout his career in Tinseltown; to cite just one example, he skimmed hundreds of thousands of dollars from the always fragile Judy Garland, much of it revolving around a non-existent nude picture of her.[489]

Some agents, like Joe Glaser, took as much as 50 percent of their mostly black clients' earnings. Glaser's alleged mob connections were instrumental in landing him the position of Louis Armstrong's manager, which led to other jazz industry figures hiring him. As the *Hollywood Reporter* noted upon Glaser's death in 1969, "After making a fortune off the musician, Glaser died and left him nothing in his will."[490] When jazz promoter and producer George Wein wrote his autobiography in 2003, he quoted a bitter Armstrong thusly: "But the minute we started to make money, Joe Glaser was no longer my friend. In all those years, he never invited me to his house. I was just a passport for him....I built Associated Booking. There wouldn't have been an agency if it wasn't for me. And he didn't even leave me a percentage of it."[491] Although the portrayal of Armstrong dying broke, in the 2015 play *Satchmo at the Waldorf*, appears to be an exaggeration, there is little question that Glaser exploited Armstrong and probably many other performers. The Band may be universally regarded as one of the greatest groups in the history of rock and roll, but they were besieged with infighting. The families of all band members except Robbie Robertson (who was aligned in most of these disputes opposite mates Levon Helm, Richard Manuel, Rick Danko and Garth Hudson) never received a penny of the estimated $39 million in profits that their filmed fare-well concert *The Last Waltz* earned from 1978-98. Garth Hudson declared bankruptcy for the third time in 2002 after his home went into foreclosure; Robertson had previously bought out his stake in the band. On February 25, 2013 *Rolling Stone* reported that Hudson's belongings had been sold off at a garage sale after he'd failed to pay rent on his loft space for seven years. Curiously, one item found was an uncashed royalty check from 1979 for $26,000. A year after her death, reports surfaced that claimed Aretha Franklin had left behind uncashed checks that totaled nearly $1 million.[492]

Bully manager Albert Grossman handled both the Band and Bob Dylan (from whom he took an astonishing 25 percent commission rather than the industry standard 15 percent, as well as an incredible 50 percent of his song publishing rights), along with other huge acts of the day, like Peter, Paul and Mary, Janis Joplin and Gordon Lightfoot. Grossman was crass enough to buy a large life insurance policy on Joplin, venturing that her excessive drug usage would eventually pay off.[493] Dylan astutely described Grossman as "kind of like a Colonel Tom Parker figure….You could smell him coming." Folk musician Jim Glover told me, in a January 12, 2021 email, "Phil (Ochs) told me Grossman was the one he was afraid of and the only one who could make him a star…" In the same email, Glover also recalled a memorable drive through Greenwich Village in the late Sixties, during which "The talk was about what I knew about Dallas. I was in the back seat between Harvey Brooks and Bob Dylan on my right. Mike Bloomfield was in front and was saying the plot involved a Major…Turns out Major Bloomfield was reported Division 5 FBI and his letters from George Bush Sr. are still withheld by Canadian Archives and my reports to the FBI and Presidents, personally to then Rep. Leon Panetta at his home in late 70's and possibly others from the thousands of records still to be released but FBI/CIA keeps telling the Presidents, No Way 'National Security.'" Bloomfield, a legendary guitarist who backed Dylan on some of his best recordings, was found dead at age thirty-seven in his car in San Francisco on February 15, 1981. An empty bottle of Valium was there, but there were no drugs in his system. And, needless to say, police concluded there was no foul play.[494]

Madonna is renowned as a serial plagiarist. Nothing about this consistently foul-natured entertainer is original. In just one case, she was forced to pay the members of Public Enemy an "undisclosed sum" for ripping off the tune to her mega-hit *Justify My Love*. If that wasn't brazen enough, apparently Madonna stole the lyrics to the same song outright from poet Ingrid Chavez, and was forced to award her a writing credit.[495] Legendary Motown songwriters Lamont Dozier, Brian Holland and Eddie Holland threatened to sue the band Aerosmith in 1989, over the similarities between their song *The Other Side* and their old Four Tops hit single *Standing in the Shadows of Love*, which resulted in them being added to the songwriting credits. It was reported in 2017 that Eddie Holland was "penniless and trying to stop the IRS from seizing his Social Security benefits to satisfy a $20 million tax debt." According to the story, "The seizure is creating an economic hardship for Holland, who is not receiving royalties from hundreds of songs and a dozen No. 1 hits."[496] Many comedians are notorious for stealing material from their peers. *South Park* poked fun at Carlos Mencia, perhaps the worst offender in this regard, a few years back. Two separate allegations of plagiarism have been filed against pop singer Brittney Spears. Shia LaBeouf's directorial debut at the 2012 Cannes Film Festival was apparently copied from a graphic novel. Jay-Z (Shawn Corey Carter) has been accused of copying parts of his 2010 memoir. The girl group the Chiffons memorably filed a lawsuit alleging former Beatle George Harrison had stolen the melody for his huge hit *My Sweet Lord* from their 1962 smash *He's So Fine*. Harrison was eventually forced to pay the Chiffons and the songwriter, Ronnie Mack, $587,000. In a scathing 2010 interview, Joni Mitchell said the following about Bob Dylan: "Bob is not authentic at all. He's a plagiarist and his name and voice are fake. Everything about Bob is a deception."[497]

Chapter Six

Hollywood, The Mob, And Government Propaganda

In all, we are looking at a vast, militarized propaganda apparatus operating throughout the screen entertainment industry in the United States...the shaping of our popular culture to promote a pro-war mindset must be taken seriously.
- Tom Secker and Matthew Alford, authors of "National Security Cinema: The Shocking New Evidence of Government Control in Hollywood."

THE 1947 MGM film depicting the story of the atomic bomb program, *The Beginning of the End,* was filmed with the express cooperation of the U.S. government. President Harry Truman even came up with the film's title. The movie was originally set to be at least relatively critical of the decision to drop nuclear weapons on Hiroshima (for whatever reason, Nagasaki was never even referenced in the film). Reporter Greg Mitchell, decades later, was granted access to early scripts that depicted the devastated ruins left in the wake of the blasts, and even a baby with a burned face. General Leslie Groves, director of the Manhattan Project, was given script approval and his influence was obvious in the final product, which portrayed the bombing bloodlessly, as an unfortunate necessity which saved a good many lives. It was shameful that Hollywood permitted President Truman and the government to exert such control over one of their products, but it certainly wouldn't be the last time they produced something with such an "official" stamp of approval.[498]

It has become public knowledge in recent years that Hollywood permits the Pentagon and the CIA to regularly control films that revolve around "national security" issues. The producers of huge movies like *Stripes* and *Top Gun* altered their scripts to please the Pentagon. In return, they are granted easy access to locations, vehicles, troops and military gear when they need them. David Robb discovered that there was, in fact, a long standing agreement between the film world and the government in this regard, which he documented in his book *Operation Hollywood*. Robb found that, while the current "agreement" was established after World War II, the government was meddling in the affairs of Hollywood going back to the very first Oscar winner, 1927's *Wings*. According to Robb, the military's primary motivation here is to promote movies that "aid in the retention and recruitment of personnel." The taxpayers footed the entire bill for everything military-related in John Wayne's pro-Vietnam War 1968 movie *The Green Berets*. By 2012, forty-five states were providing government subsidies to the film industry. The average state, in fact, spends some $31 million annually in Motion Picture Incentives. New York gives an astounding $621 million yearly in tax subsidies for film and television shoots that take place within the state.[499] Researchers Tom Secker and Matthew

Alford, authors of the book *National Security Cinema: The Shocking New Evidence of Government Control in Hollywood*, concluded, after sifting through thousands of government documents obtained via the Freedom of Information Act, that the U.S. government has worked behind the scenes on over 800 major films and more than 1,000 television programs.[500]

The television series *The Americans* had every script approved by the CIA before it could even be filmed. The FBI has an entire unit that is devoted to making sure the bureau is portrayed in the best possible light. Ex-CIA general counsel John Rizzo readily admitted to the agency's "special relationship" with the film world. "There are officers assigned to this account full-time," Rizzo declared. "Movie industry vets are receptive to helping the CIA in any way they can, probably in equal parts because they are sincerely patriotic and because it gives them a taste of real-life intrigue and excitement."[501] Directors shamelessly accept these kinds of heavy-handed restrictions on their craft. Peter Berg, while filming *Lone Survivor,* a syrupy tribute to the Navy SEALS, admitted, "The idea of a good old-fashioned combat yarn, in which the politics are very clear – we support these men – was more appealing to them." Berg even embedded himself with the SEALS prior to the making of the movie. Kathryn Bigelow, director of *Zero Dark Thirty,* a 2012 film which fancifully depicted the capture of Osama Bin Laden, defended her overt acquiescence to government control with the statement, "(The mission) was an American triumph, both heroic and nonpartisan, and there is no basis to suggest that our film will represent this enormous victory otherwise."[502]

Contrary to its popular image as a bastion of anti-war radicalism, Hollywood has overwhelmingly been pro-military and pro-war over the decades. There have been true renegades like Oliver Stone; but by and large the film colony, almost always with the imprimatur of the military and/or various intelligence agencies, inevitably portrays the military and government officials in the best possible light.

With few mostly early exceptions like the 1925 silent classic *The Big Parade* and 1930's *All Quiet on the Western Front,* there is a great deal of truth in French filmmaker Francois Truffaut's remark that, "There is no such thing as an anti-war film."[503] Even one of the films considered an anti-war classic by most, Stanley Kubrick's 1987 dark opus *Full Metal Jacket,* was scoffed at by fellow director Samuel Fuller, who sneered to critic Jonathan Rosenbaum that "it was another goddamn recruiting film."[504] Writer and director David Ayer, whose 2014 movie *Fury* glorified war and violence gratuitously, expressed profound pride in his patriotism. "Having served in the military, I've always been interested in law enforcement, the military and those people who serve society, especially those people who are franchised to exercise force on our behalf," Ayer declared. "The people who go down range and fight for us and confront the enemy so we can sleep safely in our beds ... that separates them. That creates a brotherhood and a sisterhood and separates them from the society they protect."[505]

Rekindling memories of all the pro-war propaganda spewed out by Hollywood in the World War II era, Clint Eastwood's 2014 film *American Sniper* proved that touting the government line can still be financially lucrative. The "hero" of the film, Chris Kyle, was the self-proclaimed "Most lethal sniper in U.S. military history." The film was lauded critically, even by the likes of left-leaning *Rolling Stone* magazine, which gave it three and a half stars out of four. Kyle was notable for concocting a ridiculous, slanderous story about punching out Jesse Ventura in a California bar, in response to Ventura allegedly mocking American military casualties. Ventura would later win a libel lawsuit against Kyle's estate.[506] Fittingly, considering the nature of his career, Kyle was shot and killed under suspicious circumstances at a Texas shooting range on February 2, 2013. Ben Afleck's *Argo* was not only an unabashed love letter to the CIA; First Lady Michelle Obama herself bestowed the Academy Award for Best Picture upon it, live from the White House. Television shows like *24* and *Homeland* could easily be written and produced by our own intelligence agencies, and are often indistinguishable from official, state-run propaganda. The line between government and entertainment is completely transparent; consider that former Senator Christopher Dodd is the head of the Motion Picture Association of America, which has contributed millions to members of Congress in an effort to censor the internet. Long time Lyndon B. Johnson aide Jack Valenti filled this same role for many years, and was instrumental in forcing the History Channel to stop showing the episode titled "The Guilty Men," part of the often-aired documentary series *The Men Who Killed Kennedy*.[507] In fact, none of the episodes of this series have been shown anywhere on television since Valenti and other cronies of LBJ lobbied to have that particular episode suppressed.

Mob influence in the motion picture business goes back to the days of Thomas Edison. Edison produced mundane but wholesome little films, with his Motion Picture Patents Company (referred to as the "Trust") and resented the new competition from outlaw filmmakers who were overwhelmingly Jewish. These outlaw films featured sex and violence, and were undeniably more entertaining. Edison eventually hired a squad of goons, in conjunction with cooperative Chicago police officers, to close down Jewish theaters. Edison's forces also beat up a good number of directors and actors, and forcibly removed patrons from these theaters. Gangsters like "Big" Jack Zelig and "Lefty Louie" Rosenberg retaliated with the infamous Yiddish Black Hand, stealing expensive equipment in Edison's warehouses in several cities, and then setting fires to destroy the properties.[508] In 1915, Edison disbanded his Trust and the Jewish filmmakers took their business west, to Hollywood. Some of these early film pioneers, who relied on Jewish mobsters for muscle, included Carl Laemmle, Marcus Loews, William Fox, Adolph Zukor, and the four Warner Brothers.

Johnny Roselli, well-known to JFK assassination researchers, was a hot shot Hollywood ladies' man in the 1940s and 1950s.

Among his conquests were Lana Turner and the celluloid definition of virtue and purity, Donna Reed. He could arrange murders, and also often acted as Frank Sinatra's pimp. The rumors connecting Frank Sinatra to the mafia were not fantasy. Frank's grandfather was born in the same Sicilian village as Lucky Luciano. His parents ran a small shop that was allegedly frequented by the likes of Meyer Lansky, Bugsy Siegel and Dutch Schultz. Also, his mother was a rare woman of that era who was influential in local Democratic Party politics. Sinatra was promoted relentlessly as some kind of sex symbol, which seemed a bit ludicrous given his gawky, emaciated frame. The great animator Tex Avery lampooned this nicely in one of his cartoons, by picturing Sinatra from the side completely camouflaged by the stem of a leaf. Legend has it that Sinatra's mob connections were such that the unforgettable scene in *The Godfather*, where a horses' head is found in the bed of a producer reluctant to hire a young singer, was based upon Sinatra's career. Sinatra's acting career took off with his role in *From Here to Eternity*, which notorious Columbia Studios head Harry Cohn was violently opposed to. "Who the hell wants to see that skinny asshole in a major movie?" Cohn supposedly exclaimed. After a visit from Roselli, however, who in classic gangster style advised Cohn that "certain parties" desired for Sinatra to play the role, Sinatra was hired and wound up becoming one of the unlikeliest Oscar winners in history. [509]

It was no stretch for George Raft to play all those gangster roles. He grew up the best friend of notorious New York mobster Owney Madden, and then became his personal chauffer. Raft was also friends with Meyer Lansky and Bugsy Siegel. Raft allegedly saved the lives of both Gary Cooper (whom, as noted earlier, he would come to despise after Cooper testified before the House Un-American Activities Committee and inferred he had communist connections) and James Cagney, who at differing times were scheduled to be "hit" until Raft intervened with his "friends." One of the most sensational murders in Hollywood history involved legendary leading lady Lana Turner. By the late '50s, Turner's star had faded, and MGM cancelled her contract. Already married and divorced five times, Turner began a romance with brash thug Johnny Stompanato. Stompanato had been an enforcer for Hollywood mob boss Mickey Cohen, and had already run afoul of Frank Sinatra, who pleaded in vain with Cohen to stop him from seeing Ava Gardner. He'd also taken off to the United Kingdom in a jealous rage, to threaten young Scottish actor Sean Connery with a gun on the set of *Another Time, Another Place*. The big Scot and future James Bond, a black belt in karate, quickly subdued Stompanato, who was unceremoniously deported. On April 4, 1958, Turner's fourteen-year-old daughter Cheryl Crane stabbed Stompanato to death, claiming that she had acted in an effort to stop him from further attacking her mother. It was ruled a justifiable homicide, although Turner did pay out a fairly modest settlement to Stompanato's family. Crane was sent to a school for girls in Los Angeles, to receive psychiatric therapy, from which she ran away twice. She later became an open lesbian. Oddly, Lana Turner left a mere $50,000 to her only child, who had literally killed for her. Meanwhile, the bulk of her pretty meager estate, some $1.7 million, went to her longtime maid and companion Carmen Lopez Cruz.[510]

For much of the 1930s, bouncer turned mobster Willie Bioff held a great deal of power in the film colony, from his position as co-head of the International Alliance of Theatrical State Employees. According to Kenneth Anger, "At the height of his power, Bioff ordered studio moguls around like office boys."[511] Bioff was finally brought down by courageous actor Robert Montgomery, President of the Screen Actors Guild, *Daily Variety* editor Arthur Ungar, and Hearst syndicated columnist Westbrook Pegler.[512] Bugsy Siegel threw lavish Hollywood parties and became close with huge names like Clark Gable, Gary Cooper and Cary Grant. He also dated starlets like Marie "The Body" McDonald and Wendy Barrie. One of his more intricate criminal rackets involved shaking down his movie star friends for "loans" which he didn't even pretend would ever be repaid. During his first year in Hollywood alone, Siegel is said to have been the beneficiary of an astounding $400,000 from such "loans."[513] Singer and actress Barbara McNair was married to mobster Rick Manzie, who was killed in a still unsolved gangland-style slaying in 1976. Popular Twenties' torch singer Ruth Etting married gangster Martin "Moe the Gimp" Snyder. The singer character in *The Godfather,* which was allegedly based upon Sinatra, was played by another Italian-American, Al Martino. Martino had rumored mob connections of his own. Wayne Newton launched a multimillion dollar lawsuit against NBC for stories it aired depicting his links to organized crime figures. Newton would eventually be awarded over $5 million for being libeled by the network. However, a federal appeals court reversed this decision, claiming "insufficient evidence."[514] In another show business legend concerning Frank Sinatra, some contend that Old Blue Eyes tried to contract a hit on Woody Allen, after the comedian started romancing his ex-wife Mia Farrow.[515]

Celebrated director Howard Hawks invited mobster Al Capone to see the rushes of *Scarface,* the 1932 film loosely based upon him. Capone would reciprocate when Hawks visited Chicago, throwing him a lavish party and gifting him with a miniature machine gun. George Raft, who had met Al Capone, verified that he was pleased with the film.[516] Mobster Longie Zwilmann was one of the nation's top bootleggers and a highly visible figure in early Hollywood. He had an affair with Jean Harlow, with whom he was thoroughly obsessed. Elizabeth Hurley was romantically connected to Colombo family enforcer Dominic "Donnie Shacks" Montemarano, who had an extensive criminal record and was more than thirty years her senior.[517] Hurley was also involved with very wealthy film producer Steven Bing (with whom she had a son), whose own mob connections were supposed to be the subject of an ABC News story in 2004, until it was pulled for unknown reasons. On June 22, 2020, Bing either jumped or fell to his death from a luxury high rise in Century

City. Bing had a slew of intriguing connections, including former President Bill Clinton and the late Jeffrey Epstein.[518] Action star Steven Seagal supposedly was being extorted to the tune of $150,000 for each of his films, by the Gambino crime family.[519] When *Los Angeles Times* reporter Anita Busch was investigating this story, she found a message taped on her car, which read "STOP" in red capital letters. Nearby was a tin-foil tray containing a dead fish, which brought to mind mafia-wannabe Democratic Party insider Rahm Emanuel's mailing a dead fish to a pollster who had angered him.[520] Busch was also harassed and targeted by private investigator Anthony Pellicano (who also was closely connected to Steven Bing), when she was looking into the federal indictment against Mafia don Anthony "Sonny" Ciccone. Pellicano worked with some of the biggest names in Hollywood, including Madonna and Tom Cruise. Veteran character actor Jerry Orbach was an eyewitness to the shooting of "Crazy" Joe Gallo, but refused to cooperate with the authorities. This didn't seem to affect his career at all. The best man at Gallo's wedding to his second wife was comedian David Steinberg.[521] Debbie Reynolds has long been rumored to be tied to Chicago crime families. She once responded to a question about whether people should be worried about getting killed in Las Vegas by saying, "Yeah, but only those who need killing."[522] Apparently it hasn't been much of a stretch for James Caan to portray mobsters convincingly. He was a strong supporter of John Gotti, and publicly defended "Andy Mush" Russo, who is godfather to his son. Liza Minelli allegedly dated low-level mobster Gianni Russo, who served as the go-between for New York don Joe Colombo, Sr. and Paramount Studios. Robert DeNiro spent time with "Fat Andy" Ruggiano in order to prepare for his role in 1999's *Analyze This*. Another convincing on-screen gangster, Joe Pesci, was once roughed up by mobsters hired by James Caan, over an unpaid $8,000 hotel bill.[523]

Mafia influence is strong within the recording industry. The legendary Louis Armstrong got his start playing trumpet in New

Orleans' brothels owned by the Matranga mob family.[524] Many gangsters, including Al Capone, owned clubs in Chicago and New York, which first featured the likes of King Oliver, Fletcher Henderson, and Benny Goodman. Author Dan Moldea reported that MCA records was represented at a big 1984 annual convention by reputed mobster Salvatore James Pisello. In an April 25, 1993 article headlined, "Mafia a Go-Go: The Unwritten History of Rock 'n' Roll," the *Los Angeles Times* recounted how organized crime and "payola" went back to the 1930s, when promoter Juggy Gayles plugged songs like *God Bless America* and *White Christmas* to radio stations. "The idea," Juggy said, "was to get your song played on the radio. With seven plugs, seven good shots, you could make a hit song." According to this article, Frank Sinatra once tried to kill himself in Juggy's apartment. "Booze, bribes and broads. That was rock 'n' roll," Juggy declared. Mobsters pushed the careers of entertainers openly. Lucky Luciano was singer Helen Morgan's lover and controller. Meyer Lansky, meanwhile, controlled every Wurlitzer jukebox in New York. Michael Jackson was known to have a relationship with "executive with a past" Frank Dileo. Morris Levy seems to have been the literal godfather of rock 'n' roll, who, to quote from the article, "made his fortune draining the blood, figuratively and perhaps literally, from a succession of rock 'n' roll acts that began in the early 1950s and did not end until his death in 1991." Industry legend maintains that Levy ordered the murder of James Sheppard, lead singer of the Heartbeats and Shep and the Limelights. Levy gave himself bogus, sole songwriting credit for Frankie Lyman and the Teenager's smash hit *Why Do Fools Fall in Love*, and reaped the benefits of undeserved royalties for decades. In a November 1996 article in *Vanity Fair* titled, "Tommy Boy," Robert Sam Anson directly charged Tommy Mottola, former head of Sony Music, and ex-husband of Mariah Carey, with having mob ties. Madonna's one-time boyfriend, Chris Paciello, served an incredibly light five years in prison for a mafia-related murder, before becoming an informant and entering the witness protection program. The former "night club king" is now a prosperous property owner, back once again in his former romping grounds of Miami Beach.[525]

Several books on the subject of mob infiltration of the music industry have been written, including one by huge 1960s recording artist Tommy James (*Me, The Mob, and the Music*). James, who scored several memorable hits like *Hanky Panky* and *Crimson and Clover* with his band the Shondells in the 1960s, recounted a tale about Morris Levy, who was allegedly tied to the Genovese crime family. "Morris had called all the record companies that had said yes the previous day and scared them," James said. "Finally Jerry Wexler from Atlantic Records told me the truth, that Morris had called and said (affects a mobster type voice) 'This is my fucking record. Back off.' It was right out of the movies. So we apparently were going to be on Roulette regardless. It's literally how we ended up there." James recounted how the expression around Roulette was that their accounts payable department was "the quietest place on the planet." While Levy did nothing to hide his flashy, high standard of living, James and his crew simply weren't being paid. The composer of James's early hits like *I Think We're Alone Now*, Ritchie Cordell, and the producer, Bo Gentry, were in the same position. James wrote that Gentry "hadn't been paid a dime since he started at Roulette. Morris owed both him and Ritchie a fortune in royalties as producers and writers…"[526] It was estimated that Levy owed Tommy James between thirty and forty million dollars in unpaid royalties over the years. James wasn't even given his own gold records, and eventually tore them off the walls of the studio.

Although he wound up with thousands of dollars stuffed into his coat pocket, it still must have been terrifying for Fats Waller to be taken at gunpoint and forced to play piano for three days straight, in celebration of Al Capone's birthday.[527] Tommy DeVito, one of the founding members of the huge 1960s band the Four Seasons, was childhood friends with actor Joe Pesci. The mob aura in their neighborhood was detailed in Clint Eastwood's 2014 film *Jersey Boys*. After the Four Seasons' string of hits ended, and Pesci's Holly-wood career took off, Pesci put his old friend DeVito on his payroll to "watch my back." The notorious British gangsters the Kray broth-ers built a powerful criminal enterprise in the East End of London during the 1950s and 1960s, mingling with celebrities like Judy Garland and Frank Sinatra. They extorted money for years from Brian Epstein, manager of the Beatles. The 2015 biopic based on the Krays, *Legend,* was widely criticized for portraying the duo too favorably.[528] CBS Records veteran producer Ernie Altschuler told former Yardbirds' manager Simon Napier-Bell (who also co-wrote Dusty Springfield's huge 1966 hit *You Don't Have to Say You Love Me*) that, "I've made CBS more hits than any other producer but I've never been paid a royalty or a bonus. They see me the same way they see the artists - just part of the process."[529] Napier-Bell also related another illuminating story; he once witnessed huge black recording artist Joe Tex stick his head into the office of Ahmet Ertegun, one of the brothers who owned Atlantic Records, and ask for a ten dollar loan. "You want 10 bucks," Ahmet replied. "Go downstairs to the studio, find a backing track you like and put your voice on it." Napi-er-Bell subsequently questioned Tex about royalties, and the singer admitted that he wasn't sure if got royalties at all, declaring, "I don't know exactly how it works."

Another time, Napier-Bell saw notorious music honcho Morris Levy shaking black producer Mickey Stevenson by the collar, and screaming, "You fucking black cocksucker. You promised to make me a hit record and you screwed up." Stevenson had written the mega-hit *Dancing in the Street* for Martha and the Vandellas, and produced several other successful records. In 1973 the overt bully Levy was voted Man of the Year by the United Jewish Appeal. Leg-end has it that Levy's typical refrain to questions about royalties was, "Royalties? Try Buckingham Palace." MCA Records' titan Irving Azoff once acknowledged that out of 3,000 audits conducted on record companies, "In 2,998 of them the artist was underpaid." The Dixie Chicks would later call it "Systematic thievery."[530] A veteran music industry insider who strongly wished to remain anonymous, told me another story about Levy. When singer Jimmie Rodgers, who had hits like the million-selling *Honeycomb* and *Kisses Sweeter Than Wine,* complained to Levy that he hadn't received *any* royalties for his recordings, Levy opened his desk drawer, pulled out a gun, and said, "There's your royalties." Levy's huge New York estate had a plaque on the front door which read, "A Sunny Place for Shady Characters."[531] George Lucas had to go to Levy during the making of *American Graffiti* to get the rights to all those classic songs; Levy charged a modest up-front fee, but retained sole rights for the lucrative soundtrack album release, and even demanded final say over how he was portrayed in the film. Young Martin Scorcese's connections, like so many who make it big in show business, were such that he was able to obtain the rights to several songs from Levy for his student film *Who's That Knocking?* In 1992, Levy's estate was judged posthumously liable for $4 million in a courtroom, arising from a lawsuit by Herman Santiago and Jimmy Merchant, Frankie Lymon's band mates in the Teenagers, who co-wrote the smash hit *Why Do Fools Fall in Love* with him. The two testified that they'd only received $1,000 in royalties for the 1956 hit record, which sold in excess of three million copies. Santiago stated that Levy had advised him, "Don't come down here anymore or I'll have to kill you or hurt you."[532]

The Hollywood studios were run by men who were often akin to figurative mobsters themselves, and could be as stereotypically villainous as the bad boys in any of their most garish productions. Actress Evelyn Keyes, in her memoir *Scarlett O'Hara's Younger Sister,* a bit more tactfully declared that "The major studios were each headed by a Big Daddy who reigned supreme." Industry lore holds that Jack Warner would fire anyone who didn't laugh at his lame jokes. He also had the chutzpah to tell Albert Einstein, when he was touring Warner Brothers Studios, "Doctor, you have your theory of relativity and I have mine: 'Never hire a relative.'"[533] Director Gottfried Reinhardy compared Warner to a few of his colleagues this way: "Harry Cohn was a sonofabitch but he did it for business; he was not a sadist. [Louis B.] Mayer could be a monster, but he was not mean for the sake of meanness. Jack was." Cohn was Hollywood's preeminent gambler; he was reputed to have averaged between $5,000-10,000 per day on bets. Another rumor alleges that Alfred Hitchcock cast Raymond Burr as the villain in *Rear Window* primarily because of his resemblance to David O. Selznick. Howard Hughes was so possessive that he had lovely Ava Gardner stalked when she wouldn't marry him. She purportedly retaliated by nearly killing him with an ashtray. Rita Hayworth supposedly refused Cohn's advances, and he retaliated by trying to ruin her career. "I used to have to punch a time clock at Columbia, every day of my life," Hayworth, one of the top box office draws of the 1940s, remembered.[534] Cohn is alleged to have made sleeping with him a requirement for a contract, and even installed hidden passages connected to the dressing rooms of his leading ladies. Brilliant but eccentric actress Jean Arthur used to tell friends about a scheme she'd hatched to slip into the office of Harry Cohn and shoot him with a hidden revolver. "When she began telling it my mouth opened," related close confidante Roddy McDowell, "because I realized it was a definite plan. And it was quite reasonable in her mind and could have worked out."[535] A well-known anecdote about Cohn has him betting an actor that he couldn't recite The Lord's Prayer. When the actor began, "Now I lay me down to sleep," a disgusted Cohn threw a $100 bill at him, exclaiming, "Alright you win. I didn't think you knew it." In addition to all this, Cohn had each of Columbia's sound stages bugged, and would sometimes yell, "I heard that" to his startled employees. Darryl Zanuck was alleged to have a regular four p.m. sex session with a female employee every working day. The ill-fated Carole Landis, who would crudely be known as "the studio hooker" at Fox, according to Kenneth Anger, was said to be "the most constant visitor in attendance in the back room of Darryl Zanuck's office."[536] The now mostly forgotten Anita Page was receiving 10,000 letters a week in 1929, second only to Garbo, including many from her ardent admirer Benito Mussolini. In a 2004 interview, she claimed that her very early retirement from films stemmed from her refusal to give in to the sexual demands of both Irving Thalberg and Louis B. Mayer.

Louis B. Mayer's power was such that he became the highest-paid man in America. There are those who believe that Mayer even ordered people killed, *a la* Mafiosi style. His top aide Eddie Mannix reportedly would *hit people with his car* in order to silence them. His sadism was most evident by his inexcusable treatment of poor young Judy Garland, whom he ordered to maintain a diet of coffee, cigarettes and chicken soup. Garland often worked eighteen hour days, six days per week, fortified by uppers. "After four hours they'd wake us up and give us the pep pills again," she recalled.[537] MGM actually paid Judy's mother a salary that matched her daughter's, in return for which she enforced this dangerous diet regimen. Carl Laemmle was such a notorious practitioner of nepotism that poet Ogden Nash would write, "Uncle Carl Laemmle Has a very large faemmle." Little Shirley Temple single-handedly kept Twentieth Century-Fox afloat; from 1935-1939, the youngster was the most popular movie star in the world. Despite this, she was treated like other child actors, and if she misbehaved badly enough, was locked in a windowless sound room, with only a block of ice to sit on. Shirley was dumped by Fox at age eleven, and signed by MGM. In her first visit to the new studio, producer Arthur Freed whipped out his genitals in front of her. When she giggled in response, she was unceremoniously thrown out of his office.[538]

The studios especially controlled their female stars. With the available plethora of extramarital sex, unwanted pregnancies were inevitable. Actresses were pressured by the studios to get abortions in such situations. As one anonymous actress put it, "abortions were our birth control." According to biographer Lee Israel, Tallulah Bankhead "got abortions like other women get permanent waves." One can only guess at the number of star couples who were forced to choose between parenthood and continued movie stardom. Both Lana Turner and Judy Garland allegedly became pregnant by bisexual Tyrone Power. Turner was also impregnated by bandleader Artie Shaw. She was forced to undergo a horrific abortion in a hotel, where her own mother muffled her screams with her hand. A week later, Turner was back on the set. William Powell and Jean Harlow were forbidden from marrying by their contracts, but this didn't stop her from becoming pregnant. Clark Gable supposedly knocked up Joan Crawford. Kenneth Anger claimed that Hollywood's most notorious abortionist was nicknamed "Dr. Killkare." Good Catholic Loretta Young refused to have an abortion after Clark Gable got her pregnant, and simply disappeared for a while, then "adopted" a daughter.[539]

Studio executives like MGM's Eddie Mannix covered up a variety of scandals involving their biggest stars. Clark Gable was rumored to have run over and killed actress Tosca Roulien in 1933, but Mannix supposedly persuaded screenwriter John Huston to take the rap. Predictably, Huston wasn't charged with anything due to lack of evidence.[540] Mannix kept Gable out of jail so often that the two became best friends. It was Mannix who broke the news to Gable that his wife Carole Lombard's plane had crashed, and he accompanied the devastated King of Hollywood to the crash site. Some in Loretta Young's family came to believe that Gable actually sexually assaulted her during filming of *The Call of the Wild,* and that Mannix and MGM engineered the sanitized story that resulted, as well as the behind-the-scenes legend that the affair was mutually consensual.[541] One of the great urban legends of Hollywood is the pornographic film young Joan Crawford supposedly appeared in (actually, there have long been rumors of porno films featuring some of the biggest names in the Golden Age of Hollywood). According to legend, Eddie Mannix tracked down and destroyed all copies of the film, and bought the original negative for $100,000.[542] It is known that Crawford, in an unusual move, paid MGM $50,000 when she left them in 1943. Natural speculation is that she simply was paying back the studio. "Everybody was scared of Mannix," admitted Ava Gardner, who was one of the countless actresses bullied into getting an abortion. When nineteen-year-old Gardner discovered her husband Mickey Rooney was having an affair with a fifteen-year-old, she was warned by Mannix to stay silent. He informed her that going public would mean "You'll be finished at this studio."[543] Mannix and other MGM officials would inexorably arrive at each potential crime scene involving their stars before the police.

The mob-connected Mannix was even suspected of murdering his first wife, Bernice Fitzmaurice. Mannix's biographer E.J. Fleming candidly stated, "If he hadn't fallen into the movie business he would have ended up as a knee-breaker for somebody." Mannix actually started out in life as a policeman in New Jersey, where he was probably a natural. Mannix sent a candid message to even the biggest names at the studio with the sign prominently displayed on his desk, which read, "The only star at MGM is Leo the Lion."[544] It is suspected that Mannix also played a key role in covering up the real circumstances of Ted Healey's death. Healey is best remembered today for originally forming the Three Stooges. By 1937, he was down on his luck. A heavy drinker, Healey had allegedly been involved in a drunken altercation at the Café Trocadero on the Sunset Strip, just a few days before he died. Healey was attacked by burly actor Wallace Beery, Pat DiCicco, the aforementioned mob connected figure who was married to Thelma Todd and Gloria Vanderbilt, and DiCicco's cousin Albert "Cubby" Broccoli, who would later prosper as producer of the James Bond series of films. On December 21, 1937, the alcoholic Healey was beaten so badly that he died the next day from his wounds. Healey's death at forty-one was attributed to "natural causes," related to his heavy drinking. Mannix and MGM quickly moved to protect their star Beery, and whisked him out of town for a month long vacation in Europe. Although the incident had been witnessed by numerous patrons, MGM arranged a cover up with the Trocadero staff, wherein the high profile thugs became "three drunk college boys."[545] In response to this now well accepted theory, online apologists have attempted to prove that Beery couldn't have gone to Europe at that time, or that the altercation actually took place a night earlier, in the transparent manner of official apologists for important political events. Among the pallbearers for Mannix were Robert Taylor and James Stewart.[546]

One of Hollywood's renowned attorneys for the stars, Jerry Geisler, launched his career on a high note, by getting iconic legal bastion Clarence Darrow off the hook when he was accused of bribing prospective jurors. Geisler went on to successfully defend such entertainment icons as Robert Mitchum, Errol Flynn and Charlie Chaplin. He won an acquittal for famed choreographer Busby Berkeley on his third trial (the first two trials had ended in hung juries) for the deaths of three people he caused in a 1935 car accident. He successfully represented theater magnate Alexander Pantages when he was charged with rape. He also represented mobster Bugsy Siegel, and won a verdict of justifiable homicide in the case of the aforementioned Cheryl Crane, daughter of Lana Turner, in the stabbing death of her boyfriend Johnny Stompanato. For good reason, the catchphrase "Get me Giesler" became popular in Hollywood.[547] Sidney Korshak was another renowned lawyer in Tinseltown. His legal services were sought after by the most high profile mobsters of the day, from Al Capone to Frank Nitti to Sam Giancana to Moe Dalitz. He would represent not only stars like Frank Sinatra, Ronald Reagan and Warren Beatty, producer Robert Evans, and studio head Lew Wasserman, but powerful political figures like California Governors Jerry Brown and Gray Davis. Other famous clients included doomed Teamster leader Jimmy Hoffa and Playboy founder Hugh Hefner.[548] Despite his myriad of shady connections, Korshak died at age eighty-eight without ever having been charged with a single indictment.

Clark Gable's only official child, John Clark Gable, was born after the actor died in 1960. Gable's heirs have led troubled lives; his son was arrested in 2013 and charged with drunk driving after he crashed into six parked cars in Malibu, California. Gable's grandson, Clark James Gable, was accused of pointing a laser into the cockpit of a Los Angeles police helicopter two years earlier. "Boys will be boys," Gable's manager explained to the press. "He was playing with what he thought was a toy and not a felony piece."[549] Clark James Gable died of an accidental drug overdose in 2019, at just thirty years old.[550] In 2008, Gable's granddaughter, Kayley Gable, was filmed falling down drunk, leaving her crudely exposed to photographers in skimpy beige colored underwear beneath her dress. At the time, the twenty-two-year-old Kayley was one of eighteen contestants who were competing to become the new best friend of Paris Hilton in MTV's absurd reality show, *Paris Hilton's My New BFF*.[551] It was yet another reminder that we are far, far removed from the Golden Age of Hollywood. Bette Davis became estranged from her only biological child, daughter B.D. Hyman, after she wrote the Christina Crawford-like *My Mother's Keeper,* which alleged that Davis was a cruel and abusive mother. Hyman went on to become an evangelical Christian pastor, and among her more sensational claims was that her mother regularly practiced witchcraft.[552]

Chapter Seven

More Tragedies, Inconsistencies And Legends

The ladder of success in Hollywood is usually a press agent, actor, director, producer, leading man; and you are a star if you sleep with each of them in that order.

Hedy Lamarr

THE HOLLYWOOD WALK of Fame was created in 1960, with performers like Linda Darnell, Gigi Perreau, Francis X. Bushman and Charles Coburn on hand with shovels at the ground breaking ceremony. Stanley Kramer became the first to actually have a star on the Walk.[553] The initial 500 inductees were chosen by an illustrious group that included Cecil B. DeMille, Samuel Goldwyn, Walt Disney and Hal Roach. Bob Hope and Tony Martin each had four stars on the Walk. Performers who inexplicably don't have a star on the Walk of Fame include: Clint Eastwood, Steve Martin, George Clooney, Julia Roberts, Leonardo DiCaprio, Brad Pitt, John Candy, Al Pacino, Robert DeNiro, David Letterman, Jerry Seinfeld, Jim

Carrey, Kurt Russell, Dustin Hoffman, Gene Hackman, Goldie Hawn, Mel Gibson, Meg Ryan, Jon Voight, Sean Connery, Michael Caine, Bill Murray, Dan Aykroyd, Elvis Presley, Francis Ford Coppola, Warren Beatty and Woody Allen. Actress Amy Adams does have a star there, however, as do astronaut Buzz Aldrin, actress Debbie Allen, Morey Amsterdam, who played Buddy Sorrel on *The Dick Van Dyke* Show, actor Jason Bateman, studio mogul Sherry Lansing and numerous other lesser known luminaries. It does cost $30,000 for a star on the Walk of Fame, and one must be nominated by someone (publicist, etc.).[554] Still, there was no one out there to nominate Elvis Presley, while the likes of George Lopez received a star? There is also Grauman's Chinese Theatre, with its distinctive handprints and footprints, which began in 1927 when Sid Grauman asked his friends Douglas Fairbanks and Mary Pickford to leave their imprints in cement. Some of the comments preserved for posterity there have approached legendary status on their own. Humphrey Bogart, for instance, like many of the stars directed a message to Sid Grauman, declaring, "Sid may you never die, till I kill you."[555] Myrna Loy thanked Grauman for hiring her as a dancer at the theatre in the 1920s, writing, "To Sid, who gave me my first job." During James Stewart's ceremony, the decidedly non-superstitious actor, leaving his hand prints on Friday the 13th, posed under a ladder with a black cat on a leash.[556] In January, 2016, director Quentin Tarantino left his handprints and footprints at Grauman's, now known as the TCL Chinese Theatre.[557] A close look revealed the subtle message "F*** You," in the imprints of his shoes, which the filmmaker had embedded on a character's soles during the filming of *Kill Bill: Vol. I* in 2003.

It's terribly sad that few people in the film business realized the necessity of preserving silent films. So many were damaged or lost that a 2013 study determined that an incredible seventy five percent of all silent movies are unavailable.[558] Martin Scorsese's Film Foundation puts the figure even higher, at ninety percent. Only five of Will Rogers' silent comedies exist, and classics of the genre like Tod Browning's 1927 feature *London After Midnight,* starring the incomparable Lon Chaney, are nowhere to be found. Another fascinating missing film is 1923's *Hollywood,* which was probably the industry's first film about itself. It featured lots of cameos from the biggest stars of the day, and a lead actress named Hope Drown, in her first and only film. There is no biographical data available about Drown, or why she was the star of a big movie and then never made another picture. She was described as exceptionally beautiful, but I could only find a single image of her anywhere online. This one-hit wonder of the Silents did make a handful of appearances on Broadway in the 1920s, and lived to be eighty-eight.

One could write an entire book exclusively about heartbreak and tragedy in Hollywood. 1940s-50s-era B-actress Lynn Baggett led one of the most tragic lives imaginable. She killed a nine-year-old boy in a 1954 hit and run accident, but she was the wife of producer Sam Spiegel, and thus served only a fifty day sentence.[559] Baggett would later somehow become trapped for six days under her foldaway bed, leaving her partially paralyzed, and then took her own life in 1960 at just thirty-five.[560] Dorothy Dell, an upcoming young actress who had most recently starred in Shirley Temple's film *Little Miss Marker,* died in a car crash on June 8, 1934 at just nineteen.[561] Sidney Fox, who starred with Bela Lugosi in 1932's *Murders in the Rue Morgue* and several other films, took her own life at just thirty-four. The often mean-spirited Bette Davis later quipped that the diminutive beauty (she stood only 4'11) could attribute her brief acting career to being studio mogul Carl Laemmle Jr's mistress. "Junior" Laemmle was openly scoffed at by those at the studio (Mae Clarke called him "retarded.") In fact, the scandal was the talk of Tinseltown, and the wrath she incurred undoubtedly contributed to Fox's growing depression.[562] Silent film star and boyfriend of Sarah Bernhardt, Lou Tellegen, stabbed himself to death with a pair of scissors on October 29, 1934. Critically acclaimed actor Philip Seymour Hoffman died of a heroin overdose at just forty-six in 2014. An extremely rare, undetected heart ailment took the life of John Ritter at only fifty-five-years-old. In a startling story, even for Hollywood, real life homeless man Gary Poulter was recruited for a large role in the 2013 Indie film *Joe,* which starred Nicholas Cage. Poulter turned in a powerful performance, but two months after filming was completed, he was found drowned in three feet of water in Austin, Texas.[563]

Lani O'Grady, sister of *My Three Sons* star Don Grady, led a sad life following the cancellation of the long-running TV series *Eight is Enough,* on which she portrayed the oldest daughter Mary Bradford. At the time of her death, at age forty-six, on September 25, 2001, Lani was suffering from agoraphobia and taking several different drugs. She was found dead in her mobile home, but the authorities were unable to conclude if she committed suicide or accidentally overdosed on multiple drugs.[564] Series co-star Susan Richardson fell on difficult times as well once the show ended. In January, 2013, she was interviewed by the *National Enquirer,* revealing that she was living in a rotting, unheated trailer in Wagontown, Pennsylvania. She was suffering from diabetes and a variety of other ailments. In an updated story, it was revealed that Richardson was barely getting by on a $2,000 monthly pension.[565] Richardson's slew of problems seemingly began after she came forth in 1987, claiming she'd been the victim of a kidnapping by South Korean filmmakers.[566] No real evidence for this emerged, and there is little updated information about the story. An earlier star, Ray "Crash" Corrigan, most noted for his many roles in westerns, ran Corriganville, a successful California amusement park on his ranch for years after retirement.[567] Corrigan should have profited handsomely from this, as his land was also used as a location for many film and television westerns, but he curiously died in a Brookings, Oregon mobile home. Corrigan has an unmarked grave, like so many other entertainers, despite two marriages and three children.

Poor Marie Prevost, immortalized by pop singer Nick Lowe in a late 1970s song, led a tremendously tragic life. Prevost's father died in a horrible railroad accident in 1897, shortly after she was born. The lovely young Prevost was discovered by Mack Sennett, always on the lookout for beautiful girls. By the early Twenties, she was a popular leading lady. After gaining weight, Prevost continued to work in supporting roles in some quality early talkies. Prevost had started drinking following her mother's death in a 1926 car accident. By 1937, the forty-year-old Prevost's money was mostly gone, and neighbors in her small apartment building reported hearing bill collectors knocking regularly on her door. On January 23, 1937, after not being seen by anyone recently, Prevost's body was found, and it was estimated she'd been dead for two days. She was surrounded by empty liquor bottles, an IOU to Joan Crawford (who went on to pay for her funeral), and teeth marks from her dog were found on her body.[568] Prevost's pathetic $300 estate was one of the motivating factors in the creation of the Motion Picture and Television Country House and Hospital. The legend that Prevost's dachshund actually ate some of her remains (which Lowe referenced memorably in his song) appears to be another of Kenneth Anger's more fanciful falsehoods. Marjorie White, who appeared in plum roles in early talkies and shorts, including the first Three Stooges solo effort, *Woman Haters,* was killed in an auto accident at only twenty-eight. Silent era actor, writer and director Lynn Reynolds, in a little remembered tabloid scandal, had a heated argument with his wife, former actress Kathleen O'Connor, during a welcome home party for him on February 25, 1927. He apparently became pushed over the edge when she jokingly suggested he'd had an affair with actress Renee Adoree, and shot himself in front of the assembled guests. He was only thirty-seven.[569] Adoree was a big silent film star, who sadly developed tuberculosis after making only two talkies. She died at just thirty-five, leaving behind a piddling estate of $2,429.[570] Blonde bombshell Belinda

Lee survived an accidental overdose in 1958, but three years later was killed in a car crash at just twenty-five.

Theda Bara was the original "Vamp" in the 1915 film *A Fool There Was,* and was a star that shone brighter than most, but only for a very brief time. Her famous line, "Kiss me, my fool," was parroted by young lovers of the era. For her starring role in 1917's *Cleopatra,* Bara was paid $4,000 per week. Bara abruptly retired in 1926. Incredibly, she never found a publisher for her memoirs, and a planned film about her life was never completed. She lived until 1955, but only a handful of her forty exclusively silent films survive.[571] Another leading light of the silent era, Alma Rubens, became perhaps Hollywood's biggest drug addict. She not only was hooked on heroin, but also cocaine, as well as the morphine originally prescribed to her. She tried to stab a physician, during one of her frequent visits to sanitariums. Rubens made only one part-talking picture, and died at just thirty-three after contacting pneumonia in early 1931. Her memoir, *Alma Rubens' Own Story,* published just a few months after her death, was still so popular that all forty-four chapters were serialized in *The San Antonio Light* between March and May, 1944. While she'd made as much as $3000 a week at the peak of her career, Rubens candidly described forcing her maid to become her drug supplier, since she had no money for dealers. The maid was willing to accept expensive clothes in return for the drugs.

Carmen Miranda died unexpectedly of a heart attack at only forty-six, on August 5, 1955, after taping an episode of *The Jimmy Durante Show.* It's probably a little known fact that she was the highest paid entertainer of the 1940s.[572] Bea Benaderet, fondly recalled by Baby Boomers as Kate Bradley on *Petticoat Junction* and the original voice of Betty Rubble on *The Flintstones*, died at sixty-two on October 13, 1968, from cancer. In a remarkable twist, her husband Eugene Twombly, who was eight years younger than Benaderet, suffered a heart attack at her funeral and died a day later.[573] Benaderet provided numerous voices in the old Warner Bros. Cartoons as well, but never received any screen credit due to Mel Blanc's contract stipulation that he was the only voice actor to be credited. Alexander Kirkland was briefly a leading man in early talkies like 1932's *Strange Interlude* (alongside Clark Gable and Norma Shearer). He vanished from the film world rather quickly, and was so forgotten by the 1980s that it is only presumed he died at some point during that decade. As IMDb states, "After the 1950s, very little is known of his whereabouts. Although it is unlikely that he is still alive, no reports of his death have surfaced." If he is remembered at all, it's for being briefly married to famed stripper Gypsy Rose Lee. A 1987 story noted that "at the time of his death," he was living in Mexico, and his daughter was quoted as saying he "had wasted all his money."[574] This is exceedingly strange; the exact date of his death was unknown even to his daughter?

Deanna Durbin was a shooting star sensation in the 1930s and 1940s, and at the peak of her fame was the second highest paid woman in America, behind only fellow actress Bette Davis. Like a surprising number of others, she turned her back on stardom in 1948, at only twenty-seven. She never appeared again onscreen for the rest of her life, dying at ninety-one in 2013. She was reluctant to talk about her career, granting only one interview in all those decades.[575] Roaring Twenties cowboy star legend Tom Mix never quite adapted to sound pictures. At his peak, Mix was making $17,500 weekly. His estimated $6 million in career earnings was largely whittled away on an extravagant lifestyle, leaving him with only a modest estate. Mix epitomized Hollywood excess; his huge mansion featured his name in neon lights above it. On October 12, 1940, in perfect unnatural Hollywood-style, the sixty-year-old Mix was speeding through the Arizona desert and was struck in the head by one of his aluminum suitcases, causing his car to plunge into a ravine.[576] May McAvoy was the leading lady in the classic 1925 version of *Ben-Hur* and starred opposite Al Jolson in the first talkie, 1927's *The Jazz Singer*. She experienced one of those inexplicable career plunges, as she had no more screen credits after 1929. She did appear in many uncredited bit movie roles from 1940 until 1959, with her last role being a mere crowd spectator in the 1959 remake of *Ben-Hur*.[577] The explanation is that she retired over unhappiness with the roles being offered her, and/or that it was related to her marriage. Why then, did she return to acting, but could never get any credited roles?

Writer Joseph McBride, another person who shares my interest in the JFK assassination, whose works include a biography of Frank Capra, in writing about John Ford's last film, 1966's *7 Women*, in a December 31, 2019 Facebook post, recounted an anecdote regarding one of the stars: "When I rented an apartment from Jane Chang in Beverly Hills in 1975, I thought I recognized her, but she denied she had been an actress. I went into one of my boxes and pulled out the copy of Cahiers with this picture, and she smiled and admitted she was the Mandarin princess, Miss Ling, in 7 WOMEN. We became friends. She said she loved working for Ford, who she said was the only director she ever had who allowed her to be emotional in a film or TV show. All the other directors told her, 'Orientals don't show feelings.' That's Hollywood for you. So she quit the business." Chang is apparently still alive, but has no Wikipedia page and IMDb doesn't even list the date of her birth.

Lucille Ball was devastated early in her life by a horrific accident in her backyard on July 4, 1927. The *Huffington Post* called it "The Tragic Gunshot that Ruined Lucille Ball's Childhood." An eight-year-old neighbor was shot and paralyzed when Ball's twelve-year-old brother's girlfriend accidentally fired his new gun. Ball's grandfather was financially ruined by the subsequent lawsuit. As the future television superstar described it in her memoirs: "They took our house, the furnishings that [Ball's mother] DeDe had bought so laboriously on time, week after week, the insurance— everything. My grandfather never worked again. The heart went out of him."[578] Clara Bow, the celebrated "It Girl" of the Roaring

Twenties, endured a poverty-stricken childhood marred further by a seriously ill mother. Among other things, young Clara experienced her mother falling from a second-story window, telling her she'd be better off dead than becoming an actress, and even waking up to find a butcher knife being held to her throat by her flawed maternal model. "As a kid I took care of my mother, she didn't take care of me," Clara would later declare. When her mother died from epilepsy at only forty-three, Clara became so hysterical over the hypocrisy of her grieving relatives that she tried to jump into the grave with her. Her father allegedly abused her sexually and later helped squander her considerable movie earnings. To top it off, as a child Clara witnessed a young male friend burn to death in her presence. At the height of her popularity, Bow was receiving some 45,000 letters monthly. One disputed legend regarding her voracious sexual appetite holds that she slept with the entire starting lineup of USC's 1927 football team, which included Marion Morrison, soon to become rising western star John Wayne. Clara made her last film when she was just twenty- eight, and was fired by Paramount after suffering a nervous breakdown. "A sex symbol is a heavy load to carry," Bow would write near the end of her life.[579] It is said that Bow wrote to several gossip columnists, urging them to promote young Marilyn Monroe, who became perhaps the most tragic entertainer of them all, as the new "It" girl. Clara married cowboy film star and future politician Rex Bell after she left the movies and remained married to him, albeit unhappily, for over thirty years, and had two sons. There was at least one suicide attempt, and she died at age sixty on September 27, 1965.[580] Louise Brooks was molested at age nine by a forty-five-year-old man. As she later stated, her molester "must have had a great deal to do with forming my attitude toward sexual pleasure." Brooks was as notorious a nymphomaniac as Clara Bow ever was; an employee of the Algonquin Hotel memorably referred to her room as a "bordello," and the management kicked her out.[581]

Some actors were just dealt a bad hand. Tom Tyler was an athletic star of many western films in the 1920s and 1930s. He was even considered for the role of Tarzan, which eventually went to Johnny Weissmuller. After working for smaller, "poverty row" studios, he finally found a few plum roles, starring in the lead role for Republic Pictures' Captain Marvel serial, and then played the title character in 1943's *The Phantom*. Just as his career seemed to finally be paying off, the former record-setting weightlifter rather strangely developed a severe case of rheumatoid arthritis, causing him to be able to work only sparingly in bit roles during the early days of television. He became destitute and was forced to move in with his sister, where he lived for a year before dying all too young at just fifty. Judy Carne was a busy 1960s actress best remembered for her work on *Laugh-In*. Known as the "Sock it to me" girl on the popular show, Carne would unfortunately not go on to the greener pastures co-stars Goldie Hawn and Lily Tomlin did. By the late 1970s, Carne had been arrested three times, on charges like drug possession and auto theft. Carne had been married to Burt Reynolds from 1963 to 1966, but when she tried contacting Reynolds following her arrest, the then biggest movie star in the business didn't return her calls. "At least he could have helped with the legal fees," Carne lamented. "After all, I supported him when he was out of work, and I never asked for alimony." A year after her autobiography - which was cruelly panned by critics - was published, Carne was sentenced to three months in jail for drug possession. In her book, she claimed that Reynolds was physically abusive towards her.[582] She lived to be seventy-six, but at the time of her death was financially destitute and "a bit of a recluse," to quote one of her friends.[583] Oscar nominated British actor Terry-Thomas (born Thomas Terry Stevens) was so devastated by medical bills resulting from his Parkinson's Disease, he wound up spending his final years in a tiny charity flat, assisted financially by the Actors' Benevolent Fund, until a charity concert for his benefit permitted him to move into a nicer nursing home.[584]

At the beginning of his career, in 1938, Terry-Thomas was paid just over $25 for appearing in the film *Climbing High.*

When Cary Grant's unpublished memoir was discovered a few decades after his death in 1986, it revealed how the most attractive, successful person imaginable couldn't rid himself of his childhood demons. Grant's father was an alcoholic, and his mother was institutionalized in what was then called a "lunatic" asylum. The smooth, urbane actor admitted to taking LSD more than one hundred times, and confessed to being unable to bond with women, despite being perhaps the best-looking man in the history of Hollywood. Grant's mother had simply vanished when he was eleven years old, while at the same time his father moved to the other side of Britain to start a new family with another woman. It wasn't until twenty years later that Grant discovered his mother, still alive, had actually been institutionalized by his father. "I came home from school one day and she was gone. My cousins told me she had gone to a seaside resort," Grant wrote. "I thought that odd. It seemed rather unusual but I accepted it was one of those things that adults do. I regularly haunted the Bristol wharfs and sat alone and contemplated. It gradually dawned on me that she was not coming back. She left a void in my life, a sadness of spirit that affected everything I did. I always felt my mother rejected me." His mother apparently had never recovered from accidentally closing a door on the thumb of Cary's older brother John, who went on to develop gangrene from it and died before the legendary actor was born.[585] Another manuscript that lay undiscovered for years was written by Orry George Kelly, who was the head of the costume department at Warner Brothers. Kelly had been roommates in Manhattan with the young and struggling Archibald Leach, who would go on to become movie superstar Cary Grant. Kelly painted an ugly portrait of Grant, depicting him as incredibly cheap and mean-spirited. When he ran into Grant later, after he'd morphed into a legendary film star, Kelly was shocked at his attitude. "Gone was Archie Leach full of fun," Kelly wrote. "He was adjusting the mask of Cary Grant" and didn't want to associate with people who'd known him before he was famous.[586]

Valerie Perrine never lived up to her impressive start in show business, highlighted by an Academy Award nominated performance in 1974's *Lenny.* She had memorable roles in *Superman* and *Superman II,* but while working regularly, has never approached the heights that might have logically been predicted for her. Beatrice Straight was another actress with a strange career arc. She won a Best Supporting Actress Oscar for *Network* in 1976, and had a nice supporting role in 1982's *Poltergeist,* but other than that she was relegated to lots of television work. Her last screen credit was in 1991, and she died a decade later. Kay Francis was dubbed the "Queen of Warner Brothers," and in 1935 was earning a tidy $115,000 annually (in contrast to Bette Davis's $18,200).[587] In what was probably not all that uncommon in those early days of promiscuous sex, she had seven abortions in just one two-year period, according to an article on Miles Mathis' outrageous but fascinating web site. She was also supposedly one of Hollywood's countless closeted lesbians, so she must really have been active sexually. Her career bottomed out incredibly fast, and by the mid-1940s she was forced to produce B-movies for herself at Monogram Studios. Her last screen credit, an early television appearance, was in 1952. Childless despite five marriages, she lived in virtual seclusion until her death in 1968, leaving most of her estate to the Seeing Eye, Inc., for purposes of dog training. Paulette Goddard only acted sporadically in her later years. Upon her death in 1990, the actress (childless like so many others in Hollywood) left $20 million to New York University. How did she accrue a much larger estate than huge stars like Mickey Rooney, Bette Davis and Lana Turner? Playwright Eugene O'Neill wrote all of his children out of his will. Two of his sons committed suicide, and his final split with his daughter Oona came after she married the much older Charlie Chaplin.[588]

Hedy Lamarr's biographer claimed that the Jewish actress was forced to have sex with Adolph Hitler by her first husband. Charlie Chaplin described Louise Brooks' breasts as small, "like pears," and she countered by saying his lovemaking "was suitable only for little girls." Chaplin's well known predilection for young girls resulted in multiple scandals, culminating when he married seventeen-year-old Oona O'Neill when he was fifty-three, and proceeded to have eight children with her. Chaplin was born into horrid poverty in South London. His promiscuous mother probably took to the streets at times to make ends meet, and then, *a la* Cary Grant, was sent to a mental institution when he was just eleven. He ran away from home the following year, joining a troupe of clog dancers. As Chaplin himself would state, "My childhood ended at the age of seven."[589] Chaplin's first wife, Mildred Harris, appeared nude in D.W. Griffith's *Intolerance* while still underage. Harris went on to become a silent movie star in her own right, and died at just forty-two after an operation, allegedly of pneumonia.[590] Mary Astor, scandalized when her sexually explicit diary was made public, wrote in her 1959 memoir *My Story*, about having to endure her dying, delirious mother complaining about her horrible, selfish daughter when the old woman didn't recognize her. *Rebel Without a Cause* forty-four-year-old director Nicholas Ray had an affair with sixteen-year-old star Natalie Wood.[591]

Séances were all the rage during the Roaring Twenties; Rudolph Valentino was said to be particularly enamored with them. John Barrymore was so smitten with leading theosophists Henry and Helios Hotchener that Henry became his business manager and his wife drew up the astrological charts the Great Profile relied upon. The likes of Marie Dressler, Douglas Fairbanks, and Mary Pickford swore by their astrologers. Basil Rathbone claimed to have ESP. Director Ernst Lubitsch was dependent upon his numerologist and director William Dieterle had complete faith in the psychic abilities of his wife. Superstition reigned everywhere in Tinseltown. Bruce

Cabot, chiefly remembered as Fay Wray's love interest in *King Kong*, had a clause written into his contract that stipulated he would not work on the thirteenth of any month. Bessie Love, who was nominated for an Oscar for her lead role in the early 1929 talkie *The Broadway Melody*, refused to work on Fridays. Neither Norma Shearer nor Mary Pickford would remove their wedding rings for any film role.[592]

Not everyone in show business has lots of sex. Among those who allegedly died as virgins was Andy Warhol. Benny Hill was a quintessential "Mama's Boy." He lived in the same apartment with his mother for twenty-six years, and after she died he turned it into a shrine to her. He remained in this rented apartment for the rest of his life, never owning a home or even a car. Hill's upbringing was suitably unconventional; his father insisted the children call him The Captain, and owned a small shop that exported condoms. On the shop's front counter was a giant wooden phallus. Hill proposed to three women, but was turned down each time. Legend has it that he was afraid to make a move to even kiss girls when he was out on a date. It is probably reasonable to speculate that he died a virgin, and it's quite possible that he never even kissed a woman. However, some sources counter this, claiming Hill would bring "cheap" factory girls back to his flat, and "offer poached eggs on toast and cheap lingerie in return for fellatio."[593] When Benny Hill died at sixty-seven, his body lay in his apartment, slouched before his beloved television, unnoticed for several days.[594] Tom Lester, who portrayed one of the great sitcom characters of all time, handyman Eb Dawson on *Green Acres*, was so religious that he remained a virgin until finally marrying at age sixty-eight, by which time he might very well not have been capable of consummating it. Even at the height of his fame, Lester lived in a small room over a garage, and would spend his summers off by speaking at churches and youth rallies across the country. *Diff'rent Strokes* star Gary Coleman publicly admitted to being a real life forty-year-old virgin, and declared that even two months into his marriage, he still hadn't lost his virginity.[595] Renowned authors Hans Christian Andersen and Henry David Thoreau are said to have died virgins. Lewis Carroll was only interested in prepubescent girls, and there is no evidence he ever made sexual advances towards them, thus leading most historians to conclude he never had sex. Ann B. Davis, best known for playing Alice the maid on *The Brady Bunch,* never married or was linked romantically to anyone. It is certainly reasonable speculation that she was a virgin when she died at eighty-eight in a group religious home. Betty Lynn, beloved to Baby Boomers as "Thelma Lou" on *The Andy Griffith Show*, appears not to have had any public romances and never married (although she has said she was once engaged). Lynn bought a house in 1950, shortly after the start of her film career, and lived there with her mother and grandparents. It's at least within the realm of possibility that Barney Fife's girlfriend never had sex.

Ron Howard's show business career encompassed being a child actor who played Opie on the classic *The Andy Griffith Show* to portraying Richie Cunningham on television's long-running *Happy Days* to playing the lead in the smash film *American Graffiti* to becoming one of the most respected directors in the business. Howard told Howard Stern, on his radio show back in the 1990s, that he was a virgin until he met his wife, and had never cheated on her. Frank Zappa was married to the same woman for twenty-six years, had four children by her, and seems to have been faithful to her. Paul and Linda McCartney supposedly never spent a night apart during their twenty-nine years of marriage. If this is true, presumably McCartney sowed more than enough oats during his earlier years with the Beatles. The same may be true of his ex-band mate Ringo Starr, who has been married to Barbara Bach since 1981. Rolling Stones drummer Charlie Watts claimed not to have slept with groupies, and remained faithful to his wife. Alice Cooper (born Vincent Furnier) has been married since 1976, and claims to have stayed monogamous with his wife. Jon Bon Jovi married his high school sweetheart in 1989, and they have four children. Dee Snider has been married to the same woman since 1981. "Sneaky" Pete Kleinow, a member of the Flying Burrito Brothers and a notable session musician for multiple big name artists, was married to the same woman for fifty-four years, with whom he had five children, when he died of Alzheimer's at age seventy-two in 2007. Gary Brooker, lead singer of Procol Harum, has been married to the same woman for over fifty years. Levi Stubbs, lead singer of the Four Tops, was married to the same woman (they had five children together) for forty- eight years before he died in 2008. His band mate Abdul "Duke" Fakir, the sole surviving member of the legendary Motown foursome, has been married to his second wife since 1974. Gerry Marsden, front man for the British Invasion group Gerry and the Pacemakers, had been married to the same woman since 1965, when he died in January 2021 at age seventy-eight. Brian Poole of the Tremeloes married his only and current wife in 1968. Marilyn McCoo and Billy Davis, Jr., both of the popular group The Fifth Dimension, have been married since 1969. Allan Clarke, lead singer of the very successful Sixties band The Hollies, has been married to the same woman since 1964, before all their biggest hits were recorded.

Former *SCTV* star Andrea Martin spoke candidly in her autobiography *Lady Parts* about remaining celibate for fourteen years, starting when she was just forty-two, until she met a man twenty-nine years younger than her. Martin admitted to having lots of sex in her twenties and thirties, and was busy during her period of celibacy being a single mother to two young sons, but that's still a long time. At the height of his rock stardom, Lenny Kravitz told an interviewer that he hadn't had sex for three years. Ted Gunn, the former host of *Project Runway,* publicly announced in 2012 that he hadn't had sex in twenty-nine years.[596] The late Prince Rogers Nelson, known popularly as Prince, once proclaimed, "I'm single, celibate and sexy…That's what happens with years of celibacy - it all goes into the music."[597]

Robert Taylor was one of Hollywood's most notable "Mama's boys." His overbearing mother went on a hunger strike to protest his marriage to Barbara Stanwyck. Taylor spent his wedding night with his mother, not his wife. Busby Berkeley was so close to his mother, "Queen Gertrude" that he attempted suicide a few weeks after her death and had a nervous breakdown. After being sent to the psychiatric ward at Los Angeles General, Berkeley discovered that he had only $650 to his name.[598] Milton Berle, also rumored to be one of the most well-endowed entertainers in show business, permitted his mother Sarah to live with him all her life. Fred Astaire's mother lived with him, as well. The now completely forgotten early talkie leading man Lawrence Gray was so devoted to his parents that he built a dream home to share with them, and remained with his mother until his marriage in 1935. Clifton Webb lived with his mother until she died at age ninety-one, leading Noel Coward to quip, "It must be terrible to be orphaned at 71."[599] Modern "Mama's boys" are a bit weirder about it. When he lost his virginity, *Captain America* star Chris Evans couldn't wait to tell his mother. "The first time I had sex, I raced home and was like, 'Mom, I just had sex! Where's the clit? Still don't know where it is, man,'" Evans told *Details* magazine.[600] Leonardo DiCaprio has been known to bring his mother as his date to important show business events. Ryan Gosling also brought his mother as his escort to the 2007 Academy Awards ceremony. After his father died in 2011, Bradley Cooper's mother moved in with him. Cooper described her as "a cool chick."[601] Plenty of celebrities still live at home with their parents, or did well into adulthood. Examples include *Black Panther* star Michael B. Jordan, actresses Jennifer Lawrence and Selena Gomez, actress/singer Demi Lovato, comedian Kathy Griffin, and former Reality TV stars Spencer Pratt and Heidi Montag, who moved into Pratt's parents' home after reportedly squandering a $10 million fortune.[602]

Mary Pickford had perhaps the first notable stage mother, but the mothers of Jean Harlow, Linda Darnell, Betty Grable, Loretta Young, and many others earned unpleasant reputations in the film colony. Elizabeth Taylor's overbearing mother Sara wasn't above exploiting her beautiful prepubescent daughter's budding sexual allure. She once dressed the thirteen-year-old like what a witness called a "Joan Crawford hussy" for a publicity trip to the White House.[603] Ginger Rogers had a stage mother to top all stage mothers in Lela Owens McMath. McMath was her daughter's agent, writer, wardrobe artist and nonstop promoter. Actor Lew Ayres declared that he couldn't compete with Ginger's mother during their separation. To distract her and keep her quiet, the studio put McMath in charge of its new talent school. The outspoken Ginger would passionately defend her mother, and claimed to have called her every day, wherever she was in the world, to tell her she loved her. When she died, the childless Rogers (who was also a proud nonsmoker and nondrinker) left her substantial fortune to the Christian Scientists.[604] Anissa Jones, the little girl who played Buffy on the television series *Family Affair*, was undoubtedly adversely affected by her own stage mother, whose full-time career was promoting her daughter. Jones would die of an overdose at only eighteen after predictably turning to alcohol and drugs. Gertrude Temple had Shirley listening to music while she was still in the womb. It is said that this ever-present stage mother set Shirley's hair in exactly fifty-six ringlets every morning, in an effort to match Mary Pickford's look.[605] Minnie Marx managed Groucho, Harpo, and Chico's careers, and masked the fact that she was their mother by changing her name to Palmer. As far back as 1933, Hollywood was cognizant enough of this phenomenon to produce a film entitled *Stage Mother*.

One of Hollywood's stranger success stories involved actor Charles Bickford. His biography recounts, as if it wasn't all that unusual, that *nine year old* Bickford was charged with and tried for the attempted murder of a trolley conductor after he ran over his dog. Bickford had an extensive career in Hollywood, and was nominated for three Academy Awards. This was despite an easily triggered temper; he is alleged to have knocked iconic director Cecil B. DeMille out cold for instance, over a disagreement on the set of one of his early films. Many an actor's career has ended over something far less serious than that. Bickford also supposedly pummeled a couple of strangers during the World War II era, at the Somerset House restaurant, for what he perceived as anti-patriotic comments. Bickford was mauled and nearly killed by a lion during filming of *East of Java* in 1935.[606] "Prince" Mike Romanoff started out as a garment worker named Harry Gerguson in New York. He was an open, notorious con man, and actually served time behind bars in France. He managed a magical transformation into mythical royalty in Hollywood, and was mysteriously welcomed by the studios, which paid him handsomely as a technical advisor on exotic locations. He started the first legendary restaurant that bore his name in 1938, and it never lacked for famous customers.[607]

Macho Robert Mitchum had an appropriate juvenile background; he was expelled from middle school for fighting with the principal, and later served on a real chain gang in Georgia. In 1948, Mitchum became the first celebrated figure to be arrested for smoking pot. One of those caught with him, lovely starlet Lila Leeds, served the same sixty day sentence as Mitchum, but unlike him her career never recovered.[608] While Mitchum's "bad boy" image was solidified by the incident and only increased his popularity, Leeds left Hollywood a year later after a few scattered un-credited roles. By 1974, Leeds had become a minister with Spiritual Mission, Inc., which operated a church in Hollywood, and a few years later was making personal appearances to promote Richard Lamparski's latest "Whatever Became Of . . ." book. When she died in 1999, none of the major newspapers published an obituary about her. Legendary blues singer Heddie Ledbetter, famously known as Lead Belly, was imprisoned for murder in 1918. One of those unfathomable legends has it that Lead Belly gained his early release from prison by singing the governor of Texas a song. He was incarcerated again in 1930, for attempted murder. Supposedly, he was discovered later in prison by a couple of high profile folklorists.[609] Another legendary blues figure, Robert Johnson, died under unclear circumstances at just twenty-seven. One of the same folklorists who'd discovered Lead Belly, Alan Lomax, was instrumental in promoting Johnson's music to the masses. Lomax helped to spread the fanciful legend of Johnson's midnight encounter with the Devil at a crossroads in Mississippi, where he was allegedly gifted his impressive musical skills.[610] More recently, *Mad Men* star Jon Hamm was discovered to have tortured and set afire a young pledge to his fraternity in 1990 while attending the University of Texas. He received only a slap on the wrist, and remained less than contrite years later, telling an interviewer, "It was a bummer of a thing that happened."[611] Comedian Kathy Griffin had some juicy, unkind things to say about Hamm in her 2016 book *Kathy Griffin's Celebrity Run-Ins*, claiming that he bullied her at a party.[612] Actress Amy Locane graduated from a series of commercials as a child to a blossoming adult career in the business, but rather strangely retired from acting at only thirty-five. A few years later, in 2010, Locane struck and killed a woman while driving drunk. She was sentenced to three years in prison. In a highly irregular move, especially considering her celebrity status, in 2019 Locane was summarily given twenty additional years in prison, of which she was likely to serve at least twenty months. It wasn't explained how this wasn't a case of double jeopardy, and Locane's attorney shockingly termed it "an extremely thoughtful decision in all respect."[613]

The odd case of screenwriter and playwright Wilson Mizner stands out in several respects. He came from an upper-class background, as most in tinsel town did; his father was an envoy to President Benjamin Harrison. As a young man, Mizner drifted into decidedly lurid activities. He fixed fights as a boxing manager, was arrested for running a gambling den and became an opium addict and a common swindler. Working with his brother in a typically shady way, Mizner developed Boca Raton and Palm Beach, Florida as resorts for the wealthy.[614] Despite this extremely checkered resume, he somehow received the backing of studio head Jack Warner and actress Gloria Swanson, enabling him to buy the legendary Brown Derby restaurant in Hollywood. Consistently biting the hand that fed him so well, Mizner called his time in Hollywood "a trip through a sewer in a glass bottomed boat." Mizner held a disdain for authority, and especially disliked Jack Warner, his initial benefactor in the film business. According to writer Margaret Talbot, whose father Lyle was a star in the early talkies era, Mizner was never a writer in the classic sense. His biographer, Alva Johnston, who also claimed he never stopped seeking "new suckers to trim," referred to him as "a writer who never wrote." Talbot presumably got the first-hand details from her father, as she described Mizner sleeping much of his time at the studio, ensconced in a plush red chair, where he came to be dubbed "the Archbishop." Mizner would supposedly awake long enough to utter memorable quips that the real screenwriters would incorporate into their scripts. Mizner is remembered for many lines, including "Be nice to people on the way up because you'll meet the same people on the way down." He likened working at Warner Brothers to "fucking a porcupine: it's a hundred pricks against me."[615] Talbot's book *The Entertainer: Movies, Magic, and My Father's Twentieth Century,* provides an inside look at the early years of the film business.

Women held a surprising amount of power in the early days of Hollywood. Anita Loos and Frances Marion were two of the top screenwriters during the silent era. A third renowned female screenwriter, June Mathis, has been all but forgotten. Mathis not only was a productive writer, she became the first female executive for MGM, and at age thirty-five was said to be the highest paid executive in Hollywood. Mathis, who from existing photographs appears not to have been overweight, died very suddenly while attending a Broadway play on July 26, 1927 with her grandmother. In fact, it was one of the entertainment world's most dramatic exits, as she suddenly grabbed her grandmother and screamed, "Oh mother, I'm dying!" The forty-year old Mathis was taken outside, but had already died, officially from heart disease brought on from breaking her diet.[616] Another ironic oddity is the fact that Mathis had "lent" her spot in the family crypt in what would become Hollywood Forever Cemetery to close friend Rudolph Valentino, when he died unexpectedly in 1926, a year before her. I don't think it's a stretch to say that not too many people have died from heart attacks in the presence of their grandmothers. Dorothy Arzner was Hollywood's only female director during the golden era of the 1920s -1930s. Like so many of those she directed on screen, Arzner was gay. Legend has it that her career ended prematurely when studio boss Harry Cohn fired her over a kissing scene between Merle Oberon and another actress. Lois Weber was such a respected director of the silent era that she was often mentioned in the same breath with D.W. Griffith and was credited with inventing the split screen technique. When Weber died in 1939, she was destitute, and already so forgotten the location of her ashes remains unknown.[617]

One of the most notable victims of the transition from silent to sound movies was the no longer remembered Raymond Griffith. Griffith was one of the most popular silent comedians, but had a strange malady that prevented him from speaking louder than a whisper. This was exposed in his only talking film, and he was forced to move behind the scenes, where he went on to co-found Twentieth Century-Fox. In keeping with the dark tone of this book, Griffith had a suitably Hollywood-style ending. He choked to death at a Los Angeles nightclub on November 25, 1957. Perhaps the most tragic example of a silent star failing to graduate to sound movies was Mae Murray. Murray was a huge star, earning $10,000 weekly by 1922. Legends abounded about her, crediting her with everything from discovering Rudolph Valentino to inventing the dunking of doughnuts. Murray, whose personal credo "once you become a star, you are always a star," would prove to be sadly ironic in her case, was dubbed "The Girl with the bee-stung lips." A run in with the powerful Louis B. Mayer resulted in her being fired from MGM, and blacklisted from the other studios. She made only a handful of unsuccessful talkies, and lived in extreme poverty for much of her life, with the lowlight being an arrest for sleeping on a New York City park bench. She died at seventy-five years of age, on March 23, 1965, a year after she'd been found wandering and disoriented in St. Louis.[618] Long forgotten silent star Helene Costello, sister of the better known actress Dolores Costello (grandmother of Drew Barrymore) and daughter of silent actor Maurice Costello, supposedly had a voice that was inadequate for talkies. Her life spiraled downward in the familiar pattern, and she declared bankruptcy in 1942. When she died at only fifty her funeral was attended by less than a dozen people.[619] Pretty seventeen-year-old Valerie Hobson was paid all of $800 to star in 1935's *Bride of Frankenstein*. Her second husband, prominent British politician John Profumo, would become embroiled in the sensational 1963 sex scandal with Christine Keeler.[620]

Dick York, who played the original Darren Stevens on television's *Bewitched,* led about as tragic a life as anyone in the entertainment business. A master of light comedy who also turned in memorable performances in *The Twilight Zone* and other shows, York collapsed on the set of *Bewitched* during its fifth season. Evidently, York had been living in intense pain from a back injury suffered on the set of a film in the 1950s, *They Came to Cordura.* He'd become addicted to pain-killers as a result and after the collapse, never returned to the show. York's only real tangible asset, an apartment building, was at length foreclosed on and he had to go on welfare. Understandably depressed, York ballooned up to 300 pounds and lost all but a few teeth. In an act of selfless heroism, York spent his final years advocating for the homeless, while tethered to a long oxygen life-line in his small Michigan home.[621] Another source, however, indi-cates that the Yorks lived from 1985 until York's death in 1992 at the home of his wife's parents, and that his widow Joan "Joey" Alt York, remained there until 2008.[622] According to an interview not long before his death with *People* magazine, York earned up to $4,000 per episode on *Bewitched*. Before going on welfare, York and his long-time wife Joan cleaned apartment buildings to support themselves and their five children.[623] York's *Bewitched* cast-mate David White, who played his boss Larry Tate on the show, lost his only son in the 1988 bombing of Pan Am Flight 103 over Lockerbie, Scotland.

One of the strangest episodes in the history of show business involved former *SCTV* and *Saturday Night Live* cast member Tony Rosato. Rosato apparently grew unhinged in the mid-2000s, and came to believe that his wife and infant daughter had been replaced by imposters. He spent over two years in a maximum security prison, simply for refusing to plead guilty, and another couple of years in a psychiatric facility. All the while, Rosato declined treat-ment, declaring, "It's actually enforced confinement," and calling the situation a "Catch -22." Rosato's lawyer Daniel Brodsky claimed that he'd spent more time in custody on charges of criminal harass-ment "than any other convicted prisoner in Canada has ever spent on the same charges."[624] There is nothing on the record to indicate Rosato had any sort of mental illness before the sudden onset on what the psychiatric community refers to as Capgras syndrome, wherein a person believes those close to them have been replaced by imposters. Maybe Rosato was a big fan of *Invasion of the Body Snatchers*. New York film producer Sonny Grosso described Rosa-to's situation as "the most confusing case I've ever encountered in my life." Finally free in 2009, Rosato died at only sixty-two in Jan-uary, 2017.[625] Frances Farmer was a big star whose erratic behavior resulted in her being institutionalized. In her autobiography, Farmer described horrific abuses at the hands of the psychiatric industry, including allegations of rape, beatings and even being forced to eat her own feces. When she died at age fifty-six in 1970, she was completely broke.[626]

The primary writers of the hit television series *Good Times* were Eric Monte and Mike Evans (also co-creator of the show, who acted in the original role of Lionel Jefferson on both *All in the Family* and *The Jeffersons*). Both experienced a career drop-off after the show ended. Evans eventually became a realtor, and died at only fifty-seven of throat cancer. Monte, who also produced the sitcom *What's Happening*, which was based on his screenplay for the 1975 film *Cooley High*, was discovered to be living in an east L.A. homeless shelter in 2006.[627] Monte had filed a lawsuit against Norman Lear, CBS and others for stealing his ideas in 1977, and eventually won a $1 million settlement and a small percentage of *Good Times'* residuals, much of which was lost in the funding for an unsuccessful play. Monte drank heavily and became a crack cocaine addict. At last report, he was living in Portland, Oregon. According to Demond Wilson, who played Lamont on *Sanford and Son*, he and Redd Foxx were forced to dress in the men's room when the show first started. Wilson is seemingly doing just fine financially, declaring in a 2014 interview with WTLC radio, "My shows are shown in 40 countries, my books are selling around the world and I've done several movies and I get residuals. And I get 10 grand for a speaking engagement. So I'm cool." Wilson is reported to have a pretty modest $1.5 million net worth.

One band that fizzled out quickly but saw its individual members go on to successful careers outside the business was the Cyrkle. Handled by the Beatles' famed manager Brian Epstein, the group's unusually spelled name was suggested by John Lennon himself.[628] The band had a short career, highlighted by the smash 1966 hit *Red Rubber Ball* (co-written by Paul Simon), but two of its members went on to write some memorable commercial jingles, while the others became a surgeon and attorney, respectively. The friction between John Lennon and Paul McCartney, incidentally, was most obviously detailed on Lennon's song "How Do You Sleep?" Lennon called McCartney's first solo album "rubbish" in a 1971 interview with *Rolling Stone*. Describing his feelings about the *Let it Be* film, Lennon declared, "That is one of the main reasons the Beatles ended. I can't speak for George, but I pretty damn well know we got fed up of being side-men for Paul."[629] Lennon could be refreshingly honest, once stating, "I don't bother so much about the others' songs. For instance, I don't give a damn about how 'Something' is doing in the charts -- I watch 'Come Together' (the flip side) because that's my song." In a 2015 interview, McCartney couldn't conceal his bitterness towards Lennon. "John was the witty one, sure," McCartney said. "John did a lot of great work. And post-Beatles he did more great work, but he also did a lot of not-great work. Now the fact that he's now martyred has elevated him to a James Dean, and beyond."[630]

An examination of Hollywood salaries from 1937 is very illuminating, and again illustrates the maddeningly inconsistent financial compensation in show business. Gary Cooper was the highest-paid film star, at just over $370,000 that year. Studio head and iconic cultural figure Walt Disney made a mere $39,000, while William A. Seiter, never a major film director, somehow made over $135,000. Peter Lorre barely made $15,000, and already established horror icon Boris Karloff just $40,000, while the largely forgotten Warner Baxter earned over $284,000. Baxter would later express the reality even big entertainment stars face, declaring, "I was a failure and a success three times in Hollywood, I have even had troubles paying my rent." Studio mogul Sam Goldwyn was paid only $22,000, while the little remembered Madeleine Carroll made nearly $288,000. Zeppo Marx had long stopped being a part of the brothers' act, yet he made nearly $57,000. Scenario editor Julian Johnson made over $61,000, which was $1,000 more than urbane leading man William Powell, seemingly at the peak of his career, earned. While the lovely

Loretta Young made just under $119,000, Ruth Chatterton - who was far past her prime and made only a single forgettable film that year, somehow was paid $249,500 (which was also more than Fred Astaire's $211,666, Jean Arthur's slightly over $119,000, Bing Crosby's $156,000 and Ginger Rogers' just under $125,000). Mae West made a reported $340,000 in 1935, while the king of Hollywood Clark Gable supposedly was paid a relatively modest $4,000 weekly by MGM. In contrast, Errol Flynn earned $7,000 weekly for just one of his lesser known films. Judy Garland, as always being taken advantage of, was paid $3,000 weekly during her last few years at MGM. Some of these modest salaries seem especially mystifying, considering that Mary Pickford signed a three picture contract in 1918 for $675,000 plus 50 percent of all profits. Two years earlier, Charlie Chaplin was paid $670,000 for twelve two-reel comedies. Compare this to the modest $22,500 that young sensation James Dean received for his role in *Giant* and the biggest movie star of the 1950s Marilyn Monroe, having her own production company but still being paid far less than Pickford and Chaplin had been forty years earlier, at $100,000 for four films.[631]

According to publicly released IRS statistics, Johnny "Tarzan" Weissmuller was paid a Bela-Lugosi-like $24,600 in 1935. Even costume designer Gilbert Adrian made more, at $38,666. Madeleine Carroll, at $360,000, was paid more than Gary Cooper, Bing Crosby, and Clark Gable. Miriam Hopkins earned just $86,250, and the Queen of MGM, Norma Shearer, even less, at $80,000. In contrast, notorious acting bust Anna Sten made $96,833, and Mae West topped them all, at $480,000. West made one film that year, the little remembered *Goin' to Town*. Little Shirley Temple was paid $307,014 in 1936. Fred Astaire made less that year, at $211,000. Lionel Barrymore earned $129,174. Carole Lombard's $450,000 dwarfed that of her future husband Clark Gable's $253,333. Oliver Hardy, half of a comedy duo that was already on the decline, made just $88,600, while Stan Laurel was paid $135,000. Brilliant character actor Frank

Morgan earned just $74,367, and was still making under $100,000 in 1941. Bing Crosby made $452,314 in 1940, and the seemingly over-the-hill Wallace Beery was paid $278,750. Fred MacMurray made $248,333. Cary Grant, meanwhile, certainly a bigger star than Beery or MacMurray, earned less, with $206,250 the same year. The top comedy team of its era, Abbott and Costello, earned $548,423 in 1941, while Charles Boyer made $350,000 in the same year. Cary Grant just edged Boyer out, at $351,562. Robert Young wouldn't crack the $100k barrier until 1941, when he was paid $113,208. Elizabeth Taylor would get a cool $1 million for her role in *Cleopatra* in 1963, the same amount earned by Audrey Hepburn a year later in *My Fair Lady*. Meanwhile, the biggest male star at the time, John Wayne, was only earning $600,000 per film.

John Carradine, a prolific actor who appeared in more than two hundred films, once said, "I never made big money in Hollywood. I was paid in hundreds, the stars got thousands. But I worked with some of the greatest directors in films and some of the greatest writers. They gave me freedom to do what I do best, and that was gratifying."[632] Carradine's son David was a busy actor as well, but when he died under murky circumstances in 2009 (supposedly hanged during an auto-erotic game), he left an estate of just $500,000. Karl Malden had a sixty year acting career, and lived to be ninety-seven. He claimed never to have made "the big money" until he starred on television and in commercials.[633] Ann Dvorak is a little-remembered star of some of the best pre-code talkies of the early 1930s, and her early decline and eventual retirement at barely forty years of age represented a tremendous loss for the film business. As a reminder of just how modestly some of these actors were paid, Dvorak earned only $37.50 per week for *The Hollywood Revue of 1929,* and just $250 weekly for a truly gripping performance in 1932's *Three on a Match.* When Dvorak discovered she was making the same amount of money as the five-year-old who was playing her son in *Three on a Match*, she understandably left Warner Brothers in a huff. Dvorak was perhaps Hollywood's first real rebel, but she is seldom mentioned in the same breath in this regard as the likes of Bette Davis. Her career never recovered, as the studio retaliated by placing her in substandard vehicles.[634] She later moved to England and served as an ambulance driver during World War II. She'd always been underpaid, earning just $250 a week for starring in 1932's classic *Scarface*. Shortly after her death on December 10, 1979, the *National Enquirer* ran a lurid but generally accurate story on her sad final days, depicting "a desperate, paranoid, impoverished woman living in squalor…"[635] In an interview with Alt Film Guide, Dvorak's biographer Christina Rice noted how difficult it was to get any recollections from those who'd known her: "Ann did not have any children or siblings, so there is no family to speak to. I tried placing ads in newspapers in Honolulu and Los Angeles…" Rice was relegated to interviewing a man who claimed to have taken Dvorak and her mother out to dinner in 1969. Marilyn Monroe was paid a decidedly underwhelming $1,250 weekly for 1953's *Gentlemen Prefer Blondes*. By 1956, she earned $100,000 for *Bus Stop*. At the time the first *Thin Man* was filmed in 1934, William Powell was under contract for $3,000 a week. Robert Taylor was known for being the lowest paid major movie star for decades, thanks to Louis G. Mayer's manipulation of his naive trust and willingness to work in any assigned vehicle.[636] He was making a ridiculous $35 a week for MGM in 1934, before it was increased to a still paltry $59 in 1935.

Writer and director Preston Sturges was the third highest paid man in America during the peak of his career, in the early to mid-1940s. By the end of the decade, Sturges' flame had pretty much burned out. He sunk much of his money into the Hollywood hot spot The Players, but later only the burger stand was left, and a pathetic Sturges himself could be seen behind the counter, sarcastically noting to customers, "How the mighty have fallen." The once Golden Boy of the film colony took his fall from grace philosophically, declaring, "I had so very much for so very long, it is quite natural for the pendulum to swing the other way for a while, and I really cannot or will not complain."[637] Sturges had come from a highly unusual household, led by an eccentric mother who took on many lovers, one of whom was high profile Satanist Aleister Crowley. Sturges was another "Mama's boy" who once responded to a lover's question about what had happened to his mother's remains by pointing to an urn by the bed. Sturges' colorful childhood included being spoon fed champagne as a baby by his mother's pal, dancer Isadora Duncan.[638] Sturges died suddenly of a heart attack at age sixty, alone and probably not well off financially, in a New York hotel room. The ironic title of the memoir he was working on at the time was "The Events Leading up to My Death."[639] He was buried in the rather obscure Ferncliff Cemetery in Hartsdale, New York. Sturges was one of the first in Hollywood to both write and direct his own films, although he directed only thirteen movies, less than even Stanley Kubrick.

According to celebrity net worth, at the time of former Monkee Peter Tork's death in 2019, he was worth $4 million. Tommy James claimed that the Monkees were exceptionally well-paid in comparison to even the Beatles and the Rolling Stones, in terms of concert appearances. James stated that the foursome was getting either $100,000 guaranteed, or 100 percent of the gate.[640] Ex-band mate Mike Nesmith, on the other hand, is worth $50 million. Apparently, much of Nesmith's wealth came from inheriting his mother's Liquid Paper fortune. When he died in 2012, Davy Jones was worth $5 million. In one story detailing the battle between Jones' much younger widow and his four daughters for the proceeds from his estate, it was noted that "Jones also received substantial amounts each year from royalties from the string of hits while in The Monkees..."[641] Mickey Dolenz is supposedly worth $7 million. Meanwhile, far less celebrated comedian Scott "Carrot Top" Thompson has a $75 million fortune. "Judge Judy" Sheindlin is worth an incredible $250 million. Martin Lawrence has accumulated a net worth of $110 million. Jimmy Buffet hasn't had a hit in decades, but has $430 million, undoubtedly helped by his successful restaurant chain. Gloria Estefan, another artist without a hit in a long time, has fared a lot better than more successful music performers have, with a $500 million fortune. Mick Jagger, by contrast, is worth $305 million. While Disney was paying the Sprouse twins a combined $40,000 for each episode of *The Suite Life,* young Amanda Cosgrove was earning a hefty $180,000 per episode on Nickelodeon's *ICarly* by 2010. Selena Gomez, a much bigger name, was paid $25,000 per episode during the same time period for Disney's *The Wizards of Waverly Place.*[642] And Disney's biggest star at the time, Miley Cyrus, was making even less than the Sprouse twins, at $15,000 per episode.[643] Hilary Duff was also paid just $15,000 for each episode of *Lizzie McGuire,* although she has managed to accrue a $25 million fortune while not exactly working constantly in the industry. Maybe Nickelodeon just pays better than Disney, although whatever they paid Drake Bell for starring in *Drake and Josh,* he is presently said to have only $400,000, according to Celebrity Net Worth. Drake Bell filed for bankruptcy in 2014, and claimed to have made less than $20,000 in 2013.[644] Bell and his former co-star Josh Peck, who has done much better financially (with a reported $10 million net worth), supposedly hadn't spoken for years before Bell tweeted out how hurt he was not to have been invited to Peck's 2017 wedding. Peck claimed it was a small wedding, but both the show's producer and a cast extra were invited.[645] Gary Coleman, ill-fated child star of *Diff'rent Strokes,* by contrast, worked his way up to $70,000 per episode, and that was in the 1980s.[646] The child stars of the hit Netflix series *Stranger Things* earned $30,000 per episode for the first two seasons, but were granted a dramatic increase to at least $200,000 per show for the third season.[647]

The ultra-cute Martha Quinn was a mini-icon in the '80s as one of MTV's original VJs. According to Celebrity Net Worth, she's worth a mere $750,000. That's still more than another of the original VJs, Nina Blackwood, is said to be worth - $500,000. Dwayne Hickman, who played the title role in the television series *The Many Loves of Dobie Gillis,* also has just a $500,000 net worth. Nicole Eggert, who starred on the television shows *Charles in Charge* and *Baywatch,* similarly is said to be worth just $500,000. Original VJ Mark Goodman is said to be worth $1.5 million. Will Friedle, best known for his regular role on the 1990s television series *Boy Meets World,* and also for voicing the title character in the animated series *Batman Beyond,* has remained busy over the years with regular voice work on a slew of superhero and other cartoons, but also has just $500,000, according to Celebrity Net Worth. Richard Thomas, "John-Boy" on *The Waltons,* has a modest $2 million, according to Celebrity Net Worth. Most of the rest of the cast of that long-running show seemed to fare even worse than Thomas. According to a list compiled in 2015 on the Celebrity Petal web site, Ellen Corby left an estate of only $200,000, and her onscreen husband, Will Geer, left $700,000. Most of the other actors who portrayed the *Waltons* kids are worth $500,000 or less, with David W. Harper (Jim-Bob) possessing only $100,000. An updated "Where are they now?" feature a few years back reported that Harper left acting after the show, and had worked a series of jobs, including as an employee with television brother Eric Scott's messenger service, before returning to school to study business and history. At last report, he was working an as art dealer in Los Angeles.[648] Michael Learned, mother of the brood, has a modest $3 million fortune. Her onscreen husband, Ralph Waite, left behind a $2 million estate when he died in 2014. Judy Norton-Taylor, who played Mary-Ellen on the show and did little else in the business other than posing for *Playboy* in 1985, has a higher net worth than all the rest, at $4 million. Jon Walmsley, who portrayed her brother Jason, was married to his onscreen *Waltons* wife Lisa Harrison, by Ralph Waite, who was a minister in real life. Eric Scott recounted how he went from television star to messenger boy, with the low point being when he delivered a package to Lorimar Productions, where *The Waltons* had been produced. "I walked in and saw my picture and all the Waltons in the lobby. It was an adjustment time," Scott stated. "I had to realize that that was not where I was going to be anymore. It was a humbling event." Mary McDonough, who played Erin Walton, contracted Lupus, which she attributed to her decision to get breast implants.[649]

The same Celebrity Petal web site compiled a list of the relative net worth of the *Little House on the Prairie* cast, and it was astonishing to see that Melissa Gilbert is worth only $500,000, a million less than her onscreen sister, Melissa Sue Anderson, who has acted very little since leaving the series, and the same as her arch series nemesis Alison Arngrim. James Drury starred in the title role on television's third-longest running western, *The Virginian.* I tried emailing Drury, inquiring about his experiences with royalties and residuals, but his personal assistant explained that he was a full-time caregiver for his wife and had to decline. Drury is said to have left a modest $1.5 million estate behind following his death in April 2020. The web site Celebrity Petal listed the respective net worths of all *Virginian* cast members, and as might be expected, they varied considerably. Gary Clarke, who was only on the show for a few seasons, somehow accumulated a $4 million fortune, while the late Doug McClure, a much bigger name in the film colony, died leaving an estate of only $600,000. Lee J. Cobb, who starred in the first several seasons of the show, left only $500,000 at his death, despite being in many big films prior to his television work. Charles Bickford, who replaced Cobb on the show, was an even bigger star in Hollywood, yet he left an even smaller $300,000 estate. However, this was contradicted in an online essay by Alicia Mayer, whose great uncle was Louis B. Mayer, in which she referred to Bickford "having made millions in shrewd real estate investments."[650]

The stars of the '80s series *Family Ties* fared pretty well. The parents, played by Michael Gross and Meredith Baxter, still have relatively modest net worths, considering they worked in a much better era in terms of salaries and residuals, with $6 million and $7 million respectively. Tina Yothers, despite telling Howard Stern years before that she was set for life, has an even more modest $2 million net worth. Justine Bateman is worth $5 million. Michael J. Fox, of course, dwarfs them all with his $65 million. The cast members of another iconic '80s series, *The Cosby* Show, did much better. Tempestt Bledsoe has a $13 million net worth. Her onscreen sister Keshia Knight Pulliam has $14 million, and onscreen brother Malcolm-Jamal Warner is worth $10 million, the same as their television sibling Lisa Bonet. Phylicia Rashad, who played their mother on the show, has an impressive $55 million net worth. The stars of yet another classic series from that decade, *Cheers*, lead the way financially. John Ratzenberger is worth an incredible $80 million, even more than his significantly busier co-stars Ted Danson (at $60 million) and Woody Harrelson ($65 million). Rhea Perlman has a $50 million net worth, and George Wendt is just behind her at $45 million, while Kirstie Alley has $30 million. Shelley Long, one of many television stars who've left successful series for the potential greener pastures of feature films, lags behind the rest, at $16 million. The even more recent, long-running show *Full House,* should seemingly have set up its young stars financially for life. However, Jodie Sweetin, who played Stephanie Tanner on the series, is said to have just $400,000 to her name, according to The Penny Hoarder web site. Andrea Barber, who was Kimmy Gibbler, has just a $500,000 net worth. Dave Coulier, who portrayed funnyman Joey Gladstone, has a surprisingly modest $4 million, while Scott Weinger, who had a much smaller role as D.J.'s boyfriend Steve, and has primarily provided voices for video games other than starring as the main voice in Disney's 1992 smash feature *Aladdin* in the years after the show, has nevertheless piled up a $12 million fortune. Bob Saget has a net worth of $100 million, more than the still busy John Stamos's $40 million, and the Olsen Twins, predictably, are said to be worth $150 million each.

One of my favorite shows of all time was *SCTV*. Some of the cast members, like Martin Short, Catherine O'Hara, Rick Moranis, and Eugene Levy, went on to greater fame and riches. However, some mysteriously faded from the limelight. Joe Flaherty, who played such memorable characters as station manager Guy Cabaellero and the hilarious horror movie host Count Floyd, is said to have just a $500,000 net worth. Andrea Martin is doing only slightly better, at $1 million. One of the original Not Ready for Primetime Players during the first five seasons of *Saturday Night Live,* Garrett Morris, also has just a $500,000 net worth. Tim Kazurinsky, who joined the cast in the first season after remaining originals Morris, Gilda Radner, Jane Curtin, Laraine Newman, and Bill Murray left the show, has just $1 million, according to Celebrity Net Worth. Tommy Davidson was an integral part of the cast of *In Living Color.* While Jim Carrey went on to mega-stardom, the television show *TMZ* used to poke good- natured fun at Davidson's older, unimpressive car. He is said to be worth $2 million presently. Fellow cast mate Kelly Coffield Park has a meager $300,000. Bobby Lee, one of the longest serving cast members on *MADtv* who also starred in films like *Harold & Kumar Go to White Castle* and *Pineapple Express*, has a surprisingly low $1 million net worth. Fellow cast member Aries Spears, whose post-show career appears much less impressive, is worth $8 million.

The net worth of rock stars varies wildly as well. Jackson Browne, one of the most successful singer-songwriters of the 1970s, has an estimated worth of $12 million, the same amount as the barely remembered Todd Rundgren. This is peanuts compared to the $200 million fortune of his Laurel Canyon colleague Don Henley, just one of the members of the Eagles, or Linda Ronstadt, who is so often associated with him, who amassed a $115 million fortune. It really pales in comparison to U-2 front man Bono's $600 million. Joni Mitchell, one of the greatest singer-songwriters of the rock era, has an even smaller net worth than

Browne, at just $10 million. Her seemingly less successful female peer Carly Simon has an impressive $65 million net worth. Justin Hayward, leader of the wildly successful Moody Blues, also is said to have $10 million. Cat Stevens, probably more successful than any of them, has a shockingly modest $5 million fortune, which makes his earlier quote about royalties supporting his charity work a bit perplexing. Even more remarkably, Ray Davies, front man, vocalist and songwriter of the long-lasting classic band the Kinks, is said to only have $2.6 million to show for all those years of success (although this has been updated to $12 million, it's still a pittance, considering his star stature). Davies' brother Dave, who took a clear backseat to him with the Kinks, until recently was said to be worth nearly a million more somehow. Roger McGuinn, leader of the Byrds and a successful solo act, is only marginally better at a $3 million net worth. McGuinn told a Senate Judiciary Committee, on July 11, 2000, that the Byrds had never received any royalties for *Turn, Turn, Turn* and *Mr. Tambourine Man*, their two biggest hits. Former Byrds' band mate David Crosby told the *Washington Post* in a 2013 interview that "I don't have any money at all," but seemed pretty content.[651] Celebrity Net Worth claimed at the time that Crosby had a $40 fortune. By the end of 2020, Celebrity Net Worth had lowered this figure dramatically, to $5 million. In a December 9, 2020 tweet, responding to a fan asking if he was planning to sell his musical catalog (Bob Dylan had just made headlines for selling his voluminous catalog for $300 million), Crosby stated, "I can't work... and streaming stole my record money...COVID has shut down all work live…I have a family and a mortgage and I have to take care of them so it's my only option." Crosby called his newly diminished estimate of net worth "exaggerated." Meanwhile, the never big Kiki Dee has some $10 million, and Emmylou Harris, best known for singing harmony with more famous performers, has a $15 million net worth. Nils Lofgren, who has been backing up Bruce Springsteen for years, has a $20 million fortune. That's twice as much as the $10 million accumulated by veteran singer-songwriter Nick Lowe.

Robbie Robertson, who wrote most of the classic songs recorded by The Band, also has just a comparatively modest $10 million worth. James Taylor, who sold far fewer records than the likes of Jackson Browne and Cat Stevens, has a very healthy $60 million fortune. Eric Clapton has a fantastic $300 million, but Jon Bon Jovi somehow has more, with an incredible $410 million net worth. This didn't stop Bon Jovi from once declaring, "I think record companies are criminal." Just one of the members of the group Abba, who scored with a series of hits in the late '70s through the '80s, Agneta Faltskog, has an amazing $200 million net worth. And she is worth the *least* of all the former members of the band. Her ex-husband and band mate, Bjorn Ulvaeus, has $300 million. So does Anni-Frid Lyngstad; and her former husband, the remaining member of the Abba quartet, Benny Andersson, is credited with $230 million by Celebrity Net Worth. Boomtown Rats front man turned activist Bob Geldof has a $150 million fortune, while Janis Joplin left a relatively modest $5 million estate. Mary Travers, of Peter, Paul & Mary fame, left just $3 million behind her. But Van Morrison, who is chiefly remembered for a classic album or two, has a $90 million fortune. Bobbie Gentry, known primarily for her huge 1967 hit *Ode to Billie Joe*, somehow has an incredible $100 million net worth. Gentry's one-time husband, singer Jim Stafford, who had several big hits in the 1970s like *Spiders & Snakes* and *Wildwood Weed*, lags far behind her at $8 million.

Leon Russell, for whom Elton John was once the opening act, left an estate of just $600,000. Dee Dee Ramone left even less, at only $500,000. The Doors' lead singer Jim Morrison had only a $400,000 estate, while Jimi Hendrix, with far fewer hits, left behind a $175 million fortune. Former Rolling Stones guitarist Mick Taylor is said to have only a $300,000 net worth. Joan Jett, meanwhile, a footnote to the punk-rock scene in the 1980s, has some $7 million. Mary Wilson, who spent her most productive years in the shadow of Diana Ross (who has a hefty $250 million) as a member of the Supremes, has an $8 million fortune, half of the never big Patti Smith's $16 million fortune. And the Birdman, not exactly the world's most successful rapper, nonetheless has accumulated an astounding $170 million fortune. Even session drummer Hal Blaine has a $5 million net worth. Marianne Faithfull, basically a one hit wonder with 1965's *As Tears Go By* as well as the critically acclaimed 1979 comeback LP *Broken English,* nevertheless has built a $15 million fortune, which is all the more remarkable given she once spent nearly two years homeless.[652] This is more than the $10 million estate accumulated by the late prolific singer-songwriter John Prine. Carlos Santana is worth $40 million, and Bob Seger $45 million. On the other hand, Ronnie Spector, lead singer of the Ronettes, who has worked steadily as a solo act with the some of the biggest names in the industry over the years, accrued just a $1.5 million fortune. A very similar singer, Darlene Love, despite a much smaller body of work and seemingly fewer hits, has a $5 million net worth. Mick Fleetwood, leader of the uber successful band Fleetwood Mac, has just $8.5 million, which dwarfs in comparison to band mates Lindsay Buckingham's $45 million, Christine McVie's $65 million and Stevie Nicks' $75 million fortune. Bruce Johnston, perhaps the least well known member of the Beach Boys, has built a $30 million net worth. Bonnie Bramlett was half of the husband and wife singing duo Delaney & Bonnie, who had a couple of hit singles in the early '70s, *Only You Know and I Know* and *Never Ending Song of Love,* co-wrote the Carpenters huge hit *Superstar* and the well-known Eric Clapton song *Let it Rain,* was a regular on the sitcom *Rosanne* for years, and appeared in a handful of movies, yet according to the web site vipfaq, has a net worth of just under $699,000.

Evoking memories of poor Bela Lugosi being exploited by the old studio moguls, Somalian-born actor Barkhad Abdi was reportedly paid only $65,000 for his role in the 2013 film *Captain Phillips,* while star Tom Hanks received $50 million. According to the *New Yorker,* Abdi was forced to subsist on studio per diems while living at the Beverly Hills Hotel during promotion for the movie. Author Robert Bloch received just $9,000 for the screen rights to *Psycho,*[653] and Anthony Perkins was paid a very modest $40,000 for one of the film industry's best remembered roles. Interestingly, the 1957 Ford sedan driven by Janet Leigh's character in *Psycho* was the Cleaver family vehicle on *Leave it to Beaver.* Chevy Chase, John Belushi, Dan Aykroyd, Gilda Radner, Larraine Newman, Garrett Morris and Jane Curtin were paid $750 per week during the initial 1975 season of *Saturday Night Live.* By the fourth season of *SNL,* cast members were making $4000 weekly. By 2001, Will Ferrell, on his sixth season with the show, was earning $17,500 per episode. On the other hand, when then producer Dick Ebersol signed established comedians Billy Crystal and Martin Short for the 1983-84 season, they were paid respectively a much more generous $25,000 and $20,000 per episode.[654]

Some entertainers turn their backs on show business and simply become recluses. Enterprising fans tried in vain for years to meet and talk with filmmaker John Hughes, whose body of work includes such classics as *Planes, Trains and Automobiles, The Breakfast Club* and *National Lampoon's Vacation.* Said to be severely shaken by his friend John Candy's sudden death, Hughes retreated from Hollywood in 1994, moving back to the Chicago suburbs, only occasionally granting an interview. Hughes stopped talking to his two favorite young performers, Molly Ringwald and Anthony Michael Hall, after they turned down some of his scripts. Ringwald would recall, "Most people who knew John knew that he was able to hold a grudge longer than anyone -- his grudges were almost supernatural things, enduring for years, even decades."[655] Like Candy, Hughes died without warning of a heart attack, while taking a morning stroll through Manhattan, at only fifty-nine. Celebrated authors J.D. Salinger and Thomas Pynchon each went into seclusion after initial literary successes. Original Pink Floyd front man Syd Barrett withdrew from the music world and moved back home with his mother for more than three decades.[656] Frances Bavier, beloved by television fans for her role as Aunt Bee on *The Andy Griffith Show,* spent her final years in Siler City, North Carolina, living alone in a filthy house with fourteen cats. She had a Studebaker with four flat tires in her garage, which had last been driven in 1983 to the grocery store. In 1986, her former co-stars Andy Griffith and Ron Howard visited her home, but she refused to let them inside and only spoke briefly to them from behind the front door. Bavier left behind a modest estate of $700,000.[657]

Mick Jagger summed up the nature of royalties for musical performers, most of whom now make less than their peers did decades ago, this way: "… it is a massive change and it does alter the fact that people don't make as much money out of records. But I have a take on that – people only made money out of records for a very, very small time. When The Rolling Stones started out, we didn't make any money out of records because record companies wouldn't pay you! They didn't pay anyone! Then, there was a small period from 1970 to 1997, where people did get paid, and they got paid very handsomely and everyone made money. But now that period has gone. So if you look at the history of recorded music from 1900 to now, there was a 25 year period where artists did very well, but the rest of the time they didn't."[658]

Jim Croce was reportedly earning as much as $10,000 a night on the college concert circuit during the early 1970s. However, according to his wife Ingrid, due to a misplaced trust in the man who'd discovered him, they were barely making ends meet on a $200 weekly salary.[659] Like too many other musical performers, Croce would die tragically in a plane crash on September 20, 1973. He was only thirty years old, and on the brink of superstardom. His widow battled in courts for over a decade to retrieve the rights to her husband's royalties. Croce's talented guitarist Maury Muehleisen was killed along with him. I traded several emails with Maury's sister Mary, who runs a tribute site in her brother's name. On June 7, 2018 Mary wrote, "I suppose that you may be basing your observation about Jim not faring well on things that have been said and written through the years, not all of which I personally believe to be factually accurate... Just months before Jim died, he bought a house in the Point Loma section of San Diego, one of the nicest neighborhoods in the area - in the range of about $50,000 at that time. Jim borrowed money for the down payment from his best friend Tommy Picardo, aka Tommy West, his record producer. Jim's income at the time would easily make the mortgage payments... A few years after Jim's death, a lawsuit was brought against the very people who did everything in their power to help Jim and his wife and child, both before and after his death....With regard to Maury, he received a salary from BNB Associates Ltd, who paid him in his position as Jim's lead guitarist, as they travelled together around the country and on two European tours. Maury's salary was not a fortune; but, as Jim's nest egg built up, he always insisted to his financial manager that Maury's compensation also be increased. Maury and Jim never had to worry about having large amounts of money in their pockets, as all expenses were handled for them. Maury's heirs have received royalties through the years." On January 3, 2021, upon further pursuing the facts about these royalties, Mary emailed me, "With regard to Maury....Dad was occasionally receiving checks to distribute to Maury's heirs (Mom, Dad and seven siblings). These were mostly coming from Blendingwell Music and were basically writer's royalties for Maury's 'Salon and Saloon' song. When I began to handle matters, I took a much more active role, contacting music industry entities to be certain they knew that Maury Muehleisen had heirs and that he had performed in various TV shows with Jim Croce. I also sought out any entity that may have royalties for Jim Croce songs in movies. Sure enough, unclaimed royalties were being held in Maury's name. Required paperwork was filed and unclaimed and current royalties, although dwindling, have been forthcoming." Mary Muehleisen wrote, in a January 7, 2021 email to me, "Ironically, today I received a royalty statement for $5.18 for 'Salon and Saloon' and that entity does not send checks for less than $25. That small amount will be carried forward until the $25 amount is reached." Croce's widow Ingrid didn't respond to my email or Facebook messages. There are records online of the 1984 U.S. Court of Appeals decision, which awarded Ingrid Croce over $700,000 in royalties her husband had earned.

Go-Gos member Kathy Valentine, who penned some of their biggest hits, including *Vacation* and *Head Over Heels,* sued her former band mates in 2013 for "breach of fiduciary duty and abuse of control…in an attempt to deprive her of her position and interest in the group, including the right to receive her full one-fifth, 20% share…" The other four members of the Go-Gos had crassly started a corporation without Valentine, in what looked like an obvious attempt to deny her a fair share of the band's earnings. The local Los Angeles CBS affiliate quoted the January 17, 2013 email Valentine claimed to have received from lead singer Belinda Carlisle in a May 25, 2013 story. The quote read: "We have decided, for a variety of reasons, including our musical differences with you and the disparaging comments you have made about the band on your Twitter memoir, that we no longer wish to work with you." The suit was settled out of court in 2014. By 2018, the band mates had kissed and made up, reuniting for a new tour.[660] Valentine doesn't seem to have suffered financially, as she is said to be worth $44 million. It probably won't come as a surprise to learn that Belinda Carlisle, who enjoyed a nice solo career after the breakup of the band, reportedly has a significantly smaller $16 million net worth.

Show business mirrors the rest of our winner-take-all society, with its criminally unfair distribution of wealth, a topic I explored in depth in my book *Survival of the Richest.* "Hollywood has become like a third world country," said veteran actor Kent McCord, SAG's former vice president, best recalled for his co-starring role in television's *Adam-12* series. "There are a few actors who are very rich, and a large base who can't make a living. They're turning the business into something where you have the stars, and the rest are hobbyists."[661] While guest starring roles on popular programs were once quite lucrative, even the bigger names are often now relegated to what is known in the industry as "top of show," which makes their fees per appearance as low as $8,000 or less. Many extras don't even qualify for SAG's top tier health plan, which requires a yearly income of at least $30,750. In England, things are much the same; a recent report stated that only one in fifty UK actors make more than $25,000 per year.[662] While the top stars today earn unimaginable wealth, a 2013 Department of Labor study surveyed over 155,000 actors, directors and producers, and determined that their average annual salary was $89,000. For actors alone, the average salary was a shockingly low $22.15 per hour. McCord is said to have a very modest $1.3 million net worth. His *Adam-12* co-star Martin Milner left just $500,000 behind when he died in 2015, despite also starring in another popular television series, *Route 66*.

As far back as 1923, the *Los Angeles Times* wrote, "It seems that the Chamber of Commerce statistics show that some 10,000 young men and women, less than legal age, come to this city every month to seek jobs in pictures, and of course only a small part of them have any talents or, if so, have the good fortune in the struggle to find places, for the directors are deluged with applications."[663] According to a 1934 article in the same newspaper, only a scant 2 percent of the young girls descending upon Hollywood in search of stardom ever became featured or even bit players. MGM reported that some 5,000 people auditioned with them every year, and of these just 1 percent were even given screen tests. Only a few of those earning screen tests were ever signed by the studio. As for the extras of that era, a mere thirty out of Central Casting's 17,000 worked more than *three days* in 1930.[664] Frankie Darro, once a rising young actor, would later open a restaurant he named "Try Later," as an inside joke. "Try later" was apparently the industry's phrase of choice to extras being rejected for a particular project. Darro's restaurant became in fact a popular gathering spot for extras in the film colony. Darro was unfortunate in that his very short stature (five-foot-three) limited his adult roles significantly. He never earned much money; with $5,000 for a few mid-1930s films being his high-water mark. By 1954, he would act in *The Lawless Rider* for a scant $600. In 1936, the lucky extras who were hired earned anywhere from $3.25 to $35 per day, depending upon their skill set. They could also earn an additional stunt check for falling off a horse, or for growing an impressive natural beard, or even a "wet check" for being doused with water.[665] By 1940, mobster Bugsy Siegel had taken over the extras' union.

In 1925, as many as 40,000 people, according to the now-defunct *Los Angeles Record*, were background actors, populating massive crowd scenes in biblical epics, riding horses in Westerns and so on. Each morning, a slew of men, women and children would crowd around the gates of the five major studios — Paramount, MGM, Warner Bros., 20th Century Fox and RKO Pictures. Assistant directors would come out and point to those they wanted. "A few indulge in selling real estate," the *Hollywood Citizen News* wrote, "some peddle silverware, some wash dishes in restaurants while awaiting the great opportunity they hope will come sometime." Pay was about $2 a day in the mid-1920s — around $30 in today's money. And productions might instead give vouchers to the extras, to be cashed at casting agencies — which often took a cut.[666]

Some extras do well in present day Hollywood. One of these busy commercial extras, Harold Green, candidly observed that more often than not, they spend time "doing what we do best - absolutely fucking nothing." Green even termed the work "almost like stealing." Commercial extras like Green are typically paid around $342 for less than eight hours of often not even working. This small clique of "background" actors are represented by the actors union,

SAG-AFTRA, which explains the impressive pay. While their non-union counterparts would be lucky to make $10,000 a year, background extras like Green can earn around $40,000 a year, for casual, part-time work. Another background extra, Matteo Sarria, was said be earning some $80,000 — for working maybe 100 days a year. Another prominent extra, Ron Shipp, was an LAPD officer for 15 years. For one commercial alone, Shipp earned an incredible $5,000 for 24 hours work. Union extras start getting time and a half over-time pay after eight hours of work, and double time starting with the tenth straight hour. If production goes into a 16th hour, the extras can enjoy "golden time," or $342 - the union scale for eight hours of work - for each additional hour. Another perk allows these fortunate extras to get double pay for working weekends. The luckiest break of all is to get an "upgrade;" given a spoken line or cast as a recognized feature player in the foreground. That can raise an extra's pay to as much as $40,000 for that one assignment, because these "featured roles" also earn residuals. One former television writer was said to have earned $170,000 the past year for some 140 days of work. At the other end of the spectrum, nonunion extras make essentially minimum wage, about $72 for eight hours of work.[667] Some stars started out as extras. Bruce Willis was an extra in a courtroom scene of *The Verdict*. Young Ben Affleck and Matt Damon were extras in the Fenway Park scene in *Field of Dreams*. Marilyn Monroe, Clint Eastwood, Sylvester Stallone, Brad Pitt, Clark Gable — all were extras, in the beginning. Before she was a famous novelist and the leading mind behind the philosophy of Objectivism, Ayn Rand was an extra on Cecil B. DeMille's 1927 silent epic, *The King of Kings*.

You can't make some things up. Howard Morris, veteran actor and director, probably best known for his handful of endearing appearances as Ernest T. Bass on *The Andy Griffith Show,* was a sergeant in World War II, in a unit that included both future *Hogan's Heroes* star Werner Klemperer and his eventual *Your Show of Shows* comrade Carl Reiner, who also is fondly remembered as Alan Brady on *The Dick Van Dyke Show.* Lee Marvin claimed to have served together with future *Captain Kangaroo* star Bob Keeshan at Iwo Jima although this is now said to be an urban legend. Non-show business celebrities Ted Williams and John Glenn also served in the same military unit.

Chapter Eight

Behind The Facade

I didn't have any more intention of going into pictures than I had of being president of Yale. I was living quiet and peaceful down in Amityville, Long Island, where the insane asylum is....

Will Rogers

IN ITS HEYDAY, during the 1940s, the Hollywood press corps was the third largest in the country, behind only those in New York and Washington. There were nearly four journalists for every actor in tinsel town, including has-beens and mere bit players. The publicity departments of the major studios employed an army to promote their contract players; in 1939 alone, nearly 16,000 stories were submitted to the Advertising Advisory Council, along with over 109,000 still photos.[668]

In the beginning, it wasn't quite like that. Silent stars like Gloria Swanson would swim unmolested in the ocean off Santa Monica, without being bothered for more than an occasional autograph request. F. Scott Fitzgerald was only one of many who commented on how different the earlier actors had been. He wrote about their "dignity" and humility, which changed dramatically once "pictures were bathed in a golden haze of success."[669] The Great Depression impacted the film colony like the rest of America; while Silent "King" of the movies John Gilbert had been making $250,000 per film in 1928, the new "King" Clark Gable, had to settle for a mere $350 per week under his 1931 MGM contract. Ironically, he'd been earning the same salary working in the theater. This is shockingly low considering that, in a 1996 interview, actress Anita Page recounted signing for $3000 weekly with MGM in the 1920s. In that same interview, it was mentioned that Janet Leigh would, a few decades later, sign for a paltry $50 a week with the studio. As a red hot star at Columbia in the 1940s, Rita Hayworth had to fight to get her weekly salary raised from $250 to $300. Sex symbol actress Ursula Andress signed a seven picture contract with Paramount in March 1955, starting at only $287 weekly.[670] Compare that to Mary Pickford's 1916 contract with Adolph Zukor (she would actually make more money later), paying her a weekly salary of $10,000. W.C. Fields earned $5,000 a week from Mack Sennett in his early career, more than he'd earn later from films like 1941's *Never Give a Sucker an Even Break,* for which he was paid $125,000. Even shrewd screenwriter Ben Hecht could earn more than some later leading actors; he was paid $5,000 weekly by Sam Goldwyn during the early Thirties.[671] By the end of the Roaring Twenties, even the best character actors were earning more than $1,000 weekly. Radio paid surprisingly well, especially before television took over American culture. Burns and Allen were reported to have made $9000 weekly in 1940. And in those largely segregated times, Jack Benny's Black valet Eddie "Rochester" Anderson was paid $700 for every *minute* of air time.

The Silent Era featured a number of highly publicized scandals, which caused Hollywood to take on a sordid image. One of these scandals, the mysterious November 19, 1924 death of high profile producer and director Thomas H. Ince, may have helped to launch the career of one of the film world's most powerful gossip columnists. Ince had boarded the yacht of wealthy press tycoon William Randolph Hearst, and was planning on celebrating his forty-fourth birthday there, along with guests like silent film legend Charlie Chaplin, author Elinor Glyn (the originator of the "It" craze), Hearst's longtime mistress, actress Marion Davies, and according to many people, columnist Louella Parsons. The cause of death was said to be from heart failure, or some mundane digestive disorder. However, speculation held that perhaps Hearst had caught Davies in a delicate embrace with Chaplin, and fired his gun in a jealous rage, inadvertently striking Ince instead. It is a fact that Parsons prospered tremendously afterward, as Hearst promoted her syndication nationally, and rewarded her with a lifetime contract.[672] Like many a victim connected to political subterfuge, Ince was quickly cremated before an autopsy could be performed, and there was never any inquest or investigation. Hearst repeatedly denied any rumors of foul play, as did Ince's widow Nell. In 2001, Peter Bogdanovich would make the film *The Cat's Meow*, which portrayed Ince as a murder victim. Bogdanovich claimed to have heard the scenario he based the film on from Orson Welles, who in turn is said to have heard it from Marion Davies' nephew, Charles Lederer. Hearst's granddaughter, the notorious kidnapping victim Patricia, would write a fictional account of the incident titled *Murder at San Simeon*. Richard Gully, Jack Warner's special publicity assistant, bluntly stated that "Louella knew exactly what happened in both cases," referring also to the still unsolved 1922 murder of actor-director William Desmond Taylor.[673] Taylor's body was found shot to death in his bungalow, and among the suspects were actresses Mabel Normand and Mary Miles Minter. Minter's older sister, fellow actress Margaret Shelby, openly accused their mother, Charlotte Shelby, of the murder, before heavy drinking killed her at only thirty-nine. In 1968, Director King Vidor said, "Last year I interviewed a Los Angeles police detective, William Michael Cahill, Sr., now retired, who had been assigned to the case immediately after the murder. He told me, 'We were doing all right and then, before a week was out, we got the word to lay off.'"[674]

Louella Parsons wielded an enormous amount of power, while being thoroughly unlikeable and perpetually unhappy. "The only person I cared deeply or sincerely about was me," she once remarked.[675] Getting on her bad side could destroy a career, and she could just as easily help catapult someone to stardom. Her home would be swamped with gifts on her birthday, and every Christmas, from celebrities desperate to curry favor with her. One of Hollywood's most generous souls, Carole Lombard, paid for Louella's mirrored bathroom. Parsons was semi-literate, couldn't spell, and supposedly worshiped Mussolini. She was frumpy, with an appearance to match her ugly disposition. One of Parsons' three husbands was Dr. Harry "Docky" Martin. It was said that she received much of her gossip from "Docky," whose busy workload performing abortions and treating venereal diseases provided a steady stream of salacious tidbits. Martin was paid $30,000 yearly as studio physician at Twentieth Century-Fox. Parsons appeared in the 1937 film *Hollywood Hotel,* which derived its title from her popular radio show. Though born to Jewish parents, Parsons would erase much of her biographical information, and was a fervent Catholic by middle age. She even kept an illuminated ten-foot Virgin Mary in her backyard. Much of Parsons' early work was devoted to extolling the praises of Marion Davies, the married Hearst's longtime mistress, whom he'd started an affair with when she was a fourteen-year-old chorus girl.[676]

Parsons' chief rival was Hedda Hopper, backed by none other than Louis B. Mayer himself, who desired some competition for Parsons. Unlike Parsons, Hopper was attractive and enjoyed a relatively successful acting career before concentrating all her efforts on gossip. As a chorus girl in New York, she'd been said to have the best legs in town. She could be as vindictive and foul-natured as

Parsons, and was just as capable of making or breaking an actor's career. Hopper grew into an extreme anti-communist and was also considered racist. Parsons and Hopper shared some seventy five million readers. In her autobiography, *The Whole Truth and Nothing But*, Hopper bitterly declared that Parsons "could wield power like Catherine of Russia," with Hearst's newspaper empire behind her. Like Parsons, Hedda was showered with presents from actors. Jane Powell recounted how Hedda had showed the young actress what she called "gifts of fear;" Christmas presents piled to the ceiling that filled an entire room in her home.[677] Hopper's character in the 1985 television movie *Malice in Wonderland* speculated about the rumors connecting Parsons' success to her being in the right place at the right time on Hearst's yacht, by stating, "it's the kind of story that if it isn't true it should be." Hedda's son William Hopper was an actor who will always be remembered for his role as private investigator Paul Drake on the long running television series *Perry Mason*. Hedda Hopper summed up Hollywood this way: "No matter what you say about the town, and anything you say probably is true, there's never been another like it." During their heyday, both of these powerful columnists earned some $250,000 annually. Gossip about the two columnists themselves could be pretty lurid; for instance, the disquieting claim that Parsons had suffered from lifelong incontinence, and was notorious "for leaving behind a puddle of urine wherever she sat." Both Parsons and Hopper were good soldiers, and knew when not to report a story; they shied away from things like the curious long term relationship between Spencer Tracy and Katharine Hepburn, or Norma Shearer's affair with teenager Mickey Rooney. Among the brood of Hollywood offspring that Parsons was godmother to included John Clark Gable and Mia Farrow. Joseph Cotton got even with Hopper for exposing his affair with the underage Deanna Durbin by kicking through her chair during a huge event at the Beverly Wilshire. The next day, Cotton's "house was full of flowers and telegrams from all the people who would have liked to kick Hedda in the backside but didn't have the courage. Joe pasted the telegrams on his bathroom wall." Both women had an impressive array of "spies" within the industry, to feed them gossip. Tony Curtis recalled, "We all felt that Hedda's son, Bill, was a spy. No one wanted to be his friend."[678]

Tommy James, in his memoir *Me, the Mob, and the Music,* described how creative and successful the initial publicity campaign for the Beatles was in the United States. James was working in a record shop at the time, and was intrigued, like every other young music fan, by the series of cardboard cutouts Capitol Records sent out everywhere. These cutouts at first featured only the backs of the band member's heads, with the caption, "The Beatles are Coming." The next one, a few weeks later, was slightly larger and the heads had turned a bit, so that their profiles were gradually coming into view. This process went on, until the final and biggest one featured the Fab Four in all their glory, with their faces in full front profile. The campaign worked beautifully. James recounted how "Kids came into the shop and started asking questions. Who were these guys?"[679] Whatever Capitol Records and Brian Epstein did was magical; the hype surrounding the Beatles' arrival in America was unprecedented in scope and intensity. This excitement trickled down even to seven-year-olds like me; my little friends and I all argued over our favorite Beatles. I can still recall vividly hearing *I Want to Hold Your Hand* for the first time, on Dick Clark's *American Bandstand,* during their "Rate a Record" segment. This was just prior to the Beatles hitting in big in America. The massive promotional campaign seeped into the biggest media outlets in the country; on November 15, 1963, *Time* magazine ran a piece on the "Beatlemania" sweeping the land, and on November 22, 1963, of all days (the date of the JFK assassination), the *CBS Morning News With Mike Wallace* aired a story on the Beatles. The publicity was so intense that Capitol Records cancelled all holiday leave, and issued a company-wide memo detailing the plans for a tabloid Beatles newspaper (thousands of copies of which were reprinted), Beatles buttons, Beatles stickers, Beatles wigs, and other similar items in their all-out Beatles' campaign.

The right review, or just having the right person like you, can mean everything to a performer. On May 22, 1974, Jon Landau, a producer turned music writer, wrote a review of a young artist who was still largely unknown, whom he'd seen playing at the Harvard Square. "I saw rock and roll future and its name is Bruce Springsteen," Landau would write in a small Boston free periodical called the *Real Paper*. "He made me feel like I was hearing music for the first time." Springsteen was so impressed and grateful that he sought out Landau, and subsequently made him his manager and producer. Why this particular review would have such an impact is puzzling, considering that it was published by such a small paper. The entertainment world is filled with such strange cases, however. Simple luck played a part in many an actor's career, as it does in all aspects of life. Silent film star Mae Murray was so smitten with a darling six-year-old extra named Gretchen, who would go on to become the lovely Loretta Young, she tried to adopt her. Gretchen's mother refused, but the little girl was permitted to live with Murray for a year, during which she received invaluable dance lessons from one of the best in the business, and was tutored by a German governess. Gretchen's astounding good fortune continued as a teenager, when in 1927 huge silent star Colleen Moore was so impressed by her she lobbied the head of talent at First National to sign her to a contract. The name Loretta, in fact, came from Colleen Moore's favorite doll. Both Lillian Gish and John Barrymore campaigned for a young Mary Astor with D.W. Griffith. Barrymore was always generous with new talent; he was said to be responsible for giving William Powell his start in the business. Brother Lionel Barrymore supposedly discovered Clark Gable during a Los Angeles stage performance, and arranged his screen test with MGM. Jack Warner wouldn't have signed Gable; he is purported to have called the young Gable "a jug-eared oaf with big feet, big hands, and the ugliest face

I ever saw."[680] Joel McCrea was incredibly lucky off-screen; in 1931, he purchased a ranch for $19,500. When oil was discovered on the property, he was able to lease just a small section to Union Oil for over a million dollars. Obviously, most movie stars benefited from great genetic fortune. In the case of dashing Cary Grant, he evidently was fortunate in terms of metabolism as well. His wife Dyan Cannon, in her book *Dear Cary: My Life with Cary Grant*, described how the perpetually fit and trim screen legend was obsessed with food, and could eat anything he wanted.

A year before the 1999 surprise hit movie *The Blair Witch Project* was released, efforts were underway to build a believable false history for the film, which included a mockumentary that caused many viewers, including myself initially, to believe the film was based on a real legend. This included interviews with family members, legitimate looking police photos and news coverage, and even the actors themselves being listed as "missing, presumed dead" on the influential Internet Movie Database (IMDb) web site. In a strange but certainly not uncommon twist, Heather Donohue, one of the stars of *The Blair Witch Project,* abruptly turned her back on Hollywood and devoted her life to growing medicinal marijuana. At last report, she was, ironically enough, living in the woods in a small northern California community. In a 2014 interview, Donohue, whose character memorably died onscreen in the film, told *GQ* magazine, "That will *always* be the first line of my obituary, no matter what else I do. I've done all these things since: I've published a book, I've grown weed, I've produced this independent TV pilot. I've done *so much else.*" (emphasis original). Donohue's mother received a sympathy card from a relative who, like millions of others, thought *The Blair Witch Project* was real.[681]

The music business has often utilized gimmicks to stimulate sales. I recall how excited teenagers like me were to purchase Alice Cooper's 1972 LP *School's Out*, because the record sleeve was a fresh pair of women's panties. The Raspberries incorporated a "scratch and sniff" sticker on their first album, also released in 1972. Director and producer William Castle was probably the greatest promoter of them all. In a series of delightfully kitschy horror films in the late '50s and early '60s, Castle incorporated a slew of gimmicks, like Emergo, Percepto, Illusion-O, The Fright Break, and the Punishment Poll. For his 1958 film *Macabre,* Castle handed out life insurance policies to the audience, whereby they would receive $1,000 if they "died of fright" while watching it. With 1959's *The Tingler,* Castle had select seats in theaters outfitted with small devices that caused more of a slight vibration than a shock. During 1961's *Homicidal* (a knock off of Alfred Hitchcock's classic *Psycho*), the film was paused for forty-five seconds, to allow any patrons who were too scared to continue watching to get a full refund. Theatergoers who requested this refund were obligated to go to a "Coward's Corner" in front of the audience, which was encouraged to laugh and make fun of them. For 1961's *Mr. Sardonicus,* each audience member was given a placard with a glow-in-the-dark thumbs-up and thumbs-down on it. Near the end of the movie, Castle himself came onscreen, and asked the audience to hold up their cards, seemingly allowing them to determine the fate of the villain in the film.

Alfred Hitchcock was probably the first director to both self-promote and utilize his own persona to publicize his films. Hitchcock famously made a cameo appearance in all his films, a practice directors like M. Night Shyamalan and Oliver Stone later adopted. Hitchcock produced a six-and-a-half-minute trailer for 1960's *Psycho,* in which he strolled around the set of the film, whetting the audience's appetite. He starred in a similar extended trailer for his 1963 film *The Birds,* and both he and leading lady Tippi Hedren made promotional appearances where they would dramatically release birds from cages. Regarding the legendary harassment she underwent at the hands of the brilliant but clearly disturbed Hitchcock, Hedren declared in 2012 that "If this had happened today I would be a very rich woman," in regards to the entirely different climate in the movie business, and the world at large, regarding allegations of sexual improprieties.[682] Tippi by any measure *is* a very rich woman, with a reported $20 million net worth. With his long running hit television series *Alfred Hitchcock Presents,* the portly director became a star in his own right, providing opening and closing commentary in his unique, droll style. Hitchcock developed into the most eminently marketable personality in the film colony, as his name would be affixed to a series of paperback short story collections, as well as volumes of stories for children, record albums, and the Three Investigators series of books for youngsters. It's no surprise that he left behind a $200 million estate upon his death in 1980.

Reading revelations from recent years in particular would lead one to believe that *everyone* during the Golden Age of movies was gay or at least bisexual. Bisexual Greta Garbo was a mean-spirited, penny-pinching actress with numerous physical flaws who somehow was marketed as the ultimate sex symbol. Her much ballyhooed romance with the ill-fated silent film legend John Gilbert was partially embellished, at least on her part, for public relations purposes.[683] Garbo claimed to have only been interested in Gilbert for "about fifteen minutes." One of Garbo's first lovers was the ditzy Isadora Duncan, who wrote a love poem to her. Looks were largely irrelevant to Garbo; she is alleged to have had an affair with the dowdy older actress Marie Dressler. The free-spirited Garbo was rumored to have bedded all the other countless big-name lesbians in Hollywood, like Joan Crawford, Kay Francis, Tallulah Bankhead, Louise Brooks, Lilyan Tashman and Marlene Dietrich. Gilbert himself introduced her to Tashman, and Garbo would regularly swim naked in his pool at parties, to the delight of his bathing suit-clad guests. Barbara Stanwyck, Marjorie Main, Agnes Moorehead and Claudette Colbert were just some of the notable members of Hollywood's "Sewing Circle," as the film colony's substantial lesbian/biscual contingent was referred to. Gilbert lived with Marlene Dietrich, and was crushed when she began having an affair with

Gary Cooper. Gilbert's daughter Leatrice Gilbert Fountain stated, "Marlene was unable to resist Gary Cooper. The moment father found out, he went to pieces again, and didn't stop drinking until he died."[684] Dietrich also slept with young James Stewart who, much like his onscreen image was so innocent and unsophisticated that he reportedly only read *Flash Gordon* comics.

The list of gay or bisexual male stars from Hollywood's bygone era is lengthy. Montgomery Clift, James Dean, Van Johnson, Gene Raymond, David Manners, Raymond Burr, Cesar Romero, Farley Granger, to name just a few. Now forgotten character actor Laird Cregar probably would be a household name if he hadn't died so young (and he also was gay, and connected to another of Hollywood's plentiful unnatural deaths - the murder of his boyfriend). Then there was Will "Grandpa Walton" Geer (doubly ironic in that Ellen Corby, who played Grandma Walton, has also recently been outed). Another television icon, Robert Reed, who played the patient and understanding father on *The Brady Bunch,* was a closeted gay. As noted, lesbians were everywhere, too. Beulah Bondi, who portrayed everyone's mother in films for decades. Forgotten early leading lady Margaret Lindsay. Lizabeth Scott was one of the many stars embarrassed by stories in *Confidential* magazine, which reported she'd been busted for using a high-end call girl service. Patsy Kelly, who shone in so many character roles, counted the always busy Tallulah Bankhead among her lovers, as did Hattie McDaniel. Janet Gaynor, who won the very first Academy Award for Best Actress. The early-day diva Miriam Hopkins was known to be "sexually daring" and was almost certainly bisexual. Lillian and Dorothy Gish, sister actresses who were rumored to also actually be lovers. Lilian never married or had any children, and made her friend and fellow actress Helen Hayes a beneficiary of her estate, valued at "several million dollars." Charles Laughton and Elsa Lanchester had the quintessential "lavender marriage" which lasted a lot longer than most relationships in Hollywood. William Haines, the number one box office attraction in 1930, was said to have had what Joan Crawford called "the happiest marriage in Hollywood," to his long time lover Jimmy Shields.[685] Louis B. Mayer gave Haines an ultimatum to enter into a "lavender marriage" to quell the rumors about his sexuality, but Haines refused and his promising film career was essentially over. Haines triumphed, however, and became a sought after interior decorator in Hollywood. He and Shields were together for forty-seven years. Shortly after Haines died, a despondent Shields took his own life.

The Golden Age of Hollywood was immersed in the sexual revolution decades before the 1960s. Errol Flynn was perhaps the most renowned womanizer of any era, with an absolutely insatiable libido. Jack Warner liked to vicariously share Flynn's boast of having had sex some 12,000 to 14,000 nights in his life. Flynn never appeared to have found true love. Like Charlie Chaplin, he seemed to have had a thing for underage girls, and confessed in his autobiography that he was "nothing but a phallic symbol." John Barrymore was another real ladies' man. It is said that the Great Profile lost his virginity at fourteen to his father's second wife. Barrymore was so persuasive he was even able to seduce the young, bisexual Katharine Hepburn. Everyone from Lupe Velez to Clara Bow sung Gary Cooper's praises as a lover, with Bow proclaiming he was hung like his horse. Tallulah Bankhead supposedly declared, "The only reason I went to Hollywood was to fuck that divine Gary Cooper."[686] Cooper is said to have slept with virtually all of his leading ladies. Lesser known playboys were Burgess Meredith and James Stewart. Frank Sinatra supposedly kept a secret list of his famous conquests behind his dressing room door. Contradicting what Patricia Douglas recounted about his supposed impotence, George Raft's closest confidant estimated that the star had sex with two women a day on average, for years. One of the oddest legends in Hollywood involves hot young Paulette Goddard shamelessly chasing after then seventy-nine-year-old literary legend H.G. Wells. As for Lupe Velez, she hooked up with most of the biggest actors of the day, and had such a vicious temper that many, including her Latin rival Dolores del Rio, kept their distance from her.

Forrest Tucker, who is chiefly remembered for starring in the television series *F Troop*, is rumored to have been one of the literal biggest pricks in Hollywood. Although Clark Gable, like Jean Harlow's ill-fated husband Paul Bern, was unfortunately rumored not to be so well-endowed, his long-time lover Joan Crawford would later tell interviewer David Frost that he was the sexiest man in the history of Hollywood because he had "balls." Crawford had ample experience to cast such a judgment; she is commonly linked romantically to most of the top stars, male and female, of the era. Robert Taylor, who was just one of an unlimited supply of early leading men rumored to have bisexual tendencies, bedded many of his female co-stars. Supposedly, he was unable to control his immense attraction to seventeen-year-old beauty Elizabeth Taylor on the set of *The Conspirator*, and had to ask the cameramen to only film him from the waist up to hide his persistent erections.[687] Elizabeth Taylor married eight times, and had countless other affairs. In the sensationalistic 2012 book *Elizabeth Taylor: There is Nothing Like a Dame,* authors Danforth Prince and Darwin Porter claim Taylor was caught giving Mickey Rooney a blow job at just fourteen, by the diminutive playboy's pregnant wife, lost her virginity at fifteen to Peter Lawford, slept with Ronald Reagan to get a part, and enjoyed a threesome with John F. Kennedy.[688] Gene Tierney slept around quite a bit, too, and eventually was committed to a mental institution. She would become an outspoken critic of shock treatment, claiming it had destroyed some of her memory. Promiscuousness during the Golden Age of Hollywood was such that the great screenwriter Ben Hecht could, with some justification, define a starlet as "any woman under thirty not actively employed in a brothel."[689]

Hollywood "odd couples" included the "It" girl Clara Bow and the surprisingly studly Bela Lugosi. Clark Gable's taste in women was a bit off the wall, considering he could have had his pick of anyone. His acting coach, fifteen years his senior, became his first wife, he had a two year affair with Broadway actress Pauline Frederick, who was eighteen years older than him, and he married the decidedly plain Maria Langham, even though he was seventeen years younger than her. Of course, Gable did find time to impregnate the gorgeous Loretta Young, during the shooting of *Call of the Wild*, and met the love of his life in beautiful Carole Lombard, who perished tragically in a 1942 plane crash. Lombard was known for her free use of profanity and seems to have delighted in gossiping about Gable's aforementioned modest penis size; she once said he was "not the greatest lay." The always interesting, sometimes accurate Kenneth Anger inferred that Gable bedded the wonderful frumpy character actress Edna May Oliver, but then he also claimed that Will Rogers was infatuated with prepubescent superstar Shirley Temple, and drilled a peephole into the wall of her dressing room at Twentieth Century Fox. Alfred Hitchcock was as sexually perverse as one might expect; but he was devoted to his longtime wife Alma, crediting her with saving him from "going queer." He was quite the voyeur, and in a very generous gesture, his pet icy blonde leading lady, Grace Kelly, agreed to do a striptease for him, which he watched from afar. As alluded to earlier, Hitchcock really went over the top with the ravishing Tippi Hedren, and during the shooting of *The Birds,* he sent a lifelike doll figure of her in a coffin to her young daughter Melanie Griffith, and nearly caused the actress severe injuries when he insisted that the mass bird attack on her be done with live creatures.[690] Charlie Chaplin, in addition to thanking heaven for little girls, was said to audition prospective actresses using cue cards and mime. The cards would become increasingly lewd, as he fondled their breasts in an exaggerated, silent movie-style, while they gradually removed articles of clothing, and would culminate with Chaplin throwing custard pies at the now fully unclothed women.[691] Actress Piper Laurie claimed that Ronald Reagan was a "show off" in bed who loved to deflower young virgins, and bragged to her about how long he could last as well as how expensive his condom collection was.[692]

Rock Hudson was one of many stars provided with "beards" to hide their true sexuality. It wasn't publicly known that Hudson was gay until he died of AIDS in 1985. Rumor had it that he'd been involved in a long romance with Jim "Gomer Pyle" Nabors. Often, in studio arranged marriages, the wife would be gay, too. Hudson's wife, for instance, Phyllis Gates, was a lesbian. Vincent Price was another gay actor married to a lesbian. Dolores del Rio, like her closeted male peers, had a "lavender marriage" of her own to an MGM director. Scotty Bowers' 2012 tell-all book *Full Service: My Adventures in Hollywood and the Secret Sex Lives of the Stars* contained numerous shocking claims. Inviting immediate comparisons to the work of Kenneth Anger, the book portrays the Golden Age of Hollywood as utterly, undeniably gay. The iconic writer Gore Vidal (gay himself) was a long-time friend of Bowers, and he verified that Bowers' claims were "100% true," even writing a blurb for the book. As long ago as the eighteenth century, Wolfgang Mozart wrote a little-known song, whose lyrics are as filthy as any present-day rap, with a title that translates as "Lick me in the ass nice and clean."[693]

The old studios saw to it that their stars had full heads of hair, perfect teeth, straight noses, etc. Most of the leading men during the Golden Age of Hollywood wore at least a hairpiece. Some of the women were actually in the same boat; Margaret Dumont, the comedic foil of the Marx Brothers, was bald as a cue ball. Supposedly, Harpo Marx enjoyed stealing her wig. Because of a nasty case of diphtheria, actress and director Ida Lupino was bereft of hair, including her eyebrows. Lana Turner's eyebrows were shaved when she first arrived in Hollywood, and they never grew back. Actresses like Barbara Stanwyck and Ginger Rogers, on the other hand, had hair where it shouldn't be; Rogers in particular was known for her "peach fuzz." Carole Lombard was said to have been "flat as a pancake" and resorted to drawing in a shadow line to create cleavage. Joan Crawford had to endure years of painful dental procedures to correct her flawed teeth, and the studio worked diligently to retouch publicity stills to erase all evidence of the freckles which covered her body. Leading man Brian Donlevy had to insert his dentures, put on his hairpiece, strap on his corset, and step into his elevator shoes before arriving on the set. And of course there was the crucial element of lighting, exemplified by the diffusing lens. As early as 1919, Billy Bitzer photographed twenty-two-year-old Lillian Gish through a silk net, in order to make her appear even younger. Mary Pickford's favorite photographer, Charles Rosher, used backlighting effects to maintain her image as a young girl.[694] Bill Daniels was another magical photographer, beloved by stars like Clark Gable and Norma Shearer. John Barrymore is supposed to have advised his sister Ethel, upon her arrival in Hollywood, "Get Bill Daniels. He'll make you look younger than the Mona Lisa."

Plastic surgery inevitably found a foothold in Hollywood. Facelifts and tummy tucks helped to keep aging stars looking like their former selves. However, too often celebrities still take things too far, or the procedure simply goes wrong. Now forgotten comedian Totie Fields died due to complications from a face lift. Too much collagen and tucking and scalping have left the likes of Joan Van Ark, Mickey Rourke and Daryl Hannah looking largely unrecognizable. Joan Rivers incorporated her numerous plastic surgeries into her comedy routine. Rivers would die suddenly following routine surgery, after making controversial comments about President Obama being gay and his wife being a "tranny," exciting conspiracy theorists everywhere.[695] Cher would often joke about all the cosmetic work she'd had done as well. The still lovely Helen Hunt's appearance changed dramatically circa 2017 or so. In her case, it wasn't that the plastic surgery, botox, or facelift went wrong; it's just that she suddenly looked undeniably different.

Even before the coming of sound, Hollywood had created a new breed of royalty. Groucho Marx described it as "living more luxuriously than the reigning families in Europe." Douglas Fairbanks, the biggest action star of the silent screen era, seriously suggested putting a wall around Beverly Hills. Mae Murray was said to be one of many pretentious young stars, before her Italian Count left her and, as noted earlier, she spent much of the rest of her life in struggling circumstances. While many of the often astonishingly tacky mansions of the earliest film stars have long since disappeared, some residences went through generations of celebrity occupants. Ill-fated silent icon John Gilbert's home was later owned by screen mogul David O. Selznick and his wife Jennifer Jones. John Barrymore bought and expanded director King Vidor's hacienda into sixteen separate buildings. Barrymore's eclectic trophy room included a crocodile which had been shot by his stunningly beautiful actress wife Dolores Costello, shrunken heads, and the only dinosaur egg held by a private citizen at that time.[696] Jayne Mansfield's all-pink dream home was painted white when Ringo Starr moved in, later to be supplanted by Liberace.

Of all the Golden Age movie stars, none played the part better than Joan Crawford. It is said that she even took a limousine the few hundred yards from her dressing room to the MGM photographer's studio. She pampered her poodle ridiculously, with a diet of strictly white chicken meat, ground sirloin, ice cream, and ginger ale. On the other hand, Crawford tirelessly answered every fan letter she received, and Herman Cohen, who produced her last film, the schlocky *Trog* in 1970, claimed that she got up at four a.m. every morning during filming, went to the studio to make a huge breakfast for the entire crew, and finished up by washing the dishes. Crawford was so mortified by an unflattering photo of her taken the following year, she declared, "My life as I had enjoyed living it was largely over because my life as Joan Crawford was over. I had to retire Joan Crawford from public view. What was left of me could only destroy that image. I couldn't bear people saying, 'Oh, look, she used to be Joan Crawford!'"[697] The unique Crawford was also known for bringing her own bottle of 100-proof vodka to any restaurant or any private residence where she was dining. Crawford's Brentwood mansion was one of Hollywood's most notorious allegedly haunted homes. Crawford's daughter Christina acknowledged these rumors in a 1990 interview with Brad Steiger and Sherry Hansen-Steiger. "As a child, I saw things in the house," Christina claimed. She described how, "There were places in the house that were always so cold that nobody ever wanted to go in them." Crawford's estate was only marginally better than the one left by her rival Bette Davis, at $2 million. She left her adopted twin daughters each a trust fund of $77,500. She expressly stated in her will that, "It is my intention to make no provision herein for my son Christopher or my daughter Christina for reasons which are well known to them." Crawford knew about Christina's upcoming book, *Mommie Dearest*, which portrayed her so negatively, and declared, "I think she's using my name strictly to make money...I suppose she doesn't think that I'm going to leave her enough or that I'm going to disappear soon enough...I plan not to read it...No good deed goes unpunished." Bette Davis blasted Christina, claiming it was "a terrible, terrible thing for a daughter to do." Unaware of how ironic her words would become, Davis said, "It's like trying to imagine how I would feel if my own beloved, wonderful daughter, B.D., were to write a bad book about me. Unimaginable."[698] B.D., of course, would wind up doing just that.

The homes of most stars were far more likely to be audacious than haunted. William Powell later admitted he'd made a mistake in outfitting his sprawling estate with the latest technology. Powell's home had electric switches for everything; Powell later said, "The secret panels and disappearing doors never worked right...I've been haunted by weird nightmare memories ever since." William Randolph Heart spoiled longtime mistress Marion Davies excessively; he built a three-story beach house with more than one hundred rooms in Santa Monica for her, which featured a projection room where the screen rose dramatically out of the floor. Many other celebrities owned beach front property there, and it was soon dubbed "Millionaires Row." It was Constance Talmadge's Santa Monica beach property that Cary Grant and Randolph Scott shared.[699] The predictable issues between the two older leading ladies who starred together on the 1980s television series *Falcon Crest* illustrated that vestiges of Golden Age entitlement still existed. Jane Wyman would say of Lana Turner, "I'll put up with a lot, but a limo to the loo is too much."[700]

The excesses of the silent film stars extended from their mansions to their cars. Cowboy legend Tom Mix was renowned for his gaudy vehicle, which featured a tooled saddle and steer horns on its long hood. One of Mae Murray's three luxury automobiles was an eye-grabbing canary yellow Pierce-Arrow. Clara Bow, the red-headed "It" girl, appropriately enough drove a flame-red Kissel convertible, usually with her two dogs in tow, both with their coats dyed red to match. Bow left behind an estate of only $500,000. Tragic comedian Fatty Arbuckle, who was the first actor to sign a million dollar contract (with Paramount in 1920), had a garage full of expensive vehicles, one of which was a $25,000 Pierce-Arrow equipped with a cocktail bar and toilet. Gloria Swanson's Lancia was upholstered in leopard skin. Francis X. Bushman topped even Clara Bow, as his lavender Rolls Royce included servants in lavender uniforms, and lavender cigarettes to smoke. Marlene Dietrich's chauffeur wore a mink-trimmed uniform and carried a pair of revolvers. Buster Keaton drove a yacht-like thirty-foot land cruiser, fully fitted with bunks, drawing rooms and an observation deck. Keeping in character, Keaton wore an admiral's uniform supplied by the studio wardrobe department behind the wheel. The crudely stereotyped black actor Stepin Fetchit drove a pink Rolls Royce, with his name spelled out in neon on the trunk. Again illustrating the madness of comparative celebrity wealth, Fetchit - the entertainment world's foremost example of racial discrimination - left an estate worth $10 million, the same amount as Buster Keaton, and more than many very big movie stars. During the sound era, this ostentatiousness continued, as Clark Gable insisted that his custom Duesenberg be one foot longer than Gary Cooper's identical model.[701] Personal extravagances of the stars went way beyond their means of transportation; Paulette Goddard once showed up at a party clad in a sarong decorated with ten-dollar bills. On a commensurately smaller scale, Alvy Moore, who played Hank Kimball on the television show *Green Acres,* drove a white Cadillac for many years, with the personalized license plate GRNACRS. According to actress Jane Powell, Ann Miller, probably known more for her dancing than acting, modestly wrote, under the "occupation" part of her passport: "Star." Powell also recollected, in a July 6, 2017 interview with *The Hour* that, "One time we were both on the road in shows in Houston and the apartment building we were staying in was right across the parking lot from the theater and you could just walk across the street. Not Ann. She had to have a car pick her up."

The studio bosses had ornate offices from which they reigned supreme. Sam Goldwyn once joked with Louis B. Mayer that he needed a car to drive from his office door to his desk. Moguls like Mayer and Harry Cohn had chairs behind their desks that were designed to make them look taller, and tower over their visitors. Some used special lighting to intimidate others. Cecil B. DeMille is said to have shined a disconcerting spotlight directly upon those who entered his office. Irving Thalberg was notorious for keeping visitors waiting, with some even coming back day after day, to no avail. Eddie Mannix bluntly responded to Thalberg's death at a tragically young age by stating, "Irving was a sweet guy, but he could piss ice water."[702] One delicious Hollywood anecdote has the Marx Brothers lighting a fire in Thalberg's office in order to command attention. Then they apparently sat naked baking potatoes over the fire. Daryl Zanuck's office exuded over-the-top masculinity, as the walls were filled with stuffed mementos of his African safaris. All upper management at the studios was provided with impressive trappings of power. The headquarters of Billy Grady, head of casting at MGM, was a five room bungalow. While so many performers wound up with surprisingly low net worths, those who failed to pay them fairly did much better. While none could match Walt Disney's approximately $1 billion (in today's money) fortune, the obvious wealth of show business executives must have gnawed at the musicians who sold millions of records for which they received little or no royalties, and the old actors watching their younger selves perpetually rerun on television, with no residuals or rights to their images. Jack Warner left a $300 million estate behind (adjusted for inflation), and Atlantic Records president Ahmet Ertegun was worth $300 million as well when he died in 2006, to cite just two examples.

Far more often than not, those who made it in Hollywood (and are still making it) came from at least upper middle class backgrounds, a subject I explored in my book *Survival of the Richest*. With rare exceptions like early film icons Charlie Chaplin and Joan Crawford, the backgrounds of nearly every celebrated actor contradict the propaganda that most of those in early Hollywood came from humble circumstances. To cite just some examples of this, both Spring Byington and John Carradine had mothers who were doctors, an extremely rare thing in those days. Carradine's grandfather also founded the Holy Rollers religious sect. Claudette Colbert's father was a banker, while Tallulah Bankhead's was the Speaker of the U.S. House of Representatives. Gary Cooper's father was a justice on the Montana Supreme Court. Jane Darwell's father was the president of Louisville Southern Railroad. Those who had lawyers for a father included Richard Arlen, Bette Davis, Douglas Fairbanks, Frances Farmer, Geraldine Fitzgerald, Ann Miller, and Rosalind Russell. Katharine Hepburn and Robert Tayor had fathers who were doctors. So did Humphrey Bogart, and his mother was a prestigious illustrator, which certainly must have aided the infant Bogie in winning an advertising gig for baby food. Jean Harlow's father was a dentist, and so was Ramon Novarro's.[703] There have always been very few Clara Bow types, who really did go from rags to riches, in the film colony.

The most popular stars could have clauses in their contract that reflected the power they wielded. Big-hearted Carole Lombard's contract with Paramount provided for her entire crew of favorite cameraman, electrician, grips, prop men, and others to be paid regularly along with her. Lombard also had final approval over story, director, and casting. Fastidious Joan Crawford had a written guarantee that the temperature on her sets would remain a consistent sixty-eight degrees. Although he was relatively underpaid considering his stature in the industry, Clark Gable was allowed to work a strict nine-to-five schedule, in an era when it was common for actors to work well into the night. Unlike other actresses, Gene Tierney insisted that her slightly crooked teeth not be straightened, and her Fox contract stipulated that she would never be required to alter the color or length of her hair. At the other end of the spectrum, the studio forbid early matinee idol Francis X. Bushman to reveal that he was a married father of five children. As noted, Hollywood has never been a fertile place; Bushman was in a rare class, with the likes of Maureen O'Sullivan and Charlie Chaplin, as an entertainer with a large family. The question of billing often reared its head when more than one big star appeared in the same picture. In one notable case, friends Humphrey Bogart and Spencer Tracy were anxious to do the 1955 film *The Desperate Hours* together, but neither would accept second billing. The film was eventually made with Bogart and Fredric March in Tracy's place.[704]

Dressing rooms were almost as important as billing; Mary Pickford set the standard in the silent era, with her over-the-top five-room cottage on the United Artists lot, where a butler and cook were always on duty. Colleen Moore's special bungalow featured a living room, huge bedroom, a sunken bath, and a grand piano. As the talkies took over, the perks diminished along with the salaries, at least at MGM, where the dressing rooms were situated together in an old frame building, and featured a porch that ran around the entire building. The biggest stars, like Clark Gable, Joan Crawford, and Norma Shearer, enjoyed the most elaborate rooms in the building. Lionel Barrymore wistfully recalled, "Tilting our chairs back, as drummers used to sprawl on hotel piazzas on summer nights" on the wrap-around porch. The only MGM star who was exempt from this dormitory-style arrangement was Marion Davies, who still enjoyed her fourteen-room bungalow. The bungalow was filled with Hearst antiques, courtesy of her married boyfriend, and a full staff of servants. Ginger Rogers reigned supreme at RKO Studios, with quarters that included a kitchen, bedroom, sitting room, and separate rooms for make-up, hairdressing, wardrobe, and fitting. Little Shirley Temple was the queen of Twentieth Century- Fox, with a ten-room bungalow she'd inherited from the now forgotten German expatriate Lilian Harvey. Tom Mix's suite at Universal included a gym with a regulation-sized boxing ring. Carole Lombard seems to have been exceptionally down to earth, as she was content with only a single chair and small table, where she applied her own make-up.[705]

As noted, a remarkable number of actresses remained childless in Hollywood. A lesser but still noticeable number of actors never had biological children, either. It certainly wasn't because they couldn't afford them. When they did give birth, early day actresses frequently saw their careers decline as a result. The now forgotten Helen Twelvetrees gave up a hefty $130,000 annual salary and the lead in the 1932 hit film *A Bill of Divorcement* when she became pregnant with her only child. Mae Marsh was a big star when she opted to marry and have children, against the wishes of her boss Sam Goldwyn. After she married Goldwyn's publicity agent Louis

Arms, her career waned, and she never recovered her star power, appearing instead in supporting roles later on in sound films. Those stars that did have children tended to adopt at a disproportionately high rate compared to the public at large.[706] Some stars never felt comfortable around their peers off set, and stayed away from the social gatherings that Hollywood was renowned for. Clara Bow, it is said, preferred to stay at home and play cards with her servants. Clark Gable's longtime major-domo Rufus Martin could mimic Gable's voice perfectly over the phone. Likewise, Bob Hope's long-time double, Jack Robbins, was able to impersonate his comic delivery. Many stars became good friends with their doubles, although these stand-ins were usually paid just $16.50 per day. On the other hand, Marlene Dietrich never spoke to her stand-in Lillian Kilgannon. Kilgannon, who also stood in for Mae West, Claudette Colbert, and other stars, once explained, "We are the shadows."[707] Joel McCrea was one of the rare stand-ins who went on to become a movie star.

There were genuinely nice and genuinely mean actors during the Golden Age of Hollywood. Evidently, Carole Lombard was not only incredibly generous and unassuming, but always a delight to work with. So was the ill-fated Jean Harlow. Barbara Stanwyck was beloved by everyone on the set, who referred to her affectionately as "Missy," and other favorites with the crew included Dolores del Rio, Rosalind Russell, Rita Hayworth, and Joan Blondell. Clark Gable was fond of discussing things like hunting with crew members. Gable, and other performers like Marion Davies, James Cagney and George Raft, had empathy for their lower paid brethren on the set, and would often flub their lines on purpose near the end of the day, so that extras could collect either overtime or another day of work. Marion Davies and Joan Crawford were known for their acts of kindness and generosity, and Norma Shearer donated all her earnings from radio to the National Foundation for Infantile Paralysis.[708] George Raft's generosity extended mainly to the ladies;

female guests at the flashy star's mansion would frequently discover a hundred-dollar-bill or a pricey piece of jewelry wrapped in their dinner napkins. Don Knotts, unforgettable as Barney Fife on *The Andy Griffith Show,* was voted as nicest celebrity in a long list compiled by authors Bret Saxon and Steve Stein, in their 1995 book *How to Meet and Hang Out With the Stars: A Totally Unauthorized Guide.* Their nastiest celebrity was Billy Crystal. Crystal's reputation was buttressed by what actor (*Reno 911*) and screenwriter (*Night at the Museum*) Robert Ben Garant revealed when he spoke to our writers group a few years back. When asked who the worst celebrity he'd ever met was, he named Crystal without hesitating.

On the high maintenance side, Luise Rainer was so spoiled she complained to the studio when some dirt got under her fingernails during filming of *The Good Earth.* Errol Flynn's unbelievably excessive drinking forced Jack Warner to close the studio bar. Flynn's sexual and alcoholic antics caused him to deteriorate and age rapidly; when he died at only fifty, fittingly buried with six bottles of whiskey in his coffin, he looked much older than his years. Spencer Tracy's drinking was so problematic that MGM employed a "Tracy Squad" to monitor the chronically depressed actor's behavior. E.J. Fleming, author of the book *The Fixers: Eddie Mannix, Howard Strickland and the MGM Publicity Machine,* minced no words in stating, "Spencer Tracy was an awful human being. A real nasty drunk who would punch fans in the face if they asked for an autograph." Fleming also alleged that at age thirty-eight, Tracy had slept with Judy Garland when she was in her early teens.[709] Marlon Brando was notoriously difficult, reluctant even to memorize his lines, and became increasingly hard to work with as his career progressed. Wallace Beery was the antithesis of the gruff but lovable lug he played onscreen; he was extremely hard to work with and once knocked out George Raft when he didn't pull his punch in a fight scene. Norma Shearer was so well known for her haughtiness that Joan Crawford quipped, after starring with her in 1939's *The* Women: "I love to play bitches and she helped me in the part." Other difficult personalities were Brian Donlevy (1930s leading lady Frances Drake, who retired from the screen at a young age, said he was "a very strange man. He never talked to anybody.") Paul Muni, Miriam Hopkins, Charles Laughton, Lauren Bacall, Margaret Sullavan, Grace Moore, Hedy Lamarr and especially Constance Bennett. The problems of Marilyn Monroe and Judy Garland on-set are widely known.

A 1998 online reprint of a late 1960s article raked future *Six Million Dollar Man* Lee Majors over the coals. To quote from the article: "Of all the young men and women with hands reaching for the next rung of the ladder and eyes focused on the main chance, Lee Majors is perhaps the most disliked. 'The only kind of love Lee knows,' says a member of the 'Big Valley' organization, 'is self-love. He treats members of the crew and extras - the unimportant people by Hollywood standards - as though they were less than human. Barbara Stanwyck would be kind and gracious to a visitor from skid row. Peter Breck and Dick Long are as courteous to the unimportant people they come into contact with as they are to the important.'" There are no anecdotes documenting how difficult or easy he was to work with in the early talkies he starred in, but Robert Young was not like his screen image during the *Father Knows Best* years. Young was often paralyzed by depression and had an explosive temper, which he often took out on Billy Gray, who was prone to sullenness, and Elinor Donohue's hovering stage mother. He was also, like Dick Van Dyke, an alcoholic. Young attempted suicide at the age of eighty-three, but survived and lived to be ninety-one. Joan Davis, who starred on *I Married Joan* in the 1950s, was cruel and vulgar off-camera. Her co-star, Jim Backus, remarked that "I was an indentured servant. She owned the show…."[710] Terri Garr, one of the sexiest actresses in the history of the business in my view, told an Australian interviewer that Gene Wilder was a "jerk" to work with. Garr, like another lovely actress, Annette Funicello, was stricken with multiple sclerosis and is now confined to a wheelchair. Perhaps

Wilder had his reasons; he endured an awful childhood marred by savage bullying and a sickly mother. Supposedly, a doctor advised eight-year-old Gene not to argue with his mother or "you might kill her." In his teens, the guilt-laden youth began obsessively praying in public after connecting with the controversial Theosophists. Wilder was married four times without having children, and lost the love of his life, the brilliant Gilda Radner, to cancer. Radner was filled with her own demons, starting each morning with a vodka and lemonade and continuing to drink all day, as well as struggling with bulimia; all the resultant vomiting started to rot her teeth. Wilder himself had issues with his frequent collaborator Mel Brooks, whom he accused of lusting after money and fame, and Richard Pryor, with whom he was paired in some wildly successful films. Wilder was turned off by Pryor's drug use, saying, "We were never good friends, contrary to popular belief. He was a pretty unpleasant person to be around during the time we worked together."[711]

It's said that when Warner Brothers offered Humphrey Bogart a fifteen year contract worth a minimum of $5 million, Bogart noticed in the fine print that it was only worth $4,999,999.25. He refused to sign it, and the studio's attorney tossed seventy-five cents on the table to seal the deal. Lauren Bacall supposedly grabbed the change and spent it on herself. John Barbour, by the way, told me that Bacall was one of only a few real "cunts" he'd ever met during his long show business career. One of the more unlikely wealthiest members of the film colony during the Golden era was Donald Crisp, a British born character actor, who sat on the board of Bank of America, which financed many loans to Hollywood producers. The fabulously wealthy Mary Pickford was laughingly nicknamed, "the Bank of America's sweetheart," and mogul Adolph Zukor would proclaim that she had a mind like a cash register. Pianist Arthur Rubinstein was renowned for his shockingly high fees; in 1946, he was paid $85,000 for three days work on the film *I've Always Loved You*. At the other end of the spectrum, the day after she won the

1972 Academy Award for Best Supporting Actress in *Butterflies Are Free*, Eileen Heckart paid a visit to the unemployment office, where she was cheered by the staff there who knew her well.[712]

Shelley Winters was one of Hollywood's more eccentric personalities. She was so afraid of being alone that she would regularly ask the servers at Googie's, an all-night restaurant, to come back to her home and read scripts with her. While Joan Crawford's compulsion for cleaning was legendary in Hollywood, her friend and lover Clark Gable was quite a germaphobe himself. Gable found tubs unhygienic, and didn't have any in his home. He also employed a chemical substance in his Encino, California ranch pool that turned the water bright red around any less than sanitary swimmer. Lionel Atwill was only a few steps behind horror film legends Boris Karloff, Bela Lugosi and Lon Chaney, Jr. during the 1930s and 1940s. Perhaps the quintessential celluloid mad doctor, Atwill in real life was a sex addict, giving wild parties that included the showing of early pornographic movies. Fittingly, his mansion featured a pet python, a talking macaw named copulate, and six fierce Dobermans. A 1940 Christmas Party, predictably centered on pre-Christian themes, wound up with ugly allegations revolving around a pregnant underage girl. Atwill, like most all wealthy celebrities, escaped the long arm of the law with a five-year sentence of probation for perjury. After seven months, a sympathetic judge completely exonerated him.[713] Like his fellow horror icon Bela Lugosi, Atwill wound up his career at a Poverty Row Studio. Ernie Kovacs was not only a maverick comedian who was ahead of his time, he was also wildly eccentric. Kovacs loved playing cards so much that it was not abnormal for him to unhinge his front door if he needed a gambling table. He would think nothing of calling friends in the middle of the night to organize a poker game. Kovacs was mired in debt, to a large degree because of the huge fees he paid to private investigators tasked with finding his two young daughters. His ex-wife had simply vanished with them during a weekend visitation. Eventually they were found living in a shack in Florida, behind the restaurant where their mother worked as a waitress. He owed an enormous amount of back taxes; of the $100,000 he was paid for the film *Sail on a Crooked Ship*, the government took $90,000.[714] *Green Acres* star Eddie Albert had refreshingly unconventional political views, was an extreme environmental activist and natural food advocate, and used to plant corn in the front yard of his home in Pacific Palisades. One of my favorite singers, Dusty Springfield, had an unfortunately nasty temperament, which included a fondness for tripping others up as they went on stage. She also had a unique fetish for throwing things, especially crockery and food. A closeted lesbian, Dusty regularly engaged in startlingly violent fights with her partners.[715] As her life spiraled out of control, by 1985 Dusty was relegated to miming her old songs for $500 a night in West Hollywood gay bars. She became increasingly eccentric, to the point of watching *Bonanza* reruns all day in German.[716]

One of the most macabre urban legends from the Golden Age of Hollywood concerns the corpse of John Barrymore. According to the legend, some of the Great Profile's drinking companions stole his body from the morgue and propped it up in a chair in Errol Flynn's Hollywood Hills home. Varying accounts list the participants as Errol Flynn, Raoul Walsh, Peter Lorre, Albert Dekker and John Huston.[717] One of those who recounted the incident was Paul Henreid, who also claimed that Jack Warner once commissioned a portrait of his wife from the legendary Salvador Dali. Supposedly, Dali actually painted Warner's face onto the body of a monkey, and Warner was so incensed he locked the portrait away forever, much as he was alleged to have done with films that didn't meet his standards. Barrymore's pals were generous practical jokers during his lifetime. For Barrymore's fifty-fifth birthday present, they sent him a naked girl wrapped in cellophane, tied with a big silver bow. One very real and hilarious incident involved Will Rogers reacting to Jack Warner's attempt to sign him to a contract with the following telegram: "I might fly out of here and to the Legion Convention and World Series. But if I don't and don't get a better offer, will be glad to be with you. Where is your studio?"

Blonde bombshell Jayne Mansfield was killed in a June 29, 1967 car accident, dying at just thirty-four years of age. One urban legend holds that it was no accident, but a "hit" ordered by mob connected union leader Jimmy Hoffa, because Mansfield was allegedly dating a lawyer who owed him a great deal of money. Mansfield had one decidedly odd connection that is no urban legend. She was closely affiliated, romantically or not, with Church of Satan leader Anton LaVey in the last few years of her life. There were rumors that LaVey had sworn a curse on Sam Brody, who died in the crash with girlfriend Mansfield, by proclaiming, "I pronounce that you will be dead within one year." Mansfield appeared to be a true believer in LaVey's dark powers. In a bizarre incident, the actress's six-year-old son Zoltan was attacked by a lion at a zoo, whose recovery after three surgeries was said to have been aided by LaVey's special satanic prayer recited from the top of San Francisco's Mount Tampalpais. Brody was said to despise LaVey, whom he called a "charlatan," and tried unsuccessfully to stop all contact between him and Mansfield. The relationship between the movie star and the Satanist with the shaved head and resplendent cape, thoroughly documented in numerous photos taken of them together, was undoubtedly at least partially driven for purposes of promotion. Despite all this, Mansfield issued a press release that said, "It is very interesting. I know the real basis of his church. I think he is a genius and I regard him as an interesting person. I am a Catholic and would not believe in his church. I am not a member of the black circle." LaVey, on the other hand, claimed to have made Mansfield a priestess and taught her how to cast spells. LaVey himself appears to have started the rumor that he portrayed the devil in the 1968 film *Rosemary's Baby*. Jayne Mansfield was one of the rare, extremely fertile women in Hollywood, with her three marriages producing five children.[718]

Mansfield's four oldest children went to court in 1977, to seek a proper accounting of the estate. They found it was insolvent, due to $500,000 worth of debts their mother had incurred, and the costs of estate litigation.

Television had its urban legends as well. Some were demonstrably false, like Jerry "Beaver" Mathers being killed in Vietnam (which Shelley Winters announced during an appearance on *The Tonight Show*), or his cast mate Ken "Eddie Haskell" Osmond morphing into either rock star Alice Cooper or porn star John C. Holmes, but many believed them for years. The practical joke pulled by a group of gay pranksters, which maintained that Rock Hudson and Jim Nabors of *Gomer Pyle* fame were married in 1971 resulted in the two close friends never speaking again. While there have been firm denials that Walt Disney had his body cryogenically preserved after his death on December 15, 1966, the legend that he was frozen, and not cremated, continues to persist. The quiet, very private nature of Disney's funeral only helped to ignite these rumors. Disney's daughter Diane Disney Miller resented the legend, telling the *Daily Mail* in 2012 that "Other little kids would say to my kids, 'Your grandfather is frozen, isn't he?'" The legend really took hold in 1972 when Bob Nelson, then president of the Cryonics Society of California, while stressing that Disney had in fact been cremated, told The *Los Angeles Times* that Disney had been so interested in Cryonics that his studio, before his death, called them and asked a multitude of questions about the process, their staff, and their history. "The truth is, Walt missed out," Nelson said. "He never specified it in writing, and when he died the family didn't go for it. ... Two weeks later we froze the first man. If Disney had been the first it would have made headlines around the world and been a real shot in the arm for cryonics."[719] A popular rock legend holds that singer Jack Ely of the Kingsmen simply made up lyrics for the classic 1963 song *Louie Louie* as he went along, or sang words known only to him. Anyone who has ever listened to the recording knows that the lyrics were largely unintelligible. Tommy James seemed to verify this rumor in his memoir, writing, "Years later I found out even the Kingsmen did not know what the hell they were singing."[720]

Politics and show business were often intertwined, even in the early days of the movie business. While most actors even then seemed to gravitate to leftist causes, there were plenty of conservatives like Walt Disney and Mary Pickford among the upper echelon of Tinseltown. Louis B. Mayer was a loyal Republican and such a devoted Herbert Hoover supporter that he and his wife were the first overnight guests in the new president's White House. Cecil B. DeMille's foundation channeled information to the House Un-American Activities Committee. Sam Goldwyn liked to schmooze with everyone; he became good friends with President Franklin D. Roosevelt and later President Eisenhower would stay at his home when he visited California. The same kind of elitists that run everything else, in this case the Morgans and the Rockefellers, had a monopoly on all sound equipment during the Golden Age of Hollywood. The major studios were evidently heavily involved in sabotaging writer Upton Sinclair's 1934 campaign for governor of California. Foreshadowing the dishonesty we would see in future decades from the mainstream media, this included hiring actors to portray Sinclair supporters, who would be interviewed in their fake dirty, disheveled and drunken state as "men on the street" in an effort to discredit the socialist writer. Fearing that King Vidor's 1934 film *Our Daily Bread* would evoke voter sympathy for Sinclair, the studios managed to delay its release in California until after the election. Sinclair had been very critical of the movie industry, advocating that their huge profits should be channeled to the people.[721] Meanwhile, during the propaganda buildup prior to U.S. entrance into World War II, numerous communist-tinged groups like the Hollywood Anti-Nazi League attracted some big name stars. As late as 1939, however, the son of Benito Mussolini was visiting Hollywood to learn the ropes of the film business at the Hal Roach Studio. An investigation chaired by Congressman Martin Dies defined, quite accurately, the movie industry as "a tightly controlled monopoly," and charged that their seventeen thousand theaters were basically conduits for, in the words of Senator Bennett Champ Clark, "daily and nightly mass meetings for war."[722]

Right wing "extremists" have always been an exceptionally rare breed in show business. In recent years, once superstar leading man and "Sexiest Man Alive" Mel Gibson seemed to dip a few toes into these waters. Frank Fay has been all but forgotten now, and only a few even recall that he was Barbara Stanwyck's first husband. Fay was perhaps the first standup comedian, and a real renaissance man in the entertainment world of the Roaring Twenties. His varied skill set was best shown in the early 1929 talkie *The Show of Shows*. Fay was said to be mean-spirited to everyone, and a virulent anti-Semite. His career plunge, fueled by excessive drinking, and Stanwyck's simultaneous meteoric rise, was almost certainly the main inspiration for the 1932 film *What Price Hollywood?* and the very similar *A Star is Born*, which was first filmed in 1937, and spawned three remakes, the latest in 2018, starring Lady Gaga (born Stefani Germanotta). It was also surely tied as much to his controversial politics as to his drinking. In January, 1946, some 10,000 people showed up at a white nationalist rally at Madison Square Garden that was called "The Friends of Frank Fay." Stanwyck was one of the legendary names in show business who left a startlingly meager estate behind, of just $1 million, when she died in 1990. An online forum claimed that Fay, meanwhile, left "a sizable estate." Eugene Pallette was one of those wonderful character actors whose face is remembered far more often than his name. Pallette was noted for his distinctive gravelly voice, as well as his increasingly obese frame. He actually started out in Hollywood as a much slimmer, leading man type in silent films. Pallette turned increasingly right politically, and by 1946 had constructed a veritable mountain fortress on his huge Oregon ranch, in an effort to survive what he felt was an imminent nuclear holocaust.[723] When the doomsday scenario failed to transpire, Pallette returned to Hollywood, but his right-wing politics caused him to become one of the less publicized blacklisted actors. He never appeared in another movie. Like others we mentioned earlier, Pallette's cremated remains were buried in an unmarked grave behind a monument to his parents at Green Lawn Cemetery in Kansas. Other notable right-wingers included Gloria Swanson, John Wayne, Ty Hardin (who had an un-Hollywood-like ten children), and Glen Campbell, who told *Variety* magazine that anti-war protestors who had burned their draft cards "should be hung… if you don't have enough guts to fight for your country, you're not a man."[724]

Some big movie stars made the transition to television smoothly. Fred MacMurray enjoyed great success on the small screen, and is probably best remembered for his role on *My Three Sons*. Robert Young hit it big twice, as quintessential Fifties Dad Jim Anderson on *Father Knows Best* and later as a kindly physician on *Marcus Welby, M.D.* James Stewart had a short-lived prime time series. So did Henry Fonda. Doris Day's show lasted several seasons. Robert Montgomery hosted *Robert Montgomery Presents* from 1950-1957. Eddie Albert scored with two series, the classic surrealistic comedy *Green Acres* and then *Switch,* which co-starred another Hollywood veteran, Robert Wagner. Loretta Young (who, unlike many other superstar actors, left a hefty $50 million estate behind her) had a popular television show in the 1950s. Boris Karloff hosted the *Thriller* anthology series. Barbara Stanwyck shone as always on the '60s western series *The Big Valley*. And, of course, legendary director Alfred Hitchcock was a staple on television for a decade, as host of *Alfred Hitchcock Presents.* Plenty of actors who'd played character roles in numerous films later turned up playing the same sort of characters on television. One of the greatest character actors of them all, Walter Brennan, snagged the lead role in television's *The Real McCoys*. On the other hand, some stars spurned the small screen. Clark Gable refused to appear on television at all, and even went as far as completely snubbing TV reporters. Paulette Goddard referred to television as "a premiere on Broadway that closes after opening night." Ronald Reagan was virulently opposed to the new medium initially. Ann Sheridan recalled, "I remember Ronnie telling all of us not to join TV because it was the enemy of the movies." Reagan would ignore his own advice, first appearing as host of *General Electric Theater* and then *Death Valley Days*. Rock Hudson's *MacMillan and Wife* lasted seven seasons, but he continued to look down upon the television industry. Television legends like Lucille Ball, Raymond Burr and Buddy Ebsen became much bigger stars on the small screen than they ever were in feature films. Some television stars had similar perks to those enjoyed by the biggest names during the Golden Age of Hollywood. David Janssen, star of *The Fugitive,* was paid an astronomical $4.5 million a year and had a custom-made trailer, complete with a library and a full staff, one of whom was tasked with keeping him sober.[725] In another stark example of the pay disparity in show business, Mike Connors, who starred in a similar television series, *Mannix*, was earning a comparatively low $40,000 per episode by the end of the show.[726] Fred MacMurray was permitted to shoot all of his *My Three Sons* scenes consecutively, which resulted in a much lighter work schedule for him.

The demands of some musical performers perhaps even exceeded the old movie stars at their height. Van Halen, for instance, wanted all the brown M & Ms removed from the bowl they stipulated must be backstage at their concerts. However, this was later attributed to a shrewd move on the band's part to see if their requests were actually being read. The likes of Jennifer Lopez and Mariah Carey are almost surrealistic in their diva behavior. Kanye West, perhaps the music world's foremost male diva, demands a barber chair for some reason, and has also asked for a slushy machine featuring mixed combos with alcohol.[727] The drapes in Rhianna's dressing room must be layered with "icy blue chiffon," and she must have an animal print throw rug. Katy Perry's quite specific flower demands include the stipulation that there are to be no carnations. Strict vegetarian Paul McCartney bans all animal products from his rooms, including materials like cotton and denim. All lamps must be halogen with dimmer switches, and there must not be leather seats in his stretch limo. All-time diva Madonna requires enough room for her *two hundred person* entourage and twenty international phone lines.[728] Jay Z needs *seven* separate dressing rooms for his personal use. This presumably leaves him with several places to enjoy the "good quality" peanut butter and jelly that he demands. Like other divas past and present, Mary J. Blige requires a private bathroom with a new toilet seat. Lady Gaga needs a smoothie station. Cher's classic list from 1999 included a separate wig room and another for her personal massage therapist. James "Iggy Pop" Osterberg's laughable list from 2006 included an outrageous requirement for a Bob Hope impersonator, a copy of *USA Today* that has a story about a morbidly obese person in it, and a demand that broccoli and cauliflower florets be cut up and thrown immediately into the trash because "I fucking hate that."[729]

The 1968 film *Wild in the Streets* was close to *Rebel Without a Cause* in terms of the fates that befell the lead actors. Kevin Coughlin, who'd overcome a clubfoot to become a promising young actor, was struck and killed by a speeding car as he cleaned his windshield on January 19, 1976. He was just thirty-years-old. Diane Varsi was nominated for an Academy Award in her screen debut in 1957's *Peyton Place*. Louella Parsons called her "Hollywood's Female Brando." Her anti-conformist nature earned her comparisons to James Dean as well. After more impressive roles, Varsi suffered a nervous breakdown and was reluctant to work onscreen, causing her to be suspended by Fox Studios. In 1959, she simply left Hollywood for Vermont. Her return to the film colony a couple of years later resulted in few good parts, and her role in *Wild in the Streets* represented something of a comeback for her. However, this translated into little other high profile appearances, and by 1977 she went into seclusion again. She rarely made the news again, until her death on November 19, 1992, due to complications from Lyme disease.[730] The main lead in the film, Christopher Jones, was briefly a huge young star celebrated for his physical resemblance to James Dean. Among his close friends was Sharon Tate, whose brutal murder emotionally devastated him. One of his countless lovers was Jim Morrison's long-time companion Pamela Courson, who would follow Morrison to an early grave, dying of a heroin overdose at the same age of twenty-seven. Jones inexplicably turned his back on acting for twenty-six years, until returning for a bit role in 1996's *Mad Dog Time.* Jones had come from humble origins, and spent time at a Boys Town as a youth. Continuing his unconventional narrative, Jones enlisted in the Army, but went AWOL, stole a car, and stopped at James Dean's Indiana birthplace. Dean's family, amazed at how much Jones looked like their lost loved one, invited him into their home. IMDb quotes him as recalling, "The Winslows were very nice people and made me feel right at home. They took me up to Jimmy's room, where his Levi's jeans pants were lying on the bed waiting for him to jump into them and there were several pairs of boots on the floor just where he had left them." Jones left for New York City, and turned himself in to the Army. He was court-martialed and served a six month sentence. Effectively dead for a long time, Jones managed to make it to seventy-two before succumbing to cancer. Jones, in a rarity for Tinseltown, fathered seven children.[731] As if all this wasn't enough, *Wild in the Streets* also featured the young, star-crossed comedian Richard Pryor.

In a 1977 interview, David Bowie's wife Angie told *The Evening Standard,* "Darling, we're broke. David has been robbed blind." Bowie seemed to have financially recovered nicely by the time of his death in 2016, as he left behind an estate of $100 million. Included were generous bequeaths of $2 million to his personal assistant and $1 million to a former nanny.[732] "There were millions but other people got them, not us." Rick Derringer, who hit it big with the McCoys' smash 1965 hit, *Hang on Sloopy,* and had some solo success, admitted that, "We were just following orders…we just did what we were told." Derringer is presently said to be worth $10 million, according to Celebrity New Worth, clearly rebounding from his Florida home being foreclosed on in 2010. "Anybody can be affected by this huge problem, even us," Derringer stated.[733] Carl Perkins would tell people that "'Blue Suede Shoes' was the easiest song I ever wrote," and recalled how he wrote the lyrics on a potato sack. Bo Diddley once said, "I probably made millions but I ain't never seen none of it." In 2005, he reiterated, "I've been out here for fifty years, man, and I haven't ever seen a royalty check."[734] Don Brewer, of Grand Funk Railroad, echoed the naïve sentiments of so many musical performers: "Every time a contract was brought out in front of us…we just signed."[735] One star who seemed to have done pretty well for himself was Dion DiMucci, who first hit it big at a young age fronting the band Dion and the Belmonts, with hits like *Runaround Sue* and *The Wanderer.* "On the strength of my earnings I bought an eight-room house for my folks," Dion recalled. "I also bought an elegant grey and black Thunderbird, dental capping for two front teeth, an abstract painting by a distinguished artist, a gold wristwatch for my manager Sal Bonfede, a load of presents for my old pals in the Bronx…"[736] This seems all the more amazing since Dion is known to have become a serious heroin addict starting at age sixteen. Dion is currently estimated to have a $5 million net worth. The other members of Dion's original group, the Belmonts, were said to be displeased when he was inducted by himself into the Rock and Roll Hall of Fame in 1989.[737] In an August 28, 2009 story in *The Telegraph,* the band Jethro Tull's front man Ian Anderson's 400 acre Wiltshire mansion was mentioned, and he talked about the band taking control of their management during the 1970s. Anderson noted, "I heard some bands were not making any money from their tours and, quite frankly, I thought they must be stupid." In keeping with his eccentric nature, Anderson also stated, "I don't like loud music; so I would never be in my own audience." Anderson is depicted as being financially savvy, and has a $30 million fortune according to Celebrity Net Worth.

The Rolling Stones were understandably criticized for continuing to play, with gruesome appropriateness, the song *Sympathy for the Devil* during the stabbing death of a young man at their 1969 free Altamont Speedway concert. The Stones had employed members of the notorious Hell's Angels as bodyguards for the event, so some kind of violence should have been expected. Still, Keith Richards' little-reported comment that, "People were just asking for it. All those nude, fat people. They had victims faces," was about as offensive as could be.[738] It's taken for granted that rock stars are surly and unappreciative of their adoring fans. Jerry Garcia, whose Grateful Dead band had one of the most loyal followings in the business, exemplified this stereotypical rock star persona with his, "That bullshit about the people's music, man, where's that at? It wasn't any people that sat with me when I learned to play the guitar. If the people think that way, they can play their own fucking music."[739] Jim Morrison of the Doors would snarl, "You like people? I hate them…. screw them, I don't need them."

Like the executives whose wealth is derived from the talent of artists they often don't appreciate or fairly compensate, the artists often don't appreciate the worshiping fans who make their fame possible.

Chapter Nine

Fleeting Fame

When the last dime is gone, I'll sit on the curb outside with a pencil and a ten-cent notebook and start the whole thing over again.

Preston Sturges

NAPOLEON BONAPARTE, ONE of the few historical figures to have lasting holding power, once said, "Glory is fleeting, but obscurity is forever." How many people who lived in the 1600s are still remembered today? Beyond Shakespeare, very few of the most famous and celebrated names of that era would bring more than a blank stare today from all but those who specialize in historical antiquities. How about the 1700s? Certainly far more, but still how many people would know who the greatest actors, singers, or musicians of the eighteenth century, or even the nineteenth century were? The only reason we recall John Wilkes Booth today is because of his infamous involvement in the assassination of Abraham Lincoln. But in his day, he was so famous that respected history professor Terry Alford has compared him to someone like Brad Pitt. Laura Keene, who was starring in *Our American Cousin* on April 14, 1865, at Ford's Theatre, the night Lincoln was assassinated, was probably the most popular actress of her era, but no one today remembers anything about her career in show business. While Keene died at only forty-seven, her leading man in that ill-fated play, Harry Hawk, enjoyed a long life. By 1901, he was living in obscurity in a Philadelphia suburb, and his name remains recognizable today only to the handful of Lincoln assassination scholars.[740] The man who wrote *Our American Cousin,* Tom Taylor, doesn't even have the historical notoriety of Keene or Hawk. Taylor was "one of the leading playwrights of the Sixties," in the words of Ellen Terry, the leading comic and Shakespearian actress of her era, who is now forgotten herself.

When Andy Warhol made his oft-quoted comment that "in the future, everyone will be world-famous for fifteen minutes," he distilled the transient nature of fame into a sound bite that appears as if it will last longer than anyone it applies to. Warhol himself epitomized the celebrity who is basically famous for being famous, and is remembered already almost exclusively for this one comment. But many doubt he actually said it; an April 8, 2014 article in *Smithsonian* claimed that there is little evidence for Warhol being the originator of the phrase. A misapplication like this has a rich history in show business; Bogart never said "Play it again, Sam" exactly in *Casablanca,* Jimmy Cagney never said "You dirty rat!" exactly in any film, Oliver Hardy never said the exact words, "Here's another fine mess you've gotten me into" (it was actually "another nice mess") to Stan Laurel, and extending things into the literary world, Sherlock Holmes never said, "Elementary, my dear Watson." The quote, promulgated enough times, becomes passed down as historical fact. Myths have always been more interesting than what is often a boring reality. Some off-screen quotes were mythical as well. Ava Gardner is rumored to have famously countered director John Ford's astonishment over her marrying "one hundred-twenty-pound runt" Frank Sinatra by snapping, "Well, there is only ten pounds of Frank, but there's one hundred and ten pounds of cock." In the book *Ava Gardner: The Secret Conversations,* co-author Peter Evans disclosed how upset Gardner was with this quote, which she vehe-

395 · Fleeting Fame

mently denied ever saying. "It's smut. It's sick. It's fucking obscene," the outspoken actress told him.[741] Sinatra seems to have been, more than once, the beneficiary of an extremely effective publicist.

On the other hand, truth in the entertainment business is often far stranger than fiction. Consider that Marlon Brando, who famously shouted out onscreen to Blanche DuBois' sister Stella in 1951's *A Streetcar Named Desire*, was directly descended from one.... Catharine Blanchan DuBois. Like many in show business, Brando had distinctly aristocratic lineage; other relatives include former U.S. Senator Leverett Saltonstall, former Massachusetts Governor William Weld, and JFK's niece and Arnold Schwarzenegger's wife Maria Shriver.[742] The entire Charles Manson story is exceedingly strange, but strangest of all is his firm connection to the Laurel Canyon music crowd in the late 1960s. Neil Young expressed the admiration many of his famous peers felt for Manson's musical talents when he said, "He was great, he was unreal— really, really good. He had this kind of music that nobody else was doing. I thought he really had something crazy, something great. He was like a living poet."[743] Manson had been introduced to Young and other members of the group Buffalo Springfield by Beach Boys drummer Dennis Wilson, who truly admired Manson and even allowed him to move in to his home for a while. Wilson told one interviewer, "Charlie Manson, who is another friend of mine, says he is God and the devil! He sings, plays and writes poetry."[744] Another odd couple was Vincent Fournier (like most of those in the entertainment world, from a wealthy background), better known as the front man for the group Alice Cooper, and conservative politician Barry Goldwater, who were regular golfing partners.[745] Probably the world's most famous porn star, Ron Jeremy, came from a family with connections to both the OSS (forerunner of the CIA) and mobster Bugsy Siegel. He also had future CIA director George Tenet as a high school classmate.[746] In June, 2020, Jeremy was charged with sexually assaulting four different women; by September, 20 new counts of sexual assault, on twelve women and a teenager, going back sixteen years, were added. By the end of October, the number was up to 23, including 11 counts of rape.[747]

Marilyn Monroe, perhaps as famous as any human being has ever been, once said, "Fame doesn't fulfill you. It warms you a bit, but that warmth is temporary." Many of those I've written about in this book, who once took their bows before untold numbers of fawning fans, from the stage, the screen, the radio, and the television set, meet all the criteria for obscurity. I've described more than enough examples in this book of genuine "stars" that became forgotten in their own lifetimes. Fame sometimes comes even more abruptly than it departs. Charles Dickens has often been described as becoming famous literally overnight, with the publication of his first novel *The Pickwick Papers.* The celebrated poet George Gordon, Lord Byron, described his notoriety thusly: "I awoke one morning and found myself famous." Byron established the template for most future celebrities when he later described fame as "The advantage of being known by people of whom you yourself know nothing, and for whom you care as little." With the advent of the internet, overnight sensations have become routine, due exclusively to videos that, in usually an incomprehensible fashion, went viral online. Some household names had to die in order to become celebrated. Such deaths have routinely been referred to as "a great career move." Singer-songwriter Jim Croce's fame and reputation grew by leaps and bounds after his tragic death in a plane crash at just thirty. Back in the mid-1800s, the poet Emily Dickinson wrote, "Fame is a fickle food upon a shifting plate." Dickinson lived one of the oddest lives imaginable; never leaving her home for decades, greeting her infrequent visitors from the shadows. She also spoke for the masses when she wrote, "I'm nobody! Who are you? Are you nobody, too?" Her poems were discovered and published posthumously, and she is now generally acknowledged as one of the great masters of the form. Erma Bombeck, of all people, wisely advised us, "Don't confuse fame with success. Madonna is one; Helen Keller is the other." Americans today are completely absorbed in our narcissistic celebrity culture, where those without any discernable talent are seemingly the most famous. Kim Kardashian, for example, has managed the exceptional feat of building a huge fortune and worldwide fame in the entertainment business without being able to act, sing, or dance. Kim's younger sister Kylie Jenner, with the same absence of any discernable talent, became the youngest billionaire in history, according to *Forbes,* at only twenty years old, because of the success of her cosmetics company.[748] Unlike their male counterparts Dick Clark and Ryan Seacrest, none of the Kardashians appear to have the capacity to be even an adequate game show host or master of ceremonies. Maybe it *does* take some kind of special skill to achieve great wealth and fame under those circumstances. Before the newer, trashier kind of celebrated fame, most people were content with timeless quotes on the subject like Henry Wadsworth Longfellow's:

Lives of great men all remind us
We can make our lives sublime
And departing, leave behind us
Footprints on the sands of time.

Only a fraction of human beings really leave any kind of "footprints" behind them, except in the memories of their children - if they have any - or their spouses - if they die before them. Their grandchildren - if they have any - may recollect them once in a while, but a generation after their death, all but the most famous people are essentially forgotten even by their families. Ironically, one of the first things every freshly famous person does is try to regain the anonymity the rest of us take for granted. "A celebrity is one who works all his life to become well-known and then goes through back streets wearing dark glasses so he won't be recognized," the lovely Jane Powell stated. Catherine Deneuve refreshingly admitted, "I like being famous when it's convenient for me." Bill Murray called fame "a 24 hour job." The thoroughly deluded Madonna, on the other hand, once unsurprisingly declared, "I won't be happy till I'm as famous as God." Katy Perry reflected the superficial nature of today's young celebrities with her comment, "I don't care what they say about my boobs. People are buying my songs; I have a sold-out tour."[749] The late James Gandolfini was one of many celebrities who don't understand the attention they garner. "I'm an actor. I do a job and I go home. Why are you interested in me? You don't ask a truck driver about his job," he declared, clearly not comprehending that truck drivers don't make millions of dollars and have their work broadcast repeatedly to the world. "If California is a state of mind, Hollywood is where you take its temperature. There is a peculiar sense in which this city existing mainly on film and tape is our national capital, alas, and not just the capital of California." Novelist Ross Macdonald, lauded as a master of the detective story, wrote. "It's the place where our children learn how and what to dream and where everything happens just before, or just after, it happens to us." Fittingly, Macdonald was just as illusory as the world he was describing, as his real name was Kenneth Millar.[750]

Davy Crockett, who probably achieved his greatest fame more than a hundred years after his death as a Disney film and merchandising icon, once said, "Fame is like a shaved pig with a greased tail, and it only after it has slipped through the hands of some thousands, that some fellow, by mere chance, holds on to it!" Horace Greeley defined fame as "a vapor," and noted that "the only earthly certainty is oblivion." Many celebrities have expressed a light-hearted attitude towards their fame in humorous epitaphs. "There goes the neighborhood," is carved onto Rodney Dangerfield's headstone, giving his self-deprecating humor a dose of immortality. Legendary wit Dorothy Parker (born Dorothy Rothschild) used "Excuse my dust" as an epitaph. Talk show host Merv Griffin's gravestone kept in line with his career, with "I will not be right back after this message" carved there. No dates adorn Jack Lemmon's tombstone, merely "Jack Lemmon in," expressing the actor's wish to remain in entertainment mode for eternity. Cartoon voice actor extraordinaire Mel Blanc's epitaph was a natural "That's All, Folks." One of those long, long forgotten Andy Warhol-type of transient celebrities, Sir Jeffery Hudson, achieved his notoriety from being baked into a royal pie. His gravestone reflects this, as outside of his birth and date deaths (1619-1682), all that's written on his tombstone is: "A Dwarf Presented in a Pie to King Charles I."

People often overlook the obvious; if an individual is cheered and applauded by admirers, and pampered by everyone they encounter, how could they not develop a monstrous ego? Elizabeth Taylor said what few celebrities will when she admitted, "I've been lucky all my life. Everything's been handed to me. Looks, fame, honors, wealth, love." Actor Joaquin Phoenix echoed this, stating, "If you walk into a room and one hundred people say, 'You are a lovely, beautiful person,' who isn't going to be affected by that?" Bob Dylan provided the more common perspective celebrities possess, when he said, "What good are fans? You can't eat applause for breakfast. You can't sleep with it." Barbra Streisand, whose diva behavior and scorn towards fans has been well documented by countless personal anecdotes, declared, "What does it mean when people applaud? Should I give 'em money? Say thank you? Lift my dress?" Well, I think it would be obvious to any reasonable person that, yes, you should at least say thank you. Marvin Gaye frankly stated, "I am not going to be dictated to by fans, certainly. I am dictated to enough by my record company to last me a million years."

John Barbour has told me that he made an impressive $22,000 per week during the run of the super successful television show *Real People*. He misses nothing about fame and notoriety except the fact it always brought him a good seat in a restaurant. David Bowie said the same thing, in an April 1990 interview with *Q Magazine*. When Lauren Bacall referred to stardom as "an accident," she was merely echoing what Thomas Carlyle had once written. Virginia Woolf wrote, "It is permissible even for a dying hero to think before he dies how men will speak of him hereafter…The very stone one kicks with one's boot will outlast Shakespeare." In an interview published in *Life* magazine only two days before her untimely and suspicious death, Marilyn Monroe said, "If fame goes by, so long, I've had you, fame. If it goes by, I've always known it was fickle." Representing the mindset of what passes today for celebrities, the cartoonish diva Jennifer Lopez boasted, "I have the stardom glow." Far more cerebrally, Hedy Lamarr, who ironically died with little to her name, once said, "To be a star is to own the world and all the people in it. After a taste of stardom, everything else is poverty."

Other celebrities, like my good friend John Barbour, are remarkably accessible and down to earth. Juul Haalmeyer, a noted costume designer remembered dearly by fans like me for his sometimes onscreen work on the classic television show *SCTV*, is extraordinarily cordial to everyone. Like many of those in show business, he shares wonderful inside information on Facebook. His lack of ego is best reflected in the fact he has expressed continual surprise that anyone considers him a celebrity, and gratitude for his connection to *SCTV*. He shocked everyone on Facebook by claiming he'd never had air conditioning in any place he'd lived. Martin Short used to post daily on Facebook, under the name of his famous character Jiminy Glick, sharing intimately personal photos and anecdotes. He also displayed a wide breadth of knowledge about the history of show business. Unfortunately, some years ago, he closed his account, and Facebook has never been the same. Tracy Nelson, daughter of pop music icon Rick Nelson, and a notable actress in her own right, is also a regular poster on Facebook. Like Short and others, she has shared many invaluable personal memories and photographs with all her cyber friends. Other celebrity friends on Facebook who are very generous about sharing background information about their careers include singer and Academy Award-nominated actress

Ronee Blakley, *The Donna Reed Show* star and founder of A Minor Consideration (a group that supports child actors in their adult lives), Paul Petersen, *American Graffiti* stars Candy Clark and Paul Le Mat, *Lost in Space* star Bill Mumy, *Lassie* star Jon Provost, *Leave it to Beaver* star Tony Dow, Oscar-nominated actress Sally Kirkland, and *My Three Sons* stars (and real life brothers) Stanley and Barry Livingston. Veteran actress Patti D'Arbanville is very accommodating to all on Facebook.

Sometimes, these celebrities reveal intensely personal and interesting tidbits on social media. Paul Le Mat, for instance, didn't try to conceal his animosity towards Harrison Ford, who had a much less prominent role than he did in *American Graffiti*. On October 27, 2019, Le Mat posted this comment about Ford on Facebook: "He never asks if I need anything, whenever I see him, over the years. And he has $230 million, and considering we were good friends for years after AG...and I asked him on the phone a long time ago if he could get me a job in any of his movies (he replied 'I'll keep my eyes open.'), and I called several times but he didn't return the calls...otherwise no I don't dislike him." Le Mat is a writer as well, and on December 16, 2019, referenced Ron Howard, his co-star in *American Graffiti,* thusly: "So...I doubt Ron wants to read my books and I don't know how to reach him, except by his agent which we tried before...anyway, he might be like Dreyfuss, knowing about my books but not reading any of them (as far as I know). Rock around the clock pal." To the suggestion that he try engaging Howard on Facebook, Le Mat replied, "I know but he doesn't reply or even mark 'like' to anything on there so I figure he isn't really there. The vanishing amigo. I think I tried a long time ago. Anyway, I left a message about my books. There's no tab to friend request him." Le Mat engages with everyone on Facebook, liking all their comments and responding to them, unlike many non-celebrities do.

I had become a bit perplexed from my own experience of having six books published, appearing on some big talk shows, and being interviewed by celebrated figures like Jesse Ventura, yet having virtually no acknowledgment of anything related to my writing from my own family or real life friends. I hear from people every day, from all over the world, that gratify my ego by telling me how much my book or books meant to them, or how much they love my show or one of my interviews. But every bit of attention comes from strangers, or my expanding group of cyber friends. I began to suspect that those who have achieved real fame, and not just my fledgling bit of niche notoriety, might possibly meet the same response from their own loved ones. Paul Le Mat answered my question about this with an October 18, 2020 reply on Facebook that noted, "Not really. In fact I cannot recall a word any of them said about my acting. Or career. Except my step-father called me 'star' a couple of times. My so-called mother (and my half-sister) asked me was I a millionaire. I replied in the negative, said I was in debt. They scoffed at me, both, like I was a liar...they should have asked my wife at the time. We had bought a house in the hills and went into debt doing it. The closest thing I got was a comment that she (mother) liked AG more than Aloha. After seeing Strange Invaders my so-called mother didn't comment on my acting, or how good (or not) the movie was, but asked me what was the meaning of an expression on my face in one scene, and tried to represent it to me. Yuk. It was when the character was in the church seeing the blue glow coming up from the cellar. She hadn't noticed the blue glow, I guess..." Paul Petersen appeared on another radio show I co-host with Ella Felder, daughter-in-law of Don Felder of the Eagles, and told me pretty much the same thing. During the time he was a child star on *The Donna Reed Show,* he recalled how his father hated being introduced as "Paul Petersen's father."

The great Ben Hecht wrote, "Much more frequent in Hollywood than the emergence of Cinderella is her sudden vanishing. At our party, even in those glowing days, the clock was always striking twelve for someone at the height of greatness; and there was never a prince to fetch her back to the happy scene." As I hope I've demonstrated in this book, a regular on a television series is at least as likely to have their acting career end when their show does, as they are to continue working regularly in the entertainment business. Ben Hecht's Cinderella analogy certainly holds true for the music world as well; the list of one-hit wonder performers is lengthy. As we've seen, it's possible to be a musician in the biggest band imaginable, and within a few years be forced to work a regular job.

Beau Brummell was a London sensation in the early years of the nineteenth century. The wealthy Brummell was highly influential in changing men's fashion, and his ideas evolved into the standard business suit we know today. He died in 1840 in debtor's prison and although the rock group The Beau Brummells enjoyed a few big hits in the mid-1960s, it goes without saying that the inspiration for their name is remembered by no one. Lola Montez achieved great notoriety as a Spanish dancer, had an affair with King Ludwig I of Bavaria, and eventually made her way to America. Her "Spider Dance" was provocative for the 1850s, and her fame grew as she moved to California, adopted a grizzly bear as a pet and authored a book about beauty and the "Secrets of a Lady's Toilet." She died a month before her fortieth birthday, and her name today draws a blank from everyone. Thomas Cooper was one of the first stars of the American stage. He has been lost to history with all the others of his era, despite his daughter marrying the son of President John Tyler. Thomas Hamblin, James W. Wallack, Charlotte Cushman (who was even adept at playing male roles; the *London Times* would refer to one of these portrayals as "far superior to any Romeo we have ever had"), Anna Cora Mowatt, Edwin Adams, Edwin Forrest; all of these names were "the glory of their times," to steal the title of a fantastic book Lawrence Ritter wrote about old baseball players. They, and many others like them, were the Meryl Streeps and Robert DeNiros of their day. Today, they are just as historically obscure as the actors who performed Shakespeare's plays at the Globe Theater. Even the greatest fame has a limited shelf life, except for a very few personalities (like Shakespeare himself, for instance).

Dan Rice was the most famous clown in the world, and made what was then an incredible $1,000 per week during the 1850s and 1860s. His distinctive beard was said to have been the model for Uncle Sam's. Ruined by heavy drinking, the already completely forgotten Rice died in New Jersey in 1900. Perhaps the greatest promoter and showman of them all, P.T. Barnum, was noted for saying more than "There's a sucker born every minute." There is actually no documentation for Barnum ever saying those exact words, but he undeniably once stated, "The show business has all phases and grades of dignity, from the exhibition of a monkey to the exposition of that highest art in music or the drama which secures for the gifted artists a world-wide fame princes well might envy."[751]

"An actor's popularity is fleeting. His success has the life expectancy of a small boy who is about to look into a gas tank with a lighted match," said Fred Allen, a radio star who is probably best remembered for a long-running contrived feud with Jack Benny, who in reality was his good friend. But when I say "best remembered," I am speaking to a very limited audience. In reality, Fred Allen, like all his peers during the Golden Age of radio, is an unrecognizable name today. Even looking at a more recent era, how many people today recall Ali MacGraw, who was voted the top box office star in the world in 1972? MacGraw's last screen credit was in 1997; she moved to New Mexico in 1994 and has lived there in relative obscurity ever since. MacGraw's net worth is a pretty modest $6 million. The lovely Jennifer O'Neill was also a huge star of the era, and was every teenage boy's older woman fantasy in 1971's *Summer of '42* (despite being just twenty-three at the time). While she has had sporadic roles over the years, her name today would draw a blank stare from most people. Priscilla Barnes, who replaced Suzanne Somers on the hit television show *Three's Company,* has worked fairly regularly, in mostly lower budget projects, and has only $1.5 million according to Celebrity Net Worth. Robert Hays, best known for the lead role in 1980's *Airplane!*, found stardom hard to maintain, and has a modest $3 million net worth. Glenda Jackson, a two-time Academy Award winner who starred in some of the biggest films of the 1970s, retired from show business in 1992 and launched a political career in the U.K. Her time in Parliament doesn't seem to have enriched her; she is said to presently have a net worth of between $100,000 and $1 million. She came out of retirement in 2015 and returned to the London stage and Broadway. Regardless, she is a forgotten name to the vast majority of people.

Even more recently, consider the fleeting show business success of once big names like Debra Winger, Kelly McGillis, Lori Singer, Mia Sara, Ally Sheedy and Phoebe Cates. Singer today is worth only $500,000, despite starring in the television series *Fame* and playing the lead in the 1984 hit film *Footloose*. Mia Sara, briefly a star in top films like 1984's *Ferris Bueller's Day Off*, isn't faring much better at $1.5 million. Earlier in this book I provided plenty of examples of big stars from the 1990s and even 2000s who have all but disappeared from the entertainment world, for various reasons. In the music industry, success has an even shorter shelf life. The names of the musicians in many groups remained anonymous to all but their most ardent fans, even when millions were singing along with their hit records on the radio. As we've demonstrated, a huge portion of these performers weren't properly paid during their "day in the sun," to quote Graham Parker, let alone maintained any kind of wealth in subsequent years. For every rarity like the Rolling Stones, all fabulously rich and still touring well into their seventies, there are thousands of former drummers, keyboardists, and guitarists who toil in everyday jobs alongside those who never heard the cheering crowds, or signed an autograph. Since many don't even like to discuss their show business days, often their co-workers have no idea of their connection to a distant but once vibrant celebrity. For all we know, the old guy in the cubicle across from us may have been a member of a band that sold a million records decades earlier, or a child actor in a long ago Hollywood.

This book has been an attempt to show that fame is not always what the non-famous imagine it to be, and that those who enjoy it almost always do so only temporarily. Either the business weeds them out in its curious fashion, or the entertainers themselves choose to leave the celebrity world, often for less than understandable reasons. "If a man can bridge the gap between life and death, if he can live after he's died, then maybe he was a great man. Immortality is the only true success," young rising star James Dean said, in an eerily prophetic quote, given his astounding posthumous fame. Child star extraordinaire Shirley Temple once declared, "I stopped believing in Santa Claus when I was six. Mother took me to see him in a department store and he asked for my autograph."[752] For most adult Americans, who long ago discarded Santa Claus, the Easter Bunny, and the Tooth Fairy, celebrities represent the same kind of mythological figures.

Andy Warhol grew tired of his most famous quote, saying, "I'm bored with that line. I never use it anymore. My new line is 'In 15 minutes everybody will be famous.'"[753] Fame is fleeting. Celebrities are human beings. Like the rest of us, some of them are friendly and kind, while others are nasty and egotistical. Some are just boring, seemingly unable to find their own persona in the midst of all the differing characters they've been paid to portray. Steve Martin, one of the most brilliant and innovative stand-up comedians of all time, has always been reclusive and notably unfunny in his private life. He's also notorious for being unengaging with fans; countless numbers of people have described approaching him and being given the silent treatment, while he handed out a business card that read, "This certifies that you have had a personal encounter with me and that you found me warm, polite, intelligent and funny." More recently, actor Jonah Hill has copied Martin's example, handing fans a business card that explains meeting him was "a total letdown."[754] Martin exemplifies the artist whose image is drastically different from his actual character. Others, like the late John Candy, are consistently friendly and appreciative towards fans, displaying a personality even warmer than their fans have any right to expect.

During the course of writing this book, I've spoken to and exchanged emails with many entertainers. A few have been less than cordial, but most have been at least accommodating. I'm grateful for the really friendly ones, like former *Brady Bunch* star Susan Olsen, singer-songwriter Graham Parker, actress Sally Kirkland, actress and sister of Natalie Wood, Lana Wood; and *Real People* creator and host John Barbour, who has become one of my best friends. I now regularly correspond with veteran actor Nick Mancuso, who is not only incredibly friendly and engaging, but also a brilliant, genuine renaissance man. Mancuso, like John Barbour, Susan Olsen and Lana Wood, also appeared on my radio show "I Protest." As noted earlier, Susan Olsen reminded me that it isn't necessarily "failure" when an actor switches gears and decides, for whatever reason, to pursue other ways to make a living. My emphasis on these kinds of abrupt exits from show business is only because of what should be obvious; in the vast majority of cases (many child stars with pushy stage mothers notwithstanding), those who make it in the entertainment world have achieved the ultimate goal they worked years or even decades for. A goal, needless to say, that countless others might have worked just as hard for, without ever getting to grasp that elusive golden ring. Researching this book eventually became a surrealistic experience; I had to shake my head sometimes in disbelief as I texted back and forth with Lana Wood late at night, or had Susan Olsen tell me, "I was just thinking of you," or had Nick Mancuso float the possibility of my writing a screenplay with him for a Steven Seagal project, or took phone calls from John Barbour while attending a concert, or Circus du Soleil, or simply driving about, while my wife Jeanne, a huge *Real People* fan, listened to the show's host and creator over Blue Tooth. As my wife can also readily attest, I became a shameless name-dropper.

I should probably clarify that my references to some entertainer being worth "only" $2 million or whatever, are exclusively for purposes of comparison. Obviously, working-class people who live paycheck to paycheck, and have less than $1000 in savings, would scoff at the notion that *any* celebrity has been underpaid, or cheated financially. I use the figures, which seem to be exaggerated across the board, primarily from Celebrity Net Worth, because they illustrate the wildly inconsistent nature of the business. I just question why Bette Davis, or Mickey Rooney, or Lana Turner, or Barbara Stanwyck died with so much less money (all $1 million or less) than say Clark Gable (who left behind a $100 million estate), Cary Grant ($130 million), Fred MacMurray ($150 million), or producer Aaron Spelling ($500 million), not to mention many who never approached their level of fame, and I think lots of other people will as well.

Fame doesn't cure disease, or prevent depression and unhappiness. All the suicides we've noted in this book attest to that. A 2013 study by Australian researchers found that celebrities tend to die earlier than the rest of us. From sifting through 1000 obituaries in *The New York Times* from 2009 to 2011, it was discovered that those who had gained some measure of fame died at an average age of 77.2 years. The average lifespan in the U.S. for professionals is 81.7, and 83 for business leaders and politicians. This study, published in *QJM: An International Journal of Medicine,* concluded that "Fame and achievement in performance-related careers may be earned at the cost of a shorter life expectancy." The researchers studied both famous athletes and entertainers.[755] A disproportionately high percentage of celebrities, including younger ones, still smoke cigarettes. Smoking is also prevalent in the modeling world, as many female models especially use cigarettes as a form of weight control.

William Shatner, despite being the butt of many jokes over his ham-handed acting, as well as having a horrible reputation with fans, nevertheless issued this refreshing and self- deprecating statement about the transient nature of fame: "What have I done? I've blundered my way through life. So I have my picture on the wall. The minute I die, that picture will start to yellow and fade and eventually be gone. Blown in the wind and become part of the molecular structure of something else. These things we see as 'success,' they're non-accomplishments." Irreverent comedian George Carlin once remarked, "My tombstone? I'm thinking something along the lines of 'Geez, he was just here a minute ago.'"[756]

Most of us fantasize about being famous. We dream of cheering throngs idolizing us, as we stand on a stage, or patrol a ballfield. During their marriage, one of the most star-studded unions of the 1950s or any era, Marilyn Monroe is alleged to have once cavalierly said to her equally famous husband, Hall of Famer Joe DiMaggio, "Oh Joe, you never heard a crowd cheering like that..."[757] To those at the level of fame that Monroe and DiMaggio achieved, it must be difficult to see yourself as a human being, unlike the millions worshiping you in the stands, in the streets, in the restaurants and stores, who see you as something superhuman.

I love the Kinks, but despite the proclamation in their classic 1972 song *Celluloid Heroes*, everybody isn't a star. Of the incalculable number of people who have walked the earth over the centuries, only a very tiny percentage achieved any semblance of fame. Far fewer still found any lasting celebrity. Almost all of us are anonymous souls, trying to do our best, with "a good conscience our only sure reward," to quote John F. Kennedy. Hopefully, within these pages I was able to explore what life is like for those rare individuals who broke free of their anonymity, for however brief a time, heard the cheers, and lived on borrowed fame.

Bibliography

Anger, Kenneth, *Hollywood Babylon II,* 1990, New York, Plume

Anger, Kenneth, *Hollywood Babylon,* 1975, New York, Straight Arrow Press/Simon & Schuster

Astor, Mary, *My Story: An Autobiography,* 1959, New York, Doubleday

Barbour, John, *Your Mother's Not a Virgin: The Bumpy Life and Times of the Canadian Dropout Who Changed the Face of American TV!,* 2019, Oregon, Trine Day

Belzer, Richard and Wayne, David, *Dead Wrong: Straight Facts on the Country's Most Controversial Cover-Ups,* 2012, New York, Skyhorse Publishing

Boone, Steve and Moss, Tony, *Hotter Than a Match Head: Life on the Run With the Lovin' Spoonful,* 2014, Toronto, ECW Press

Bowers, Scotty and Friedberg, Lionel, *Full Service: My Adventures in Hollywood and the Secret Sex Lives of the Stars,* 2013, New York, Grove Press

Bresler, Fenton, *Who Killed John Lennon?,* 1989, New York, St. Martin's

Cannon, Dyan, *Dear Cary: My Life With Cary Grant,* 2011, London, Biteback Publishing

Christy, Jim, *The Long Slow Death of Jack Kerouac,* 1998, Toronto, ECW Press

Crane, Robert, and Fryer, Christopher, *Crane: Sex, Celebrity, and my Father's Unsolved Murder,* 2015, Lexington, University of Kentucky Press

Davis, Ivor, *The Beatles and Me on Tour,* 2014, Ventura, Cockney Kid Publishing

Eden, Barbara and Leigh, Wendy, *Jeannie Out of the Bottle: A Memoir,* 2012, New York, Crown

Finch, Christopher and Rosenkrantz, Linda, *Gone Hollywood*, 1979, New York, Doubleday

Fleming, E.J., *The Fixers: Eddie Mannix, Howard Strickland and the MGM Publicity Machine,* 2004, North Carolina, McFarland and Company

Foster, Buddy and Wagener, Leon, *Foster Child: A Biography of Jodie Foster,* 1998, New York, Signet

Foster, Charles, *Stardust and Shadows: Canadians in Early Hollywood,* 2000, Toronto, Dundurn Press

Fountain, Leatrice Gilbert, *Dark Star: The Untold Story of the Meteoric Rise and Fall of Legendary Silent Screen Star John Gilbert,* 1985, New York, St. Martin's Press

Garbus, Martin, *Ready for the Defense,* 1971, New York, Farrar, Straus and Giroux

Gardner, Ava and Evans, Peter, *Ava Gardner: The Secret Conversations,* 2013, Simon & Schuster

Garver, Kathy and Ascher, Fred, *X Child Stars: Where are They Now?,* 2016, Maryland, Taylor Trade Publishing

Gerron, Peggy Sue and Cameron, Glenda, *Whatever Happened to Peggy Sue?: A Memoir by Buddy Holly's Peggy Sue,* 2008, Oklahoma City, TogiEntertainment

Goldman, Albert, *The Lives of John Lennon,* 1988, New York, William Morrow and Co.

Green, Jonathan, *The Book of Rock Quotes,* 1982, New York, Music Sales Corp

Griffin, Kathy, *Kathy Griffin's Celebrity Run-Ins: My A-Z Index,* 2016, New York, Flatiron Books

Harrison, Louise, *My Kid Brother's Band...a.k.a The Beatles!,* 2014, Sikeston, Missouri, Acclaim Press

Jacobson, Laurie, *Hollywood Heartbreak: The Tragic and Mysterious Deaths of Hollywood's Most Remarkable Legends,* 1984, New York, Simon & Schuster

James, Tommy and Fitzpatrick, Martin, *Me, the Mob, and the Music: One Helluva Ride With Tommy James & the Shondells,* 2011, New York, Scribner

Kruth, John, *Rhapsody in Black: The Life and Music of Roy Orbison,* 2013, London, Backbeat Books

Lamparski, Richard, *Whatever Became of...* series, 1967-1986, New York, Crown

Law, William Matson, *In the Eye of History: Disclosures in the JFK Assassination Medical Evidence,* 2004, Dallas, JFK Lancer Productions & Publications

Leigh, Suzanna, *Paradise, Suzanna Style,* 2000, Brighton, England, Pen Press

Linna, Miriam and Fuller, Randall, *I Fought the Law: The Life and Strange Death of Bobby Fuller,* 2015, Brooklyn, Kicks Books

Maltin, Leonard and Bann, Richard W., *Our Gang: The Life and Times of the Little Rascals,* 1984, New York, Crown

Martin, Andrea, *Lady Parts,* 2014, New York, Harper

Marx, Samuel, *Jean Harlow and the Murder of Paul Bern,* 1991, New York, Dell

McGowan, David, *Weird Scenes Inside the Canyon: Laurel Canyon, Covert Ops and the Dark Heart of the Hippie Dream,* 2014, Manchester, England, Headpress

Polly, Matthew, *Bruce Lee: a Life,* 2018, New York, Simon & Schuster

Ranone, Dee Dee, Korman, Veronica, and McNeil, Legs, *Lobotomy: Surviving the Ramones,* 2000, Cambridge, Massachusetts, Da Capo Press

Ribowsky, Mark, *Ain't Too Proud to Beg: The Troubled Lives and Enduring Soul of the Temptations,* 2010, Hoboken, New Jersey, Wiley Publishing

Robb, David L., *Operation Hollywood: How the Pentagon Shapes and Censors the Movies,* 2004, Buffalo, Prometheus Books

Saxon, Bret and Stein, Steve, *How to Meet and Hang Out With the Stars: A Totally Unauthorized Guide,* 1995, New York, Citadel Press

Seaman, Frederic, *Last Days of John Lennon,* 1992, New York, Dell

Secker, Tom and Alford, Matthew, *National Security Cinema: The Shocking New Evidence of Government Control in Hollywood,* 2017, Amazon, CreateSpace Independent Publishing

Shales, Tom and Miller, James Andrew, *Live From New York: The Complete, Uncensored History of Saturday Night Live as Told by Its Stars, Writers, and Guests,* 2002, New York, Little, Brown and Company

Short, Martin, *I Must Say: My Life as a Humble Comedy Legend,* 2015, New York, Harper

Slatzer, Robert F., *The Curious Death of Marilyn Monroe,* 1975, New York, Pinacle

Spector, Ronnie and Waldron, Vince, *Be My Baby: How I Survived Mascara, Miniskirts, and Madness,* 1990, New York, Harmony Books

Stallings, Penny and Mandelbaum, Howard, *Flesh and Fantasy: The Truth Behind the Fantasy- The Fantasy Behind the Truth,* 1978, 1978, New York, St. Martin's

Staples, Peter, *Wild Thing: A Rocky Road,* 2017, Nottinghamshire, UK, New Haven Publishing Ltd

Stenn, David, *Bombshell: The Life and Death of Jean Harlow,* 1993, New York, Doubleday

Strongman, Phil, *John Lennon - Life, Times, and Assassination,* 2010, Liverpool, Bluecoat Press

Summers, Antony, *Goddess: The Secret Life of Marilyn Monroe,* 1985, New York, New American Library

Talbot, Margaret, *The Entertainer: Movies, Magic, and my Father's Twentieth Century,* 2013, New York, Riverhead Books

Thomas, Dave, *SCTV: Behind the Scenes,* 1997, Toronto, McClelland & Stewart

Tranberg, Charles, *Fred MacMurray: A Biography,* 2007, Georgia, BearManor Media

White, Charles, *The Life and Times of Little Richard,* 1984, New York, Harmony Books

Wilson, Mary, *Dreamgirl: My Life as a Supreme,* 1986, New York, St. Martin's

Wright, Lawrence, *Going Clear: Scientology, Hollywood, and the Prison of Belief,* 2013, New York, Vintage

Endnotes

1   *UK Independent,* July 3, 1993

2   *St. Augustine Record,* June 8, 2010

3   *People,* July 19, 1993

4   *UK Independent,* July 3, 1993

5   *The Immortal Count: The Life and Films of Bela Lugosi* by Arthur Lennig, p. 133

6   *Time,* July 7, 1980

7   *Chicago Tribune,* April 6, 1999

8   *TribLive,* June 28, 2009

9   Stephen Foster letter, January 27, 1857

10 *Smithsonian,* October 7, 2014

11 *Firsts Magazine,* September 1999

12 *The Irish Times,* October 26, 2019

13 *Sotheby's,* August 16, 2018

14 *The Long Slow Death of Jack Kerouac* by Jim Christy, p. 7

15 *Lansing State Journal,* November 25, 1975

16 *Sydney Morning Herald,* June 21, 2013

17 *Forbes,* September 19, 2015

18 *The New Yorker,* July 22, 2010

19 *New York Times,* August 4, 1966

20 *NPR,* March 24, 2006

21 *UK Daily Mail,* March 25, 2015

22 *Philadelphia Weekly,* October 22, 2008

23   *UK Express,* March 31, 2014

24   *Rolling Stone,* October 14, 1971

25   *UK Daily Mail,* July 5, 2009

26   *Forbes,* June 30,2017

27   *New York Times,* November 1, 2005

28   *The Guardian,* July 10, 2000

29   *UK Daily Mail,* September 14, 2007

30   *Mental Floss,* June 4, 2008

31   *Los Angeles Times,* November 1, 2001

32   *The Guardian,* August 10, 2008

33   *Magazine of the Oklahoma Hall of Fame,* August 29, 2017

34   *The Spokesman-Review,* May 15, 1968

35   *Los Angeles Times,* September 2, 1948

36   *Las Vegas Sun,* October 22, 2002

37   *Three Stooges: The Triumphs and Tragedies of the Most Popular Comedy Team of All Time* by Jeff Forrester, p. 80

38   *Associated Press,* August 4, 1995

39   *Entertainment Weekly,* January 22, 2019

40   *Los Angeles Times,* October 27, 2010

41   *The Baltimore Sun,* November 7, 2012

42   *LA Weekly,* January 22, 2015

43   *The Lives of John Lennon* by Albert Goldman, pp. 690-691

44   *UK Express,* September 23, 2016

45   *Los Angeles Daily News,* November 9, 1950

46   *ABC News,* July 4, 2012

47   *Hollywood Reporter,* July 3, 2012

48   *Weird Scenes Inside the Canyon: Laurel Canyon, Covert Ops & the Dark Heart of the Hippie Dream* by David McGowan, p. 226

49   *Variety,* October 10, 1928

50   *Daily Caller,* November 23, 2018

51   *Yahoo,* November 26, 2014

52   *Chicago Tribune,* April 24, 1996

53   *MSN,* August 10, 2018

54   *Star-News,* December 11, 1965

55   *Santa Cruz Sentinel,* July 13, 1985

56   *New York Post,* December 29, 2006

57   *ETonline,* December 2, 2015

58   *TMZ,* September 25, 2018

59   *UK Times,* April 30, 2019

60   *People,* November 1, 1993

61   *X Child Stars: Where Are They Now?* By Kathy Garver and Fred Ascher, p. 12

62   Ibid, p. 33

63   *Variety,* December 10, 2019

64   *UK Daily Mail,* September 27, 2013

65   *Chicago Tribune,* November 6, 1990

66   *Us,* January 29, 2014

67   *UK Daily Mail,* February 11, 2020

68   *Mr. Tambourine Man: The Life and Legacy of the Byrds' Gene Clark* by John Einarson, p. 75

69   *Weird Scenes Inside the Canyon: Laurel Canyon, Covert Ops & the Dark Heart of the Hippie Dream* by David McGowan, p. 193

70   Ibid, p. 197-198

71   *CNN,* May 15, 1997

72   *New York Daily News,* April 10, 2016

73   *TMZ,* June 23, 2015

74   *Chicago Tribune,* January 10, 2018

75   *The List,* February 1, 2021

76   *Daily Herald,* March 15, 2008

77   *Town & Country Magazine,* April 26, 2017

78   *The Guardian,* October 25, 2006

79   *New York Post,* April 6, 2019

80   *USA Today,* June 7, 2019

81   *TMZ,* June 7, 2019

82   *USA Today,* July 7, 2019

83   *Everyday Health,* November 14, 2017

84   *LA Weekly,* October 19, 2017

85   *The Guardian,* September 23, 2010

86   *Rolling Stone,* April 22, 2015

87   *New York Times,* December 1, 2015

88   *UK Sunday Mirror,* April 2, 2007

89   *The Times,* November 10, 2007

90   *Los Angeles Times,* September 18, 2018

91   *Billboard,* August 22, 2015

92   *USA Today,* November 17, 2016

93   *Vanity Fair,* December 1, 2010

94   *E Online,* November 12, 2010

95   *National Enquirer,* February 18, 2018

96   *Orlando Sentinel,* August 2, 1991

97   *ENews,* March 12, 2010

98   *NPR,* July 13, 2019

99   *Evening Independent,* November 10, 1980

100 *UK Daily Mail,* April 1, 2015

101 *The immortal Count: The Life and Films of Bela Lugosi* by Arthur Lennig, p. 396

102 *UK Daily Mail,* July 10, 2015

103 *BBC,* January 11, 2015

104 *John Ford: A Bio-Bibliography* by Bill Levy, p. 36

105 *Montreal Gazette,* June 26, 1974

106 *UPI,* March 31, 1994

107 *Santa Fe New Mexican,* January 13, 2008

108 *Los Angeles Times,* November 7, 1989

109 *New York Post,* March 25, 2011

110 *Tennessean,* April 24, 2018

111 *CBS News,* January 26, 2006

112 *UK Express,* March 9, 2009

113 *Los Angeles Times,* January 21, 2010

114 *Mental Floss,* February 27, 2012

115 *Forbidden Channels* by Penny Stallings, p. 103

116 *Slant Magazine,* September 20, 2011

117 *The Guardian,* October 22, 2009

118 *Showbiz CheatSheet,* July 27, 2020

119 *People,* December 7, 2017

120 *Los Angeles Times,* March 16, 2016

121 *New York Daily News,* August 5, 2009

122 *New York Times,* February 16, 2009

123 *Variety,* February 17, 1993

124 *The Guardian,* April 14, 2003

125 *Detroit Metro Times,* August 27, 2008

126 *The New Yorker,* July 1, 2013

127 *The Australian,* June 5, 2014

128 *Tampa Bay Times,* February 12, 2018

129 *Los Angeles Times,* February 24, 1965

130 *Time,* July 20, 2010

131 *Orlando Sentinel,* July 16, 1988

132 *Los Angeles Times,* March 24, 1964

133 *UK Independent,* February 3, 1999

134 *New York Times,* February 28, 1994

135 *Medium,* November 9, 2018

136 *NPR,* December 9, 2010

137 *Weird Scenes Inside the Canyon: Laurel Canyon, Covert Ops & the Dark Heart of the Hippie Dream* by David McGowan, p. 258

138 *UK Independent,* December 1, 2017

139 *The Guardian,* June 30, 2015

140 *Free Speech Project,* November 15, 2017

141 *UK Independent,* November 7, 2017

142 *San Francisco Chronicle,* February 22, 2006

143 *Los Angeles Times,* July 29, 2016

144 *The Telegraph,* July 30, 2009

145 *Huffington Post,* November 4, 2014

146 *Charlotte Observer,* August 26, 2016

147 *Daily Finance,* September 29, 2011

148 *Chicago Tribune,* January 31, 1981

149 *The Evening Independent,* December 10, 1936

150 *Vogue,* April 17, 2016

151 *LA Weekly,* February 10, 2017

152 *Los Angeles Times,* December 9, 1952

153 *Washington Post,* August 28, 1961

154 *New York Times,* March 16, 1978

155 *Los Angeles Times,* November 22, 1987

156 *Hollywood Reporter,* September 20, 2012

157 *Des Moines Register,* April 28, 2015

158 *Lubbock Avalanche-Journal,* March 3, 2015

159 *Daily News Media,* February 3, 2019

160 *UK Daily Mail,* January 19, 2008

161 *Texas Monthly,* October 1995

162 *The Australian,* December 26, 2019

163 *Liverpool Echo,* April 16, 2011

164 *Beatle!: The Pete Best Story* by Pete Best and Patrick Doncaster, p. 179

165 *Weird Scenes Inside the Canyon: Laurel Canyon, Covert Ops & the Dark Heart of the Hippie Dream* by David McGowan, pp. 35-36

166 *LA Weekly,* March 6, 2015

167 *Los Angeles Magazine,* July 11, 2013

168 *Variety,* February 2, 1974

169 *Entertainment Weekly,* June 27, 2019

170 *Brooklyn Daily Eagle,* January 4, 1937

171 *Milwaukee Sentinel,* December 22, 1947
172 *Miami Herald,* June 6, 2018
173 *Daily Telegraph* Australia, April 4, 2008
174 *New York Times,* March 18, 2009
175 *Nashville Tennessean,* September 20, 1980
176 *Core DJ Radio,* January 13, 2015
177 *Rolling Stone,* December 27, 2010
178 *Today Show,* March 27, 2007
179 *People,* May 1, 1995
180 *Reuters,* April 11, 2008
181 *People,* July 17, 1995
182 *UK Telegraph,* April 14, 2017
183 *Reuters,* September 14, 2009
184 *New Musical Express,* July 4, 2019
185 *Billboard,* January 24, 2017
186 *UK Daily Mail,* May 6, 2017
187 *The Inquisitir,* May 7, 2017
188 *The Stars of Hollywood Forever* by Tony Scott, p. 19
189 *People,* September 29, 1980
190 *Rolling Stone,* August 7, 1997
191 *Melody Maker,* November 26, 1994
192 *Lobotomy: Surviving the Ramones* by Dee Dee Ramone, pp. 232-233
193 *BBC News,* May 3, 2010
194 *UK Daily Mail,* January 17, 2015
195 *New York Daily News,* January 16, 2016
196 *Variety,* January 7, 2013
197 *Variety,* December 29, 1937
198 *Los Angeles Times,* February 24, 2017
199 *UK Telegraph,* March 13, 2016
200 *Hollywood Reporter,* July 4, 2016
201 *South China Morning Post,* July 4, 2018
202 *Fox News,* March 21, 2019
203 *The Book of Rock Quotes,* complied by Jonathan Green, p. 116
204 *Los Angeles Times,* June 23, 1998
205 *New York Times,* February 4, 2018
206 *Washington Post,* October 6, 1996
207 *Los Angeles Times,* February 28, 1990
208 *UK Independent,* January 5, 2015
209 *UK Daily Mail,* August 13, 2015

210 *Los Angeles Times,* December 5, 1991

211 *Essence,* June 18, 2012

212 *Philadelphia Sun,* June 24, 2012

213 *New York Post,* July 6, 2016

214 *TMZ,* September 27, 2012

215 *Variety,* June 7, 2018

216 *UK Independent,* April 30, 1994

217 *Orlando Sentinel,* June 3, 1991

218 *Detroit News,* June 28, 2011

219 *New York Times,* October 22, 1938

220 *Mothers, Mammies and Old Maids: Twenty-Five Character Actresses of Golden Age Hollywood* by Axel Nissan, p. 8

221 *The Agony Booth,* April 29, 2014

222 *New York Times,* September 9, 1979

223 *New York Times,* April 26, 1972

224 *National Enquirer,* February 22, 2015

225 *New York Times,* September 18, 1971

226 *Orlando Sentinel,* May 12, 1993

227 *Entertainment Weekly,* May 15, 1992

228 *USA Today,* February 1, 2018

229 *Los Angeles Times,* October 13, 1999

230 *Andrea Martin's Lady Parts,* p. 197

231 *Rolling Stone,* March 1, 1984

232 *Variety,* May 10, 1999

233 *The Irish Times,* May 18, 2002

234 *New York Times,* December 10, 1978

235 *ABC News,* May 13, 2010

236 *AP,* July 29, 1996

237 *Boston Herald,* December 18, 2015

238 *Financial Post,* November 29, 2017

239 *Rolling Stone,* February 10, 1994

240 *JAM!,* October 15, 1999

241 *UK Independent,* April 26, 2013

242 Official Inquest Into the Death of Michael Kelland Hutchence, February 6, 1998

243 *UK Independent,* July 23, 2014

244 *Rolling Stone,* May 17, 2013

245 *Shuffling to Ignominy: The Tragedy of Stepin Fetchit* by Champ Clark, p. 115

246   *Newsmax,* April 8, 2013

247   *Yahoo Celebrity,* November 8, 2016

248   *People,* November 11, 2015

249   *Discovery,* April 4, 2014

250   *Hollywood Babylon* II, p. 203

251   *Weird Scenes Inside the Canyon: Laurel Canyon, Covert Ops & the Dark Heart of the Hippie Dream* by David McGowan, p. 94

252   *Los Angeles Daily News,* December 5, 2008

253   *Daily Express,* September 24, 2009

254   *The Guardian,* April 28, 2009

255   *Weird Scenes Inside the Canyon: Laurel Canyon, Covert Ops & the Dark Heart of the Hippie Dream* by David McGowan, pp. 27-28

256   *UPI,* October 17, 1990

257   *Chicago Tribune,* May 5, 1991

258   *Baltimore Sun,* January 21, 2017

259   *Los Angeles Times,* February 4, 1941

260   *New York Times,* October 1, 1935

261   *Detroit News,* September 12, 1935

262   *Weird Scenes Inside the Canyon: Laurel Canyon, Covert Ops & the Dark Heart of the Hippie Dream* by David McGowan, p. 32

263   *Rolling Stone,* August 5, 1971

264   *Rolling Stone,* January 26, 1989

265   *Weird Scenes Inside the Canyon: Laurel Canyon, Covert Ops & the Dark Heart of the Hippie Dream* by David McGowan, pp. 30, 32-39

266   *Deadline Hollywood,* June 20, 2016

267   *Entertainment Weekly,* July 21, 2016

268   *Washington Post,* March 22, 2018

269   McGowan, p. 181

270   McGowan, p. 34

271   McGowan, p. 35

272   McGowan, pp. 35-37

273   *Fox News,* January 27, 2017

274   *CTV News,* January 6, 2009

275   *Mercury News,* January 24, 2019

276   *UK Telegraph,* July 31, 2015

277   *Live Journal,* November 1, 2008

278   *Kansas City Times,* February 7, 1959

279   *New York Times,* May 9, 1968

280   *People,* August 31, 2018

281 *New York Times,* April 25, 1990

282 *Agence France-Presse,* June 6, 2018

283 *Fresno Bee,* June 28, 1965

284 McGowan, pp. 90-91

285 Ibid, p. 92

286 Ibid, pp. 114-115

287 *Los Angeles Times,* January 3, 1989

288 *AP,* January 14, 1985

289 *Variety,* May 27, 2010

290 *UPI,* November 17, 1992

291 *The Guardian,* October 11, 2002

292 *People,* June 13, 1988

293 *AP News,* February 4, 1988

294 *Los Angeles Times,* December 3, 1986

295 *KSEQ News Channel,* November 16, 2015

296 *Weird Scenes Inside the Canyon* by David McGowan, p. 57

297 *New York Times,* November 6, 1989

298 *Tuscaloosa News,* December 3, 1978

299 *Milwaukee Journal,* August 12, 1973

300 *NPR,* April 7, 2015

301 *Me, the Mob, and the Music: One Helluva Ride With Tommy James & The Shondells* by Tommy James, p. 72

302 *On This Day in Music History* by Jay Warner, p. 166

303 *New York Times,* February 3, 1994

304 *Time,* February 20, 1978

305 *The New Yorker,* May 16, 2005

306 *New York Times,* March 30, 2003

307 *Hollywood Babylon* by Kenneth Anger, p. 219

308 *Forbidden Channels* by Penny Stallings, p. 104

309 *The Life of Dick Haymes: No More Little White Lies* by Ruth Prigozy, p. 177

310 *Los Angeles Times,* February 24, 1935

311 *New York Times,* January 5, 1931

312 *Los Angeles Times,* November 17, 1981

313 *Miami Herald,* January 10, 2017

314 *UK Metro,* November 2, 2017

315 *People,* July 18, 2018

316 *UK Daily Mail,* August 12, 2015

317 *Washington Post,* October 12, 1991

318 McGowan, p. 260

319 *The Guardian,* February 7, 2018

320 *Rolling Stone,* January 20, 2018

321 *Rolling Stone,* January 19, 2018

322 *BBC News,* September 6, 2018

323 *Yahoo Entertainment,* May 10, 2019

324 *UK Independent,* December 12, 2019

325 *UK Daily Mail,* December 28, 2019

326 *New York Times,* November 1, 1938

327 *Fox News,* May 23, 2018

328 *CNN Money,* December 6, 2000

329 *Fox News,* February 10, 2019

330 *Life,* April 25, 1938

331 *How the Beatles Destroyed Rock 'n' Roll: An Alternative History of American Popular Music* by Elijah Wald, p. 211

332 *Yahoo Finance,* August 15, 2019

333 *Hudson Valley Magazine,* July 23, 2019

334 *Hollywood Reporter,* July 6, 2012

335 *Huffington Post,* November 10, 2012

336 *The Sun,* April 30, 2017

337 *Forbes,* June 7, 2004

338 *The Hollywood Reporter,* July 23, 2014

339 *Chicago Tribune,* February 4, 1969

340 *Reuters,* August 11, 2008

341 *The Arts in the 1970s* by B.J. Moore-Gilbert, pg. 247

342 *The Scotsman,* October 14, 2016

343 *Rolling Stone,* September 5, 2018

344 *Billboard,* April 1, 2017

345 *Allen Klein: The Man Who Bailed out the Beatles, Made the Stones, and Transformed Rock & Roll* by Fred Goodman, pp. 66-68

346 *The Telegraph,* May 18, 2015

347 *UK Independent,* January 21, 2008

348 *They Left Their Hearts in San Francisco: The Lives of Songwriters George Cory and Douglass Cross* by Bill Christine, p. 168

349 *BBC,* May 5, 2004

350 *Los Angeles Times,* January 16, 2002

351 *Los Angeles Times,* March 7, 2015

352 *LA Weekly,* March 3, 2015

353 *Newsweek,* March 14, 2015

354 *Chicago Tribune,* August 30, 2007

355 *UK Daily Mail,* July 11, 2019

356 *NPR,* July 29, 2009

357 *Vibe,* January 17, 2017

358 *Chicago Tribune,* October 13, 1991

359 *Rolling Stone,* August 7, 2018

360 *Orlando Sentinel,* August 4, 1986

361 *The Guardian,* January 30, 2016

362 *Digital Music News,* November 25, 2014

363 *CNBC,* January 26, 2018

364 *Digital Music News,* December 10, 2018

365 *CNBC,* January 26, 2018

366 *Los Angeles Times,* August 19, 2006

367 *National Enquirer,* October 19, 2010

368 *Washington Post,* October 24, 2010

369 *Huffington Post,* February 16, 2012

370 *Fox News,* September 20, 2018

371 *TMZ,* September 5, 2018

372 *Hollywood Reporter,* December 30, 2020

373 *The New York Times,* September 8, 2003

374 *Fox News,* March 9, 2011

375 *Forbes,* September 28, 2017

376 *Yahoo,* December 16, 2017

377 *Vanity Fair,* November 2016

378 *Parade,* August 25, 2019

379 *Los Angeles Times,* September 5, 1989

380 *Los Angeles Times,* August 10, 2004

381 *UK Independent,* December 30, 1998

382 *Mental Floss,* December 17, 2018

383 *Los Angeles Times,* October 20, 2009

384 *A Textbook of Cultural Economics* by Ruth Towse, p. 490

385 *New York Post,* January 27, 2017

386 *Aol.Com,* October 15, 2009

387 *The Guardian,* June 5, 2002

388 *Yuma Sun,* January 10, 2015

389 *BBC,* July 4, 2014

390 *New Musical Express,* October 1964

391 *TMZ,* November 6, 2017

392 *Slate,* February 11, 2013

393   *Wall Street Journal,* May 22, 2014

394   *Huffington Post,* April 5, 2012

395   *Billboard,* June 15, 1996

396   *Hollywood Reporter,* March 7, 2014

397   *Variety,* August 21, 2015

398   *Los Angeles Times,* January 6, 1977

399   *New York Times,* August 2, 1976

400   *Your Mother's Not a Virgin: The Bumpy Life and Times of the Canadian Dropout Who Changed the Face of American TV!* By John Barbour, p. 126

401   *Rolling Stone,* October 24, 2011

402   *UK Daily Mail,* July 1, 2014

403   *USA Today,* August 28, 2016

404   *New York Post,* March 30, 2015

405   *Bossip,* February 20, 2011

406   *The Guardian,* December 14, 2018

407   *UK Daily Mail,* November 26, 2013

408   *Riverfront Times,* March 18, 2015

409   *Hollywood Reporter,* December 17, 2013

410   *San Francisco Chronicle,* May 17, 2009

411   *UK Telegraph,* December 21, 2017

412   *UK Daily Mail,* July 13, 2008

413   *Vanity Fair,* November 20, 2006

414   *The Oklahoman,* March 12, 1958

415   *Hollywood Reporter,* April 20, 2017

416   *UPI,* March 17, 1983

417   *Forbes,* March 20, 2016

418   *TV Guide,* March 24, 2000

419   *UK Metro,* October 12, 2017

420   *Chicago Tribune,* August 24, 1997

421   *Chicago Sun-Times,* June 10, 2005

422   *Hollywood Reporter,* February 8, 2018

423   *UK Daily Mail,* March 30, 2018

424   *Rolling Stone,* April 25, 2019

425   *TMZ,* January 15, 2017

426   *Arizona Daily Sun,* May 14, 2019

427   *TMZ,* August 1, 2018

428   *The Sun,* November 11, 2017

429   *NBC News,* June 19, 2019

430 *Fox News,* April 5, 2019

431 *Yahoo Entertainment,* April 8, 2019

432 *New York Times,* October 27, 2020

433 *Yahoo Entertainment,* December 18, 2019

434 *Fox News,* December 30, 2019

435 *The Hollywood Reporter,* October 27, 2017

436 *Los Angeles Review of Books,* December 6, 2013

437 *Los Angeles Times,* May 8, 2011

438 *Los Angeles Times,* April 26, 1961

439 *Los Angeles Times,* November 14, 1973

440 *Oakland Tribune,* March 18, 1962

441 *Irish News,* January 4, 2019

442 *People,* September 15, 1986

443 *New York Post,* November 5, 2005

444 *The Ireland Independent,* September 16, 2007

445 *Time,* August 10, 2006

446 *Your Mother's Not a Virgin* by John Barbour, p. 401

447 *Hollywood Reporter,* January 11, 2012

448 *People,* November 10, 2017

449 *CNN,* July 21, 2010

450 *Hollywood Reporter,* January 11, 2012

451 *Celebitchy.com,* November 20, 2013

452 *Huffington Post UK,* January 19, 2013

453 *Time,* September 3, 2014

454 *UK Daily Mail,* December 20, 2019

455 *A Case for Murder* by Jay Margolis, p. 10-11

456 *UK Telegraph,* March 4, 2011

457 *People,* August 10, 1992

458 *UK Independent,* October 29, 2006

459 *Los Angeles Times,* August 6, 1962

460 *Los Angeles Times,* October 29, 1985

461 *Dead Wrong: Straight Facts on the Country's Most Controversial Cover-Ups* by Richard Belzer and David Wayne, p. 46

462 *Marilyn Monroe: A Case for Murder* by Jay Margolis, p. 140

463 *UK Daily Mail,* December 28, 2012

464 *Variety,* April 20, 2017

465 *UK Independent,* January 11, 2018

466 *New York Times,* June 13, 2014

467 *Smithsonian,* February 24, 2012

468 *Hollywood Reporter,* December 12, 2017

469 *NPR,* October 8, 2010

470 *The Guardian,* August 1, 2005

471 John Marks, *The Search for the "Manchurian Candidate"*(New York: W. W. Norton & Company, 1979), 1991 paperback edition, p. 204.

472 *Los Angeles Free Press,* August 15, 1975

473 *The Covert War Against Rock: What You Don't Know About the Deaths of Jim Morrison, Tupac Shakur, Michael Hutchence, Brian Jones, Jimi Hendrix, Phil Ochs, ... Tosh, John Lennon, and The Notorious B.I.G.* by Alex Constantine, p. 118

474 Ibid, p. 118

475 *Instant Karma,* December 1991

476 *Constantine,* p. 122

477 Ibid, p. 123

478 Ibid, pp. 123-124

479 Ibid, pp. 127-128

480 *UK Daily Mail,* December 3, 2010

481 *New York Post,* August 4, 2018

482 *Daily Telegraph,* April 1, 2015

483 *The Guardian,* December 11, 2009

484 *UK Mirror,* December 21, 2014

485 *UK Mirror,* January 1, 2012

486 *The Sunday Herald,* August 22, 2014

487 *Jerusalem Post,* April 14, 2011

488 *Los Angeles Times,* February 7, 2001

489 *New Republic,* September 15, 2011

490 *Hollywood Reporter,* May 30, 2015

491 *Pops: A Life of Louis Armstrong* by Terry Teachout, p. 363

492 *Fox News,* August 24, 2019

493   Amburn, Ellis. *Pearl: The Obsessions and Passions of Janis Joplin,* Warner Books, 1992, p. 216

494 *Fort Worth Star-Telegram,* March 3, 1981

495 *Irish Examiner,* May 31, 2004

496 *Detroit News,* December 6, 2017

497 *UK Independent,* April 24, 2010

498 *The Nation,* September 27, 2012

499 *Village Voice,* October 11, 2017

500 *UK Independent,* September 3, 2017

501 *UK Daily Mail,* February 17, 2016

502 *Salon,* August 29, 2011

503 *Sydney Morning Herald,* October 24, 2011

504 *BBC,* July 10, 2014

505 *World Socialist Web Site,* November 1, 2014

506 *Minnesota Star Tribune,* December 1, 2017

507 *New York Times,* February 4, 2004

508 *A Renegade History of the United States* by Thaddeus Russell, p. 238

509 *UK Express,* August 18, 2018

510 *Los Angeles Times,* September 5, 1999

511 *Hollywood Babylon II* by Kenneth Anger, p. 66

512 *Los Angeles Times,* July 5, 1987

513 Turkus, Burton B.; Feder, Sid, *Murder, Inc.: The Story Of The Syndicate,* Cambridge, Massachusetts: Da Capo Press, 2003, p. 270

514 *Los Angeles Times,* August 31, 1990

515 *UK Daily Mail,* October 30, 2015

516 Yablonsky, Lewis , *George Raft.* McGraw-Hill Book Company, Hew York, 1974, p. 76

517 *New York Post,* June 18, 2001

518 *Hollywood Reporter,* June 30, 2020

519 *New York Times,* July 12, 2002

520 *UK Daily Express,* September 18, 2012

521 *NPR,* July 21, 2009

522 *Lipstick Alley,* February 10, 2019

523 *Thrillist,* july 31, 2015

524 *UK Express,* November 13, 2009

525 *Miami Herald,* January 19, 2018

526 *Me, the Mob, and the Music* by Tommy James, p. 136

527 *UK Independent,* August 12, 1995

528 *UK Daily Mail,* September 3, 2015

529 *The Observer,* January 20, 2008

530 *The Guardian,* January 20, 2008

531 *Huffington Post,* June 19, 2014

532 *Associated Press,* November 18, 1992

533 *Wall Street Journal,* February 5, 2016

534 *St. Petersburg Times,* June 23, 1968

535 *Jean Arthur: The Actress Nobody Knew* by John Oller, p. 100

536 *Hollywood Babylon II* by Kenneth Anger, p. 79

537 *UK Express,* April 5, 2010

538 *New York Times,* October 14, 2017

539 *Vanity Fair,* July 15, 2016

540 *The Sun,* April 6, 2016

541 *UK Express,* July 21, 2015

542 *UK Daily Mail,* April 10, 2017

543 *UK Express,* February 5, 2016

544 *The Sun,* February 16, 2016

545 *Chicago Tribune,* April 4, 2002

546 *UK Express,* February 5, 2016

547 *Los Angeles Times,* January 4, 1998

548 *Chicago Tribune,* September 16, 2006

549 *CNN,* July 31, 2011

550 *USA Today,* April 18, 2019

551 *UK Daily Mail,* October 9, 2008

552 *Vanity Fair,* March 20, 2017

553 *Los Angeles Times,* March 29, 1960

554 *Business Insider,* December 1, 2015

555 *Los Angeles Magazine,* August 20, 2012

556 *Los Angeles Times,* May 18, 2017

557 *Reuters,* January 6, 2016

558 *The Atlantic,* December 4, 2013

559 *Los Angeles Times,* July 10, 1954

560 *UPI,* March 23, 1960

561 *Los Angeles Times,* June 9, 1934

562 *Women in Horror Films, 1930s* by Gregory William Mank, pp. 104-105

563 *The Austin Chronicle,* April 11, 2014

564 *ENews,* January 16, 2002

565 *National Enquirer,* July 25, 2014

566 *Associated Press,* December 29, 1987

567 *Los Angeles Times,* December 27, 1998

568 *The Sarnia Observer,* April 21, 2014

569 *Sarasota Herald,* February 26, 1927

570 *New York Times,* October 11, 1933

571 *The Guardian,* January 10, 2008

572 *Tampa Bay Times,* June 17, 1946

573 *Los Angeles Times,* October 18, 1968

574 *New York Magazine,* September 14, 1987

575 *UK Independent,* May 1, 2013

576 *Arizona Republic,* April 29, 2014

577 Lamparski, Richard, *Whatever Became Of...?*, New York: Crown Publishers, 1982, pp. 190–191

578 *Huffington Post,* January 15, 2016

579 *International Business Times,* June 1, 2015

580 *The Guardian,* June 21, 2016

581 *List Verse,* April 9, 2015

582 *New York Times,* September 7, 2015

583 *Washington Post,* September 8, 2015

584 *UK Daily Express,* August 2, 2007

585 *UK Daily Mail,* May 15, 2017

586 *UK Daily Mail,* February 18, 2016

587 *Dark Victory: The Life of Bette Davis* by Ed Sikov, p. 82

588 *New York Times,* December 7, 1977

589 *UK Daily Mail,* April 4, 2014

590 *St. Petersburg Times,* July 21, 1944

591 *Hollywood Reporter,* November 24, 2011

592 *Gone Hollywood,* p. 348

593 *The Scotland Sunday Herald,* July 9, 2011

594 *New York Times,* April 21, 1992

595 *EOnline,* January 8, 1999

596 *Business Insider,* January 25, 2012

597 *USA Today,* September 25, 2008

598 *Los Angeles Times,* January 25, 1998

599 *The Gay Almanac,* November 19, 2017

600 *Celebitchy,* April 12, 2012

601 *US Magazine,* April 16, 2013

602 *CNBC,* July 5, 2018

603 *UK Daily Mail,* October 16, 2015

604 *Los Angeles Times,* April 26, 1995

605 *The Guardian,* February 11, 2014

606 *Variety,* November 15, 1967

607 *Time,* October 12, 2018

608 *St. Petersburg Times,* September 2, 1948

609 *New York Times,* February 21, 2015

610 *Mother Jones,* June 21, 2010

611 *Yahoo Celebrity,* April 5, 2018

612 *Us Magazine,* November 23, 2016

613 *Fox News,* February 16, 2019

614 *Sarasota Herald Tribune,* January 27, 2008

615   *The New Yorker,* October 1, 2012

616   *The Stars of Hollywood Forever* by Tony Scott, p. 1978

617   *Los Angeles Times,* November 17, 1939

618   *Ottawa Citizen,* February 21, 1964

619   *Milwaukee Journal,* January 29, 1957

620   *UK Telegraph,* September 2, 2006

621   *Los Angeles Times,* February 8, 1989

622   *The Rockford Squire,* June 28, 2012

623   *People,* March 6, 1989

624   *Toronto Star,* May 13, 2007

625   *New York Times,* January 15, 2017

626   *Washington Post,* January 23, 1983

627   *NPR,* July 29, 2006

628   *Port Arthur Texas News,* June 8, 1966

629   *Associated Press,* January 30, 2019

630   *UK Telegraph,* July 4, 2015

631   *Marilyn Monroe: The Biography* by Donald Spoto, pp. 339-340

632   *Los Angeles Times,* November 28, 1988

633   *Hollywood Remembered: An Oral History of Its Golden Age* by Paul Zollo, p. 74

634   *LA Weekly,* December 5, 2013

635   *Ann Dvorak: Hollywood's Forgotten Rebel* by Christina Rice, p. 293

636   *Pushing the Envelope: All the Way to the Top* by Harvey Mackay, p. 100

637   *UK Independent,* May 5, 2000

638   *Los Angeles Times,* May 6, 1990

639   *New York Times,* March 24, 1988

640   *Me, the Mob, and the Music* by Tommy James. P. 109

641   *UK Daily Mail,* August 19, 2012

642   *MTV,* May 11, 2010

643   *Seventeen,* January 18, 2018

644   *Showbiz CheatSheet,* March 16, 2019

645   *US Magazine,* Jun 21, 2017

646   *Washington Post,* May 29, 2010

647   *Deadline Hollywood,* March 19, 2018

648   *MSN,* February 6, 2019

649   *New York Post,* July 24, 2002

650   *The Film Colony,* September 15, 2012

651   *Washington Post,* January 31, 2014

652   *UK Express,* September 7, 2014

653 *Milwaukee Record,* May 6, 2015

654 *Live From New York: An Uncensored History of Saturday Night Live* by Tom Shales and James Andrew Miller, pp. 177-179

655 *New York Daily News,* August 13, 2009

656 *Rolling Stone,* July 7, 2016

657 *Los Angeles Times,* January 17, 1990

658 *Baltimore Sun,* May 28, 2010

659 *San Diego Union Tribune,* July 14, 2012

660 *Los Angeles Times,* June 28, 2018

661 *Lipstick Alley,* September 3, 2018

662 *UK Independent,* May 28, 2014

663 *LA Weekly,* February 18, 2015

664 *The Entertainer: Movies, Magic and My Father's Twentieth Century* by Margaret Talbot, p. 134

665 *Gone Hollywood* by Christopher Finch & Linda Rosenkrantz, p. 95

666 *LA Weekly,* February 18, 2015

667 Ibid

668 *Gone Hollywood* by Christopher Finch and Linda Rosenkrantz, p. xi

669 Ibid, p. 7

670 *Los Angeles Times,* March 11, 1955

671 *Gone Hollywood* by Christopher Finch and Linda Rosenkrantz, p. 62

672 *Los Angeles Times,* April 12, 2002

673 *Vanity Fair,* April 1, 1997

674 Robert Giroux, *A Deed of Death: The Story Behind the Unsolved Murder of William Desmond Taylor,* New York Knopf, 1990, p. 180

675 *Film Star Facts,* July 24, 2015

676 *Vanity Fair,* April 1, 1997

677 *The Hour,* July 6, 2017

678 *Vanity Fair,* April 1, 1997

679 *Me, The Mob, and the Music* by Tommy James, p. 30

680 *UK Express,* March 4, 2010

681 *GQ,* September 16, 2016

682 *UK Daily Mail,* August 2, 2012

683 *Slate,* October 9, 2015

684 *New York Times,* April 21, 1985

685 *Vanity Fair,* March 17, 2017

686 *The Advocate,* August 8, 2012

687 *UK daily Mail,* October 16, 2015

688 Ibid

689 *The Hollywood Sign: Fantasy and Reality of an American Icon* by Leo Braudy, p. 92

690 *Huffington Post,* Setpember 26, 2012

691 *The Times of India,* March 16, 2005

692 *UK Daily Mail,* November 11, 2011

693 *SPY Hollywood,* February 25, 2017

694 *Gone Hollywood* by Christopher Finch and Linda Rosenkrantz, p. 27

695 *CNN,* October 20, 2014

696 *Architectural Digest,* August 6, 2018

697 *Vanity Fair,* April 24, 2017

698 *Vanity Fair,* March 2008

699 *Gone Hollywood,* p. 146-150

700 *The Times,* May 6, 2013

701 *Gone Hollywood*, pp. 33-36

702 *Lion of Hollywood: The Life and Legend of Louis B. Mayer* by Scott Eyman, p. 145

703 *Gone Hollywood*, pp. 226-231

704 *Gone Hollywood*, pp.62-67

705 *Gone Hollywood*, pp. 88-92

706 *Gone Hollywood*, p. 37

707 *Mae West Blogspot,* January 25, 2016

708 *Arizona Sun,* January 3, 1947

709 *The Sun,* February 26, 2016

710 *Forbidden Channels* by Penny Stallings, p. 172-173

711 *UK Daily Mail,* August 31, 2016

712 *Chicago Tribune,* March 27, 1992

713 *Los Angeles Times,* July 5, 2013

714 *Vulture,* September 22, 2017

715 *UK Express,* June 26, 2014

716 *The Spectator,* August 2, 2014

717 *National Enquirer,* August 4, 2014

718 *UK Daily Mail,* July 21, 2017

719 *Mental Floss,* December 15, 2013

720 *Me, The Mob, and the Music* by Tommy James, p. 29

721 *Smithsonian,* March 1, 2016

722 *Daily Express,* September 11, 1941

723 *Einstein's Beets* by Alexander Theroux, p. 202

724 *Weird Scenes Inside the Canyon* by David McGowan, p. 255

725 *Entertainment Weekly,* August 27, 1993

726   *Seattle Times,* January 26, 2017

727   *Insider,* September 6, 2016

728   *Huffington Post,* June 16, 2012

729   *UK Telegraph,* October 13, 2015

730   *Variety,* November 23, 1992

731   *Hollywood Reporter,* February 1, 2014

732   *Forbes,* February 1, 2016

733   *South Florida Sun Sentinel,* October 7, 2010

734   *Rolling Stone,* August 25, 2005

735   *Rolling Stone,* October 12, 1972

736   *The Book of Rock Quotes,* compiled by Jonathan Green, p. 99

737   *Billboard,* January 3, 2012

738   *Rolling Stone,* January 23, 2015

739   *Creem,* November 1970

740   *St. Louis Republic,* April 14, 1901

741   *Ava Gardner: The Secret Conversations* (paperback edition) by Peter Evans, Ava Gardner, p. 228

742   *Weird Scenes Inside the Canyon* by David McGowan, p. 94

743   *Weird Scenes Inside the Canyon* by David McGowan, p. 159

744   Ibid, p. 257

745   Ibid, p. 168

746   Ibid, p. 214

747   *The Guardian,* October 28, 2020

748   *Forbes,* March 5, 2019

749   *Vanity Fair,* June 2011

750   *New York Times Book Review,* March 14, 1999

751   *New York Times,* April 8, 1891

752   *UK Telegraph,* December 24, 2017

753   *Poker Tilt* by Dutch Boyd, Laurence Samuels, p. 144

754   *New York Daily News,* December 1, 2015

755   *New York Daily News,* April 18, 2013

756   *Forbes,* May 6, 2014

757   *People,* February 12, 1996

Index

CPSIA information can be obtained
at www.ICGtesting.com
Printed in the USA
LVHW081202271121
704492LV00004B/3

9 781629 338071